BRIDGING THE GAP

FIFTH EDITION

BRIDGING THE GAP

COLLEGE READING

Brenda D. Smith
Georgia State University

LONGMAN

An imprint of Addison Wesley Longman, Inc.

New York • Reading, Massachusetts • Menlo Park, California • Harlow, England
Don Mills, Ontario • Sydney • Mexico City • Madrid • Amsterdam

Acquisitions Editor: Ellen Schatz
Director of Development: Patricia Rossi
Developmental Editor: Susan Moss
Project Coordination and Text Design: Ruttle, Shaw & Wetherill, Inc.
Cover Designer: Kay Petronio
Cover Photograph: PhotoDisk, Inc.
Photo Researcher: Feldman & Associates, Inc.
Electronic Production Manager: Christine Pearson
Manufacturing Manager: Helene G. Landers
Electronic Page Makeup: Ruttle, Shaw & Wetherill, Inc.
Printer and Binder: R. R. Donnelley & Sons Company
Cover Printer: The Lehigh Press, Inc.

Library of Congress Cataloging-in-Publication Data
Smith, Brenda D., [date]
    Bridging the gap : college reading / Brenda D. Smith.—5th ed.
    p. cm.
    Includes bibliographical references and index.
    ISBN 0–673–99810-X (student ed.).–ISBN 0–673–99811–8 (teacher ed.)
    1. Reading (Higher education)   2. Study skills.   I. Title.
LB2395.3.S64 1997   96–438
428.4'3—dc20   CIP

ISBN 0-673-99810-X (student ed.)
ISBN 0-673-99811-8 (teacher ed.)

345678910—DOC—999897

To
My Mother
and Father

Contents

3 Main Idea

4 Organizing Textbook Information

5   Inference

6   Point of View

7 | Critical Thinking

8 | Graphic Illustrations

9 Rate Flexibility

10 Test Taking

11 Textbook Application

Preface

Ultimately, reading should be liberating. What may start as a basic skill should quickly lead to such processes as higher-level thinking, networking, and evaluating. Reading enables learners to gain independence and self-confidence, to solve problems, and to make decisions. My aim in this text is—and has always been—for students to become capable readers and thinkers who take ownership of their learning.

The fifth edition emphasizes metacognitive awareness. Learning Logs are included at the end of each chapter to encourage students to reflect on their own progress as learners. Conscientious use of the Learning Logs can help them recognize the relevance of what they have learned, analyze their own strengths and weaknesses, and communicate their thoughts on learning to themselves and their instructors. Armed with knowledge of the process, each student can be his or her own best teacher.

Many colleges cite the ability to think critically as one of the essential academic outcome goals for graduates. Along these lines, the Critical Thinking chapter (Chapter 7) has been revised and expanded to offer a more systematic method of applying previously learned skills and making decisions. Each part in the four-step method that is advanced includes an explanation, model, and practice exercises. To further reinforce critical thinking and promote group collaboration, Collaborative Critical Thinking exercises are included in each chapter.

The intent of the fifth edition, as with previous editions, is to personally involve the reader, to build and enrich the knowledge networks that become so important in academic study, to stimulate engaging class discussions, and to elicit independent learning and thinking. I hope that students both learn from and enjoy this text.

CONTENT AND ORGANIZATION

The fifth edition continues the tradition of previous editions by using actual college textbook material for teaching and practice. Designed for an upper-level course in college reading, each chapter introduces a new skill, provides short practice exercises to teach the skill, and then offers practice through longer selections. For vocabulary development, words are presented in context after most of the longer selections, as well as in short Word Bridge sections within selected chapters.

Presentation of skills in the text moves from the general to the specific. Initial chapters discuss concentration, study strategies, main idea, and organization, while later chapters teach inference, point of view, critical thinking, graphic illustrations and rate flexibility. The reading and study skills discussions in the first portion of the book stress the need to construct the main idea of a passage and select significant supporting details. Exercises encourage "engaged thinking" before reading, while reading, and after reading. Four different methods of organizing textbook information for later study are explained.

The expanded Critical Thinking chapter is a culmination and application of main-idea, inference, and point-of-view skills. The chapter on test taking is designed to help students gain insights into text construction and the testing situation. The book concludes with an opportunity to apply all the skills to an actual chapter from a college textbook.

NEW FEATURES

Significant improvements in the fifth edition include the following:

- Fourteen new longer reading selections (a 60 percent change)
- Learning Logs at the end of each chapter for students to learn about themselves, reflect on their strengths and weaknesses, and monitor their progress as learners
- An expanded chapter on critical thinking that focuses on the systematic application of previously introduced skills
- Discussion and practice exercises on barriers to critical thinking that include cultural conditioning, self-deception, and oversimplication
- Practice in identifying fallacies in critical thinking and in evaluating arguments
- In most chapters, Collaborative Critical Thinking activities to encourage connecting ideas from the longer reading selections to new information and sharing group resources for problem solving
- Additional practice readings for main idea, patterns of organization, and summaries
- The option of multiple-choice as well as essay questions for all longer reading selections
- Recasting of main idea questions into a multiple-choice format
- Incorporation of new selections that reflect the cultural diversity of student readers
- Recasting of end-of-chapter prose summaries into bulleted summary points

CONTINUING FEATURES

Other features of the book include the following:

- Actual textbook selections are used for practice exercises.
- Many academic disciplines are represented throughout, including psychology, history, business, allied health, biology, anthropology, sociology, and English literature.
- Each selection has both explicit and inferential questions.
- Selections include essay questions for writing practice.
- Vocabulary is presented in context, and exercises on prefixes, suffixes, and roots are included.
- Although skills build and overlap, each chapter can be taught as a separate unit to fit individual class or student needs.
- Pages are perforated so that students can tear out and hand in assignments.
- Short Word Bridge sections are included for vocabulary development.
- At the end of the text, the chapter-length selection "Racial and Ethnic Minorities" explores the history of ethnic groups in America. Taken from a freshman sociology textbook, this longer selection provides the opportunity to practice the transfer of skills while still including study questions and strategy suggestions. Both multiple-choice and essay questions are provided.

The *Instructor's Manual,* which is included in the Teacher's edition, contains the answers to all exercises, suggestions for additional practice, and true-false comprehension exercises.

An interactive computer software program and a test packet are also available from the publisher. The test packet includes quizzes and reading selections for additional practice and is available in computerized form, for both DOS and Mac. The computer software provides the student with opportunities to apply specific strategies and receive immediate feedback from the program.

ACKNOWLEDGMENTS

I appreciate the leadership and support of my editorial friends at Longman, Basic Skills Editor Ellen Schatz and Developmental Editor Susan Moss. Ellen is sensitive to the needs of teachers and students and has made valuable suggestions that are incorporated into this edition. Susan and I have worked on many books together, and I value her advice. She selects excellent reviewers and works with me on making major and minor decisions. I am indebted to both Ellen and Susan for their help.

Again, I feel extremely privileged to have received advice from so many learned colleagues in the college reading profession. The book is strengthened by their insightful, sincere, and constructive comments. Their students are lucky to have these knowledgeable and concerned instructors:

Ellen Bell
Manatee Community College

Jane Brackett
Spartanburg Methodist College

Jim Bernarducci
Middlesex County College

Helen R. Carr
San Antonio College

Dianne Cates
Central Piedmont
   Community College

Richard Harms
Rogue Community College

Bonnie Rittenbach
Mesa College

Melissa Rust
Frederick Community College

Robert L. Stamps
City College of San Francisco

Sylvia Ybarra
San Antonio College

Karen Haas
Manatee Community
   College

Lane C. Johnson
North Harris College

Annice L. Ritter
Athens Technical Institute

Madeleine St. Romain
Clayton State College

Jane Thielemann
University of Houston,
   Downtown

Brenda D. Smith
Learning Support Programs
1 Park Place
Georgia State University
Atlanta, GA 30327
404-651-3360

CHAPTER

1

Concentration

What is it?
How can you improve it?
How does the brain "pay attention"?
Can you do two things at once?
What are common distractors?
What are the cures?

WHAT IS CONCENTRATION?

Answer the following questions honestly:

1. Do you believe the power of concentration is an innate gift that some are born with and others lack? *yes*
2. Do you believe that the ability to concentrate is hereditary, like having blue eyes or brown hair? *yes*
3. If your father's side of the family is fidgety and can't concentrate, does that mean that you will be the same? *no*

The answer to all three questions is an obvious *no*. Concentration is a skill that is developed through self-discipline and practice—not a mystical power, a hereditary gift, or a defective gene. It is a **habit** that requires time and effort to develop and careful planning for consistent success. Athletes have it, surgeons have it, and successful college students must have it. *Concentration is essential for good reading comprehension.* Your college success depends on your willingness and your ability to concentrate.

Concentration is no more than **paying attention**—that is, focusing your full attention on the task at hand. Someone once said that the mark of a genius is the ability to concentrate completely on one thing at a time. This is easy if the task is fun and exciting, but it becomes more difficult when you are required to read something that is not very interesting to you. At this point your mind begins to wander, and the words on the page remain just words for the eyes to see rather than becoming meaningful thoughts and ideas to engage your imagination.

When you are "trying hard to concentrate," what is your brain actually doing? To explain this mystery, cognitive psychologists hypothesize and conduct data-collecting experiments to test theories about our many mental processes. They then make inferences or educated guesses about how the brain operates.

WHAT IS COGNITIVE PSYCHOLOGY?

Cognitive psychology is the body of knowledge that describes how the mind works, or at least how experts think the mind works. Fortunately or unfortunately, the activity of the bran in concentrating, reading, and remembering cannot be directly observed. These cognitive processes are invisible, just as thinking and problem solving are also invisible.

Since so little is actually known about thinking, the ideas of cognitive psychologists are frequently described as *models* or designs of something else we understand. For the last thirty years, for example, the computer has been a popular model for describing how the brain processes information. The human brain is more complex than a computer, but the analogy provides a comparison that can help us understand.

HOW DOES THE BRAIN SCREEN MESSAGES?

Cognitive psychologists use the word **attention** rather than concentration to describe a student's uninterrupted mental focus. Thinking and learning, they say, begin with attention. During every minute of the day the brain is bombarded with millions of sensory messages. How does the brain decide which messages to pay attention to and which to overlook? At this moment, are you thinking about the temperature of the room, outdoor noises, or what you are reading? Since all of this information is available to you, how are you able to set priorities?

The brain relies on a dual command center to screen out one message and attend to another. According to a researcher at UCLA, receptor cells send millions of messages per minute to your brain.[1] Your reticular activating system (RAS), a network of cells at the top of the spinal cord that runs to the brain, tells the cortex in the brain not to bother with most of the sensory input. Your RAS knows that most sensory inputs do not need attention. For example, you are probably not aware at this moment of your back pressing against your chair or your clothes pulling on your body. Your RAS has decided not to clutter the brain with such irrelevant information unless there is an extreme problem, like your foot going to sleep because you are sitting on it.

The cortex can also make attention decisions. When you decide to concentrate your attention on a task, like reading your history assignment, your cortex tells your RAS not to bother it with trivial information. While you focus on learning, your RAS follows orders and "holds" the messages as if you were on an important long-distance call. The cortex and the RAS cooperate in helping you block out distractions and concentrate on learning.

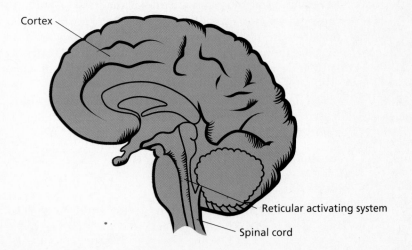

Cortex

Reticular activating system

Spinal cord

[1]H. W. Magoun, *The Waking Brain*, 2nd ed. (Springfield, Ill.: Charles C. Thomas, 1963).

IS DIVIDED ATTENTION EFFECTIVE?

Students often ask if it is possible to do two things at once, such as watching television and doing homework. Most psychologists agree that you can attend to only one thing at a time. An early researcher used a "switch model" to describe his belief, saying that attention operates like the on-off switch of a light fixture in that only one channel is "on" at a time.[2] The "cocktail party effect" illustrates this model. At a party with many available conversations within your listening range, you would probably attend to only one person at a time. If your name were spoken in a nearby group, however, your attention would be diverted. You would probably "switch" your attention to the nearby group to seek more information on such a fascinating topic while only pretending to listen to the original conversation. According to Broadbent's model, you would not be able to listen intently to both conversations at the same time.

Two later researchers conducted an experiment to test the effectiveness of divided attention.[3] They asked subjects to watch two televised sports events with one superimposed over the other. When subjects were instructed to attend to only one of the games, they did an excellent job of screening out the other and answering questions accurately. When asked to attend to both games simultaneously, subjects made eight times more mistakes than when focusing on only one game. This research seems to confirm the old adage, "You can't do two things at once and do them well."

CAN TASKS BECOME AUTOMATIC?

How can you walk and chew gum at the same time? Does every simple activity require your undivided attention? Many tasks—walking, tying shoelaces, and driving a car, for example—begin under controlled processing, which means that they are deliberate and require concentrated mental effort. After much practice, however, such tasks become automatic. Driving a car is an overlearned behavior that researchers would say becomes an automatic process after thousands of hours of experience. You can probably drive, change radio stations, and talk at the same time. Driving no longer requires your full cognitive capacity unless conditions are hazardous. Similarly, a skilled athlete can dribble a basketball automatically while also attending to strategy and position. Attention is actually not divided because it can shift away from tasks that have become automatic.

Automatic Aspects of Reading

The idea of doing some things automatically is especially significant in reading. As a first-grade reader you had to concentrate on recognizing letters, words,

[2]D. E. Broadbent, *Perception and Communication* (London: Pergamon Press, 1958).
[3]U. Neisser and R. Becklen, "Selective Looking: Attending to Visually Significant Events," *Cognitive Psychology* 7 (1975), pp. 480–494.

and sentences, as well as trying to construct meaning. After years of practice and overlearning, much of the recognition aspect of reading became automatic. You no longer stop laboriously to decode each word or each letter. For example, why can you look at the word *child* without processing the meaning? Because you automatically think the meaning. This way you can focus your mental resources on understanding the *message* in which the word appears, rather than on understanding the word itself.

College textbooks tend to contain unfamiliar words that are not automatically processed. Attention to the message can be interrupted by the need to attend to an individual unit of thought. Such breaks are to be expected in college reading because of the newness of the material. You can become caught in the dilemma of trying to do two things at once; that is, trying to figure out word meaning as well as trying to understand the message. When this happens, your attention shifts to defining and then back to comprehending. After such a break, you can regain your concentration, and little harm is done if the breaks are infrequent. However, frequent lapses in this automatic aspect of reading can undermine your ability to concentrate on the message.

Learning Styles

Did you know that many experts believe that your ability to concentrate on learning may be affected by the manner in which the information is presented to you? For example, could you be a right-brain thinker in a left-brain classroom? Are you an intuitive type working with concrete details? Do you have a learning style preference?

Many psychologists believe that individuals develop a preference for a particular style or manner of learning at an early age and that these preferences affect concentration and learning. For example, some people learn easily by reading, but others benefit more readily from a demonstration or a diagram. Similarly, engineers like to work with details whereas politicians prefer broad generalizations. Learning style theorists focus on strengths, not weaknesses; there is no right or wrong way. These researchers believe that instruction is best when it matches the learner's particular preference.

Some college orientation programs offer resources and information concerning learning styles. Although knowing your preferences will probably not affect the manner in which your classes are taught, such knowledge can improve your attitude about yourself as a learner and your ability to focus by building on your strengths.

Learning Style Preferences. One popular measure of individual learning style preferences is the Myers-Briggs Type Indicator (MBTI). Based on psychologist Carl Jung's theory of personality types, it measures individual learning style preferences in four categories. Although the MBTI is not accepted by all educators, the following brief description of its four categories gives an idea of the kinds of issues that its proponents consider significant:

1. *Extroverted—Introverted*

   Extroverts prefer to talk with others and learn through experience, whereas introverts prefer to think alone about ideas.

2. *Sensing—Intuitive*

   Sensing types prefer working with concrete details and tend to be patient, practical, and realistic. Intuitive types like abstractions and are creative, impatient, and theory oriented.

3. *Thinking—Feeling*

   Thinking types tend to base decisions on objective criteria and logical principles. Feeling types are subjective and consider the impact of the decision on other people.

4. *Judging—Perceiving*

   Judging types are time-oriented and structured, whereas perceivers are spontaneous and flexible.

Right- versus Left-Brain Dominance. Another popular learning style theory is concerned with right- or left-brain dominance. Proponents of this theory believe that left-brain dominant people are analytical and logical and excel in verbal skills. Right-brain people, on the other hand, are intuitive, creative, and emotional, and tend to think in symbols. Albert Einstein, for example, said that he rarely thought in words, but that his concepts appeared in symbols and images.

Learning style theorists offer another way of looking at attention and learning. If you are "turned off" by an assignment, maybe it is the manner in which the material is presented and not the topic itself. Perhaps a presentation more in tune with your learning preferences would capture your attention and engender enthusiasm. A compatible approach may "turn on" your imagination.

© 1997 Addison-Wesley Educational Publishers Inc.

POOR CONCENTRATION: CAUSES AND CURES

The type of intense concentration that forces the RAS and cortex to close out the rest of the world is the state we would all like to achieve each time we sit down with a textbook. Too often, however, the opposite is true.

Students frequently ask, *How can I keep my mind on what I'm doing?* or say *I finished the assignment, but I don't know a thing I read.* The solution is not a simple mental trick to fool the brain; rather, it involves a series of practical short- and long-range planning strategies targeted at reducing external and internal distractions.

External Distractions

External distractions are the temptations of the physical world that divert your attention away from your work. They are the people in the room, the noise in the background, the time of day, or your place for studying. To control these external distractions, create an environment that says, "Now this is the place and the time for me to get my work done."

Place. Start by establishing your own private study cubicle; it may be in the library, on the dining room table, or in your bedroom. Wherever it is, choose a straight chair and face the wall. Get rid of gadgets, magazines, and other temptations that trigger the mind to think of *play*. Stay away from the bed because it triggers *sleep*. Spread out your papers, books, and other symbols of studying and create an atmosphere in which the visual stimuli signal *work*.

Time. To be successful, your study hour must be as rigid and fixed in your mind as your class hours. Leave nothing to chance because too often an unplanned activity never gets done. At the beginning of each new term, establish a routine study time for each day of the week and stick scrupulously to your schedule.

Use a Pocket Calendar or Assignment Book. At the beginning of the quarter or semester record dates for tests, term papers, and special projects on a calendar that you can keep with your books. Use the planner to organize all course assignments. A look at the calendar will remind you of the need for both short- and long-term planning. Assigned tests, papers, and projects will be due whether you are ready or not. Your first job is to devise a plan for getting ready.

Schedule. A weekly activity chart appears on page 8. Analyze your responsibilities and in the squares on the chart write your fixed activities such as class hours, work time, mealtime, and bedtime. Next, think about how much time you plan to spend studying and how much on recreation, and plug those into the chart. For studying, indicate the specific subject and exact place involved.

Make a fresh chart at the beginning of each week since responsibilities and assignments vary. Learn to estimate the time usually needed for typical assignments. As the term progresses, include time for a regular review of lecture notes. Examinations require special planning. Many students do not realize how much time it takes to study for a major exam. Spread your study out over several days and avoid last-minute cramming sessions late at night. Plan additional time for special projects and term papers, so as not to get caught in a deadline crisis.

Successful people do not let their time slip away; they manage time, rather than letting time manage them. Plan realistically and then follow your schedule.

Ratio. Even though it is not necessary to write this on the chart, remember that you need short breaks. Few students can study uninterrupted for two hours without becoming fatigued and losing concentration. Try the *50:10 ratio*—study hard for fifty minutes, take a ten-minute break, and then promptly go back to the books for another fifty minutes.

Habit. Forming study habits is similar to developing the habit of brushing your teeth; the important word is *consistency*. Always study in the same places at the same times and do not tolerate exceptions. After a number of repeated experiences, the places and times should become subconscious psychological signals for concentration.

Time	Sunday	Monday	Tuesday	Wednesday	Thursday	Friday	Saturday
7:00–8:00							
8:00–9:00							
9:00–10:00							
10:00–11:00							
11:00–12:00							
12:00–1:00							
1:00–2:00							
2:00–3:00							
3:00–4:00							
4:00–5:00							
5:00–6:00							
6:00–7:00							
7:00–8:00							
8:00–9:00							
9:00–10:00							
10:00–11:00							
11:00–12:00							

Internal Distractions

Internal distractions are the concerns that come repeatedly into your mind as you try to keep your attention focused on the assignment. Rather than the noise or the conversations in a room, they are the nagging worries or doubts in your mind that disrupt your work.

Unfortunately, students, just like everyone else, have to run errands, pick up laundry, make telephone calls, and pay bills. The world does not stop just because George has to read four chapters for a test in "Western Civ." by Wednesday. Consequently, when George sits down to read, he worries about getting an inspection sticker for his car or about picking up tickets for Saturday's ball game rather than concentrating completely on the assignment.

Make a List. For the most part, the interferences that pop into the mind and break reading concentration are minor concerns rather than major problems. To gain control over these mental disruptions, make a list of what is bothering you. What is on your mind that is keeping you from concentrating on your studies? Jot down on a piece of paper each mental distraction and then analyze each to determine if immediate action is possible. If so, get up and take action. Make that phone call, write that letter, or finish that chore. Maybe it will take a few minutes or maybe half an hour, but the investment will have been worthwhile if the quality of your study time—your concentration power—has improved. Taking action is the first step in getting something off your mind.

For the big problems that you can't tackle immediately, ask yourself, "Is it worth the amount of brain time I'm dedicating to it?" Take a few minutes to think and make notes on possible solutions. Jotting down necessary future action and forming a plan of attack will help relieve the worry and clear the mind for studying.

Right now, list five things that are on your mind that you need to remember to do. Alan Lakein, a specialist in time management, calls this a **to-do list.** In his book, *How to Get Control of Your Time and Your Life,*[4] Lakein claims that successful business executives start each day with such a list. Rank the activities on your list in order of priority and then do the most important things first.

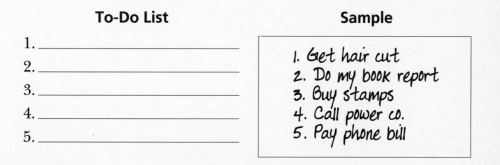

To-Do List	**Sample**
1. _____	1. Get hair cut
2. _____	2. Do my book report
3. _____	3. Buy stamps
4. _____	4. Call power co.
5. _____	5. Pay phone bill

[4]A. Lakein, *How to Get Control of Your Time and Your Life* (New York: Signet, 1974).

At the end of the day all the tasks may not be completed, but the leftovers can be transferred to tomorrow's list. Keep your to-do lists in a booklet, rather than on different scraps of paper, so that you can refer back to a previous day's activity as well as make notes for several days ahead. If you can't think of five things you need to do, think harder! In fact, most students will probably come up with more than five items.

Increase Your Self-Confidence. Saying "I'll never pass this course" or "I can't get in the mood to study" is the first step to failure. Concentration requires self-confidence. If you didn't think you could do it, you would not be in a college class reading this book. Getting a college degree is not a short-term goal. Your enrollment indicates that you have made a commitment to a long-term goal. Ask yourself the question, "Who do I want to be in five years?" In the following space, describe how you view yourself, both professionally and personally, five years from now.

Five years from now I hope to be ___*a elementary school*___
___*teacher*___

Sometimes identifying the traits you admire in others can give you further insight into your own values and desires. Think about the traits you respect in others and your own definition of success. Answer the two questions that follow and consider how your responses mirror your own aspirations and goals.

Who is the person that you admire the most? ___*my mother*___

Why do you admire this person? ___*She is a hard*___
___*worker and she is not a*___
___*quitter.*___
___
___

Improve Your Self-Concept. Have faith in yourself and in your ability to be what you want to be. How many people do you know who have passed the particular course that is worrying you? Are they smarter than you? Probably not. Can you do as well as they did? Turn your negative feeling into a positive attitude. What are some of your positive traits? Are you a hard worker, an honest person, a loyal friend? Take a few minutes to pat yourself on the back. Think about your good points and, in the following spaces, list five positive traits that you believe you possess.

Positive Traits

1. ___*Prayer*___
2. ___*love*___
3. ___*fun*___

4. _Cork_

5. _friend_

What have you already accomplished? Did you participate in athletics in high school, win any contests, or master any difficult skills? Recall your previous achievements, and in the following spaces, list three accomplishments that you view with pride.

Accomplishments

1. _son_

2. _Sunday School teacher_

3. _going back to school_

Reduce Anxiety. Have you ever heard people say, "I work better under pressure?" This statement contains a degree of truth. A small amount of tension can help you to force yourself to direct full attention on an immediate task. For example, concentrated study for an exam is usually more intense two nights before, rather than two weeks before, the test.

Yet too much anxiety can cause nervous tension and discomfort, which interfere with the ability to concentrate. Students operating under too much tension sometimes "freeze up" mentally and experience nervous physical reactions. The causes can range from fear of failure to lack of organization and preparation; the problem is not easily solved.

Anxiety is a behavior that is learned in response to situations that engender feelings of inadequacy. Because it is learned, it can also be unlearned. As an immediate, short-term response to tension, try muscle relaxation and visualization. For example, if you are reading a particularly difficult section in a chemistry book and are becoming frustrated to the point that you can no longer concentrate, stop your reading and take several deep breaths. Use your imagination to visualize a peaceful setting in which you are calm and relaxed. Imagine yourself rocking back and forth in a hammock or lying on a beach listening to the surf. Use the image you created and the deep breathing to help relax your muscles and regain control. Take several deep breaths and allow your body to release the tension so that you can resume reading and concentrate on your work.

As a long-term solution, nothing works better than success. Just as failure fuels tension, success tends to weaken it. Each successful experience helps to diminish feelings of inadequacy. Early success in a course can make a big psychological difference between final success and failure. Starting off with a passing grade on the first examination means that for the rest of the course you are working to maintain a passing grade rather than fighting to overcome a failure. Maintaining a good grade creates far less tension and pressure than trying to overcome a bad one. The counseling centers of most colleges offer special help for stress management and test anxiety.

Spark an Interest. Potentially dull material, like seemingly dull people, needs some background work. Ask some questions, get some ideas, and do some thinking before starting to read. If the material was assigned, it must have merit, and finding it will make your job easier. Make a conscious effort to stimulate your curiosity before reading, even if in a contrived manner. Make yourself want to learn something. First look over the assigned reading for words or phrases that attract your attention, glance at the pictures, check the number of pages, and then ask yourself the following question: What do *I* want to learn about this?

With practice, this method of thinking before reading can create a spark of enthusiasm that will make the actual reading more purposeful and make concentration more direct and intense.

Set a Time Goal. An additional trick to spark your interest is to set a time goal. Study time is not infinite and short-term goals create a self-imposed pressure to pay attention, speed up, and get the job done. After looking over the material, project the amount of time you will need to finish it. Estimate a reasonable completion time and then push yourself to meet the goal. The purpose of a time goal is not to "speed read" the assignment, but rather to be realistic about the amount of time to spend on a task and to learn how to estimate future study time.

FOCUS ON SUCCESSFUL ACADEMIC BEHAVIORS

Good concentration geared toward college success involves more than the ability to comprehend reading assignments. College success demands concentrated study, self-discipline, and the demonstration of learning. If the "focused athlete" can be successful, so can the "focused student." Begin to evaluate and eliminate behaviors that waste your time and divert you from your goals. Direct your energy toward activities that will enhance your chances for success. Adopt the following behaviors of successful students.

Attend Class. At the beginning of the quarter or semester, most college professors have an outline of what they plan to cover during each class period. Although they may not always check class attendance, the organization of the daily course work assumes perfect attendance. College professors *expect* you to attend class, and they usually do not repeat lecture notes or give makeup lessons for those who are absent. Be responsible and set yourself up for success by coming to class. You paid for it!

Be on Time. Professors usually overview the day's work at the beginning of each class, as well as answer questions and clarify assignments. Arriving late puts you at an immediate disadvantage. You are likely to miss important "class business" information. In addition, tardy students distract both the professor and other students. Put on a watch and get yourself moving.

Be Aware of Essential Class Sessions. Every class session is important, but never *ever* miss the last class before a major test. Usually students will ask questions about the exam that will stimulate your thinking. In reviewing, answering questions, and rushing to finish uncovered material, the professor will often drop important clues to exam items. Unless you are critically ill, take tests on time because "make ups" are usually more difficult, and be in class when the exams are returned to hear the professor's description of an excellent answer.

Read Assignments Before Class. Activate your knowledge on the subject before class by reading homework assignments. The lecture and class discussion can thus be used to build your knowledge network rather than create it. Jot down several questions that you would like to ask the professor about the reading.

Review Lecture Notes Before Class. Always review your lecture notes before the next class period. This recitation helps you to learn rather than merely to accumulate information. Fill in gaps if you remember unrecorded details or make notes to ask questions to resolve confusion. Some students like to review their notes during a break, after class, or on the phone with another classmate.

Consider Using a Tape Recorder. If you are temporarily unable to concentrate, with the professor's permission tape-record the lecture. Take notes at the same time as you record, and you can review your notes while listening to the recording.

Pass the First Test. Stress interferes with concentration. Do yourself a favor and over-study for the first exam. Passing the first exam will help you avoid a lot of tension while studying for the second one.

Predict the Exam Questions. Never go to an exam without first predicting test items. Turn chapter titles, subheadings, and boldface print into questions, and then brainstorm the answers. Feeling prepared boosts self-confidence.

Network with Other Students. You are not in this alone; you have lots of potential buddies who can offer mutual support. Collect the names and phone numbers of a few classmates who are willing to help you if you do not understand the homework, miss a day of class, or need help on an assignment. Be prepared to help your classmates in return for their support.

Classmate ———————————————— Phone —————

Classmate ———————————————— Phone —————

Classmate ———————————————— Phone —————

Form a Study Group. Research experiments involving college students have shown that study groups can be very effective. Students learn to collaborate and form academic bonds that increase their chances of academic success. Studying with others is not cheating; it is a wise use of available resources. In many colleges such groups have become so popular that counselors assist students in finding study partners. If asked, many professors will assist networking

© 1997 Addison-Wesley Educational Publishers Inc.

efforts by distributing copies of the class roll on which willing participants have provided phone numbers. A developmental studies student testified on receiving a scholarship as a dean's list junior, "I call my study buddy when I have a problem. One time I called about an English paper because I couldn't think of my thesis. She asked what it was about. I told her and she said, 'That's your thesis.' I just couldn't see it as clearly as she did."

Learn from Other Student Papers. Talking about an excellent paper is one thing but actually reading one is another. In each discipline we need models of excellence. Always read an "A" paper. Don't be shy. Ask the "A" students (who should be proud and flattered to share their brilliance) or ask the professor. Don't miss this important step in becoming a successful student.

Collaborate. When participating in group learning activities, set expectations for group study so that each member contributes, and try to keep the studying on target. As a group activity, ask several classmates to join you in discovering the resources that are available for students on your campus. First, brainstorm with the group to record answers that are known to be true. Next, divide responsibilities among group members to seek information to answer unknown items. Reconvene the group to complete the responses.

Exercise 1   CAMPUS FACTS

1. Where are the academic advisors located?

_____

2. Where is the learning lab, and what kind of help is offered?

_____

3. When does the college offer free study skills workshops?

_____

4. Where can you use a word processor?

_____

5. Where do you get an identification number for the Internet?

_____

6. Where is your professor's office, and what is the phone number?

_____

7. What kind of financial aid is available, and where can you find this information?

_____

8. What services does the dean's office offer to students?

_____

9. How late is the library open on weekends?

_____

10. What free services does the counseling center offer?

_____

Use the Syllabus. The syllabus is a general outline of the goals, objectives, and assignments for the entire course. The syllabus includes examination dates, course requirements, and an explanation of the grading system. Most professors distribute and explain the syllabus on the first day of class.

Ask questions to help you understand the "rules and regulations" in the syllabus. Keep it handy as a ready reference and use it as a plan for learning. Devise your own daily calendar for completing weekly reading and writing assignments.

The following is a syllabus for Psychology 101. Study the course syllabus and answer the questions that follow.

INTRODUCTION TO PSYCHOLOGY

Class: 9:00–10:00 a.m. daily   Dr. Julie Wakefield
10-Week Quarter   Office: 718 Park Place
Office Hours: 10:00–12:00 daily   651–3361

Required Texts
Psychology: An Introduction by Josh R. Gerow
Paperback: Select one book from the attached list for a report.

Course Content
The purpose of Psychology 101 is to overview the general areas of study in the field of psychology. An understanding of psychology gives valuable insights into your choices and behaviors and those of others. The course will also give you a foundation for later psychology courses.

Methods of Teaching
Thematic lectures will follow the topics listed in the textbook assignments. You are expected to read and master the factual material in the text, as well as take careful notes in class. Tests will cover both class lectures and textbook readings.

Research Participation

All students are required to participate in one psychological experiment. Details and dates are listed on a separate handout.

Grading

Grades will be determined in the following manner:

Tests (4 tests at 15% each)	60%
Final Exam	25%
Written Report	10%
Research Participation	5%

Tests

Tests will consist of both multiple-choice and identification items as well as two essay questions.

Important Dates

Test 1: 1/13
Test 2: 1/29
Test 3: 2/10
Test 4: 2/24
Report: 3/5
Final Exam: 3/16

Written Report

Your written report should answer one of three designated questions and reflect your reading of a book from the list. Each book is approximately 200 pages long. Your report should be at least eight typed pages. More information to follow.

Assignments

Week 1: Ch. 1 (pp. 1–37), Ch. 2 (pp. 41–75)
Week 2: Ch. 3 (pp. 79–116)
   Test 1: Chapters 1–3
Week 3: Ch. 4 (pp. 121–162), Ch. 5 (pp. 165–181)
Week 4: Ch. 5 (pp. 184–207), Ch. 6 (pp. 211–246)
   Test 2: Chapters. 4–6
Week 5: Ch. 7 (pp. 253–288), Ch. 8 (pp. 293–339)
Week 6: Ch. 9 (pp. 345–393)
   Test 3: Chapters 7–9
Week 7: Ch. 10 (pp. 339–441), Ch. 11 (pp. 447–471)
Week 8: Ch. 11 (pp. 476–491), Ch. 12 (pp. 497–533)
   Test 4: Chapters 10–12
Week 9: Ch. 13 (pp. 539–577), Ch. 14 (pp. 581–598)
   Paper
Week 10: Ch. 14 (pp. 602–618), Ch. 15 (pp. 621–658)
   Exam: Chapters 1–15

Exercise 2   REVIEW THE SYLLABUS

Refer to the syllabus to answer the following items with *T* (true) or *F* (false).

_____ 1. Pop quizzes count five percent of the final grade.

_____ 2. The written report is due about a week before the final exam.

_____ 3. The professor is not in her office on Thursdays.

_____ 4. Each of the four tests covers two weeks of work.

_____ 5. Two books are required for the course.

Exercise 3   REVIEW YOUR OWN CLASS SYLLABUS

Examine your syllabus for this college reading course and answer the following questions.

1. How many weeks are in the quarter or semester?

   _____

2. When is your next test and how much does it count?

   _____

3. Will your next major exam have a multiple-choice or essay format?

   _____

4. What is the professor's policy about absences?

   _____

5. What test or assignment constitutes the largest portion of your final grade?

   _____

   Explain._____

Do you have questions that did not seem to be answered on your syllabus? List two issues that you would like to ask the professor to clarify.

1. _____

2. _____

SUMMARY POINTS

- Concentration is focusing your full attention on the job at hand. A critical skill that is developed through self-discipline and practice, it promotes efficient and effective reading.

- Research indicates that the brain has two cooperating systems, the RAS and the cortex, that allow it to selectively attend to certain inputs and to block out others.
- The ability to do several tasks at once depends on the amount of cognitive resources required for each.
- Experienced readers automatically process word meaning and thus use cognitive resources to comprehend ideas.
- Many psychologists suggest that individuals develop a preference for a particular style or manner of learning.
- Common causes of poor concentration come from external and internal sources.
- External distractions are physical temptations that divert your attention. You can manipulate your environment to remove these distractions.
- Internal distractions are mental wanderings that vie for your attention. You can learn to control these by organizing your daily activities, planning for academic success, and striving to meet your goals for the completion of assignments.
- Concentration requires self-confidence, self-discipline, and persistence.
- Adopt successful academic behaviors, including networking with other students and collaborating on assignments, to focus your energy and enhance your chances for success.
- Use your syllabus as a guide for learning.

SELECTION 1

PSYCHOLOGY

Skill Development: Concentration

Preview

Directions: Before reading the first selection, take a few moments to analyze your potential for concentration, preview the selection, and answer the following questions.

1. Look at your physical environment. Where are you and what time is it?

   _____

   Is this your usual study time and place or are you deviating today for some special reason?

   _____

   What, if any, are your external distractions?

   _____

   _____

   _____

2. Is anything popping into your mind that you need to remember to do? Do you feel confident that you understand the assignment and can do well? What, if any, are your internal distractions?

   _____

   _____

   _____

3. Now the big question is "Do you have any interest in what you are about to read?" The title of the selection is "Critical-Period Hypothesis," and it is taken from a book on human behavior. Do you know what *imprinting* means? Glance over the selection and see what words attract your attention. You may notice words and phrases like critical-period hypothesis, Lorenz, goslings, baby chicks, the maternal instinct in rats, overcoming the critical period, baby geese, and others. What do you think you would like to know about the topic? What about it is of interest to you?

   _____

   _____

   _____

   _____

4. Set approximate time goals for yourself. How long do you think it will take you to read this selection? —————— minutes. Look at the comprehension and vocabulary questions that follow the selection. How long do you think it will take you to answer the questions? ——————— minutes

Learning Strategy

Even though most of this excerpt describes animal behavior, the textbook is concerned with human behavior; therefore, be alert to links between the two. Be able to define and give examples of the two major terms in this selection.

Word Knowledge

Are you familiar with the following words in this selection?

hypothesis	restrained
incubator	inseminate
genetic	disrupt
instinctive	irreversible
sustain	coax

Your instructor may choose to ask ten true-false questions from the *Instructor's Manual* to stimulate your thinking using these words.

As you begin to read, record your starting time: _10:00 pm_

Critical-Period Hypothesis
From James V. McConnell, *Understanding Human Behavior*

There is some evidence that the best time for a child to learn a given skill is at the time the child's body is just mature enough to allow mastery of the behavior in question. This belief is often called the *critical-period hypothesis*—that is, the belief that an organism must have certain
5   experiences at a *particular time* in its developmental sequence if it is to reach its mature state.

There are many studies from animal literature supporting the critical-period hypothesis. For instance, German scientist Konrad Lorenz discovered many years ago that birds, such as ducks and geese, will follow
10   the first moving object they see after they are hatched. Usually the first thing they see is their mother, of course, who has been sitting on the eggs when they are hatched. However, Lorenz showed that if he took goose eggs

away from the mother and hatched them in an incubator, the fresh-hatched *goslings* would follow him around instead.

15   After the goslings had waddled along behind Lorenz for a few hours, they acted as if they thought he was their mother and that they were humans, not geese. When Lorenz returned the goslings to their real mother, they ignored her. Whenever Lorenz appeared, however, they became very excited and flocked to him for protection and affection. It was as if the

20 visual image of the first object they saw moving had become so strongly *imprinted* on their consciousness that, forever after, that object was "mother."

During the past 20 years or so, scientists have spent a great deal of time studying *imprinting* as it now is called. The effect occurs in many but not in all types of birds, and it also seems to occur in mammals such as sheep and

25 seals. Whether it occurs in humans is a matter for debate. Imprinting is very strong in ducks and geese, however, and they have most often been the subjects for study.

The urge to imprint typically reaches its strongest peak 16 to 24 hours after the baby goose is hatched. During this period, the baby bird has an

30 innate tendency to follow anything that moves, and will chase after its mother (if she is around), or a human, a bouncing football or a brightly painted tin can that the experimenter dangles in front of the gosling. The more the baby bird struggles to follow after this moving object, the more strongly the young animal becomes imprinted to the object. Once the goose

35 has been imprinted, this very special form of learning cannot easily be reversed. For example, the geese that first followed Lorenz could not readily be trained to follow their mother instead; indeed, when these geese were grown and sexually mature, they showed no romantic interest in other geese. Instead, they attempted to court and mate with humans.

40   If a goose is hatched in a dark incubator and is not allowed to see the world until two or three days later, imprinting often does not occur. At first it was thought that the "critical period" had passed and hence the bird could never become imprinted to anything. Now we know differently. The innate urge to follow moving objects does appear to reach a peak in geese

45 24 hours after they are hatched, but it does not decline thereafter. Rather, a second innate urge—that of fearing and avoiding new objects—begins to develop, and within 48 hours after hatching typically overwhelms the prior tendency the bird had to follow after anything that moves. To use a human term, the goose's *attitude* toward strong things is controlled by its genetic

50 blueprint—at first it is attracted to, then it becomes afraid of, new objects in its environment. As we will see in a moment, these conflicting "attitudes" may explain much of the data on "critical periods" in both animals and humans.

How might these two apparently conflicting behavioral
55   **tendencies help a baby goose survive in its usual**
or natural environment?

In other experiments, baby chickens have been hatched and raised in the dark for the first several days of their lives. Chicks have an innate tendency to peck at small objects soon after they are hatched—an
60 instinctive behavior pattern that helps them get food as soon as they are born. In the dark, of course, they cannot see grain lying on the ground and hence do not peck (they must be hand-fed in the dark during this period of time). Once brought into the light, these chicks do begin to peck, but they do so clumsily and ineffectively, as if their "critical period" for learning the
65 pecking skill had passed. Birds such as robins and blue jays learn to fly at about the time their wings are mature enough to sustain flight (their parents often push them from the nest as a means of encouraging them to take off on their own). If these young birds are restrained and not allowed to fly until much later, their flight patterns are often clumsy and they do not
70 usually gain the necessary skills to become good fliers.

The "Maternal Instinct" in Rats

Suppose we take a baby female rat from its mother at the moment of its birth and raise the rat pup "by bottle" until it is sexually mature. Since it has never seen other rats during its entire life (its eyes do not open until several
75 days after birth), any sexual or maternal behavior that it shows will presumably be due to the natural unfolding of its genetic blueprint—and not due to learning or imitation. Now, suppose we inseminate this hand-raised female rat artificially—to make certain that she continues to have no contact with other rats. Will she build a nest for her babies before they are
80 born, following the usual pattern of female rats, and will she clean and take care of them during and after the birth itself?

The answer to that question is yes—*if.* If, when the young female rat was growing up, there were objects such as sticks and sawdust and string and small blocks of wood in her cage, and which she played with. Then, when
85 inseminated, the pregnant rat will use these "toys" to build a nest. If the rat grows up in a bare cage, she won't build a nest *even though we give her the materials to do so once she is impregnated.* If this same rat is forced to wear a stiff rubber collar around her neck when she is growing up—so that she cannot clean her sex organs, as rats normally do—she will not usually lick her
90 newborn babies clean *even though we take off the rubber collar a day or so before she gives birth.* The genetic blueprint always operates best within a particular environmental setting. If an organism's early environment is abnormal or particularly unusual, later "innate" behavior patterns may be disrupted.

Overcoming the "Critical Period"

95 All of these examples may appear to support the "critical-period" hypothesis—that there is one time in an organism's life when it is best suited to learn a particular skill. These studies might also seem to violate the general rule that an organism can "catch up" if its development has been

delayed. However, the truth is more complicated (as always) than it might
100 seem from the experiments we have cited so far.

Baby geese will normally not imprint if we restrict their visual
experiences for the first 48 hours of their lives—their fear of strange objects
is by then too great. However, if we give the geese tranquilizing drugs to
help overcome their fear, they can be imprinted a week or more after
105 hatching. Once imprinting has taken place, it may seem to be irreversible.
But we can occasionally get a bird imprinted on a human to accept a goose
as its mother, if we coax it enough and give it massive rewards for
approaching or following its natural mother. Chicks raised in darkness
become clumsy eaters—but what do you think would happen if we gave
110 them special training in how to peck, rather than simply leaving the matter
to chance? Birds restrained in the nest too long apparently learn other ways
of getting along and soon come to fear heights; what do you think would
happen if we gave these birds tranquilizers and rewarded each tiny
approximation to flapping their wings properly?

115 There is not much scientific evidence that human infants have the
same types of "critical periods" that birds and rats do. By being born
without strong innate behavior patterns (such as imprinting), we seem to
be better able to adjust and survive in the wide variety of social
environments human babies are born into. Like many other organisms,
120 however, children do appear to have an inborn tendency to imitate the
behavior of other organisms around them. A young rat will learn to press a
lever in a Skinner box much faster if it is first allowed to watch an adult rat
get food by pressing the lever. This learning is even quicker if the adult rat
happens to be the young animal's mother. Different species of birds have
125 characteristic songs or calls. A European thrush, for example, has a song
pattern fairly similar to a thrush in the United States, but both sound quite
different from blue jays. There are *local dialects* among songbirds, however,
and these are learned through imitation. If a baby thrush is isolated from its
parents and exposed to blue jay calls when it is very young, the thrush will
130 sound a littlelike a blue jay but a lot like other thrushes when it grows up.
And parrots, of course, pick up very human-sounding speech patterns if
they are raised with humans rather than with other parrots.

Record reading time: _10:15_

Do you remember what you read? Your instructor may ask ten true-false
questions from the *Instructor's Manual* to stimulate your thinking.

COMPREHENSION QUESTIONS

After reading the selection, answer the following questions with *a, b, c,* or *d.*

_____ 1. The best statement of the main idea of this selection is
   a. studies show that goslings can be imprinted on humans.
   b. a particular few days of an animal's life can be a crucial time for developing long-lasting "natural" behavior.
   c. imprinting seems to occur in mammals but is very strong in ducks and geese.
   d. the "crucial period" of imprinting is important but can be overcome with drugs.

_____ 2. The critical-period hypothesis is the belief that
   a. there is a "prime time" to develop certain skills.
   b. most learning occurs during the first few days of life.
   c. fear can inhibit early learning.
   d. the "maternal instinct" is not innate but is learned.

_____ 3. In Lorenz's studies, after the goslings imprinted on him, they would do all of the following except
   a. follow him around.
   b. flock to him for protection.
   c. return to their real mother for affection.
   d. become excited when Lorenz appeared.

_____ 4. The author points out that in Lorenz's studies the early imprinting of geese with humans
   a. was easily reversed with training.
   b. caused the geese to be poor mothers.
   c. produced later sexually abnormal behavior in the geese.
   d. made it difficult for the goslings to learn to feed themselves.

_____ 5. The author suggests that after 24 hours the innate urge to imprint in geese is
   a. decreased significantly.
   b. increased.
   c. overwhelmed by the avoidance urge.
   d. none of the above.

_____ 6. In its natural environment the purpose of the avoidance urge that develops within 48 hours of hatching might primarily be to help a small gosling
   a. learn only the behavior of its species.
   b. follow only one mother.
   c. escape its genetic blueprint.
   d. stay away from predators.

_____ 7. The author suggests that there is a critical period for developing all of the following except
   a. desire to eat.
   b. pecking.
   c. flying.
   d. cleaning the young.

_____ 8. The studies with rats suggest that nest building and cleaning behavior are
   a. totally innate behaviors.
   b. totally learned behaviors.
   c. a combination of innate and learned behaviors.
   d. neither innate nor learned behaviors.

_____ 9. Abnormal imprinting during the critical period can later be overcome by using all of the following except
   a. tranquilizing drugs.
   b. natural tendencies.
   c. special training.
   d. massive reward.

_____ 10. Because humans do not seem to have strong innate behavior patterns, the author suggests that humans
   a. are better able to adapt to changing environments.
   b. have more difficulty learning early motor skills.
   c. find adjustment to change more difficult than animals.
   d. need more mothering than animals.

Answer the following with *T* (true) or *F* (false).

_____ 11. The author states that whether imprinting occurs in humans is a matter of debate.

_____ 12. The author implies that a goose can be imprinted on a painted tin can.

_____ 13. In the author's opinion, studies show that organisms can catch up adequately without special training when skill development has been delayed past the critical period.

_____ 14. If an abandoned bird egg is hatched and raised solely by a human, the author suggests that the bird will be abnormal.

_____ 15. The author suggests that the urge to imitate is innate in both humans and animals.

VOCABULARY

According to the way the italicized word was used in the selection, select *a, b, c,* or *d* for the word or phrase that gives the best definition.

_b_ 1. "The critical-period *hypothesis*" (03)
a. association
b. tentative assumption
c. law
d. dilemma

_a_ 3. "its *genetic* blueprint" (49)
a. sexual
b. emotional
c. hereditary
d. earned

_d_ 5. "to *sustain* flight" (66)
a. support
b. imitate
c. begin
d. imagine

_b_ 7. "suppose we *inseminate*" (77)
a. imprison
b. artificially impregnate
c. injure
d. frighten

_c_ 9. "seem to be *irreversible*" (105)
a. temporary
b. changeable
c. frequent
d. permanent

_d_ 2. "in an *incubator*" (13)
a. cage
b. electric enlarger
c. nest
d. artificial hatching apparatus

_b_ 4. "an *instinctive* behavior pattern" (60)
a. desirable
b. innate
c. early
d. newly acquired

_b_ 6. "birds are *restrained*" (68)
a. pressured
b. pushed
c. held back
d. attacked

_a_ 8. "may be *disrupted*" (93)
a. thrown into disorder
b. repeated
c. lost
d. destroyed

_a_ 10. "*coax* it enough" (107)
a. encourage fondly
b. punish
c. feed
d. drill

Record total time for reading and responding: ――――

WRITTEN RESPONSE

Use information from the text to respond to the following:
Does a critical period exist during which an organism must have certain experiences in order to reach its normal mature state?

Response Strategy: Define the critical-period hypothesis and describe three to five examples from the text that support the hypothesis. (Use your own paper for this response.)

SKILL DEVELOPMENT: CONCENTRATION

When you have finished each part of the assignment, evaluate your reading and study time.

How long did you take to read the selection? —————— minutes

How long did you take to answer the questions? —————— minutes

Did you work steadily or were you interrupted? _Yes_

Did setting a time goal help you keep your mind on your work? _Yes_

If you had been given the concentration pop quiz while reading this selection, would your score have been high —————, medium —————, or low —————?

Now that you have completed this selection, how much time would you plan for the next selection? _24_ minutes

SELECTION 2

PSYCHOLOGY

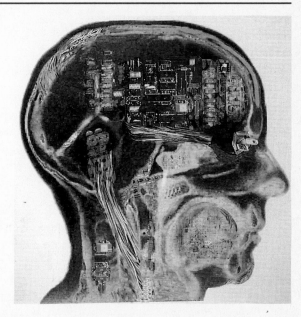

Skill Development: Concentration

Directions: Before reading the second selection, take a few moments to analyze your potential for concentration, preview the selection, and answer the following questions.

1. Where are you? —————— What time is it? _9:05_
   Is this study time and place written on your weekly time schedule? What, if any, are your external distractions?

   _no_

   things on my mind

2. Is anything special on your mind at the moment? Are you ready to "attack" the material? What, if any, are your internal distractions?

   Yes, no staying fences

3. What do you think you will find interesting about the next selection on memory? Do you have a good memory? Do you use "tricks" to help you remember things? Looking over the pages, are you intrigued by levels of processing, retrieval cues, schemas, and reading a textbook? Do these phrases stimulate your interest?

4. Set approximate time goals for yourself. How long do you think it will take you to read this selection? —————— minutes. Look at the comprehension and vocabulary questions that follow the selection. How long do you think it will take you to answer the questions? —————— minutes

Learning Strategy

Even though most of this excerpt describes animal behavior, the textbook is concerned with human behavior; therefore, be alert to links between the two. Be able to define and give examples of the two major terms in this selection.

Word Knowledge

Are you familiar with the following words in this selection?

intentionally	proactive	facilitated
pursuing	retroactive	urge
hindered	perspective	
devised	parenthetical	

Your instructor may ask ten true-false questions from the *Instructor's Manual* to stimulate your thinking using these words.

As you begin to read, record your starting time: ———————

Build a Better Memory
Douglas A. Bernstein et al., *Psychology*, 3rd ed.

Mathematician John Griffith estimated that, over the course of the average person's lifetime, he or she will have stored roughly five hundred times as much information as can be found in all the volumes of the *Encyclopedia Britannica* (Hunt, 1982).

Types of Memory

5   No one is sure, but most research suggests that there are at least three basic types. Each type of memory is named for the kind of information it handles: episodic, semantic, and procedural (Reed, 1992).

Any memory of a specific event that happened while you were present
10   is an **episodic memory**—such as what you had for dinner yesterday, what you did last summer, or where you were last Friday night. **Semantic memory** contains generalized knowledge of the world that does not involve memory of a specific event. For example, you can answer a question like "Are wrenches pets or tools?" without remembering any specific episode in which
15   you learned that wrenches are tools. As a general rule, people convey episodic memories by saying, "I remember when . . . ," whereas they convey semantic memories by saying, "I know that . . . " (Tulving, 1982). **Procedural memory,** which involves *skill learning,* provides the memory for how to do things—how to ride a bicycle, read a map, or tie a shoelace, for example.
20   Often, a procedural memory consists of a complicated sequence of movements that cannot be described adequately in words. For example, a gymnast might find it impossible to describe the exact motions in a particular routine.

LEVELS OF PROCESSING   The **levels-of-processing model** suggests that the
25   most important determinant of memory is how extensively information is encoded or processed when it is first received. Consider situations in which a person intentionally tries to memorize something by *rehearsing* it—that is, by repeating it to themselves. There appear to be two basic types of mental rehearsal: maintenance and elaborative. **Maintenance rehearsal** involves
30   simply repeating an item over and over. This method can be effective for re-membering information for a short time. If you needed to look up a phone number, walk across the room, and then dial the number, maintenance rehearsal would work just fine. But what if you needed to remember some-

thing for hours or months or years? Far more effective in these cases is **elab-**
35 **orative rehearsal,** which involves thinking about how new material relates to
information already stored in memory. For example, just repeating a new
person's name to yourself is not a very effective strategy for memorizing it.
Instead, if you have difficulty remembering new names, try thinking for a
moment about how the new person's name is related to something you
40 already know. If you are introduced to a man named Jim Crews, you might
think, "He reminds me of my Uncle Jim, who always wears a crew cut."
Study after study has shown that memory is enhanced when people use
elaborative rather than maintenance rehearsal (Anderson, 1990). The
levels-of-processing model says that this enhancement occurs because of the
45 degree or "depth" to which incoming information is mentally processed
during elaborative rehearsal. The more you think about new information,
organize it, and relate it to existing knowledge, the "deeper" the processing,
and the better memory becomes.

PARALLEL DISTRIBUTED PROCESSING MODELS OF MEMORY Over the last thirty
years, virtually all approaches to memory have conceptualized it as a system
50 in which individual pieces of information are put in and taken out (Roedi-
ger, 1990). Today, some theorists are pursuing a new approach based on
parallel distributed processing (or **PDP**) models of memory. These models
suggest that new experiences don't just provide new facts that are later re-
55 trieved individually; they also change people's overall knowledge base, altering in a more general way their understanding of the world and how it operates. For example, if you compare your knowledge of college life today with
what it was when you first arrived, chances are it has changed day by day in a
way that is much more general than any single new fact you learned.

60 ### Retrieval Cues

Stimuli that help people retrieve information from long-term memory
are called **retrieval cues.** They allow people to recall things that were once
forgotten and help them to recognize information stored in memory. In
general, recognition tasks are easier than recall tasks because they contain
65 more retrieval cues. For example, it is usually easier to recognize the correct
alternative on a multiple-choice exam than to recall material on an essay
test.

Context

In general, people remember more when their efforts at recall take
70 place in the same environment in which they learned, because they tend to
encode features of the environment where the learning occurred (Bjork &
Richardson, Klavehn, 1989). These features later act as retrieval cues.

Members of a university diving club provided one demonstration of this
principle. They first learned lists of words while they were either on shore or
75 submerged twenty feet underwater. They then tried to recall as many of
the words as possible, again either on shore or underwater. Those who

originally learned underwater scored much better when they were tested underwater than when they were tested on shore. Similarly, those who had learned the words on shore did better when tested on shore (Godden & Baddeley, 1975).

When memory can be helped or hindered by similarities in context, it is termed **context-dependent.** One study found that students remember better when tested in the classroom in which they learned the material than when tested in a different classroom (Smith, Glenberg & Bjork, 1978).

SCHEMAS **Schemas** are mental representations of categories of objects, events, and people. For example, most Americans have a schema for *baseball game,* so that simply hearing these words is likely to activate whole clusters of information in long-term memory, including the rules of the game, images of players, bats, balls, a green field, summer days, and, perhaps, hot dogs and stadiums. The generalized knowledge contained in schemas provides a basis for making inferences about incoming information during the encoding stage. So if you hear that a baseball player was injured, your schema about baseball might prompt you to encode the player as a male, even though gender information was not mentioned. As a result, you are likely to recall the injury episode as involving a male player.

Improving Your Memory

In psychology, as in medicine, physics, and other sciences, practical progress does not always require theoretical certainty. Even though some basic questions about what memory is and how it works resist final answers, psychologists know a great deal about how people can improve their memories (Bellezza, 1981).

Classical Mnemonics

People with normal memory skills (Harris & Morris, 1984) as well as brain-damaged individuals (Wilson, 1987) can benefit from **mnemonics,** which are strategies for placing information into an organized context in order to remember it. For example, to remember the names of the Great Lakes, you might use the acronym HOMES (for Huron, Ontario, Michigan, Erie, and Superior). Verbal organization is the basis for many mnemonics. You can link items by weaving them into a story or a sentence or a rhyme. To help customers remember where they have parked their cars, some large garages have replaced section designations such as "A1" or "G8" with labels such as color names or months. Customers can then tie the location of their cars to information already in long-term memory—for example, "I parked in the month of my mother's birthday."

One simple but powerful method for remembering almost anything is the *peg-word system.* To use this method, first learn a list of words to serve as memory "pegs," such as "one is a bun, two is a shoe, three is a tree, four is a door, five is a hive, six is a stick, seven is heaven," and so on. Next, create an image or association between each item to be remembered and a peg word.

120 In general, the more novel and vivid you make the images and the better they tie all of the objects together, the more effective they will be (Zoller, Workman & Kroll, 1989).

One of the authors was introduced to another popular mnemonic while he was an undergraduate. His roommate, who was known to brag a
125 bit, said that he could remember any one hundred words if he had enough time to think about them. A bet of $100 was made, the words were read, and the author lost. The author's friend had used a powerful and ancient mnemonic called the *method of loci* (pronounced "low-sigh"), or the method of places. To use this method, first think about a set of familiar geographic
130 locations. For example, if you use your home, you might imagine walking along the sidewalk, up the steps, through the front door, around all four corners of the living room, and through each of the other rooms. Next, imagine each item to be remembered in one of these locations. Whenever you want to remember a list, use the same locations, in the same order. As
135 with the peg-word system, particularly vivid images seem to be particularly effective (Kline & Groninger, 1991). For example, tomatoes smashed against the front door or bananas hanging from the bedroom ceiling might be helpful in recalling items on a grocery list.

These and other mnemonic systems share one characteristic: each
140 requires that you have a well-learned body of knowledge (such as peg words or locations) that can be used to provide a *context* for organizing incoming information (Hilton, 1986). The success of these strategies demonstrates again the importance of relating new information to knowledge already stored in memory.

145 ### Guidelines for More Effective Studying

Most of the procedures discussed so far were devised for remembering arbitrary lists. When you want to remember more organized material, such as a chapter in a textbook, the same principles apply (Palmisano & Hermann, 1991). Memory for text material is facilitated when people first
150 create an overall context for learning it, such as an outline (Glover et al., 1990). Resist the urge simply to read the material. Repetition may seem effective, because maintenance rehearsal keeps material in short-term memory; but it is not effective, no matter how much time you spend on it, for retaining information over long periods (Bjorklund & Green, 1992).
155 Don't be subject to the "labor in vain effect" (Nelson & Leonesio, 1988). Instead, think about the material and elaborate it into an organized, meaningful context. What you learn will then be less subject to both proactive and retroactive interference (Anderson, 1990).

In addition, plan ahead and spend your time wisely. *Distributed practice* is
160 much more effective than *massed practice* for learning new information. If you are going to spend ten hours studying for a test, you will be much better off studying for ten one-hour blocks (separated by periods of sleep and

other activity) than "cramming" for one ten-hour block. By scheduling more study sessions, you will stay fresh and tend to think about the material
165 from a new perspective each session. This method will help you elaborate the material and remember it.

READING A TEXTBOOK More specific advice for remembering textbook material comes from a study that examined how successful and unsuccessful college students approach their reading (Whimbey, 1976). Unsuccessful stu-
170 dents tend to read the material straight through; they do not slow down when they reach a difficult section; and they keep going even when they do not understand what they are reading. In contrast, successful college students monitor their understanding, reread difficult sections, and periodically stop to review what they have learned. In short, effective learners en-
175 gage in a very deep level of processing. They are active learners, thinking of each new fact in relation to other material, and they develop a context in which many new facts can be organized effectively.

Based on what is known about memory, we suggest two specific guidelines for reading a textbook. First, make sure that you understand
180 what you are reading before moving on (Hermann & Searleman, 1992). Second, use the *SQ3R method* (Thomas & Robinson, 1972), which is one of the most successful strategies for remembering textbook material (Anderson, 1990). SQ3R stands for five activities to follow when you read a chapter: survey, question, read, recite, review. These activities are designed
185 to increase the depth to which you process the information you read.

1. *Survey* Take a few minutes to skim the chapter. Look at the section headings and any boldface or italicized terms. Obtain a general idea of what material will be discussed, how it is organized, and how its topics relate to one another and to what you already know. Some
190 people find it useful to survey the entire chapter once and then survey each major section in a little more detail before reading it.

2. *Question* Before reading each section, ask yourself what content will be covered and what information should be extracted from it.

3. *Read* Read the text, but think about the material as you read. Are
195 the questions you raised earlier being answered? Do you see the connections between the topics?

4. *Recite* At the end of each section, recite the major points. Resist the temptation to be passive by mumbling something like, "Oh, I remember that." Put the ideas into your own words.

200 5. *Review* Finally, at the end of the chapter, review all the material. You should see connections not only within a section but also among the sections. The objective is to see how the author has organized the material. Once you grasp the organization, the individual facts will be far easier to remember.

_____ 7. A schema is
   a. a network or cluster of knowledge.
   b. a new idea.
   c. an unrelated concept.
   d. an experience that is not yet connected.

_____ 8. The author suggests that the most effective method of spending four
   hours studying a chapter for an exam would be to
   a. read it once and then recite and relate.
   b. read it once, recite, and then read it again.
   c. read it twice and then recite.
   d. read it three times.

_____ 9. The difference between distributed practice and mass practice is
   a. the number of hours spent studying.
   b. the complexity of the material studied.
   c. the time intervals between study periods.
   d. the amount of material that can be studied.

_____ 10. The author suggests that the most efficient study technique for a college student to use in remembering material is
   a. rereading.
   b. maintenance rehearsal.
   c. elaborative rehearsal.
   d. semantic memory.

Answer the following with _T_ (true) or _F_ (false).

_____ 11. In the parallel distributed processing model of memory, the individual pieces of information change the overall knowledge base.

_____ 12. Research suggests that your memory might be adversely affected if
   your professor changes the location of the final exam from your regular classroom to a new location.

_____ 13. The author suggests that recitation is similar to a self-imposed examination.

_____ 14. According to the author's explanation, answering a true-false test is
   considered an easier task than taking a test that provides a name and
   asks you to identify it.

_____ 15. According to the author, research has shown that students remember
   a professor's jokes better than the main lecture points.

VOCABULARY

According to the way the italicized word was used in the selection, select _a,_
_b, c,_ or _d_ for the word or phrase that gives the best definition.

—— 1. "person *intentionally* tries" (27)
   a. deliberately
   b. suddenly
   c. hopelessly
   d. laboriously

—— 2. "*pursuing* a new approach" (52)
   a. inventing
   b. evaluating
   c. offering
   d. following

—— 3. "*hindered* by similarities" (81)
   a. employed
   b. designed
   c. controlled
   d. condensed

—— 4. "*devised* for remembering" (146)
   a. altered
   b. enriched
   c. hurt
   d. refined

—— 5. "Memory . . . is *facilitated*" (149)
   a. focused
   b. expanded
   c. accelerated
   d. assisted

—— 6. "*proactive* . . . interference" (158)
   a. existing during
   b. existing afterward
   c. existing beforehand
   d. always existing

—— 7. "*retroactive* interference" (158)
   a. existing beforehand
   b. existing afterwards
   c. existing during
   d. always existing

—— 8. "from a new *perspective*" (165)
   a. chapter
   b. unit
   c. block
   d. viewpoint

—— 9. "jokes and *parenthetical* remarks"(211)
   a. off-color
   b. inserted
   c. nasty
   d. sarcastic

—— 10. "resist the *urge*" (233)
   a. rule
   b. commitment
   c. desire
   d. emotion

WRITTEN RESPONSE

Student study guides frequently have a selection entitled "Steps to a Better Memory." Such sections typically contain five to ten suggestions for improving memory for college study. Pretend that you are the author of a study guide for memory. Use the information in this selection and your own knowledge to list five steps to a better memory. For each of your steps, explain your reasoning and give an example of a student applying the technique in college learning.

SKILL DEVELOPMENT: CONCENTRATION

When you have finished each part of the assignment, evaluate your reading and study time.

How long did you take to read the selection? ———————— minutes

How long did you take to answer the questions? ———————— minutes

Did you work steadily or were you interrupted? ————————

Did setting a time goal help you keep your mind on your work? ————————

If you had been given the concentration pop quiz while reading this selection, would your score have been high ————————, medium ————————, or low ————————?

How much time do you think you will need to complete the next selection? ———————— minutes

**COLLABORATIVE
CRITICAL
THINKING**

Using Mnemonics for Learning

Form a collaborative study group for this activity on memory. Work as a group to discuss and divide the assignment. Use the ideas in the selection, as well as the ideas and resources of the group, to devise ways to remember the following typically memorized facts from history and science.

First, add meaning to each item through group discussion. Network your new knowledge from the group by connecting it to your existing knowledge. Next, weigh the strength of different mnemonics for each learning task, and then select the mnemonic that the group believes is most appropriate for remembering each item or groups of items. Share your strategies with the class.

History
1492   Columbus discovers America
1620   *Mayflower* lands English Pilgrims in Plymouth, Massachusetts
1776   Declaration of Independence
1865   Civil War ends
1929   Stock market crash and start of Great Depression
1945   World War II ends
1955   Rosa Parks refuses to give up her seat on the bus
1973   Vietnam War ends

Science

The four lobes of the brain are:

frontal	occipital
lateral	parietal

The elements that make up the vast majority of molecules in living things are:

carbon	nitrogen	phosphorus
hydrogen	oxygen	sulphur

The classification of the major drugs is as follows:

Stimulants: amphetamines, nicotine, caffeine, cocaine
Depressants: barbiturates, opium, alcohol
Hallucinogens: marijuana, LSD

Read the following passage to expand your knowledge on schemata and memory. Develop and share group strategies for remembering the dates with the class.

Schemata and Expert Memorizers

Sometimes experts in a particular area seem to have remarkable memories for information in their own specialty. For example, the famous conductor Toscanini is reported to have had an extraordinary memory for music. Just before the start of a concert, an agitated
5 musician appeared before him. The musician reported that the key for the lowest note on his bassoon was broken—how would he play the concert? Toscanini shaded his eyes, thought for a moment, and then said, "It's all right—the note does not occur in tonight's concert." Not only did Toscanini know every note for every instrument in that concert,
10 but it has been estimated that he knew by heart every note for every instrument in about 250 symphonic works, the words and music for 100 operas, plus a volume of chamber music, piano music, cello and violin pieces, and songs. How could Toscanini memorize so much information? One view holds that experts can memorize information in
15 their field because they already have well-developed schemata or frameworks to place the information in.

A study by Chiesi, Spilich, and Voss demonstrated the role of schemata in memory. This experiment showed that people who knew a lot about baseball could remember more about a fictitious baseball
20 game than those who knew less about the sport. Baseball knowledge was first assessed by a test used to divide subjects into high- and low-knowledge groups. Both groups were given an account of one-half of an inning in a fictitious baseball game and were then asked to recall the information. Presumably because they could more easily map the new
25 information onto their existing knowledge structure or schema, the high-knowledge subjects remembered significantly more.

Schemata may also be helpful to students. For example, you may have noticed that when you are first studying a subject it is difficult to

30 learn and remember the new terms and concepts. Yet the more you study the subject, the easier it becomes to learn additional information. Perhaps you have developed schemata for the material that help you to organize and remember the new information.

From Andrew B. Crider et al., *Psychology*

WORD BRIDGE

Remembering New Words

While reading, you come across the following words:

autocrat   monotonous   prenatal

What do they mean? Should you stop reading immediately, look up each word in the dictionary, and jot down the definitions for future drill? That's ambitious, but unrealistic.

Your purpose for reading is to get information and ideas from the text, not to make word lists. Stopping to look up a particular word in the dictionary may improve your vocabulary, but it interrupts your train of thought and detracts from your comprehension of the material. Good readers use several strategies to get an approximate meaning of a word before going to the dictionary. They begin by using context and structural clues and then seek further clarification in the glossary or dictionary if necessary.

How to Remember New Words

Have you ever made lists of unknown words that you wanted to remember? Did you dutifully write down the word, a colon, and a definition, and promise to review the list at night before going to bed? Did it work? Probably not! Memorization can be an effective cramming strategy, but it does not seem to produce long-term results. Recording only the word and definition does not establish the associations necessary for long-term memory.

The best way to expand your vocabulary is to place yourself in an environment where challenging words are used. As children, this is the way we learn new words. Although changing households may not be an option, books afford a similarly rich verbal environment for those who are willing and eager to learn. Books both introduce and reinforce new words. The more you read, the more you will notice new words. With a little effort, these "new" words will gradually become "old." Once you start noticing words, you will probably be surprised at how often they recur. The following suggestions can help you make new words into old friends.

Associate Words in Phrases. Never record a word in isolation. Think of the word and record it in a phrase that suggests its meaning. The phrase may be part of the sentence in which you first encountered the word, or it may be a vivid creation of your own imagination. Such a phrase provides a setting for the word and enriches the links to your long-term memory.

For example, the word *caravel* means a "small sailing ship". Record the word in a phrase that creates a memorable setting, like "a caravan of gliding caravels shimmering on the sea."

Associate Words in Families. Words, like people, have families that share the same names. In the case of words, the names are called **prefixes, roots,** and **suffixes.** A basic knowledge of word parts can help you unlock the meaning to thousands of associated family members.

The prefix *ambi* means "both", as in the word *ambivert,* which means being both introverted and extroverted. Although this word is seldom used, it can be easily remembered because of its association with the other two more common words. A useful transfer occurs, however, when the knowledge of *ambi* is applied to new family members like *ambidextrous, ambiguous,* and *ambivalence.*

Associate Words in Images. Expand the phrase chosen for learning the word into a vivid mental image. Create a situation or an episode for the word. Further, enrich your memory link by drawing a picture of your mental image. Such a picture may ultimately prove to be a more useful memory tool than writing the word in a sentence.

The "caravan of gliding caravels on the shimmering sea" is an engaging illustration. Another example is the word *candid,* which means "frank and truthful." A suggestive phrase for learning the word might be "his candid reply hurt her feelings."

Seek Reinforcement. Look and listen for your new words. As suggested previously, you will probably discover that they are used more frequently than you ever thought. Notice them, welcome them, and congratulate yourself on your newfound wisdom.

Create Concept Cards. The following blocks represent the front and back of index cards for recording information on new words. Each word is already presented in a phrase on the front of the card, along with a notation of where the word was encountered. On the back of each card, write an appropriate definition, use the word in a sentence, and draw an image illustrating the word. Review the cards to reinforce the words.

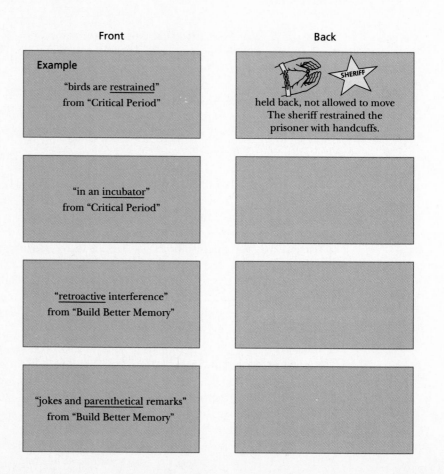

Front   Back

Example

"birds are <u>restrained</u>"
from "Critical Period"

held back, not allowed to move
The sheriff restrained the
prisoner with handcuffs.

"in an <u>incubator</u>"
from "Critical Period"

"<u>retroactive</u> interference"
from "Build Better Memory"

"jokes and <u>parenthetical</u> remarks"
from "Build Better Memory"

Name _____

To improve your skills, you must seriously reflect on the daily choices you make and your progress as a learner. Be your own best teacher by questioning your academic behaviors, your understanding of the material, and your academic performance. Take ownership of new ideas and strategies by finding a way to make them a part of you.

Many experts believe that writing is a mode of learning. In other words, writing about something helps a person understand it. With that purpose in mind, record your reflections in the following "learning log" to communicate to yourself and your instructor. Use the log to learn about yourself.

Where have you decided to do most of your studying? Why?

_____

_____

If the telephone is a distraction, how are you managing your calls?

_____

Which television programs have you decided to watch during the week and which are you dropping?

_____

_____

When and where do you tend to waste time?

_____

_____

When do you write your "To Do" list for the day?

_____

_____

Which classmates would you feel comfortable calling about an assignment?

_____

_____

When have you successfully collaborated with other students? What was the purpose?

_____

_____

Have some of your classmates been late for class? How were these tardy students put at a disadvantage?

_____

_____

What two "success behaviors" have you observed in fellow classmates that you would like to copy?

_____

_____

Reflect on the Longer Selections

Total your short-answer responses for the two longer selections.

Comprehension scores:
completed = _____ # correct = _____ # incorrect = _____ accuracy = _____%

How would you categorize the questions that you missed?

_____

_____

Did you make any careless errors? Where?

_____

_____

What reminders will you give yourself to improve your scores in the next chapter?

_____

_____

Clip out and explain two questions that you missed. Attach these questions and your analysis to the Learning Log for your instructor.

Reflect on the Vocabulary

Total your vocabulary responses for the two longer selections.

Vocabulary Scores:
completed = _____ # correct = _____ # incorrect = _____ accuracy = _____%

List the words that you missed.

_____

_____

Describe how you plan to remember two of the new words in the selections.

_____

_____

Using the perforations, tear out the Learning Log for your instructor.

© 1997 Addison-Wesley Educational Publishers Inc.

CHAPTER

2

Reading and Study Strategies

Why use a study system?

What is a study system?

What are the three stages of reading?

How do you preview?

Why should you activate your schemata?

How do good readers think?

What is metacognition?

Why recall or self-test what you have read?

WHY USE A STUDY SYSTEM?

When a professor ends a class by saying, "Read the assigned pages for your next class meeting," both the students and the professor know the real message is, "Read *and study* the assigned pages for our next class meeting." Reading a textbook means "reading to learn," which means studying and thus includes a number of steps required to master the material.

Textbook reading therefore demands an organized approach. To be successful, the techniques for reading novels and textbooks must differ. Reading a murder mystery may provide an escape into intrigue and adventure, whereas the purpose of textbook reading is to learn and remember a body of information. Each chapter, and even each page, of a textbook may contain a heavy load for the reader.

Students need to be aware of the activities involved in the learning process. According to experts on learning theory, students should first analyze the reading task to determine appropriate prereading strategies. As reading progresses, these strategies should be monitored and may need to be altered. To enhance understanding and recall while reading, students should engage in predicting, summarizing, self-testing, and establishing relationships to prior knowledge.[1] Obviously, all of these activities involve more than simply opening a book and moving from one word to another.

WHAT IS A STUDY SYSTEM?

In 1946, after years of working with college students at the Ohio State University, Francis P. Robinson developed the textbook-study system called SQ3R. The system was designed to help students efficiently read and learn from textbooks and effectively recall relevant information for subsequent exams. The letters in Robinson's acronym, SQ3R, stand for the following five steps: survey, question, read, recite, and review.

Numerous variations have been developed since SQ3R was introduced. One researcher, Norman Stahl, analyzed 65 textbook study systems and concluded that there are more similarities than differences among the systems.[2] The commonalities in the systems include a previewing stage, a reading stage, and a final self-testing stage. In the *previewing* stage students ask questions, activate past knowledge, and establish a purpose for reading. During the *reading* stage, students answer questions and continually integrate old and new knowledge. The *self-testing* stage of reading involves review to improve recall, evaluation to accept or reject ideas, and integration to blend new information with existing knowledge networks. Strategies used in these stages are depicted in the chart on the following page and are discussed in this chapter.

[1]A. L. Brown, J. C. Campione, and J. E. Day, "Learning to Learn: On Training Students to Learn from Text," *Educational Researcher* 10 (1981), pp. 14–21.
[2]N. A. Stahl, *Historical Analysis of Textbook Study-Systems* (Ph.D. diss., University of Pittsburgh, 1983).

STAGE 1: PREVIEWING

What Is Previewing?

Previewing is a method of assessing your knowledge and needs before starting to read. When you preview, you decide what the material is about, what you already know about the topic, what needs to be done, and how to go about doing it. You formulate a reading strategy and then read to meet those goals. Even though previewing may take a few extra minutes in the beginning, the increased involvement that results makes it worth the time.

How to Preview

What to Ask. To preview, look over the material, think, and ask questions. The process is similar to the concentration technique of sparking an interest before reading, except that in previewing, the questions are more directly related

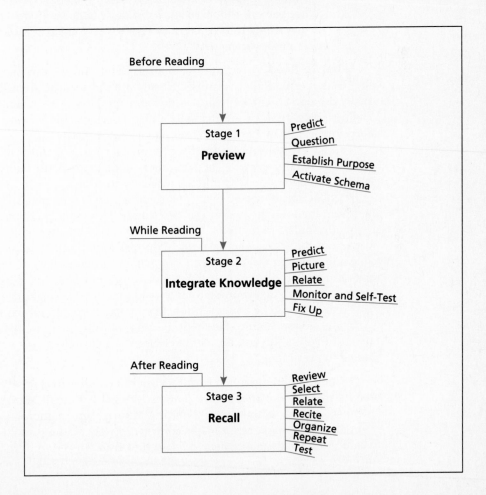

to the purpose. The focus is, "What do I already know, what do I need to know, and how do I go about finding it out?"

More specifically, ask the following questions before beginning to read:

1. What is the topic of the material?

    What does the title suggest? What do the subheadings, italics, and summaries suggest?

2. What do I already know?

    What do I already know about this topic or a related topic?

    Is this new topic a small part of a larger idea or issue that I have thought about before?

3. What is my purpose for reading?

    What will I need to know when I finish?

4. How is the material organized?

    What is the general outline or framework of the material? Is the author listing reasons, explaining a process, or comparing a trend?

5. What will be my plan of attack?

    What parts of the textbook seem most important? Do I need to read everything with equal care? Can I skim some parts? Can I skip some sections completely?

What to Read. A narrative tells a story and moves from one event to another in the resolution of a conflict. Novels and short stories are narratives. They usually develop in chronological order and rarely have such signposts as subheadings, italic type, or even chapter titles. Therefore, previewing a novel or a short story is difficult because of the lack of reader signposts.

Textbooks, however, are written in an expository manner in order to inform, explain, and discuss. They use many signposts to assist the reader in previewing the material so as to anticipate what is to come.

A public speaking rule says, "Tell them what you are going to tell them, tell them, and then tell them what you told them." This same organizational pattern frequently applies to textbook material. Typically, a chapter begins with a brief overview of the topic. The ideas are then developed in paragraphs or sections. Concluding statements at the end summarize the important points the author wants remembered. Although this pattern does not apply in every case, it can serve as a guide in determining what to read when previewing textbook material.

Previewing can be a hit-or-miss activity since there may or may not be an introductory or concluding statement. Because of differences in writing styles, no one set of rules will work for all materials. The following points should be considered in previewing.

Title. Titles are designed to attract attention and reflect the contents of the material. The title of an article, a chapter, or a book is the first and most obvious clue to its content. Think about the title and turn it into a question. If the article is entitled "Acupuncture," a major concern in your reading would probably be to find out "What is acupuncture?" Use the "five-*W* technique" that newspaper stories often use in the first paragraph: Ask *who, what, when, where,* and *why* of the title.

Introductory Material. To get an overview of an entire book, refer to the table of contents and preface. Sophisticated students use the table of contents as a study guide, turning the chapter headings into possible exam items. When you are seeking specific information in a book for research, the table of contents can help you to locate relevant material quickly. For novels, read the book jackets or paperback covers for a preview.

The first paragraphs in textbook chapters and articles frequently introduce the topic to be covered and give the reader a sense of perspective. For both articles and chapters, italicized inserts are sometimes used to overview and highlight the contents.

Subheadings. Subheadings are titles for sections within chapters. The subheadings, usually appearing in **boldface print** or *italics,* outline the main points of the author's message and thus give the reader an overview of the organization and the content. Turn these subheadings into questions that need to be answered as you read.

Italics, Boldface Print, and Numbers. Italics and boldface print are used to highlight words that merit special attention and emphasis. These are usually new words or key words that students should be prepared to define and remember. For example, a discussion of sterilization in a biology text might emphasize the words *vasectomy* and *tubal ligation* in italics or boldface print. Numbers usually signal a list of important details. In another book on the same subject, the two forms of sterilization might be emphasized with enumeration, by indicating (1) vasectomy and (2) tubal ligation.

Concluding Summary. Many textbooks include summaries at the end of the chapters to highlight the important points within the material. The summary can serve not only as a review to follow reading, but also as an introduction for overviewing the chapter.

Exercise 1   PREVIEWING THIS TEXTBOOK FOR THE BIG PICTURE

To get an overview of this textbook, look over the table of contents to get an idea of the scope and sequence of the book. Think about how the different chapter topics fit into the goals of college reading. Glance through the chapters to get a sense of the organization, and then use your previewing to answer the following questions.

1. Who is the author? Is the author a teacher?

2. The book is divided into how many major sections?

3. What seems to be the purpose of the reading selections?

4. List seven different college disciplines that are represented in the longer reading selections.

5. What seems to be the purpose of the "Collaborative Critical Thinking" segments?

6. Which chapter do you think you need the most?

7. Which chapter do you think you will like the most?

8. Why does the last chapter have only one reading selection?

9. Does the text have any study aids such as an index, a glossary, or summaries?

10. Which reading selection do you think will be most interesting?

Exercise 2   PREVIEWING THIS CHAPTER

To get an overview of this chapter, look first at the table of contents at the beginning of the book and then read the list of questions at the beginning of the chapter. Read the chapter summary and scan to understand the subheadings and italicized words. Use your previewing to answer the following questions.

1. What is a study system?

2. Why are questions listed at the beginning of this chapter?

3. Why is reading considered in three stages rather than one stage?

4. What is a schema?

5. What is metacognition?

6. What is the purpose of a recall diagram?

7. Why does this chapter have a list of summary points?

8. Which reading selection do you think will be most interesting?

9. What is a context clue?

10. What are the five thinking strategies used by good readers?

Preview to Activate Schemata

Despite what you may sometimes think, you are not an empty bucket into which the professor is pouring information. You are a learner who already knows a lot, and you are actively selecting, eliminating, and connecting information.

What do you bring to the printed page? As a reader, you have a responsibility to think and interact before, during, and after reading. Your previewing of material helps you predict the topic. Then, as a further part of the prereading stage, you need to activate your schema for what you perceive the topic to be.

A **schema** is the skeleton of knowledge in your brain on a particular subject. As you learn more about the subject, you flesh out the skeleton with new information, and the skeleton grows. A schema is like a computer chip in your brain that holds all you know on a subject. Each time you learn something new, you pull out the computer chip on that subject, add the new information, and return the chip to storage.

The depth of the schema or the amount of information on the chip varies according to previous experience. A scientist would most likely have a more detailed computer chip for DNA than would a freshman biology student. If the student can define the concept or recall an instance in which DNA appeared, however, the beginning of a rather sketchy schema exists.

All college students have a schema for Shakespeare. Suppose your previewing of a ten-page essay led you to predict that the discussion focused on the strength of the main characters in five of Shakespeare's plays. Next you would ask, "What existing knowledge do I have on the subject?" or "What is on my computer chip labeled 'Shakespeare'?" Most students would immediately think of *Macbeth* and *Hamlet,* both the characters and the plays. Others who have studied Shakespeare more might recall *King Lear,* the comedies, and a model of the Globe Theater. The richness of your background determines the amount you can activate. In general, the more you are able to activate, the more meaningful the reading will be.

STAGE 2: INTEGRATING KNOWLEDGE WHILE READING

Importance of Relating Prior Knowledge

Is it easier to understand a passage if you already know something about the topic? You already know that the answer is *yes.* Read the following paragraphs for a demonstration.

Passage A: Water Balance

Water may be the single most important nutrient for athletic performance. The body may be able to survive weeks or even months without certain vitamins and minerals, but without water, performance may be compromised in as little as 30 minutes. Our bodies are approximately 60% water, and our muscles are approximately 70%. For an athlete exercising vigorously, water's main function is to remove the heat (calories) generated by exercise. The body's metabolic rate may increase 20 to 25 times during intense exercise. The body gets rid of this heat by picking it up in the circulation and transporting it to the skin, where it is lost through evaporation.

S. Fike, et al., "Fluid and Electrolyte Requirements of Exercise,"
Sports Nutrition, ed. by Dan Benardot

Passage B: Echinoderms (i kī' nə dərms')

Echinoderms have protective skeletal elements embedded in their body walls. They also have an unusual feature called a water vascular system, which is used as a kind of hydraulic pump to extend the soft, pouchlike *tube feet,* with their terminal suckers. They are sluggish creatures with poorly developed nervous systems. However, they are tenacious foragers. Some species feed on shellfish, such as oysters. They wrap around their prey and pull relentlessly until the shells open just a bit. Then they evert their stomachs, squeezing them between the shells, and digest the flesh of the oysters on the spot.

Robert Wallace, Biology: The World of Life

Even if you are a biology major, the first passage is probably easier to read than the second. People tend to be interested in the health of the human body. Thus, most people have greater prior knowledge of the water balance needs of the human body than those of echinoderms. This prior knowledge makes reading more interesting, easier to visualize, and therefore easier to understand. Linking the old with the new provides a schema on which to hang the new ideas.

Before and while reading, good readers ask, "What do I already know about this topic?" and "How does this new information relate to my previous knowledge?" Although textbook topics may at times seem totally unfamiliar, seldom are all of the ideas completely new. Usually there is a link, an old bit of knowledge that you can associate with the new ideas. For example, although you may not be familiar with the echinoderms described in Passage B, you probably know what an oyster looks like and can visualize the tenacity needed to open its shell.

On the other hand, your choice of Passage A or B might have been different if you had known before reading the second paragraph that starfish are echinoderms. You might have found the description of mealtime downright exciting. Reread the passage with this knowledge and visualize the gruesome drama.

Later in this chapter you will read another passage on echinoderms. Be ready to pull out your already developed "echinoderm knowledge network."

Expanding Knowledge

Most experts agree that the single best predictor of your reading comprehension is what you already know. In other words, **the rich get richer.** The good news about this conclusion is that once you have struggled and learned about a subject, the next time you encounter the subject, learning about it will be easier. Forming new schemata is much more difficult than adding to existing ones. Does this help to explain why some experts say that the freshman year is the hardest? Frequently, students who barely make C's in introductory courses end up making A's and B's during their junior and senior years. Although the later courses are more advanced than the introductory ones, the students profit from the initial struggle of building schemata. Their intellectual energies during the junior and senior years can go into assimilating and arranging new information into previously established frameworks rather than striving to build schemata. Be comforted to know that during that initial struggle with new subjects, you are building schemata that you will later reuse. Tell yourself, "The smart get smarter, and I'm getting smart!"

Integrating Ideas: How Do Good Readers Think?

Understanding and remembering complex material requires as much thinking as reading. Both consciously and subconsciously, the good reader is predicting, visualizing, and drawing comparisons in order to assimilate new knowledge. The following list, devised by a reading researcher, represents the kind of thinking strategies good readers employ.[3]

1. *Make predictions.* (Develop hypotheses.)

   "From the title, I predict that this section will give another example of a critical time for rats to learn a behavior."

   "In this next part, I think we'll find out why the ancient Greeks used mnemonic devices."

   "I think this is a description of an acupuncture treatment."

2. *Describe the picture you're forming in your head from the information.* (Develop images during reading.)

   "I have a picture of this scene in my mind. My pet is lying on the table with acupuncture needles sticking out of its fur."

3. *Share an analogy.* (Link prior knowledge with new information in text.) We call this the "*like-a*" step.

   "This is like my remembering, 'In 1492 Columbus sailed the ocean blue.'"

4. *Verbalize a confusing point.* (Monitor your ongoing comprehension.)

   "This just doesn't make sense."

   "This just doesn't make sense. How can redwoods and cypress trees both be part of the same family?"

   "This is different from what I had expected."

5. *Demonstrate fix-up strategies.* (Correct your lagging comprehension.)

   "I'd better reread."

   "Maybe I'll read ahead to see if it gets clearer."

   "I'd better change my picture of the story."

   "This is a new word to me—I'd better check the context to figure it out."

The first three thinking strategies used by good readers are perhaps the easiest to understand and the quickest to develop. Young readers quickly learn to predict actions and outcomes as the excitement of an adventure escalates. Vivid descriptions and engaging illustrations nurture the imagination to create exciting mental images. Questions, discussions, and feelings of self-worth encourage the inclusion of past experience.

Up until this point, reading is like going to the movies, whether the reading is about Mafia gangsters or cholesterol's slow accumulation in the blood vessels. The moviegoer, as well as the reader, can be totally absorbed and integrated into the topic. When the ideas get more complicated, however, the last two thinking strategies become essential elements in the pursuit of meaning. College textbooks are tough and require constant use of monitoring strategies and frequent use of correction strategies.

© 1997 Addison-Wesley Educational Publishers Inc.

[3]B. Davey, "Think Aloud–Modeling for Cognitive Processes of Reading Comprehension," *Journal of Reading* 27 (October 1983), pp. 44–47.

These last two strategies involve a higher level of thinking than just picturing an oyster. They reflect a deeper understanding of the process of getting meaning and suggest a reader who both knows and controls. This ability to know and control is called *metacognition*.

Metacognition

When you look at the following words, what is your reaction?

feeet   thankz   supplyyied

Your reaction is probably, "The words don't look right. They are misspelled." The reason for your realizing the errors so quickly is that you have a global understanding of the manner in which letters can and cannot occur in the English language. You instantly recognize the errors, and immediately scan your knowledge of words and the rules of ordering letters. Through your efficient recognition and correction, you have used global information that goes beyond knowing about each of the three individual words. You have demonstrated a metacognitive awareness and understanding of lettering in the English language.[4]

The term **metacognition** is a coined word. **Cognition** refers to knowledge or skills that you possess. The Greek prefix *meta-* suggests an abstract level of understanding as if viewed from the outside. Thus, metacognition not only means having the knowledge but also refers to your own awareness and understanding of the processes involved and your ability to regulate and direct the processes. In reading, if you know how to read, you are operating on the cognitive level. To operate on a metacognitive level, you must know the processes involved in reading and be able to regulate them. If you are reading a chemistry assignment and are failing to understand, you must first of all recognize that you are not comprehending. Then you must identify what and why you don't understand. Remember, you can do this because you understand the skills involved in the reading process. Next, you select another tactic. You attempt a fix-up strategy. If it does not work, you try another and remain confident that you will succeed. The point is to understand how to get meaning, to know when you don't have it, and to know what to do about getting it. One researcher calls this "knowing about knowing."[5]

Comparing reading to a similar activity, do you know when you are really studying? Do you know the difference between really studying and simply going through the motions of studying? Sometimes you can study intensely for an hour and accomplish a phenomenal amount. Other times you can put in twice the time with books and notes but learn practically nothing. Do you know the difference and do you know what to do about it? Some students do not.

[4]The author is grateful to Professor Jane Thielemann, University of Houston (Downtown), for inspiring this paragraph.
[5]A. L. Brown, "The Development of Memory: Knowing, Knowing about Knowing, and Knowing How to Know," in H. W. Reese, ed., *Advances in Child Development and Behavior*, vol. 10 (New York, NY: Academic Press, 1975), pp. 104–146.

Metacognition

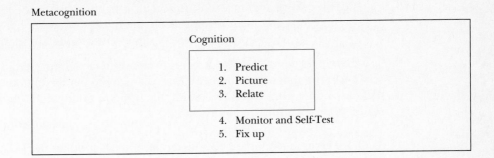

Many poor readers do not know that they don't know. They seem unaware that gaps of knowledge exist. They continue to read and do not notice comprehension failures. Not only do they fail to monitor and recognize, but they probably do not know enough about the reading process to be able to attempt a fix-up strategy to correct faulty comprehension.

Poor readers see their failure to comprehend as a lack of ability and feel that nothing can be done about it. Successful readers see failure only as a need to reanalyze the task. They know they will eventually correct their problems and succeed.

Develop a Metacognitive Sense for Reading

Research studies indicate that students can learn to develop a metacognitive sense for reading. With instruction and practice, students can improve their total reading performance. Awareness and improvement activities center around the following areas:

1. *Knowing about reading.* Good readers are aware of the many strategies they use to comprehend. These include knowledge about words, main ideas and supporting details, and implied ideas. They also understand the organization of the text and where meaning can be found. In other words, they understand the underlying elements of process and presentation.
2. *Knowing how to monitor.* Monitoring is the ongoing process of predicting, clarifying, questioning, and self-testing. The advocates of SQ3R focus on predicting and questioning in the preview stage, while metacognitive proponents stress the occurrence of these activities throughout the reading. Monitoring is an ongoing process of questioning and predicting with subsequent corroborations or discards. Clarification and self-testing both reinforce learning and pinpoint gaps in comprehension.
3. *Knowing how to correct failures.* Knowledge of the reading process offers choices for correction. Perhaps rereading to reprocess a complex idea systematically will solve the comprehension failure. Maybe the writing style is confusing, and the idea must be unraveled on a sentence level. Then again, perhaps the idea is slowly unfolding, and reading ahead

will bring enlightenment. In some cases, correction may lie beyond the text. You may need to consult the dictionary for additional word knowledge or peruse other sources to fill in background knowledge you lack.

Examples Apply both your cognitive and metacognitive knowledge to the reading of the following sentences. Interact with the material, monitor, and predict the ending phrase before reading the options. Some of the thoughts of the reader are highlighted in handwriting.

Picture

How horrible

1. Leeches used to be a favorite means of treating bruises (especially black eyes) and were also used for bloodletting. Pharmacies in some countries still stock them

   Didn't work   *not here*

   At the drugstore

   Key word?

   a. for historical value.

   b. but they are never used.

   c. to entertain customers.

   d. for medicinal purposes.   *The word still suggests some use*

   Picture   *pollutes and kills*

2. What is euphemistically called an "oil spill" can very well become an oil disaster for marine life. This is particularly true when refined or semirefined

   Wants to make more money

   products are being transported. As the tankers get bigger, so do the accidents, yet we continue to

   Key word

   a. fight for clean water.

   b. search for more oil.

   c. use profits for cleanup.

   d. build larger vessels.   *shows a parallel idea*

   Robert Wallace, *Biology: The World of Life*

The following passage illustrates the use of these thinking strategies with longer textbook material. The thoughts of the reader are highlighted in handwriting. Keep in mind that each reader reacts differently to material, depending on background and individual differences. This example merely represents one reader's attempt to integrate knowledge.

what have I already read about this?

Dehydration and Fluid Replacement Guidelines

what's that in cups?

An athlete exercising under hot and humid conditions may lose more than 2 L of water per hour. Research has shown, under experi-

How much for a 150 lb. guy?

mental conditions in subjects wearing football equipment, a loss of 1.8% of body weight in 30 minutes. Marathon runners have been shown to

How much for a 130 lb. girl? →

lose 6% to 10% of body weight during a race. A 2% loss of body weight by dehydration can impair the body's ability to dissipate heat, and a 4% loss can cause exhaustion. Besides impairing the body's thermoregulatory functions, dehydration can harm performance by causing reductions in strength, power, endurance, and aerobic capacity. Unreplaced fluid losses will eventually raise the body's core temperature to the point of heat exhaustion or even life-threatening heat stroke.

when do athletes replace fluid? →

Fortunately, most coaches and athletes now understand the importance of fluid replacement, and fluid restriction is seldom practiced. An exception is in the sport of wrestling, where fluid restriction or voluntary dehydration still appears prominent. Although the importance of fluid intake may be understood, a recent survey reported that 53% of athletes did not know how much fluid to drink. Thirst is not a reliable indicator of the need for fluid. Individuals exercising in the heat who are given water ad libitum replace only about two thirds of their fluid losses. Exercise blunts the thirst mechanism. Consequently, the most reliable indicator for fluid needs is body weight.

why wrestling? →

← *Do they get sick?*

what is? →

P. 38-39 → *Is there a chart?*

S. Fike, et al., "Fluid and Electrolyte Requirements of Exercise,"
Sports Nutrition, ed. by Dan Benardot

The example may be confusing to read because many of the thoughts that are highlighted normally occur on the subconscious level rather than the conscious level. Stopping to consciously analyze these reactions seems artificial and interrupting. It is important, however, to be aware that you are incorporating these thinking strategies into your reading. The following exercises are designed to make you more aware of this interaction.

Exercise 3   INTEGRATING KNOWLEDGE WHILE READING

For the following passage, demonstrate with written notes the way you use the five thinking strategies as you read. The passage is double-spaced so that you can insert your thoughts and reactions between the lines. Make a conscious effort to experience all of the following strategies as you read:

1. Predict (Develop hypotheses.)

2. Picture (Develop images during reading.)

3. Relate (Link prior knowledge with new ideas.)

4. Clarify points (Monitor your ongoing comprehension.)

5. Use fix-up strategies (Correct your lagging comprehension.)

Sea Stars

Let's take a look at one class of echinoderms—the sea stars. Sea stars (starfish) are well known for their voracious appetite when it comes to gourmet foods, such as oysters and clams. Obviously, they are the sworn enemy of oystermen. But these same oystermen may have inadvertently helped the spread of the sea stars. At one time, when they caught a starfish, they chopped it apart and vengefully kicked the pieces overboard. But they were unfamiliar with the regenerative powers of the starfish. The central disk merely grows new arms, and a single arm can form a new animal.

Stars are slow-moving predators, so their prey, obviously, are even slower-moving or immobile. Their ability to open an oyster shell is a testimony to their persistence. When a sea star finds an oyster or clam, the prey clamps its shell together tightly, a tactic that discourages most would-be predators, but not the starfish. It bends its body over the oyster and attaches its tube feet to the shell, and then begins to pull. Tiring is no problem since it uses tube feet in relays. Finally, the oyster can no longer hold itself shut, and it opens gradually—only a tiny bit, but it is enough. The star then protrudes its stomach out through its mouth. The soft stomach slips into the slightly opened shell, surrounds the oyster, and digests it in its own shell.

Robert Wallace, *Biology: The World of Life*

At first glance, you probably recognized *echinoderm* as an old friend and activated your newly acquired schema from a previous page. The description of the starfish lends itself to a vivid visualization. Were some of your predictions corroborated as you read the passage? Did you find yourself monitoring to reconcile new facts with old ideas? Did you need to use any fix-up strategies? Has your computer chip been expanded?

STAGE 3: RECALLING FOR SELF-TESTING

What Is Recalling?

Recalling is telling yourself what you have learned, what you wish to remember, and relating it to what you already know. It is taking those few extra minutes to digest what you have read and having a short conversation with yourself or a friend about the new material. Rather than being formal, long, and involved, the recalling process is a brief overviewing that helps you "pull together" what you have learned, as well as fill in any gaps. Before saying, "Hallelujah, I've finished!" good readers invest a few more minutes in remembering and arranging. Researchers have proven that recalling pays off. In experiments students who actively recalled what they had read scored higher on tests than students who did not recall or who merely reread the material. Recall is part of the monitoring in metacognition. It is the final self-testing good readers require of themselves.

Recall also involves arranging new information into old schemata and creating new schemata. Not only are you recalling what you just read, but you are also recalling old knowledge and seeking to make connections. While "sorting through" ideas, you are accepting and rejecting information, making decisions about storage, rearranging old networks, and creating new ones. Good readers make an effort to make connections.

Why Recall?

Engaging in recall immediately after reading forces the reader to select the most important points and to relate new with existing information.

1. *Pinpoint the topic.*
   Sift through the generalities and the nonessentials to get focused on the subject. Use the title and the subheading to help you recognize and narrow down the topic of the material.
2. *Select the most important points.*
   The poor student wants to remember everything—facts have equal importance and thus no priorities are set. In short, no decisions have been made, and the student has failed to sift through the reading and pull out the important issues.
   Good readers look for order and importance. They recognize issues and identify significant support information.
3. *Relate the information.*
   Facts are difficult to learn in isolation. For example, many first-year college students have difficulty with history courses because they

have no framework or schemata into which to fit new information. Events appear to be isolated happenings rather than results of previous occurrences or parts of ongoing trends. Yet juniors and seniors, who have worked hard to establish knowledge networks, can more readily relate historical happenings into existing frameworks.

How to Recall

To recall, simply take a few minutes after that last "*Hallelujah!* period" to recap what you have learned. This can be done in your head or on paper. To visualize the main points graphically, make a recall diagram. On a straight line across the top, briefly state the topic, or what the selection seems to be mainly about. Indented underneath the topic, state the supporting details that seem to be most significant. Next, take a few seconds to make a connection. What do you already know that seems to relate to this information? Each reader's answer will be unique because you are connecting the material to your own knowledge networks. Draw a dotted line, your thought line, and recall a related idea, issue, or concern. The following is an example of a recall diagram.

RECALL DIAGRAM

What is the material mainly about?

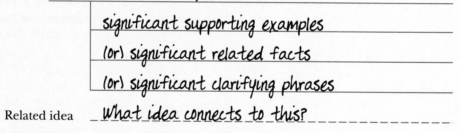

significant supporting examples

(or) significant related facts

(or) significant clarifying phrases

Related idea   What idea connects to this?

Example: Autopsies

Today, many dead people receive some form of **autopsy** or postmortem examination. At least two main reasons for this are (1) the desire of the family to know the exact cause of death, and (2) the fact that increased medical knowledge results. Because of the important moral and legal restrictions on human experimentation, much of our knowledge of pathology comes from autopsies. This fact prompts many people to donate their bodies to medical schools and/or donate certain organs for possible transplantation.

John Cunningham, *Human Biology*

Remember that the recall diagram is a temporary and artificial format. The diagram graphically demonstrates a process that you will learn to do in your

(topic) **Why autopsies are done**

(significant
details)
> **To know exact cause of death**
>
> **To increase medical knowledge**
>
> **- thus donations**

(related idea) **Will this relieve the need for much animal research?**

head. Practice using the diagram will help you learn to organize and visualize
your reading.

Exercise 4   RECALL DIAGRAMS

After reading each of the following passages, stop to recall what the passage
contained. Use the recall diagrams to record what the passage seems to be
mainly about, list significant supporting details, and identify a related idea, issue,
or concern to which you feel the information is connected.

Passage A: Wholesale Clubs Grow

The success of the wholesale club can be attributed to many factors.
Jack Shoemaker, former vice chairman of Wal-Mart Stores, Incorporated,
has suggested that success stems from three factors. First, because fast
turnover items sell before vendors are paid, clubs have an incentive to stock
high-volume, fast-turnover items. Second, packaging saves costs for the club,
and therefore the consumer. Manufacturers, for example, might shrink-
wrap five items and put a tag on them, thus minimizing labor costs once the
items are in the store. The third factor, suggests Shoemaker, is the lower
costs for labor incurred by wholesale clubs. These lower labor costs result
from the need for fewer personnel to provide service functions and the use
of more efficient check-out and check verification systems.

Thomas C. Kinnear et al., *Principles of Marketing*

(topic)

(significant
details)

(related idea)

Passage B: Kangaroos

Kangaroos and Australia are synonymous for most people, and the abundance of the large kangaroos has gone up since the British colonized Australia. The increase in kangaroo populations has occurred in spite of intensive shooting programs, since kangaroos are considered pests by ranchers and are harvested for meat and hides. The reason seems to be that ranchers have improved the habitat for the large kangaroos in three ways. First, in making water available for their sheep and cattle, the ranchers have also made it available for the kangaroos, removing the impact of water shortage for kangaroos in arid environments. Second, ranchers have cleared timber and produced grasslands for livestock. Kangaroos feed on grass, and so their food supply has been increased as well as the water supply. Third, ranchers have removed a major predator, the dingo. The dingo is a doglike predator, the largest carnivore in Australia. Because dingoes eat sheep, ranchers have built some 9,660 kilometers of fence in southern and eastern Australia to prevent dingoes from moving into sheep country. Intensive poisoning and shooting of dingoes in sheep country, coupled with the dingo fence that prevents recolonization, has produced a classic experiment in predator control.

Charles Krebs, The Message of Ecology

(topic) _____

(significant
details)

(related idea) _____

SUMMARY POINTS

- Reading is an active rather than a passive process and requires that thinking occur before, during, and after the act.
- All study systems include a previewing stage to ask questions and establish a purpose for reading, a reading stage to answer questions and integrate knowledge, and a final stage of self-testing and reviewing to improve recall.
- Previewing is a way to assess your needs before you start to read by deciding what the material is about, what needs to be done, and how to go about doing it.
- Activate your schemata before reading; the more you are able to activate, the more meaningful the reading will become.
- The second stage of reading involves thinking while reading. The thinking strategies are to predict, to picture, to relate, to monitor, and to fix up.

- Good readers operate on a metacognitive level, which means they control and direct these thinking strategies as they read.
- Recalling what you have read immediately after reading is the last stage. It forces you to select the most important points, to relate the supporting details, and to connect new information into existing networks of knowledge.

SELECTION 1

ALLIED HEALTH

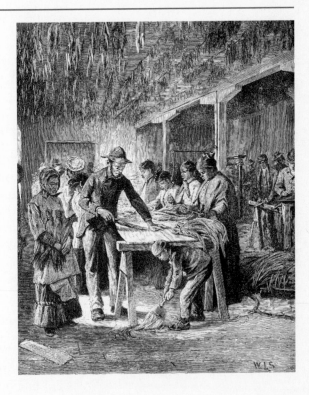

Skill Development

Stage 1: Preview

Preview the next selection to predict purpose, organization, and a learning plan.
The author probably reviews the history of tobacco usage.

agree ☐   disagree ☐

After reading this passage, I will need to know

_____

Activate Schema

How has the American attitude toward smoking changed in your lifetime?

Do you smoke? Why or why not?

In what areas on campus is smoking allowed?

© 1997 Addison-Wesley Educational Publishers Inc.

Learning Strategy

Are you able to explain how the attitudes toward and public acceptance of tobacco have changed since its discovery?

Word Knowledge

Are you familiar with the following words in this selection?

abscesses   diatribes

enamored   volatile

indigenous   oxidation

transition   mimicked

aromatic   chronic

Your instructor may choose to ask ten true-false questions from the *Instructor's Manual* to stimulate your thinking using these words.

Stage 2: Integrate Knowledge While Reading

Since each reader interacts with material in a unique manner, it is artificial to require certain thinking strategies to be used in certain places. In order to heighten awareness, however, several questions have been inserted within this selection. Briefly respond in the margin to the inserted questions. In addition, make a note in the margin of at least one other instance when you used each of the following strategies:

1. Predict   2. Picture   3. Relate   4. Monitor   5. Fix up

Tobacco
From Oakley Ray and Charles Ksir, *Drugs, Society & Human Behavior*

Tobacco was a plant just waiting for civilization to discover it—so it could conquer civilization. Long before Columbus stumbled onto the Western Hemisphere, the Indians here were using tobacco. It was one of the many contributions of the New World to Europe: corn, sweet potatoes,
5   white potatoes, chocolate, and—so you could lie back and enjoy it all—the hammock. Christopher Columbus recorded that the natives of San Salvador presented him with tobacco leaves on October 12, 1492. A fitting birthday present.

In 1497 a monk who had accompanied Columbus on his second trip
10   wrote a book on native customs that contained the first printed report of tobacco smoking. It wasn't called tobacco, and it wasn't called smoking. Inhaling smoke was called drinking. In that period you either "took" (used snuff) or "drank" (smoked) tobacco.

The word "tobacco" came from one of two sources. "Tobaco" referred
15   to a two-pronged tube used by natives to take snuff. Some early reports confused the issue by applying the name to the plant they incorrectly thought was being used. Another idea is that the word developed its current

usage from the province of Tobacos in Mexico where everyone used the herb.
Be that as it may, in 1598 an Italian-English dictionary published in London
20 translated the Italian "Nicosiana" as the herb "Tobacco," and that spelling
and usage gradually became dominant.

One member of Columbus's party was the poor fellow who introduced
tobacco drinking to Europe. He was also the first European to touch Cuba
and possibly the first to smoke tobacco. When he continued his habit in
25 Portugal, his friends were convinced the devil had possessed him as they saw
the smoke coming out his mouth and nose. The priest agreed, and Rodrigo
spent the next several years in jail, only to find on his release that people
were doing the same thing for which he had been jailed!

What are the laws against smoking today?

30 ### *Early Medical Uses*
Tobacco was formally introduced to Europe as an herb useful for
treating almost anything. A 1529 report indicated that tobacco was used for
"persistant headaches," "cold or catarrh," and "abscesses and sores on the
head." Between 1537 and 1559, 14 books mentioned the medicinal value of
35 tobacco.

Jean Nicot was sent to Lisbon, Portugal in 1559 to arrange a royal
marriage that never took place, but he became enamored with the medical
uses of tobacco. He tried it on enough people to convince himself of its
value and sent glowing reports of the herb's effectiveness to the French
40 court. He was successful in "curing" the migraine headaches of Catherine
de Medici, Queen of Henry II of France, which made tobacco use very
much "in." It was called the *herbe sainte,* holy plant, and the *herbe a tous les
maux,* the plant against all evils. The French loved it, and although tobacco
had been introduced earlier to Paris, Nicot received the credit. By 1565 the
45 plant had been called nicotiane, and Linnaeus sanctified it in 1753 by
naming the genus *Nicotiana.* When a pair of French chemists isolated the
active ingredient in 1828, they acted like true nationalists and called it
nicotine.

Tobacco Use Spreads
50 To fully appreciate the history of tobacco you must know that there are
more than 60 species of *Nicotiana,* but only two major ones. ***Nicotiana
tobacum,*** the major species grown today in more than 100 countries, is large
leafed. Most importantly, *tobacum* was indigenous only to South America, so
the Spanish had a monopoly on its production for more than a hundred
55 years. ***Nicotiana rustica*** is a small-leaf species and was the plant existing in
the West Indies and eastern North America when Columbus arrived.

The Spanish monopoly on tobacco sales to Europe was a thorn in the
side of the British. When the settlers returned to England in 1586 after
failing to colonize Virginia, they brought with them seeds of the *rustica*

60 species and planted them in England, but this species never grew well. The English crown again attempted to establish a tobacco colony in 1610 when they sent John Rolfe as leader of a group to Virginia. From 1610 to 1612 Rolfe tried to cultivate *rustica*, but the small-leafed plant was weak, poor in flavor, and had a sharp taste.

65 **What probably happened with the seed?**

In 1612 Rolfe's wife died, but, more important, he somehow got hold of some seeds of the Spanish *tobacum* species. This species grew beautifully and sold well in 1613. The colony was saved, and every available plot of land was planted with *tobacum*. By 1619, as much Virginia tobacco as Spanish tobacco 70 was sold in London. That was also the year that King James prohibited the cultivation of any tobacco in England and declared the tobacco trade a royal monopoly.

Tobacco became one of the major exports of the American colonies to England. The Thirty Years' War spread smoking throughout central Europe, 75 and nothing stopped its use. Measures such as one in Bavaria in 1652 probably slowed tobacco use, but only momentarily. This law said that "tobacco-drinking was strictly forbidden to the peasants and other common people" and made tobacco available to others only from a druggist on a doctor's prescription. During the eighteenth century smoking gradually 80 diminished, but the use of tobacco did not. Snuff replaced the pipe in England. At the beginning of that century the upper class was already committed to snuff. The middle and lower classes only gradually changed over, but by 1770 very few people smoked. The reign of King George III (1760 to 1820) was the time of the big snuff. His wife Charlotte was so 85 addicted to the powder that she was called "Snuffy Charlotte," although for obvious reasons not to her face. On the continent Napoleon had tried smoking once, gagged horribly, and returned to his 7 pounds of snuff a month.

Picture how dirty this would be.

90 ### *Tobacco in Early America*
Trouble developed in the colonies, which, being democratic, made the richest man in Virginia (perhaps the richest in the colonies) commander in chief of the Revolutionary Army. In 1776 George Washington said in one of his appeals, "If you can't send money, send tobacco." Tobacco played an 95 important role in the Revolutionary War, since it was one of the major products for which France would lend the colonies money. Knowing the importance of tobacco to the colonies, one of Cornwallis's major campaign goals in 1780 and 1781 was the destruction of the Virginia tobacco plantations.

© 1997 Addison-Wesley Educational Publishers Inc.

100   ### Chewing Tobacco
          Chewing was a suitable activity for a country on the go; it freed the
hands, and the wide open spaces made an adequate spittoon. There were
also other considerations: Boston, for example, had passed an ordinance in
1798 forbidding anyone from being in possession of a lighted pipe or
105 "segar" in public streets. The original impetus was a concern for the fire
hazard involved in smoking, not the individual's health, and the ordinance
was finally repealed in 1880. Today it is difficult to appreciate how much of
chewing country we were in the nineteenth century. In 1860 only 7 of 348
tobacco factories in Virginia and North Carolina manufactured
110 smoking tobacco. The amount of tobacco for smoking did not equal the
amount for chewing until 1911 and did not surpass it until the 1920s.

                    What motivated the change?

          ### Cigars and Cigarettes
          The transition from chewing to cigarettes had a middle point, a
115 combination of both smoking and chewing: cigars. Cigarette smoking was
coming, and the cigar manufacturers did their best to keep cigarettes under
control. They suggested that cigarettes were drugged with opium so you
could not stop using them and that the paper was bleached with arsenic and
thus was harmful to you.
120   By the turn of the century there was a preference for cigarettes with an
aromatic component, that is, Turkish tobacco. A new cigarette in 1913
capitalized on the lure of the Near East while rejecting it in actuality.
Camels were a blend of burley and bright with just a hint of Turkish
tobacco—you had the camel and pyramid on the package, what more could
125 you want? Besides, eliminating most of the imported tobacco made the
price lower. Low price was combined with a big advertising campaign: "The
Camels are coming. Tomorrow there'll be more CAMELS in town than in
all of Asia and Africa combined." By 1918 Camels had 40% of the market
and stayed in front until after World War II.
130   The year 1919 was marked by the first ad showing a woman smoking.
To make the ad easier to accept, the woman was Oriental looking and the
ad was for Turkish-type cigarettes. King-size cigarettes appeared in 1939 in
the form of Pall Mall, which became the number-one seller. Filter cigarettes
as filter cigarettes, not cigarettes that happen to have filters along with a
135 mouthpiece, appeared in 1954 with Winston, which rapidly took over the
market and continued to be number one until the mid–1970s. Filter
cigarettes captured an increasing share of the market, and now represent
more than 90% of all U.S. cigarette sales.

          Over the years, how have advertisements manipulated the public?

140 A Social and Economic Dilemma

It is now clear that cigarette smoking is deadly, but acceptance of the facts may have been slowed to some extent because tobacco, like alcohol and other substances, has long been the subject of emotional diatribes. In 1604 King James of England (the same one who had the Bible translated) 145 wrote and published a strong antitobacco pamphlet stating that tobacco was "harmfull to the braine, dangerous to the lungs." Never one to let morality or health concerns interfere with business, he also supported the growing of tobacco in Virginia in 1610.

Nicotine Absorption

150   How easily does it get into your blood stream?

Nicotine is a naturally occurring liquid alkaloid that is colorless and volatile. On oxidation it turns brown and smells much like burning tobacco. Tolerance to its effects develops, along with the dependency that led Mark Twain to remark how easy it was to stop smoking—he'd done it several 155 times!

Inhalation is a very effective drug-delivery system, with 90% of inhaled nicotine being absorbed. The physiological effects of smoking one cigarette have been mimicked by injecting about 1 mg of nicotine intravenously.

Acting with almost as much speed as cyanide, nicotine is well 160 established as one of the most toxic drugs known. In humans, 60 mg is a lethal dose, and death follows intake within a few minutes. A cigar contains enough nicotine for two lethal doses (who needs to take a second one?), but not all of the nicotine is delivered to the smoker or absorbed in a short enough period of time to kill a person.

165 Causes for Concern

Although the first clear scientific evidence linking smoking and lung cancer appeared in the 1950s, acceptance was slow. Each decade brought clearer evidence and more forceful warnings from the Surgeon General. By now it is abundantly clear that tobacco is America's true "killer weed," and is 170 a bigger public health threat than all the other drug substances combined, including alcohol.

If we add it all up it comes out like this: although lung cancer is not common, almost all lung cancers occur in smokers. Among deaths resulting from all types of cancer, smoking is estimated to be related to 30%, or about 175 129,000 premature deaths per year. However, cancer is only the second leading cause of death in the United States. It now appears that smoking may also be related to about 30% of deaths from the leading killer, coronary heart disease, or about 170,000 premature deaths per year. In addition, cigarette smoking is the cause of 80% to 90% of deaths resulting from 180 chronic obstructive lung disease—another 62,000 cigarette-related premature deaths per year. The total from these three causes is more than

185 360,000 premature deaths per year in the United States. No wonder these reports keep saying that "cigarette smoking is the chief, single, avoidable cause of death in our society and the most important public health issue of our time."

Stage 3: Recall

Stop to self-test and relate. Use the subheadings in the recall diagram to guide your thinking. For each subheading, jot down a key idea that you feel is important to remember. (In addition, your instructor may choose to ask ten true-false questions to stimulate your recall.)

History of Tobacco's Popularity

Discovery

Early medical uses

Tobacco use spreads

Early America

Chewing tobacco

Cigars and cigarettes

Social and economic dilemma

Nicotine absorption

Causes for concern

Related idea or question? _____

COMPREHENSION QUESTIONS

After reading the selection, answer the following questions with *a, b, c,* or *d.*

_____ 1. The best statement of the main idea of this selection is
   a. tobacco was a major contribution to the Old World from the New World.
   b. the popularity of tobacco brought a damaging disease to Europe.
   c. the success of the colonies and the American Revolution can be attributed to tobacco.
   d. the usage and importance of tobacco have varied historically, but it is now known to be deadly.

_____ 2. The author's attitude in the first paragraph could be described as
   a. intellectual.
   b. nostalgic.
   c. sarcastic.
   d. respectful.

_____ 3. The word "tobacco" probably came from
   a. a town in Portugal called Tobacos.
   b. a tube for taking snuff.
   c. the Italian word for nicotine.
   d. the name of the monk who first wrote about it.

_____ 4. Tobacco was successfully introduced as a medical cure in Europe by
   a. Rodrigo.
   b. Columbus.
   c. Nicot.
   d. Rolfe.

_____ 5. The author implies that the supremacy of the American colonies in tobacco production depended greatly on
   a. acquisition of seeds for the rustica species.
   b. the prohibition on cultivation in England.
   c. the Spanish monopoly on tobacco sales.
   d. the Thirty Years' War.

_____ 6. The author suggests that tobacco played an important role in the Revolutionary War in all of the following except
   a. it created wealth for the colonies.
   b. it influenced the direction of military action.
   c. it could be used as collateral for debts.
   d. the British were hindered by the trade monopoly.

_____ 7. The author suggests that the reason for the camel on Camel cigarettes was
   a. to more strongly suggest Turkish tobacco while using less.
   b to create an image suitable for the Asian and African market.
   c. to open the Oriental market.
   d. to advertise that only Turkish tobacco was used.

_____ 8. Nicotine is a toxic drug and can be lethal in humans when
   a. 1 mg is injected intravenously.
   b. 60 mg are injected intravenously.
   c. the nicotine from one cigarette is injected intravenously.
   d. the smoke from one cigar is delivered quickly to the smoker.

_____ 9. The statistics on smoking-related deaths reveal that
   a. lung cancer causes 360,000 premature deaths per year.
   b. 60 percent of the premature deaths are smoking related.

    c. smoking is estimated to be related to 30 percent of the coronary heart disease deaths.

    d. lung cancer is the second leading cause of death in the United States.

_____ 10. The product "timeline" in the sequential progression of the highest popularity of smoking products in Europe and the United States would be

    a. pipe, snuff, chewing tobacco, cigarettes.

    b. snuff, chewing tobacco, pipe, cigarettes.

    c. chewing tobacco, pipe, snuff, cigarettes.

    d. pipe, snuff, cigarettes, chewing tobacco.

Answer the following with *T* (true) or *F* (false).

_____ 11. In the first printed report on tobacco smoking, inhaling smoke was called drinking.

_____ 12. The author suggests that George Washington's wealth contributed to his position as Commander-in-Chief.

_____ 13. Prior to the 1900s, no information about the effects of tobacco on the lungs was in print.

_____ 14. The author suggests that chewing tobacco became popular because of concerns about fires.

_____ 15. Winston introduced the king-size cigarette to the market.

VOCABULARY

According to the way the italicized word was used in the selection, select *a, b, c,* or *d* for the word or phrase that gives the best definition.

_____ 1. "*abscesses* and sores" (33)

    a. dandruff

    b. boils

    c. hair

    d. freckles

_____ 2. "*enamored* with medical uses" (37)

    a. fascinated

    b. enlightened

    c. educated

    d. obsessed

_____ 3. "*indigenous* only to South America" (53)

    a. useful

    b. important

    c. hardy

    d. native

_____ 4. "*transition* from chewing to cigarettes" (114)

    a. consumption

    b. change

    c. rebirth

    d. response

—— 5. "an *aromatic* component"
(121)
a. foreign
b. scented
c. innovative
d. deceptive

—— 6. "emotional *diatribes*"
(143)
a. bitter speeches
b. decisions
c. medical articles
d. pamphlets

—— 7. "colorless and *volatile*" (151)
a. explosive
b. clear
c. expensive
d. addictive

—— 8. "On *oxidation* it turns" (152)
a. consumption
b. exposure to light
c. chemical change process
d. absorption

—— 9. "*mimicked* by injection" (158)
a. increased
b. imitated
c. transferred
d. released

—— 10. "*chronic* obstructive lung
disease" (180)
a. painful
b. hidden
c. aggravated
d. continuous

WRITTEN RESPONSE

Use information from the text to respond to the following: **Create a time line beginning in 1492 that outlines the significant events, attitudes, or people related to the history of tobacco.**

Response Strategy: Use your pen to circle the times, events, and attitudes that are chronicled by the author. Select the ones that seem to be milestones and put them in chronological order in your timeline.

COLLABORATIVE CRITICAL THINKING

An Investigation of Smoking

Smoking is a personal and family concern for many, but for all of us it is a national concern. The dangers of smoking are irrefutable and the cost of addiction is high. To investigate the problem, form a collaborative group and seek answers to the following questions. Develop a format such as a paper or presentation to present each group's findings to the class.

1. *Who is now smoking?*

Search the Internet for recent statistics on smoking. Try to find data on the age and gender of smokers. Describe what categories of people are most likely to smoke.

2. *What are the national costs of smoking?*

Brainstorm with group members to list ways in which smoking costs money that eventually comes out of the pockets of fellow citizens.

3. *Why do people start smoking?*

Ask at least ten smokers why they started the habit. List their reasons and comment on any patterns that you sense emerging.

4. *What can be done to discourage smoking?*

Brainstorm to suggest ways in which the government, organizations, and individuals can discourage people from smoking. List your suggestions.

The following selection addresses the personal and family concerns of smoking. Read the selection to help you understand these sometimes emotional issues.

Passive Smoking

The right of nonsmokers to a smoke-free environment has become an emotional issue. The controversy centers around how seriously the nonsmoker is threatened by **passive smoke,** also called "second-hand"
or "side-stream" smoke.

Studies have shown that the danger from passive smoking is very real. The smoke rising from a burning cigarette resting in an ashtray or in a smoker's hand is *not* the same as the smoker is inhaling. The smoker is inhaling smoke that has been filtered through the tobacco along the length of the cigarette (and usually by its filter) while the nonsmoker is inhaling smoke that is totally unfiltered. Of course, the smoker also inhales this unfiltered smoke. Unfiltered "side-stream" smoke contains 50 times the amounts of carcinogens, is twice as high in tar and nicotine, has five times the carbon monoxide, and has 50 times as much ammonia as smoke inhaled through the cigarette. Although the nonsmoker does not usually inhale side-stream smoke in the concentration that the smoker inhales the **mainstream smoke,** the concentration inhaled still amounts to, for the average person in the United States, the equivalent of smoking one cigarette per day. For people working in very smoky places, such as a bar or office, passive smoking can reach the equivalent of 14 cigarettes per day.

Cancer Affecting Passive Smokers

In January 1993, a long-awaited Environmental Protection Agency (EPA) report classified passive cigarette smoke as a human carcinogen that causes lung cancer in nonsmokers. According to the report, passive

smoking causes somewhere between 700 and 7000 lung cancer deaths a year in the United States. The agency said that the most likely number is about 3000 deaths a year. This report is expected to result in additional limits on smoking in public places and federal regulations on smoking
30 in the workplace. Predictably, the tobacco industry said that the report was based on inadequate scientific data.

Other Effects

Passive tobacco smoke is a major lung irritant. At the very least, breathing second-hand smoke causes discomfort and coughing.
35 Research has demonstrated that children raised in homes of smokers show early signs of conditions known to lead to heart disease in adulthood. For example. they show increased stiffness of the arteries, thickened walls of the heart chambers, and an unfavorable change in the blood's ratio of high-density lipoprotein to low-density lipoprotein.
40 For people susceptible to **asthma** (attacks of difficult breathing caused by narrowing of the bronchioles), passive smoking can bring on a full-blown asthma attack. This is especially true for children. The incidence of asthma is higher among children who live in homes where someone smokes than among those from homes in which no one
45 smokes. One estimate is that passive smoking may cause up to 100,000 new cases of childhood asthma in the United States each year. Further, asthmatic children from homes in which someone smokes are likely to be in poorer health than asthmatic children from homes where no one smokes. Infants living in homes with smokers also experience twice as
50 many respiratory infections as other infants.
Many people do not enjoy the smell of burning tobacco, do not want to have the taste of their dinner spoiled by the smell of smoke, do not want their clothing or hair contaminated with the smell of stale smoke, and consider it very rude to be subjected to these intrusions.
55 Conversely, many smokers are addicted to nicotine and are thus uncomfortable if required to forego smoking for extended periods. Many have tried to quit smoking without success. To be denied the right to smoke in public places makes it difficult or impossible for them to enjoy restaurant dining and other activities. As long as there are both
60 smokers and nonsmokers we can expect to see conflicts regarding the rights of each group.

BUSINESS

Skill Development

Stage 1: Preview

Preview the next selection to predict purpose, organization, and a learning plan.

The author probably emphasizes the accident rate and dangers of riding motorcycles.

agree ☐   disagree ☐

After reading this passage, I will need to know

Activate Schema

What is the average price of a motorcycle?

Why do you think Harley-Davidson is a good motorcycle?

Learning Strategy

Are you able to explain how the Harley-Davidson company has become successful?

Word Knowledge

Are you familiar with the following words in this selection?

crest	intangible
espouse	prominent
devastated	stringent
enhanced	defray
consummate	spectrum

Your instructor may choose to ask ten true-false questions from the *Instructor's Manual* to stimulate your thinking using these words.

Stage 2: Integrate Knowledge While Reading

Since each reader interacts with material in a unique manner, it is artificial to require certain thinking strategies to be used in certain places. In order to heighten awareness, however, several questions have been inserted within this selection. Briefly respond in the margin to the inserted questions. In addition, make a note in the margin of at least one other instance when you used each of the following strategies:

1. Predict   2. Picture   3. Relate   4. Monitor   5. Fix up

The Story of Harley-Davidson Motorcycles
From Thomas C. Kinnear, Kenneth Bernhardt, and Kathleen Krentler, *Principles of Marketing*

Overview

Harley-Davidson, Incorporated, the only remaining major American manufacturer of motorcycles, is riding the crest of success as measured by consumer demand, revenue, and profits. The company produces
5   motorcycles and related products that espouse a unique attitude and inspire power, excitement, and individuality both in Harley-Davidson riders and in much of the nonriding public.

As a company, Harley-Davidson has evolved through stages of development that have affected business throughout the past century. When
10   Harley first began to produce motorcycles in 1903, it entered the *production concept* stage, during which a company presumes that supply will create its own demand for a product. During this stage, there was no conscious effort to increase mass market sales; Harley-Davidson's primary goal was simply to develop a technically superior motorcycle. However, as the firm's success
15   became more evident, it moved into the *sales concept* stage, during which improved manufacturing processes allowed supply to outpace demand. The natural response was to increase sales efforts, and at this time Harley-Davidson developed its worldwide dealership network.

Over the last two decades, Harley-Davidson has entered into the
20   *marketing concept* stage, which involves a strong focus on consumer needs and has included developing the Harley Owners Group (H.O.G.), the world's largest organization of motorcycle enthusiasts.

> Can you visualize the activities of the company during the three concept periods?

25   How Did It Happen?

Harley-Davidson's success did not come overnight nor has it been sustained continuously. In the early 1900s, Harley-Davidson was one of more

than 100 U.S. motorcycle manufacturers on the scene. However, when Ford
Motor Company first introduced its Model T car, the motorcycle market was
30   devastated, and most of the companies folded by 1920. Harley-Davidson did
well in the 1960s and early 1970s in selling to an often misunderstood
market. However, the company went from claiming 100 percent of the U.S.
heavyweight motorcycle market to less than 15 percent in the early 1980s,
when higher-quality and lower-priced Japanese offerings dominated.
35   At the time, Harley-Davidson maintained that Japanese manufacturers
were producing motorcycles at record rates and flooding the U.S. market,
despite the fact that a sharp decline in new motorcycle purchases had been
occurring. As a result, dealers of imported motorcycles resorted to intense
price discounting to relieve their inventories, which created an unfair
40   selling environment for Harley-Davidson. In late 1982, Harley-Davidson
appealed to the International Trade Commission (ITC) to increase tariffs
on imported heavyweight motorcycles to help support the company against
Japanese competition. Based on the ITC's recommendations, in 1983 the
United States imposed additional tariffs, effective for five years. Buoyed by
45   the tariffs, Harley-Davidson had regained the top position in the U.S.
heavyweight market by the end of 1986. On firm financial footing, Harley-
Davidson felt confident enough to petition the ITC for early termination of
the tariffs in 1987.

        What other major companies have received government support
50   **to get on a firm financial footing?**

The Harley-Davidson Family

        The first Harley-Davidson motorcycle was built in 1903 in Milwaukee,
Wisconsin. There William Harley and the Davidson brothers (Walter,
Arthur, and William) designed and built high-quality motorcycles from
55   scratch. The reputation of the bikes spread, and throughout the 1920s and
1930s police department, postal workers, and even the U. S. military began
to use the motorcycles. In World War II, all of Harley-Davidson's production
(more than 90,000 units) was sold to the U. S. government for military use.

                Why were motorcycles useful in World War II?

60   ### Primary Segments and Targets

        As a result of good market analysis and customer research, Harley-
Davidson was able to design and sell the right product to the right group.
From 1983 to 1992 it increased its share in the heavyweight market from less
than 15 percent to more than 60 percent.
65   The average Harley-Davidson buyer is male, 41.6 years old, and shares an
average household income of about $45,000 per year. Aging baby boomers
are the heavyweight motorcycle's future lifeblood. Sales figures show this

group increasing at least until the year 2000. Interestingly, Harley-Davidson
does not target women differently than it does men. Rather, it finds that
70   rider characteristics are not gender-specific, and that women ride their
motorcycles for basically the same reasons that men do. However, the
company provides an extension line of women's apparel and also sponsors
the Ladies of Harley organization of motorcycle enthusiasts.

Do you know women who ride motorcycles?

75   Harley-Davidson sells about 70 percent of its bikes in the United States
and roughly 30 percent abroad. The company has a strong international
reputation. Riders abroad are usually professionals who can afford to pay up
to $25,000 for a motorcycle and who thrill to the classic American image. In
fact, export sales in 1993 equaled $283 million (24 percent of sales, up from
80   14 percent in 1989).

What would you predict to be the targeted personality traits or
"attitude" of Harley owners?

Product Considerations

The core strength of Harley-Davidson is its excellent product—one that
85   many thousands of people want to buy, and others who can't buy, still want.
When purchasing a Harley-Davidson, you are not just buying a motorcycle,
but also the heritage, image, service, and attitude that come with it. In order
to stress their commitment to service, employees and dealers strive to build
long-term relationships with customers. Management makes it a policy to
90   attend Harley-Davidson's frequent "Town Hall Meeting," where Harley
Owners Groups (HOGs) meet and share Harley stories and ideas for
improvements in products and services.

Why would the company promote HOG meetings?

Production Process

95   Today, demand for Harley-Davidson motorcycles exceeds the
company's supply of bikes. This fact reflects well on the product, but puts
pressure on production to make more bikes more quickly. Under such
circumstances, a keen eye must be kept on maintaining the high quality of
the bikes. Harley-Davidson continues to invest millions of dollars in
100   production to ensure quality and consistency in the end product.

Ancillary and Licensed Products

Licensing the trademark emblem and logos creates and increases an
awareness of the brand among the riding and nonriding public and
reinforces the company's image with customers. Harley-Davidson
105   motorcycles are complemented in the secondary market with licensing
arrangements to create such products and services as T-shirts and other

apparel, motorcycle collectibles, restaurants, and children's toys. These are target-specific; not all consumers respond to each of these items. Harley-Davidson is regarded as a consummate promoter with an excellent product
110   in high demand.

Which of these products have you seen?

Advertising

In 1993, Harley-Davidson was recognized for its creative ads by *Adweek* magazine. One example of the company's advertising is the following ad
115   placed in a number of magazines to celebrate Harley-Davidson's 90th anniversary in 1993. The ad copy playfully expresses the attitude at the core of the Harley-Davidson mystique:

> We've survived four wars, a depression, a few recessions, 16 U.S. presidents, foreign and domestic competition, racetrack competition, and
120   one Marlon Brando movie. Sounds like a party to us.

Why do you like or dislike the ad?

Public Relations

The patronage of famous personalities is usually a dependable boon to sales. Jay Leno of *The Tonight Show* rides a Harley-Davidson and has
125   appeared at charitable benefits sponsored by the company. The late Malcolm Forbes, owner and publisher of *Forbes* magazine, was a great lover of Harley-Davidson motorcycles. His trip on a Harley-Davidson through China with other prominent dignitaries was well publicized.

Can you name another celebrity who rides a Harley?

130   ### Sales

Much of Harley-Davidson's recent boost in sales is due to improved quality and manufacturing systems and increased employee involvement. However, while quality and sales are up and production has nearly tripled in the past six years, the company has not been able to supply enough
135   motorcycles to satisfy total demand in the marketplace. Because Harley-Davidson knows that reliability and service play a critical role in its competition advantage, it refuses to sacrifice quality for the sake of increased production and sales. Moreover, Harley-Davidson has learned from experience about the cyclical nature of market and customers'
140   demand. By keeping growth under control, Harley-Davidson carefully avoids overexpansion. Meanwhile, the company develops parts, services, and accessories to maintain sales volume and profits for dealers.

Why doesn't Harley build more motorcycles?

Premium Product at a Premium Price

145 Pricing is taken very seriously at Harley Davidson. Managers and employees recognize that not everyone can afford the price of a Harley-Davidson motorcycle, which ranges from $5,600 to $16,000 (without accessories). The company knows it must produce such an excellent product that enough customers say the price is worth it. Harley-Davidson

150 has been able to prove the worth of its bikes with more than 600,000 registered in the United States alone.

How do consumers react to a premium price? Relate an example.

While Harley-Davidson management recognizes that its motorcycles occupy the high end of the price spectrum, it is continuously evaluating the

155 possible development of smaller, entry-level-priced motorcycles. The hope is that these new bikes will attract more customers to the Harley-Davidson brand. Some of these new customers might eventually decide to buy a larger, more traditional Harley-Davidson model.

Stage 3: Recall

Stop to self-test and relate. Use the subheadings in the recall diagram to guide your thinking. For each subheading, jot down a key idea that you feel is important to remember. (In addition, your instructor may choose to ask ten true-false questions to stimulate your recall.)

The Success of Harley-Davidson

| How did it happen? |
| Harley-Davidson family |
| Primary segments and targets |
| Product considerations |
| Ancillary products |
| Advertising |
| Public relations |
| Sales |
| Premium product |

Related idea _____

COMPREHENSION QUESTIONS

After reading the selection, answer the following questions with *a, b, c,* or *d.*

_____ 1. The best statement of the main idea of this selection is
   a. Harley-Davidson is the only remaining major American motorcycle manufacturer.
   b. Harley-Davidson targets customers who are upscale and independent.
   c. Harley-Davidson increased profits by licensing the trademark and logo to ancillary products.
   d. Harley-Davidson's success is built on an excellent product and on marketing that inspires an attitude and excitement.

_____ 2. According to the passage, the product concept stage is a period during which
   a. mass marketing efforts occur.
   b. the goal is to create a superior product that wins sales.
   c. the company develops a network of dealerships.
   d. demand outstrips supply.

_____ 3. The stage of marketing that develops organizations to discuss the needs and concerns of customers is called the
   a. productions concept stage.
   b. dealership network stage.
   c. sales concept stage.
   d. marketing concept stage.

_____ 4. The authors suggest that Harley-Davidson outdistanced the Japanese competition in the mid 1980s through
   a. producing products at a faster rate.
   b. intense discount pricing.
   c. the protection provided by import tariffs on Japanese goods.
   d. direct and unprotected market competition.

_____ 5. According to the authors, Harley-Davidson does not advertise differently for women and men because
   a. women are motivated to buy for similar reasons as men.
   b. women do not buy as many bikes as men.
   c. women buy more apparel than men.
   d. women and men customers are approximately the same age and income level.

_____ 6. In 1993 the percentage of total Harley-Davidson sales outside the United States was
   a. 70 percent.
   b. 30 percent.
   c. 24 percent.
   d. 14 percent.

_____ 7. The advertisement includes the reference to a Marlon Brando movie for the purpose of
 a. humor.
 b. clarity.
 c. comparison.
 d. identifying owners.

_____ 8. The authors suggest that the Harley-Davidson marketing image promotes all of the following except
 a. status.
 b. historical tradition.
 c. speed.
 d. membership in a group.

_____ 9. The author suggests that Jay Leno and Malcolm Forbes
 a. were employed by Harley-Davidson.
 b. stimulated sales through their personal bike choices.
 c. sought avenues for promoting the motorcycles.
 d. advertised regularly for Harley-Davidson.

_____ 10. The authors suggest that currently the Harley-Davidson motorcycle is
 a. overproduced.
 b. underproduced.
 c. sacrificing quality for quantity.
 d. overexpanding.

Answer the following with _T_ (true) or _F_ (false).

_____ 11. The trade tariffs originally requested still remain on Japanese motorcycles.

_____ 12. Harley and Davidson were the two brothers who designed and built the first Harley-Davidson motorcycle.

_____ 13. The authors suggest that the company knowingly promotes an image of status.

_____ 14. Currently the demand for Harley-Davidson motorcycles exceeds the supply.

_____ 15. The average Harley owner is a baby boomer born after 1945.

VOCABULARY

According to the way the italicized word was used in the selection, select _a_, _b_, _c_, or _d_ for the word or phrase that gives the best definition.

—— 1. "*crest* of success" (3)
   a. roar
   b. cost
   c. peak
   d. smell

—— 2. "demand, *revenue,* and profits" (4)
   a. income
   b. tax
   c. pensions
   d. overhead

—— 3. "*espouse* a unique attitude" (5)
   a. repeat
   b. demand
   c. buy
   d. support

—— 4. "*evolved* through stages" (8)
   a. matured
   b. floundered
   c. held the market
   d. manipulated

—— 5. "*Buoyed* by the tariffs" (44)
   a. bought out
   b. supported
   c. overwhelmed
   d. disregarded

—— 6. "early *termination* of the tariffs" (47)
   a. payout
   b. recognition
   c. resumption
   d. end

—— 7. "market was *devastated*" (29)
   a. ruined
   b. tapped
   c. shot
   d. divided

—— 8. "a *consummate* promoter" (109)
   a. authentic
   b. wealthy
   c. accomplished
   d. educated

—— 9. "*prominent* dignitaries" (128)
   a. foreign
   b. well-known
   c. hard-working
   d. promising

—— 10. "end of the price *spectrum*" (154)
   a. array
   b. image
   c. ticket
   d. increase

WRITTEN RESPONSE

Use information from the text to respond to the following:

What has the Harley-Davidson company "done right" in each of the three stages of business concept development?

Response Strategy: Define each of the three stages and give examples from the text for each.

SELECTION 3

SOCIOLOGY

Skill Development

Stage 1: Preview

Preview the next selection to predict purpose, organization, and a learning plan.

Unity in diversity is a paradox. What does it seem to mean?

_____

After reading this selection, I will need to know

_____

Activate Schema

Is it wrong for primitive tribal people to wear no clothes?

Does social status exist in primitive cultures?

Could you eat insects if doing so meant survival?

Learning Strategy

How do the examples explain the different principles and the overall idea of cultural unity?

Word Knowledge

Are you familiar with the following words in this selection?

curb	smirk
naïveté	abstained
adornments	postpartum
articulate	agile
bizarre	consign

Your instructor may choose to ask ten true-false questions from the *Instructor's Manual* to stimulate your thinking using these words.

Stage 2: Integrate Knowledge While Reading

Since each reader interacts with material in a unique manner, it is artificial to require certain thinking strategies to be used in certain places. In order to heighten awareness, however, several questions have been inserted within this selection. Briefly respond in the margin to the inserted questions. In addition, make a note in the margin of at least one other instance when you used each of the following strategies:

1. Predict   2. Picture   3. Relate   4. Monitor   5. Fix up

Unity In Diversity
From Donald Light, Jr., and Suzanne Keller, *Sociology**

Does this title make sense or are these words opposites?

What is more basic, more "natural" than love between a man and woman? Eskimo men offer their wives to guests and friends as a gesture of hospitality; both husband and wife feel extremely offended if the guest

5 declines (Ruesch 1951, pp. 87–88). The Banaro of New Guinea believe it would be disastrous for a woman to conceive her first child by her husband and not by one of her father's close friends, as is their custom.

> The real father is a close friend of the bride's father. . . . Nevertheless the first born child inherits the name and possessions of the husband. An
> 10 American would deem such a custom immoral, but the Banaro tribesmen would be equally shocked to discover that the first born child of an American couple is the offspring of the husband. (Haring 1949, p. 33)

The Yanomamö of Northern Brazil, whom anthropologist Napoleon A. Chagnon (1968) named "the fierce people," encourage what we would

15 consider extreme disrespect. Small boys are applauded for striking their mothers and fathers in the face. Yanomamö parents would laugh at our

*From *Sociology*, 4th edition, by Donald Light and Suzanne Keller, pages 74–77. Copyright © 1986 by McGraw-Hill, Inc. Reproduced by permission of McGraw-Hill, Inc.

efforts to curb aggression in children, much as they laughed at Chagnon's
naïveté when he first came to live with them.

20   **What would your parents do if you slapped either of
them in the face?**

The variations among cultures are startling, yet all peoples have
customs and beliefs about marriage, the bearing and raising of children,
sex, and hospitality—to name just a few of the universals anthropologists
have discovered in their cross-cultural explorations. But the *details* of
25   cultures do indeed vary: in this country, not so many years ago, when a girl
was serious about a boy and he about her, she wore his fraternity pin over
her heart; in the Fiji Islands, girls put hibiscus flowers behind their ears
when they are in love. The specific gestures are different but the impulse to
symbolize feelings, to dress courtship in ceremonies, is the same. How do
30   we explain this unity in diversity?

Cultural Universals

Cultural universals are all of the behavior patterns and institutions that
have been found in all known cultures. Anthropologist George Peter
Murdock identified over sixty cultural universals, including a system of
35   social status, marriage, body adornments, dancing, myths and legends,
cooking, incest taboos, inheritance rules, puberty customs, and religious
rituals (Murdock 1945, p. 124).

The universals of culture may derive from the fact that all societies must
perform the same essential functions if they are to survive—including
40   organization, motivation, communication, protection, the socialization of
new members, and the replacement of those who die. In meeting these
prerequisites for group life, people inevitably design similar—though not
identical—patterns for living. As Clyde Kluckhohn wrote, "All cultures
constitute somewhat distinct answers to essentially the same questions posed
45   by human biology and by the generalities of the human situation" (1962,
p. 317).

The way in which a people articulates cultural universals depends in
large part on their physical and social environment—that is, on the climate
in which they live, the materials they have at hand, and the peoples with
50   whom they establish contact. For example, the wheel has long been
considered one of the humankind's greatest inventions, and
anthropologists were baffled for a long time by the fact that the great
civilizations of South America never discovered it. Then researchers
uncovered a number of toys with wheels. Apparently the Aztecs and their
55   neighbors did know about wheels; they simply didn't find them useful in
their mountainous environment.

Describe your mental picture.

Adaptation, Relativity, and Ethnocentrism

Taken out of context, almost any custom will seem bizarre, perhaps
60 cruel, or just plain ridiculous. To understand why the Yanomamö encourage
aggressive behavior in their sons, for example, you have to try to see things
through their eyes. The Yanomamö live in a state of chronic warfare; they
spend much of their time planning for and defending against raids with
neighboring tribes. If Yanomamö parents did *not* encourage aggression in a
65 boy, he would be ill equipped for life in their society. Socializing boys to be
aggressive is *adaptive* for the Yanomamö because it enhances their capacity
for survival. "In general, culture is . . . adaptive because it often provides
people with a means of adjusting to the physiological needs of their own
bodies, to their physical-geographical environment and to their social
70 environments as well" (Ember and Ember 1973, p. 30).

In many tropical societies, there are strong taboos against a mother
having sexual intercourse with a man until her child is at least two years old.
As a Hausa woman explains,

> A mother should not go to her husband while she has a child such is
75 > sucking . . . if she only sleeps with her husband and does not become
> pregnant, it will not hurt her child, it will not spoil her milk. But if another
> child enters in, her milk will make the first one ill. (Smith, in Whiting 1969,
> p. 518)

Undoubtedly, people would smirk at a woman who nursed a two-year-
80 old child in our society and abstained from having sex with her husband.
Why do Hausa women behave in a way that seems so overprotective and
overindulgent to us? In tropical climates protein is scarce. If a mother were
to nurse more than one child at a time, or if she were to wean a child before
it reached the age of two, the youngster would be prone to *kwashiorkor,* an
85 often fatal disease resulting from protein deficiency. Thus, long postpartum
sex taboos are adaptive. In a tropical environment a postpartum sex taboo
and a long period of breast-feeding solve a serious problem (Whiting, in
Goodenough 1969, pp. 511–24).

No custom is good or bad, right or wrong in itself; each one must be
90 examined in light of the culture as a whole and evaluated in terms of how it
works in the context of the entire culture. Anthropologists and sociologists
call this *cultural relativity.* Although this way of thinking about culture may
seem self-evident today, it is a lesson that anthropologists and the
missionaries who often preceded them to remote areas learned the hard
95 way, by observing the effects their best intentions had on peoples whose way
of life was quite different from their own. In an article on the pitfalls of
trying to "uplift" peoples whose ways seem backward and inefficient, Don
Adams quotes an old Oriental story:

> Once upon a time there was a great flood, and involved in this flood
100 > were two creatures, a monkey and a fish. The monkey, being agile and
> experienced, was lucky enough to scramble up a tree and escape the raging

waters. As he looked down from his safe perch, he saw the poor fish struggling against the swift current. With the very best intentions, he reached down and lifted the fish from the water. The result was inevitable
105   (1960, p. 22).

What is the difference between adaptation and relativity?

Ethnocentrism is the tendency to see one's own way of life, including behaviors, beliefs, values, and norms as the only right way of living. Robin Fox points out that "any human group is ever ready to consign another
110   recognizably different human group to the other side of the boundary. It is not enough to possess culture to be fully human, you have to possess *our* culture" (1970, p. 31).

Values and Norms
The Tangu, who live in a remote part of New Guinea, play a game
115   called *taketak,* which in many ways resembles bowling. The game is played with a top that has been fashioned from a dried fruit and with two groups of coconut stakes that are driven into the ground (more or less like bowling pins). The players divide into two teams. Members of the first team take turns throwing the top into the batch of stakes; every stake the top hits is
120   removed. Then the second team steps to the line and tosses the top into their batch of stakes. The object of the game, surprisingly, is not to knock over as many stakes as possible. Rather, the game continues until both teams have removed the *same* number of stakes. Winning is completely irrelevant (Burridge 1957, pp. 88–89).

120   ### What will be covered in this next part?

In a sense games are practice for "real life"; they reflect the values of the culture in which they are played. *Values* are the criteria people use in assessing their daily lives, arranging their priorities, measuring their pleasures and pains, choosing between alternative courses of action. The
130   Tangu value equivalence: the idea of one individual or group winning and another losing bothers them, for they believe winning generates ill-will. In fact, when Europeans brought soccer to the Tangu, they altered the rules so that the object of the game was for two teams to score the same number of goals. Sometimes their soccer games went on for days! American games, in
135   contrast, are highly competitive; there are *always* winners and losers. Many rule books include provisions for overtime and "sudden death" to prevent ties, which leave Americans dissatisfied. World Series, Superbowls, championships in basketball and hockey, Olympic Gold Medals are front-page news in this country. In the words of the late football coach Vince
140   Lombardi, "Winning isn't everything, it's the only thing."
Norms, the rules that guide behavior in everyday situations, are derived from values, but norms and values can conflict. You may recall a news item

that appeared in American newspapers in December 1972, describing the discovery of survivors of a plane crash 12,000 feet in the Andes. The crash
145 had occurred on October 13; sixteen of the passengers (a rugby team and their supporters) managed to survive for sixty-nine days in near-zero temperatures. The story made headlines because, to stay alive, the survivors had eaten parts of their dead companions. Officials, speaking for the group, stressed how valiantly the survivors had tried to save the lives of the injured
150 people and how they had held religious services regularly. The survivors' explanations are quite interesting, for they reveal how important it is to people to justify their actions, to resolve conflicts in norms and values (here, the positive value of survival vs. the taboo against cannibalism). Some of the survivors compared their action to a heart transplant, using parts of a dead
155 person's body to save another person's life. Others equated their act with the sacrament of communion. In the words of one religious survivor, "If we would have died, it would have been suicide, which is condemned by the Roman Catholic faith" (Read 1974).

Stage 3: Recall

Stop to self-test and relate. Recall important points in the selection. Use the recall diagram to record what the passage seems to be mainly about, list significant supporting details, and name a related idea, issue, or concern to which you feel the information is connected.

(topic) _____

(significant
details)

(related idea) _____

COMPREHENSION QUESTIONS

After reading the selection, answer the following questions with *a, b, c,* or *d.*

_____ 1. The best statement of the main idea of this selection is
   a. the variety of practices and customs in society show few threads of cultural unity.
   b. the unusual variations in societies gain acceptability because of the cultural universals in all known societies.

    c. a variety of cultural universals provides adaptive choices for specific societies.

    d. cultural universals are found in all known societies even though the details of the cultures may vary widely.

_____ 2. The author believes that the primary cultural universal addressed in the Eskimo custom of offering wives to guests is

    a. bearing and raising of children.

    b. social status.

    c. hospitality.

    d. incest taboos.

_____ 3. The custom of striking practiced by the Yanomamö serves the adaptive function of

    a. developing fierce warriors

    b. binding parent and child closer together.

    c. developing physical respect for parents.

    d. encouraging early independence from parental care.

_____ 4. *Cultural universals* might be defined as

    a. each culture in the universe.

    b. similar basic living patterns.

    c. the ability for cultures to live together in harmony.

    d. the differences among cultures.

_____ 5. The author implies that universals of culture exist because of

    a. a social desire to be more alike.

    b. the differences in cultural behavior patterns.

    c. the competition among societies.

    d. the needs of survival in group life.

_____ 6. The author suggests that the wheel was not a part of the ancient Aztec civilization because the Aztecs

    a. did not need wheels.

    b. were not intelligent enough to invent wheels.

    c. were baffled by inventions

    d. did not have the materials for development.

_____ 7. The underlying reason for the postpartum sexual taboo of the Hausa is

    a. sexual.

    b. nutritional.

    c. moral.

    d. religious.

_____ 8. The term *cultural relativity* explains why a custom can be considered

    a. right or wrong regardless of culture.

    b. right or wrong according to the number of people practicing it.

    c. right in one culture and wrong in another.

    d. wrong if in conflict with cultural universals.

_____ 9. The author relates Don Adams's oriental story to show that missionaries working in other cultures
   a. should be sent back home.
   b. can do more harm than good.
   c. purposefully harm the culture to seek selfish ends.
   d. usually do not have a genuine concern for the people.

_____ 10. The tendency of ethnocentrism would lead an American to view the Eskimo practice of wife sharing as
   a. right.
   b. wrong.
   c. right for Eskimos but wrong for Americans.
   d. a custom about which an outsider should have no opinion.

Answer the following questions with *T* (true) or *F* (false).

_____ 11. An American's acceptance of the Banaro tribal custom of fathering the firstborn is an example of an understanding by cultural relativity.

_____ 12. The author feels that the need to symbolize feelings in courtship is a cultural universal.

_____ 13. The author feels that culture is not affected by climate.

_____ 14. The author states that all societies must have a form of organization if they are to survive.

_____ 15. The author implies that the rugby team that crashed in the Andes could have survived without eating human flesh.

VOCABULARY

According to the way the italicized word was used in the selection, select *a*, *b*, *c*, or *d* for the word or phrase that gives the best definition.

_____ 1. "efforts to *curb* aggression" (17)
   a. stabilize
   b. release
   c. promote
   d. restrain

_____ 2. "at Chagnon's *naïveté*" (18)
   a. lack of knowledge
   b. gentle manner
   c. jolly nature
   d. clumsiness

_____ 3. "body *adornments*" (35)
   a. ailments
   b. treatments
   c. scars
   d. decorations

_____ 4. "*articulate* cultural universals" (47)
   a. remember
   b. design
   c. express clearly
   d. substitute

—— 5. "will seem *bizarre*" (59)
   a. phony
   b. unjust
   c. grotesque
   d. unnecessary

—— 6. "*smirk* at a woman" (79)
   a. refuse to tolerate
   b. smile conceitedly
   c. lash out
   d. acknowledge approvingly

—— 7. "*abstained* from having sex" (80)
   a. matured
   b. regained
   c. refrained
   d. reluctantly returned

—— 8. "long *postpartum* sex taboos" (85)
   a. after childbirth
   b. awaited
   c. subcultural
   d. complicated

—— 9. "being *agile* and experienced" (100)
   a. eager
   b. nimble
   c. young
   d. knowledgeable

—— 10. "ready to *consign*" (109)
   a. assign
   b. remove
   c. reorganize
   d. overlook

WRITTEN RESPONSE

Use the information in this selection and your own ideas to answer the following question.

For each of the following, define the terms and describe two examples of each that are not mentioned in the selection:

adaptation   values   ethnocentrism

relativity   norms

Response Strategy: Define the cultural concepts in your own words and relate examples from today's society.

WORD BRIDGE

Context Clues

Context clues are the most common method of unlocking the meaning of unknown words. The context of a word refers to the sentence or paragraph in which it appears. Readers use several types of context clues. In some cases, words are defined directly in the sentences in which they appear; in other instances, the sentence offers clues or hints that enable the reader to arrive indirectly at the meaning of the word. The following are examples of how each type of clue can be used to figure out word meaning in textbooks.

1. Definition

Complex scientific material has a heavy load of specialized vocabulary. Fortunately, new words are often directly defined as they are introduced in the text.

Do you know the meaning of *erythrocytes* and *oxyhemoglobin*? Read the following textbook sentence in which these two words appear, and then select the correct definition for each word.

When oxygen diffuses into the blood in external respiration, most of it enters the red blood cells, or erythrocytes, and unites with the hemoglobin in these cells, forming a compound called oxyhemoglobin.

Willis H. Johnson et al., *Essentials of Biology*

_____ *Erythrocytes* means
    a. diffused oxygen.
    b. red blood cells.
    c. respiration process.

_____ *Oxyhemoglobin* means
    a. hemoglobin without oxygen.
    b. dominant oxygen cells.
    c. combination of oxygen and hemoglobin.

The answers are *b* and *c*. Notice that the first word is defined as a synonym in an appositive phrase, and the second is defined in the sentence.

2. Elaborating Details

In political science you will come across the term *confederation*. Keep reading and see if you can figure out the meaning from the hints in the following sentence.

There is a third form of governmental structure, a *confederation*. The United States began as such, under the Articles of Confederation. In a confederation, the national government is weak and most or all the power is in the hands of its components, for example, the individual states. Today, confederations are rare except in international organizations such as the United Nations.

Robert Lineberry, *Government in America*

_____ A *confederation* is a governmental structure with
    a. strong federal power.
    b. weak federal power.
    c. weak state power.
    d. equal federal and state power.

The answer is *a* and can be figured out from the details.

3. Examples

In psychology you will frequently encounter a complicated word describing something you have often thought about but not named. Read the following sentence to find out what *psychokinesis* means.

Another psychic phenomenon is *psychokinesis*, the ability to affect physical events without physical intervention. You can test your powers of psychokinesis by trying to influence the fall of dice from a mechanical shaker. Are you able to have the dice come up a certain number with a greater frequency than would occur by chance?

Douglas W. Matheson, Introductory Psychology: The Modern View

_____ *Psychokinesis* means
- a. extrasensory perception.
- b. an influence on happenings without physical tampering.
- c. physical intervention affecting physical change.

The answer is *b*. Here the word is first directly defined in a complicated manner and then the definition is clarified by a simple example.

4. Comparison

Economics uses many complex concepts that are difficult to understand. The use of a familiar term in a comparison can help the reader relate to a new idea. Can you explain a *trade deficit?* The following comparison will help.

When the United States imports more than it exports, we have a trade deficit rather than a trade balance or surplus. Similarly, a store manager who buys more than she sells will create a financial deficit for the company.

_____ A *trade deficit* means that the nation
- a. sells more than it buys.
- b. buys more than it sells.
- c. sells what it buys.

The answer is *b*. The comparison explains the definition by creating a more understandable situation.

5. Contrast

Can you explain what *transsexuals* are and how they differ from *homosexuals?* The following sentences will give you some clues.

Transsexuals are people (usually males) who feel that they were born into the wrong body. They are not homosexuals in the usual sense. Most homosexuals are satisfied with their anatomy and think of themselves as appropriately male or female; they simply prefer members of their own sex. Transsexuals, in contrast, think of themselves as members of the opposite sex (often from early childhood) and may be so desperately unhappy with their physical appearance that they request hormonal and surgical treatment to change their genitals and secondary sex characteristics.

Rita Atkinson et al., Introduction to Psychology

_____ A *transsexual* is a person who thinks of himself as

a. a homosexual.

b. a heterosexual.

c. a member of the opposite sex.

d. a person without sex drive.

The answer is *c*. By comparing *homosexual* and *transsexual,* the reader is better able to understand the latter and distinguish between the two.

Limitations of Context Clues

While the clues in the sentence in which an unknown word appears are certainly helpful in deriving the meaning of a word, these clues will not always give a complete and accurate definition. To understand totally the meaning of a word, it is frequently necessary to take some time after your reading is completed to look the word up in a glossary or a dictionary. Context clues operate just as the name suggests; they are hints and not necessarily complete definitions.

Exercise 5 THE POWER OF CONTEXT CLUES

The purpose of this exercise is to demonstrate how context clues assist the reader in clarifying or unlocking the meaning of unknown words. For each of the following vocabulary items, make two responses. First, without reading the sentence containing the unknown word, select *a, b, c,* or *d* for the definition that you feel best fits each italicized word. Then, read the material in which the word is used in context and answer again. Check your answers and compare the accuracy with and without context clues. Did reading the word in context help? Were you uncertain of any word as it appeared on the list, but then able to figure out the meaning after reading it in a sentence?

Word List

_____ 1. *usurped*

a. shortened

b. acknowledged

c. aggravated

d. seized

_____ Henry, to the end of his life, thought of himself as a pious and orthodox Catholic who had restored the independent authority of the Church of England *usurped* centuries before by the Bishop of Rome.

Shepard B. Clough et al., *A History of the Western World*

_____ 2. *assimilationist*
  a. one who adopts the habits of a larger cultural group
  b. a machinist
  c. typist
  d. one who files correspondence

  _____ When members of a minority group wish to give up what is distinctive about them and become just like the majority, they take an *assimilationist* position. An example is the Urban League.

  Reece McGee et al., *Sociology: An Introduction*

_____ 3. *dyad*
  a. star
  b. two-member group
  c. opposing factor
  d. leader

  _____ George Simmel was one of the first sociologists to suggest that the number of members in a group radically transforms its properties. He began with an analysis of what happens when a *dyad,* a two-member group, becomes a triad, a three-member group.

  Ibid.

_____ 4. *self-actualization*
  a. imitation of self
  b. reality counseling
  c. achievement to fullest degree
  d. evaluation of past experiences

  _____ Rogers believes that everyone has a tendency toward *self-actualization,* the realization of one's potentials, and stresses that the human need for acceptance and approval is essential if self-actualization is to occur.

  Ibid

_____ 5. *gastrovascular*
  a. relating to arteries of petroleum
  b. explosive
  c. digestive and circulatory
  d. cellular interaction

  _____ The gut is essentially an elaborate *gastrovascular* cavity.

  Willis H. Johnson et al., *Essentials of Biology*

_____ 6. *planarians*
   a. meteorites
   b. small worms
   c. birds
   d. lizards

   _____ Locomotion ranges from the generally nonmotile tapeworms to freely moving flatworms such as *planarians,* that glide on a slime they secrete by ciliary action of their epidermal cells and generalized muscular contractions of the body.

   Ibid.

_____ 7. *anticoagulants*
   a. demonstrators
   b. substances against clotting
   c. coal-mining disease agents
   d. germs

   _____ The body can produce some natural *anticoagulants* such as heparin or dicumarol, which are formed in the liver. Also, some animals that depend on blood for nutrition—such as fleas and leeches—secrete substances to inhibit clotting.

   Ibid.

_____ 8. *expropriated*
   a. taken from its owners
   b. industrialized
   c. approximated
   d. increased in size

   _____ Under a decree of September 1952, the government *expropriated* several hundred thousand acres from large landholders and redistributed this land among the peasants.

   Jesse H. Wheeler, Jr., et al., *Regional Geography of the World*

_____ 9. *adherents*
   a. children
   b. followers
   c. instigators
   d. detractors

   _____ One of the fundamental features of Hinduism has been the division of its *adherents* into the most elaborate caste system ever known.

   Ibid.

_____ 10. *stimulus*
   a. writing implement
   b. distinguishing mark
   c. something that incites action
   d. result

   _____ While we are sleeping, for example, we are hardly aware of what is happening around us, but we are aware to some degree. Any loud noise or other abrupt *stimulus* will almost certainly awaken us.

   Gardner Lindzey et al., Psychology

_____ 11. *debilitating*
   a. weakening
   b. reinforcing
   c. exciting
   d. enjoyable

   _____ However, anyone who has passed through several time zones while flying east or west knows how difficult it can be to change from one sleep schedule to another. This "jet lag" can be so *debilitating* that many corporations will not allow their executives to enter negotiations for at least two days after such a trip.

   Ibid.

_____ 12 *autocratic*
   a. automatic
   b. democratic
   c. self-starting
   d. dictatorial

   _____ *Autocratic* leadership can be extremely effective if the people wielding it have enough power to enforce their decisions and if their followers know that they have it. It is especially useful in military situations where speed of decision is critical. Among its disadvantages are the lack of objectivity and the disregard for opinions of subordinates.

   David J. Rachman and Michael Mescon, Business Today

_____ 13. *incentive*
   a. debt
   b. sensory agent
   c. encouragement
   d. suggestion

   _____ Many social critics decry profits as an *incentive* but have proposed no practical alternative in a free society. The only other incentive that has worked is the one used most often in com-

munist countries: severe punishment for nonproductive persons.

Ibid.

_____ 14. *disseminated*
   a. dissolved
   b. spread
   c. destroyed
   d. originated

   _____ Disseminated Magmatic Deposits are the simplest of the magmatic deposits. The valuable mineral is *disseminated* or scattered throughout the igneous body. In the diamond deposits
   of South Africa, for example, the diamonds are disseminated
   in unusual rock, somewhat similar to peridotite.

   Robert J. Foster, *Physical Geology*

_____ 15. *me-toos*
   a. new products to the marketplace
   b. new products to the company
   c. franchise companies
   d. companies that are second from the top

   _____ Companies create *me-toos* because they believe there is room in
   the market for another competitor, and the projected returns
   outweigh the risks. For example, when McDonald's decided to
   enter the fast-food breakfast business, its product was new to
   the company even though a fast-food breakfast was not new to
   the market.

   Thomas Kinnear et al., *Principles of Marketing*

Exercise 6   CONTEXT CLUES IN SENTENCES

The following sentences appeared in this chapter. Use your memory of the
passage and the context of the sentence to determine the meaning, or an approximate guess at the meaning, of each of the following italicized words.

1. Then they *evert* their stomachs, squeezing them between the shells, and digest the flesh of the oyster on the spot.

Robert Wallace, *Biology: The World of Life*

Evert means _____.

2. But they were unfamiliar with the *regenerative* powers of the starfish. The central disk merely grows new arms, and a single arm can form a new animal.

Ibid

Regenerative means —————————————————————————————

3. To our delight, the *planarians* that had eaten educated victims learned much faster than did the worms that had consumed their untrained brethren.

Ibid.

Planarians are —————————————————————————————

4. Belle Starr, the *moniker* of one Myra Belle Shirley, was immortalized as "the bandit queen," as pure in heart as Jesse James was socially conscious.

Ibid.

Moniker means —————————————————————————————

5. Calamity Jane (Martha Cannary), later said to have been Wild Bill's *paramour,* wrote her own romantic autobiography in order to support a drinking problem.

Ibid.

A *paramour* is —————————————————————————————

Name _____

Answer the following questions to learn about your own learning and reflect on your progress. Your instructor may collect your responses.

What do you enjoy reading on a regular basis? Why?

_____

_____

How do you preview a book or magazine before purchasing it?

_____

_____

What do you plan to do to "train" yourself to use the Recall Stage?

_____

_____

Which of the five thinking strategies do you tend to use the most while reading? Explain.

_____

_____

What seems to be the main cause of confusion in your comprehension?

_____

_____

Reflect on the Longer Selections

Total your short-answer comprehension responses for the longer selections.

Comprehension scores:
completed = _____   # correct = _____   # incorrect = _____   accuracy = _____%

Which selection did you enjoy the most? Why?

_____

Describe two of your comprehension errors in this chapter.

_____

Describe a question that you thought was difficult to understand.

_____

Clip out and explain three questions that you missed. Attach these questions and your analysis to the Learning Log for your instructor.

Reflect on the Vocabulary

Vocabulary scores:

\# completed = ____   \# correct = ____   \# incorrect = ____   accuracy = ____%

List the words that you missed.

_____

_____

_____

Describe an item that you answered correctly by guessing. How did you guess correctly?

_____

_____

_____

Which vocabulary word is one that you recognize but seldom use?

_____

_____

_____

Which word would you like to remember and use? Why?

_____

_____

_____

Using the perforations, tear out the Learning Log for your instructor.

Main Idea

What is a topic?

What is a main idea?

What are significant details?

What is an organizational pattern?

What is a summary?

WHAT IS THE POINT?

Many experts agree that the most important skill in reading is understanding the **main idea**, or the particular point the author is trying to convey about the subject in a passage. They say that comprehending the main idea is crucial to the comprehension of text. In fact, if all reading comprehension techniques were reduced to one basic question, that question might be, "What is the main idea the author is trying to get across?"

To answer the question, the reader must first determine the **topic** being discussed; that is, the general subject under which the key ideas in a passage may be grouped. Then, after considering the contributing details, he or she must decide what point or statement the author is trying to make about the topic. For example, if a friend commented favorably on a recent article, your first question would be, "What was it about?" and then you would ask, "What was the point?" The first answer is the topic and the second is a statement of the main idea. *The point being made about the topic is the main idea.*

MAIN IDEA STATEMENTS

Reading specialists use several different terms in referring to the author's main idea. In this book, all of the following terms are synonymous with *main idea.*

main point

central focus

gist

controlling idea

central thought

thesis

In all cases, the reader's statement of the main idea of a passage must be in a complete sentence. Constructing anything less, such as expanding a phrase or narrowing in on a subject, remains only a designation of the topic.

IMPORTANCE OF PRIOR KNOWLEDGE IN MAIN IDEA

Although identifying the main idea is proclaimed as the most important reading skill, until recently little research has been done on the processes readers use to construct main ideas. One researcher asked graduate students and university professors to "think aloud" as they read passages on both familiar and unfamiliar topics.[1] These expert readers spoke their thoughts to the researcher

[1]P. Afflerbach, "How Are Main Idea Statements Constructed? Watch the Experts!," *Journal of Reading* 30 (1987): 512–518; and "The Influence of Prior Knowledge on Expert Readers' Main Idea Construction Strategies," *Reading Research Quarterly* 25 (1990): 31–46.

before, during, and after they had finished reading. From these investigations, Afflerbach concluded that expert readers use different strategies for familiar and unfamiliar materials.

This research showed that *already knowing something about the topic is the key to easy reading.* When the readers were already familiar with the material, constructing the main idea was effortless and, in many cases, automatic. These readers quickly assimilated the unfolding text into already well-developed knowledge networks. They seemed to organize text into chunks for comprehension and later retrieval. These "informed" readers did not have to struggle with an information overload.

By contrast, expert readers with little prior knowledge of the subject were absorbed in trying to make meaning out of unfamiliar words and confusing sentences. Because they were struggling to recognize ideas, few mental resources remained for constructing a main idea. These "uninformed" experts were reluctant to guess at a main idea and to predict a topic. Instead, they preferred to read all of the information before trying to make sense out of it. Constructing the main idea was a difficult and deliberate task for these expert readers.

MAIN IDEA STRATEGIES

The following strategies for getting the main idea were reported by Afflerbach's expert readers. Can you see the differences in the thinking processes of the informed and uninformed experts?

"Informed" Expert Readers

Strategy 1: The informed expert readers skimmed the passage before reading and took a guess at the main idea. Then they read for corroboration.

Strategy 2: The informed experts automatically paused while reading to summarize or reduce information. They frequently stopped at natural breaks in the material to let ideas fall into place.

"Uninformed" Expert Readers

Strategy 1: Expert readers who knew very little about the subject were unwilling to take a guess at the main idea. Instead, they read the material, decided on a topic, and then looked back to pull together a main idea statement.

Strategy 2: The uninformed experts read the material and then reviewed it to find key terms and concepts. They tried to bring the key terms and concepts together into a main idea statement.

Strategy 3: The uninformed experts read the material and then proposed a main idea statement. They double-checked the passage to clarify or revise the main idea statement.

Since introductory college textbooks address many topics that are new and unfamiliar, freshmen readers will frequently need to use the last three strategies listed above to comprehend the main ideas of their college texts. Until prior knowledge is built for the different college courses, main idea construction for course textbooks is likely to be a conscious effort rather than an automatic phenomenon.

WHAT IS A TOPIC?

The topic of a passage is like a title. It is a word or phrase that labels the subject but does not reveal the specific contents of the passage. The topic is a general, rather than specific, term and forms an umbrella under which the specific ideas or details in the passage can be grouped. For example, what general term would pull together and unify the following items?

Items: carrots

lettuce

onions   Topic? _____

potatoes

Exercise 1   IDENTIFYING TOPICS

Each of the following lists includes four specific items or ideas that could relate to a single topic. At the end of each list, write a general topic that could form an umbrella under which the specific ideas can be grouped.

1. shirt	2. psychology	3. democracy	4. Bermuda	5. coffee
pants	history	autocracy	Cuba	tea
jacket	sociology	oligarchy	Haiti	cola
sweater	political science	monarchy	Tahiti	chocolate
_____	_____	_____	_____	_____

HOW DO TOPICS AND MAIN IDEAS DIFFER?

Topics are general categories, like titles, but they are not main ideas. In the previous list, caffeine is a general term or topic that unifies the items, *coffee, tea, cola,* and *chocolate.* If those items were used as details in a paragraph, the main idea could not be expressed by simply saying "caffeine." The word *caffeine* would answer the question, "What was the passage about?" but not the second question, "What is the author's main idea?"

A writer could actually devise several very different paragraphs about caffeine using the same four details as support. If you were assigned to write a paragraph about caffeine, using the four items as details, what would be the main idea or thesis of your paragraph?

Topic: Caffeine

Main idea or thesis: _____

Read the following examples of different main ideas that could be developed in a paragraph about caffeine.

1. Consumption of caffeine is not good for your health. (Details would enumerate health hazards associated with each item.)
2. Americans annually consume astonishing amounts of caffeine. (Details would describe amounts of each consumed annually.)
3. Caffeine can wake up an otherwise sluggish mind. (Details would explain the popular use of each item as a stimulant.)
4. Reduce caffeine consumption with the decaffeinated version of popular caffeinated beverages. (Details would promote the decaffeinated version of each item.)

Below are examples of a topic, main idea, and supporting detail.

Topic
Main Idea

Detail

Early Cognitive Development

Cognitive psychologists sometimes study young children to observe the very beginnings of cognitive activity. For example, when children first begin to utter words and sentences, they overgeneralize what they know and make language more consistent than it actually is.

Christopher Peterson, *Introduction to Psychology*

The topic pulls our attention to a general area, and the main idea provides the focus. The detail offers elaboration and support.

Exercise 2 DIFFERENTIATING TOPIC, MAIN IDEA, AND DETAILS

This exercise is designed to check your ability to differentiate statements of main idea from topic and specific supporting details. Compare the items within each group and indicate whether each one is a statement of main idea (*MI*), a topic, (*T*), or a specific supporting detail (*D*).

Group 1

_____ a. In New Mexico, Governor Tony Anaya called himself the nation's highest elected Hispanic officer and worked to create a national "Hispanic force."

———— b. Hispanics slowly extended their political gains as well.

———— c. Hispanic political progress

Gary B. Nash et al., The American People

Group 2

———— a. For poor farm families, life on the plains meant a sod house or a dugout carved out of the hillside for protection from the winds.

———— b. One door and usually no more than a single window provided light and air.

———— c. Sod houses on the plains

James W. Davidson et al., Nation of Nations

Group 3

———— a. As individuals, Americans tend to value the knowledge and skills transmitted by the schools, not for their own sake but because they hope to translate those skills into good jobs and money.

———— b. Social mobility through education

———— c. As one study indicates, many students are attracted to college because of job and career considerations.

Alex Thio, Sociology

Group 4

———— a. For example, human babies require about twice as many calories per unit of body weight than adults.

———— b. Although children need less total food than adults, their metabolic needs exceed those of adults in proportion to their body weight.

———— c. Metabolic needs of children

John Cunningham, Human Biology

Group 5

———— a. The question of a Bill of Rights

———— b. First, Hamilton wrote in Federalist 84 that a Bill of Rights might be necessary to restrict a king, but not a government established by the people; such a government, he said, possesses only the powers given to it by the people.

_____ c. A serious objection raised against the Constitution by those who opposed its ratification was that it contained no Bill of Rights.

Fred Harris et al., *Understanding American Government*

QUESTIONING FOR THE MAIN IDEA

To determine the main idea of a paragraph, an article, or a book, ask the three basic questions listed in the box below. The order of the questions may vary depending on your prior knowledge of the material. If the material is familiar, main idea construction may be automatic and thus a selection of significant details would follow. If the material is unfamiliar, as frequently occurs in textbook reading, identifying the details through key terms and concepts would come first and from them you would form a main idea statement.

Read the following example, and answer the questions for determining the main idea.

New high-speed machines also brought danger to the workplace. If a worker succumbed to boredom, fatigue, or simple miscalculation, disaster

FINDING THE MAIN IDEA

1. Establish the topic. Ask, "Who or what is this about?" The response is a general word or phrase that names the subject. The topic should be broad enough to include all the material, yet restrictive enough to reflect the details. For example, identifying the topic of an article as "politics," "federal politics," or "corruption in federal politics" might all be correct, but the last may be the most descriptive of the actual contents.

2. Ask the question, "What are the major details?" The response should include key terms and concepts within the passage. List the details that seem to be significant to determine if they point in any one particular direction. If so, this direction could be the topic or focus that leads to the main idea. Details such as kickbacks to senators, overspending on congressional junkets, and lying to the voters could support the idea of "corruption in federal politics."

3. Sharpen the impact of the topic. Ask, "What is the main idea the author is trying to convey about the topic?" This statement of the main idea should be:

a. a complete sentence;
b. broad enough to include the significant details; and
c. slanted enough to reflect the author's treatment of the topic.

In the example about corruption in federal politics, the author's main idea might be that voters need to ask for an investigation of seemingly corrupt practices by federal politicians.

could strike. Each year of the late nineteenth century some 35,000 wage earners were killed by industrial accidents. In Pittsburgh iron and steel mills alone, in one year 195 men died from hot metal explosions, asphyxiation, and falls, some into pits of molten metal. Men and women working in textile mills were poisoned by the thick dust and fibers in the air; similar toxic atmospheres injured those working in anything from twine-making plants to embroidery factories. Railways, with their heavy equipment and unaccustomed speed, were especially dangerous. In Philadelphia over half the railroad workers who died between 1886 and 1890 were killed by accidents. For injury or death, workers and their families could expect no payment from employers, since the idea of worker's compensation was unknown.

James W. Davidson et al., Nation of Nations

1. Who or what is this about? *Injuries from machines*
2. What are the major details? *35,000 killed, 195 died from explosions, etc., poisoned by dust: Half of rail workers killed.*
3. What is the main idea the author is trying to convey about the topic? *New high-speed machines brought danger to the workplace.*

Stated and Unstated Main Ideas

Like paragraphs, pictures also suggest main ideas. Artists compose and select to communicate a message. Look at the picture on the following page, and state the topic of the picture, the details that seem important, and the main idea that the artist is trying to convey.

What is the general topic of the picture? _____

_____

What details seem important? _____

_____

What is the main idea the artist is trying to convey about the topic? _____

_____

The topic is smoking or, more specifically, a plea for women to stop smoking. The details show a daughter using a crayon or pencil to mimic her mother's movements with a cigarette. The picture suggests what the caption directly states, "Like Mother, Like Daughter." The mother is the role model that the child will imitate. The main idea is that women should stop smoking—not only for their own health, but also for the welfare of their daughters. In this advertise-

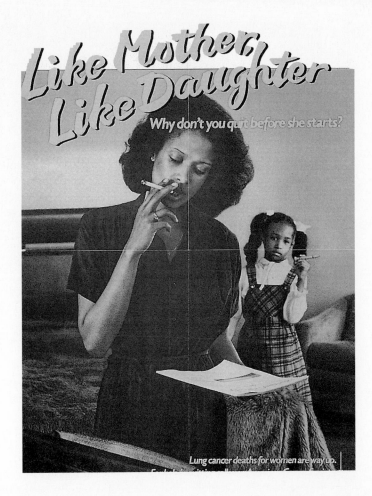

Like Mother, Like Daughter

Why don't you quit before she starts?

Lung cancer deaths for women are way up.

ment by the American Cancer Society, the main idea is stated in a question that can be restated as "You should quit before she starts."

Now look at the picture on page 112, which does not include a slogan or directly stated appeal. Again, state the topic of the picture, the important details, and the main idea the artist is trying to get across.

What is the general topic of the picture? _____

_____

What details seem important? _____

_____

What is the main idea the artist is trying to convey about the topic? _____

_____

The topic is homelessness. The details show a faceless person wrapped in blankets sitting on a park bench by a public trash can with a lake in the background. The assorted bags appear to be all the worldly possessions of the homeless person. The pillow implies that the person spent the night on the bench. The main idea is that the homeless are destitute and forced to sleep unsheltered on public park benches. Although the point is unstated, do you sense the despair and the hardships of the homeless?

As in the pictures, an author's main point can either be directly stated in the material or it can be unstated. When the main idea is stated in a sentence, the statement is called a **topic sentence or thesis statement.** Such a general statement is helpful to the reader because it provides an overview of the material. It does not, however, always express the author's opinion of the subject. For that reason, although helpful in overviewing, the topic sentence may not always form a complete statement of the author's main point.

Frequency of Stated Main Idea. Research shows that students find passages easier to comprehend when the main idea is directly stated within the passage. How often do stated main ideas appear in college textbooks? Should the reader expect to find that most paragraphs have stated main ideas?

For psychology texts, the answer seems to be about half and half. In a recent study,[2] stated main ideas appeared in *only 58 percent* of the sampled paragraphs in introductory psychology textbooks. In one of the books, the main idea was directly stated in 81 percent of the sampled paragraphs, and the researchers noted that the text was particularly easy to read.

Given these findings, we should recognize the importance of being skilled in locating and, especially, in constructing main ideas. In pulling ideas together to construct a main idea, you will be looking at the big picture and not be bound to the text in search of any single suggestive sentence.

Location of Stated Main Ideas. Should college readers wish for all passages in all textbooks to begin with stated main ideas? Indeed, research indicates that when the main idea is stated at the beginning of the passage, the text tends to be most easily comprehended. In their research, however, Smith and Chase found only 33 percent of the stated main ideas to be positioned as the first sentence of the paragraph.

Main idea statements can be positioned at the beginning, in the middle, or at the end of a paragraph. Both the beginning and concluding sentences of a passage can be combined for a main idea statement. The following examples and diagrams demonstrate the different possible positions for stated main ideas within paragraphs.

1. An introductory statement of the main idea is given at the beginning of the paragraph.

main idea
  1. detail
  2. detail
  3. detail
  4. detail

Under hypnosis, people may recall things that they are unable to remember spontaneously. Some police departments employ hypnotists to probe for information that crime victims do not realize they have. In 1976, twenty-six young children were kidnapped from a school bus near Chowchilla, California. The driver of the bus caught a quick glimpse of the license plate of the van in which he and the children were driven away. However, he remembered only the first two digits. Under hypnosis, he recalled the other numbers and the van was traced to its owners.

David Dempsey and Philip Zimbardo, *Psychology and You*[3]

---

[2]B. Smith and N. Chase, "The Frequency and Placement of Main Idea Topic Sentences in College Psychology Textbooks," *Journal of College Reading and Learning* 24 (1991): 46–54.

[3]From *Psychology and You* by David Dempsey and Philip G. Zimbardo. Copyright © 1978 by Scott, Foresman and Company, HarperCollins College Publishers.

2. A concluding statement of the main idea appears at the end of the paragraph.

1. detail
2. detail
3. detail
4. detail
main idea

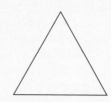

Research is not a once-and-for-all-times job. Even sophisticated companies often waste the value of their research. One of the most common errors is not providing a basis for comparisons. A company may research its market, find a need for a new advertising campaign, conduct the campaign, and then neglect to research the results. Another may simply feel the need for a new campaign, conduct it, and research the results. Neither is getting the full benefit of the research. When you fail to research either the results or your position *prior* to the campaign, you cannot know the effects of the campaign. *For good evaluation you must have both before and after data.*

Edward Fox and Edward Wheatley, *Modern Marketing*[4]

3. Details are placed at the beginning to arouse interest, followed by a statement of main idea in the middle of the paragraph.

1. detail
2. detail
main idea
3. detail
4. detail

What happens when foreign materials do enter the body by breaking through the skin or epithelial linings of the digestive, circulatory, or respiratory systems and after the clotting process is complete? The next line of defense comes into action. Phagocytic cells (wandering and stationary) may engulf the foreign material and destroy it. But there is another and very complicated aspect of the process. *This is the production of specific antibody molecules. Antibodies may circulate in the blood as mentioned or they may be bound to cells;* less is known about these cell-bound antibodies. Antibodies inactivate or destroy the activity of antigens by combining with them. The reaction is a manifestation of the immune response, and the discipline primarily devoted to its study is immunology. Generally immunity is

[4]From *Modern Marketing* by Edward J. Fox and Edward W. Wheatley. Copyright © 1978 by Scott, Foresman and Company, HarperCollins College Publishers.

considered to be peculiar to the vertebrates, but recent evidence suggests that a form of immunity occurs in invertebrate animals also.

Willis H. Johnson et al., Essentials of Biology

4. Both the introductory and concluding sentences state the main idea.

main idea
  1. detail
  2. detail
  3. detail
  4. detail
main idea

A speech of tribute is designed to create in those who hear it a sense of appreciation for the traits or accomplishments of the person or group to whom tribute is paid. If you cause your audience to realize the essential worth or importance of the person or group, you will have succeeded. But you may go further than this. You may, by honoring a person, arouse deeper devotion to the cause he or she represents. Did this person give distinguished service to community or country? Then strive to enhance the audience's sense of patriotism and service. Was this individual a friend to young people? Then try to arouse the conviction that working to provide opportunities for the young deserves the audience's support. Create a desire in your listeners to emulate the person or persons honored. *Make them want to develop the same virtues, to demonstrate a like devotion.*

Douglas Ehninger et al., Principles of Speech Communication[5]

Unfortunately, readers cannot always rely on a stated main idea being provided. For example, fiction writers rarely, if ever, use stated main ideas. The following is an example of a paragraph with an unstated main idea.

5. Details combine to make a point but the main idea is not directly stated.

  1. detail
  2. detail
  3. detail
  4. detail

    This creature's career could produce but one result, and it speedily followed. Boy after boy managed to get on the river. The minister's son became an engineer. The doctor's sons became "mud clerks"; the wholesale liquor dealer's son became a bar-keeper on a boat; four sons of the chief

---

[5]From Principles of Speech Communication, 9th Brief Edition, by Douglas Ehninger, Bruce E. Gronbeck, and Alan H. Monroe. Copyright © 1984, Scott, Foresman and Company, HarperCollins College Publishers.

merchant, and two sons of the county judge, became pilots. Pilot was the grandest position of all. The pilot, even in those days of trivial wages, had a princely salary—from a hundred and fifty to two hundred and fifty dollars a month, and no board to pay. Two months of his wages would pay a preacher's salary for a year. Now some of us were left disconsolate. We could not get on the river—at least our parents would not let us.

Mark Twain, Life on the Mississippi

Main idea: Young boys in the area have a strong desire to leave home and get a job on the prestigious Mississippi River.

WHAT DO DETAILS DO?

Look at the details in the picture on page 117 to decide what message the photographer is trying to communicate. Determine the topic of the picture, propose a main idea using your prior knowledge, and then list some of the significant details that support this point.

What is the topic? _____

_____

What are the significant supporting details? _____

_____

What is the point the photograph is trying to convey about the topic?

_____

The topic of the picture is the destruction of homes by fire. The details show the remains of houses that have been burned. Brick chimneys mark the places where houses once stood and where families once lived. Nothing seems to have been saved from the fire. The trees were charred, and the other chimneys suggest that an entire neighborhood went up in flame. A lone man views the devastation and perhaps mourns his losses. Notice that a Christmas bow has been ironically placed on the front chimney. The main idea of this picture is that the fire totally destroyed the homes and, perhaps, the dreams of an entire neighborhood.

Details support, develop, and explain a main idea. Specific details can include reasons, incidents, facts, examples, steps, and definitions. The task of a reader is to recognize the major details and to pull them together into a main idea. Being able to pick out major details implies that the reader has some degree of prior knowledge on the subject and has probably already begun to form some notion of the main idea.

Textbooks are packed full of details, but fortunately all details are not of equal importance. Major details tend to support, explain, and describe main

ideas, whereas minor details tend to support, explain, and describe the major details. Ask the following questions to determine which details are major in importance and which are not:

1. Which details logically develop the main idea?
2. Which details help you understand the main idea?
3. Which details validate the main idea?

Noticing key words that form transitional links from one idea to another can sometimes help the reader distinguish between major and minor details. The following terms are frequently used to signal significance:

Key words for major details: one, first, another, furthermore, also, finally

Key words for minor details: for example, to be specific, that is, this means

Example of Stated Main Idea

Managers can regain control over their time in several ways. One is by meeting whenever possible in someone else's office, so that they can leave as soon as their business is finished. Another is to start meetings on time without waiting for late-comers. The idea is to let late-comers adjust their schedules rather than everyone else adjusting theirs. A third is to set aside a block of time to work on an important project without interruption. This may require ignoring the telephone, being protected by an aggressive secretary, or hiding out. Whatever it takes is worth it.

Reitz and Jewell, *Managing*

1. Who or what is this about?
   (The passage is about managers controlling their time.)
2. What are the major details?
   (The details are: meet in another office, start meetings on time, and block out time to work.)
3. What is the main idea the author is trying to convey about the topic?
   (The main idea, stated in the first sentence, is that managers can do things to control their time.)

Exercise 3   STATED MAIN IDEAS

Read the following passages and use the three-question system to determine the author's main idea. For each passage in this exercise, the answer to the third question will be stated somewhere within the paragraph.

Passage A

Courting behavior in birds is also believed to be instinctive. In one experiment Daniel Lehrman of Rutgers University found that when a male blond ring dove was isolated from females, it soon began to bow and coo to a stuffed model of a female—a model that it had previously ignored. When the model was replaced by a rolled-up cloth, he began to court the cloth; and when this was removed the sex-crazed dove directed his attention to a corner of the cage, where it could at least focus its gaze. It seems that the threshold for release of the behavior pattern became increasingly lower as time went by without the sight of a live female dove. It is almost as though some specific "energy" for performing courting behavior were building up within the male ring dove.

Robert Wallace, *Biology: The World of Life*

1. Who or what is this about?

   _____

   _____

2. What are the major details?

   _____

   _____

© 1997 Addison-Wesley Educational Publishers Inc.

3. What is the main idea the author is trying to convey about the topic? Underline the main idea.

Passage B

Branding has many advantages for marketers. Retailers, wholesalers, manufacturers, and other marketers can develop loyal customers who identify what to buy through branding. Advertising a brand encourages consumers to buy and continue buying products. Branding allows marketers to introduce new products more efficiently. For example, in 1993 when Skippy introduced peanut butter cookies, the product required less advertising and achieved faster consumer acceptance than it would have if it had not used Skippy's name. BankAmericard changed its brand name to VISA so it would be more effective in marketing the credit card throughout the world. Nissan introduced the brand name Datsun in the United States because it felt it would be more acceptable to American buyers, but eventually changed back to Nissan to establish a single brand name worldwide.

Thomas C. Kinnear et al., *Principles of Marketing*

1. Who or what is this about? _____

_____

2. What are the major details?

_____

_____

3. What is the main idea the author is trying to convey about the topic? Underline the main idea.

Passage C

To retrieve a fact from a library of stored information, you need a way to gain access to it. In recognition tests, retrieval cues (such as photographs) provide reminders of information (classmates' names) we could not otherwise recall. Retrieval cues also guide us where to look. If you want to know what the pyramid on the back of a dollar bill signifies, you might look in *Collier's Encyclopedia* under "dollar," "currency," or "money." But your efforts would be futile. To get the information you want, you would have to look under "Great Seal of the United States." Like information stored in encyclopedias, memories are inaccessible unless we have cues for retrieving them. The more and better learned the retrieval cues, the more accessible the memory.

David G. Myers, *Psychology*

1. Who or what is this about? _____

_____

© 1997 Addison-Wesley Educational Publishers Inc.

2. What are the major details?

_____

_____

3. What is the main idea the author is trying to convey about the topic? Underline the main idea.

Passage D

Most of the Plains Indians believed that land could be utilized, but
never owned. The idea of owning land was as absurd as owning the air
people breathed. To some, the sacredness of the land made farming against
their religion. Chief Somohalla of the Wanapaun explained why his people
refused to farm. "You ask me to plow the ground! Shall I take a knife and
tear my mother's bosom? . . . You ask me to cut grass and make hay and sell
it, and be rich like white men! But how dare I cut off my mother's hair?"

James Kirby Martin et al., *America and Its People*

1. Who or what is this about? _____

_____

2. What are the major details?

_____

_____

3. What is the main idea the author is trying to convey about the topic? Underline the main idea.

Passage E

Ironically, large predators have never been a significant cause of human
death (unless you happened to be the one they were chasing). Our greatest
threat has always come from the microscopic side of the eat-and-be-eaten
continuum. By far, our most deadly enemies are the tiny viruses, bacteria,
protozoans, fungi, and parasitic worms and flukes that are responsible for
the diseases and infections afflicting our species.

Carl E. Rischer and Thomas A. Easton, *Focus on Human Biology*

1. Who or what is this about? _____

_____

2. What are the major details?

_____

_____

3. What is the main idea the author is trying to convey about the topic? Underline the main idea.

Example of an Unstated Main Idea

Michael Harner proposes an ecological interpretation of Aztec sacrifice and cannibalism. He holds that human sacrifice was a response to certain diet deficiencies in the population. In the Aztec environment, wild game was getting scarce, and the population was growing. Although the maize-beans combination of food that was the basis of the diet was usually adequate, these crops were subject to seasonal failure. Famine was frequent in the absence of edible domesticated animals. To meet essential protein requirements, cannibalism was the only solution. Although only the upper classes were allowed to consume human flesh, a commoner who distinguished himself in a war could also have the privilege of giving a cannibalistic feast. Thus, although it was the upper strata who benefited most from ritual cannibalism, members of the commoner class could also benefit. Furthermore, as Harner explains, the social mobility and cannibalistic privileges available to the commoners through warfare provided a strong motivation for the "aggressive war machine" that was such a prominent feature of the Aztec state.

Serena Nanda, *Cultural Anthropology*

1. Who or what is this about?
   (This passage is about Aztec sacrifice and cannibalism.)

2. What are the major details?
   (The major details are: diet deficiencies occurred, animals were not available, and upper class members and heros could eat human flesh.)

3. What is the main idea the author is trying to convey about the topic?
   (The author's main idea is that Aztec sacrifice and cannibalism met protein needs of the diet and motivated warriors to achieve.)

Exercise 4　UNSTATED MAIN IDEAS

Read the following passages and use the three-question system to determine the author's main idea. Pull the ideas together to state the main ideas in your own words.

Passage A

When our children are adults there will be no more Siberian tigers, African elephants, or cheetahs left in the wild. The major sources of diversity and evolution on this planet, the tropical rain forests, are falling at the rate of 100 acres a minute. At the rate we are going today, there will be no wilderness left on the planet within 30 years. The only remnants will be tiny islands which we set aside as parks and reserves—but when you have an island of wilderness, extinction within that island goes on. We are the *last* generation that will have any decision to make about wilderness because within our lifetimes it's all going to be gone. Around the world the skin of life is being torn apart by the deadliest predator ever known in the history of life on earth. (David Suzuki, biologist and anchor of Canadian Broadcasting Corporation series "Improving on Nature," in his keynote address at 1989 UCLA Conference on the Environment).

Richard P. Appelbaum and William J. Chambliss, Sociology

1. Who or what is this about? _____

_____

2. What are the major details?

_____

_____

3. What is the main idea the author is trying to convey about the topic? _____

_____

_____

Passage B

Prior to the time of Jan Baptiste van Helmont, a Belgian physician of the 17th century, it was commonly accepted that plants derived their matter from materials in the soil. (Probably, many people who haven't studied photosynthesis would go along with this today.) We aren't sure why, but van Helmont decided to test the idea. He carefully stripped a young willow sapling of all surrounding soil, weighed it, and planted it in a tub of soil that had also been carefully weighed. After five years of diligent watering (with rain water), van Helmont removed the greatly enlarged willow and again stripped away the soil and weighed it. The young tree had gained 164 pounds. Upon weighing the soil, van Helmont was amazed to learn that it had lost only 2 ounces.

Robert Wallace et al., Biology: The Science of Life, 3rd edition

1. Who or what is this about? _____

_____

2. What are the major details?

_____

_____

3. What is the main idea the author is trying to convey about the topic? _____

_____

_____

Passage C

The Aswan High Dam, built in Egypt with Russian support, was supposed to provide hydroelectric power and to increase Egypt's food supply by controlling the unpredictable Nile River. The project meant that great art treasures were flooded as submerged land was drained for cultivation. However, only one-tenth of an acre of land was made available for each person added to Egypt's population during the period of construction. One result of the dam was that the Nile no longer flooded the delta farmlands annually. These annual floods served to restore the farmland fertility with deposited silt. This no longer the case, the quality of the farmland decreased. The dam also cut off the nutrients that had been washed to the Mediterranean Sea as a result of the annual floodings. Because of this, or the change in the salinity of the sea that the dam produced, the sardine catch dropped from 18,000 tons per year to 500 tons per year. The stable lake created by the dam allowed aquatic snails to flourish. The snails serve as an intermediate host to a blood fluke that bores into humans causing the dreaded disease, schistosomiasis. The construction of the dam had important political implications at the time. These tombs had to be moved to be saved from the dam's waters. The political scene has changed now. So has the environmental one.

Robert Wallace, *Biology: The World of Life*

1. Who or what is this about? _____

_____

2. What are the major details?

_____

_____

3. What is the main idea the author is trying to convey about the topic? _____

_____

_____

Passage D

If using sunscreen, apply it at least 30–45 minutes before exposure, then reapply it periodically, especially after you swim or sweat. It is especially important to protect children. One or more severe sunburns with blisters in childhood or adolescence can double the risk of the skin cancer melanoma later in life. Additional protection can be provided by a wide-brimmed hat to protect your head and face, and opaque clothing to cover those body areas you wish to protect. Any fabric or material you can see through, including some beach umbrellas, does not give full protection. You should stay out of the sun between 10 AM and 2 PM when the rays are strongest.

Curtis O. Byer and Louis W. Shainberg, Living Well

1. Who or what is this about? _____

_____

2. What are the major details?

_____

_____

3. What is the main idea the author is trying to convey about the topic? _____

_____

_____

Passage E

In 1979 when University of Minnesota psychologist Thomas Bouchard read a newspaper account of the reuniting of 39-year-old twins who had been separated from infancy, he seized the opportunity and flew them to Minneapolis for extensive tests. Bouchard was looking for differences. What "the Jim twins," Jim Lewis and Jim Springer, presented were amazing similarities. Both had married women named Linda, divorced, and married women named Betty. One had a son James Alan, the other a son James Allan. Both had dogs named Toy, chainsmoked Salems, served as sheriff's deputies, drove Chevrolets, chewed their fingernails to the nub, enjoyed stock car racing, had basement workshops, and had built circular white benches around trees in their yards. They also had similar medical histories: Both gained 10 pounds at about the same time and then lost it; both suffered what they mistakenly believed were heart attacks, and both began having late-afternoon headaches at age 18.

Identical twins Oskar Stohr and Jack Yufe presented equally striking similarities. One was raised by his grandmother in Germany as a Catholic and a Nazi, while the other was raised by his father in the Caribbean as a Jew. Nevertheless, they share traits and habits galore. They like spicy foods and sweet liqueurs, have a habit of falling asleep in front of the television, flush the toilet before using it, store rubber bands on their wrists, and dip buttered toast in their coffee. Stohr is domineering toward women and yells at his wife, as did Yufe before he was separated.

David G. Myers, Psychology

1. Who or what is this about? _____

   _____

2. What are the major details?

   _____

   _____

3. What is the main idea the author is trying to convey about the topic? _____

   _____

   _____

GETTING THE MAIN IDEA OF LONGER SELECTIONS

Understanding the main idea of longer selections requires a little more thinking than finding the main idea of a single paragraph. Since longer selections such as articles or chapters involve more material, the challenge of tying the ideas together can be confusing and complicated. Each paragraph of a longer selection usually represents a new aspect of a supporting detail. In addition, several major ideas may contribute to developing the overall main idea. The reader, therefore, must fit the many pieces together under one central theme.

For longer selections, the reader needs to add an extra step between the two questions, "What is the topic?" and "What is the main idea the author is trying to convey?" The step involves organizing the material into manageable subunits and then relating those to the whole. Two additional questions to ask are, "Under what subsections can these ideas be grouped?" and "How do these subsections contribute to the whole?"

Use the following suggestions to determine the main idea of longer selections. The techniques are similar to those used in previewing and skimming, two skills that also focus on the overall central theme.

1. Think about the significance of the title. What does the title suggest about the topic?
2. Read the first one or two paragraphs for a statement of the topic or thesis. What does the selection seem to be about?
3. Read the subheadings and, if necessary, glance at the first sentences of some of the paragraphs. From these clues what does the article seem to be about?

4. Look for clues that indicate how the material is organized.
   a. Is the purpose to define a term, to prove an opinion, or explain a concept, to describe a situation, or to persuade the reader toward a particular point of view?
   b. Is the material organized into a list of examples, a time order or sequence, a comparison or contrast, or a cause-and-effect relationship?
5. As you read, organize the paragraphs into subsections. Give each subsection a title. These become your significant supporting details.
6. Determine how the overall organization and subsections relate to the whole, and answer the question, "What is the main idea the author is trying to convey in this selection?"

PATTERNS OF ORGANIZATION

The main idea and the pattern of organization chosen by a writer to deliver this idea are closely interwoven. Identifying one will often help identify the other, because the message can dictate the structure. A **pattern of organization** is a vehicle or structure for a message. Before beginning to write, an author must ask, "If this is what I want to say, what is the best way to organize my message?"

From a number of possible patterns, an author chooses the organizational structure that seems most appropriate. For example, if he or she wanted to convey the message or main idea that freshmen receive more support at junior colleges than at large universities, the author would probably organize the message through a pattern of comparison and contrast. On the other hand, if the writer wanted to explain that a college degree can lead to expanded opportunities, upward mobility within companies, later salary increases, and ultimately greater job satisfaction, the idea might best be communicated through a pattern of cause and effect, although words like *expanded* and *greater* also suggest a comparison.

Suppose you were writing an orientation article describing support services available at your own college. You could summarize the resources in a list pattern, or you could discuss them in the order in which a freshman is likely to need them. Within your article, you might use a separate paragraph to describe or define a relatively unknown service on campus, with examples of how it has helped others. Thus, one long article might have an overall list pattern of organization yet contain individual paragraphs which follow other patterns. The organizational pattern is a choice you make for structuring your message.

The importance of identifying organizational patterns is that they signal how facts will be presented. They are blueprints for you to use while reading. The number of details in a textbook can be overwhelming. Identifying the author's pattern can help you to master the complexities of the material by allowing you to predict the format of upcoming information.

Although key words can signal a particular pattern, the most important clue to the pattern is the main idea itself. In a single selection several patterns can be employed. Your aim as a reader is to anticipate the overall pattern and place the supporting details into its broad perspective.

The following are examples of the patterns of organization that are found most frequently in textbooks.

Simple Listing

With a simple listing, items are randomly listed in a series of supporting facts or details. These supporting elements are of equal value, and the order in which they are presented is of no importance. Changing the order of the items does not change the meaning of the paragraph.

Signal words, often used as transitional words to link ideas in a paragraph with a pattern of simple listing, are: *in addition, also, another, several, for example, a number of.*

Example:
Work-Related Stress

Work-related stress has increased significantly in the last few years. People are spending more hours at work and bringing more work home with them. Job security has decreased in almost every industry. Pay, for many, has failed to keep up with the cost of living. Women are subject to exceptionally high stress levels as they try to live up to all of the expectations placed upon them. Finally, many people feel that they are trapped in jobs they hate, but can't escape.

Curtis O. Byer and Louis W. Shainberg, *Living Well*

Definition

Frequently in a textbook, an entire paragraph is devoted to defining a complex term or idea. The concept is defined initially and then expanded with examples and restatements.

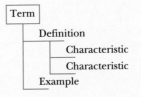

Example:
Ultrasound

Ultrasound is a relatively new technique that uses sound waves to produce an image that enables a physician to detect structural abnormalities. Useful pictures can be obtained as early as 7 weeks. Ultrasound is frequently used in conjunction with other techniques such as amniocentesis and fetoscopy.

John Dacey and John Travers, Human Development

Description

Description is like listing; the characteristics that make up a description are no more than a definition or a simple list of details.

Example:
Caribbean

Caribbean America today is a land crowded with so many people that, as a region (encompassing the Greater and Lesser Antilles), it is the most densely populated part of the Americas. It is also a place of grinding poverty and, in all too many localities, unrelenting misery with little chance for escape.

H. J. De Blij and Peter O. Muller, Geography

Time Order or Sequence

Items are listed in the order in which they occurred or in a specifically planned order in which they must develop. In this case, the order is important, and changing it would change the meaning.

Signal words often used for time order or sequence: *first, second, third, after, before, when, until, at last, next, later.*

Example:
Napoleon

In May 1803, just two weeks after Napoleon sold Louisiana to the United States, France declared war on Britain. For the next 12 years, war engulfed Europe. In 1805 France defeated the armies of Austria and Russia at Austerlitz thereby winning control of much of the European continent. Napoleon then massed his troops and assembled a fleet of flat boats for an invasion of England.

James Kirby Martin et al., America and Its People

Comparison-Contrast

Items are presented according to similarities and differences among them. Signal words often used for comparison-contrast: *different, similar, on the other hand, but, however, bigger than, in the same way, parallels.*

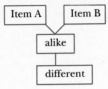

Example:
Oranges

An orange grown in Florida usually has a thin and tightly fitting skin, and it is also heavy with juice. Californians say that if you want to eat a Florida orange you have to get into a bathtub first. California oranges are light in weight and have thick skins that break easily and come off in hunks.

John McPhee, Oranges

Exercise 5   PATTERNS OF ORGANIZATION AND MAIN IDEA

Read the following passages and use the three-question system to determine the author's main idea. In addition, indicate the dominant pattern of organization used by the author. Select from the following list:

Simple listing

Definition

Description

Time order

Comparison-contrast

Cause and effect

Passage A

Let us follow the story of how rabbits were introduced into Australia. European rabbits reached Australia with the first European settlers in 1788 and repeated introductions followed. By the early 1800s rabbits were being kept in every large settlement and had been liberated many times. All the early rabbit introductions either died out or remained localized. No one knows why.

On Christmas Day, 1859, the brig HMS *Lightning* arrived at Melbourne with about a dozen wild European rabbits bound for an estate in western Victoria. Within three years rabbits had started to spread, after a bush fire destroyed the fences enclosing one colony. From a slow spread at first the colonization picked up speed during the 1870s, and by 1900 the European rabbit had spread 1000 miles to the north and west, changing the entire economy of nature in southeastern Australia.

Charles Krebs, *The Message of Ecology*

1. Who or what is this about? _____

   _____

   _____

2. What are the major details? _____

   _____

   _____

   _____

3. What is the overall pattern of organization? _____

4. What is the main idea the author is trying to convey about the topic? _____

   _____

   _____

Passage B

Sloppy people can't bear to part with anything. They give loving attention to every detail. When sloppy people say they're going to tackle the surface of a desk, they really mean it. Not a paper will go unturned; not a rubber band will go unboxed.

Neat people are bums and clods at heart. They have cavalier attitudes toward possessions, including family heirlooms. Everything is just another dust-catcher to them. If anything collects dust, it's got to go and that's that.

Suzanne Britt, *Neat People vs. Sloppy People*

1. Who or what is this about? _____

   _____

   _____

2. What are the major details? _____

   _____

   _____

   _____

3. What is the overall pattern of organization? _____

4. What is the main idea the author is trying to convey about the topic? _____

_____

_____

Passage C

The disadvantage faced by children who attempt morning schoolwork on an empty stomach appears to be at least partly due to hypoglycemia. The average child up to the age of ten or so needs to eat every four to six hours to maintain a blood glucose concentration high enough to support the activity of the brain and nervous system. A child's brain is as big as an adult's, and the brain is the body's chief glucose consumer. A child's liver is considerably smaller, and the liver is the organ responsible for storing glucose (as glycogen) and for releasing it into the blood as needed. The liver can't store more than about four hours' worth of glycogen; hence the need to eat fairly often. Teachers aware of the late-morning slump in their classrooms wisely request that a midmorning snack be provided; it improves classroom performance all the way to lunch time. But for the child who hasn't had breakfast, the morning may be lost altogether.

Eva May Nunnelley Hamilton et al., *Nutrition*

1. Who or what is this about? _____

_____

_____

2. What are the major details? _____

_____

_____

_____

3. What is the overall pattern of organization? _____

4. What is the main idea the author is trying to convey about the topic? _____

_____

_____

Passage D

In office, Jackson greatly enhanced the power and prestige of the presidency. He was the first president to fire a cabinet officer, the first to use federal troops to put down a labor strike, the first to open diplomatic relations with the Far East, and the first to declare that the president, and not Congress, represented the people. He was also the first president to declare that the Union could not be peacefully dissolved.

James Kirby Martin et al., *America and Its People*

1. Who or what is this about? _____

_____

_____

2. What are the major details? _____

_____

_____

_____

3. What is the overall pattern of organization? _____

4. What is the main idea the author is trying to convey about the topic? _____

_____

_____

Passage E

Patronage is one of the key inducements used by machines. A patronage job is one that is given for political reasons rather than for merit or competence alone. Jobs are not the only form of patronage. In return for handsome campaign contributions, machines have been known to give out government contracts. Today, though, such activity has been greatly curtailed and the party machines are a relic of the past.

Robert L. Lineberry et al., *Government in America*

1. Who or what is this about? _____

_____

_____

2. What are the major details? _____

_____

_____

_____

3. What is the overall pattern of organization? _____

4. What is the main idea the author is trying to convey about the topic? _____

_____

_____

Cause and Effect

In this pattern, one element is shown as producing another element. One is the *cause* or the "happening" that stimulated the particular result or *effect*.

Signal words often used for cause and effect: *for this reason, consequently, on that account, hence, because.*

Example:
Steroids

There has been a great deal of discussion about "'roid rage," a kind of manic rage that has been reported by some steroid users. We should be careful on the basis of uncontrolled retrospective reports to attribute instances of violence to a drug, especially when the perpetrator of a violent crime may be looking for an excuse. However, there is a sufficient number of reports of violent feelings and actions among steroid users for us to be concerned and to await further research. According to Dr. William Taylor, a leading authority on anabolic steroids, "I've seen total personality changes. A passive, low-key guy goes on steroids for muscle enhancement, and the next thing you know, he's being arrested for assault or disorderly conduct."

Oakley Ray and Charles Ksir, *Drugs, Society, and Human Behavior*

SUMMARY WRITING: A MAIN IDEA SKILL

What Is a Summary?

A summary is a brief, concise statement in your own words of the main idea and the significant supporting details. The first sentence should state the main idea or thesis, and subsequent sentences should incorporate the significant details. Minor details and material irrelevant to the learner's purpose should be omitted. The summary should be in paragraph form and should always be shorter than the material being summarized.

Why Summarize?

Summaries can be used for textbook study and are particularly useful in anticipating answers for essay exam questions. For writing research papers, summarizing is an essential skill. Using your own words to put the essence of an article into concise sentences requires a thorough understanding of the material. As one researcher noted, "Since so much summarizing is necessary for writing papers, students should have the skill before starting work on research papers. How much plagiarism is the result of inadequate summarizing skills?"[6]

Writing a research paper may mean that you will have to read as many as thirty articles and four books over a period of a month or two. After each reading you want to take enough notes so you can write your paper without returning to the library for another look at the original reference. Since you will be using so many different references, the notetaking should be done carefully. The complete sentences of a summary are more explicit than underscored text or the highlighted topic-phrase format of an outline. Your summary should demonstrate a synthesis of the information.

How to Summarize

1. Keep in mind the purpose of your summary. Your projected needs will determine which details are important and how many should be included.
2. Decide on the main idea the author is trying to convey. Make this main idea the first sentence in your summary.
3. Decide on the major ideas and details that support the author's point. Include in your summary the major ideas and as many of the significant supporting details as your purpose demands.
4. Do not include irrelevant or repeated information in your summary.
5. Use appropriate transitional words and phrases to show relationships between points.
6. Use paragraph form.
7. Do not add your personal opinion as part of the summary.

Example of Summarizing

Read the following excerpt on political authority as if you were researching for a term paper and writing a summary on a notecard. Mark key terms that you would include in your summary. Before reading the example provided, anticipate what you would include in your own summary.

[6]K. Taylor, "Can College Students Summarize?," *Journal of Reading* 26 (March 1983): 540–544.

Types of Authority

Where is the source of the state's authority? Weber described three possible sources of the right to command, which produce what he called traditional authority, charismatic authority, and legal authority.

Traditional Authority

In many societies, people have obeyed those in power because, in essence, "that is the way it has always been." Thus, kings, queens, feudal lords, and tribal chiefs did not need written rules in order to govern. Their authority was based on tradition, on long-standing customs, and it was handed down from parent to child, maintaining traditional authority from one generation to the next. Often, traditional authority has been justified by religious tradition. For example, medieval European kings were said to rule by divine right, and Japanese emperors were considered the embodiment of heaven.

Charismatic Authority

People may also submit to authority, not because of tradition, but because of the extraordinary attraction of an individual. Napoleon, Gandhi, Mao Tse-tung, and Ayatollah Khomeini all illustrate authority that derives its legitimacy from **charisma**—an exceptional personal quality popularly attributed to certain individuals. Their followers perceive charismatic leaders as persons of destiny endowed with remarkable vision, the power of a savior, or God's grace. Charismatic authority is inherently unstable. It cannot be transferred to another person.

Legal Authority

The political systems of industrial states are based largely on a third type of authority: legal authority, which Weber also called *rational authority*. These systems derive legitimacy from a set of explicit rules and procedures that spell out the ruler's rights and duties. Typically, the rules and procedures are put in writing. The people grant their obedience to "the law." It specifies procedures by which certain individuals hold offices of power, such as governor or president or prime minister. But the authority is vested in those offices, not in the individuals who temporarily hold the offices. Thus, a political system based on legal authority is often called a "government of laws, not of men." Individuals come and go, as American presidents have come and gone, but the office, "the presidency," remains. If individual officeholders overstep their authority, they may be forced out of office and replaced.

Alex Thio, *Sociology*

To begin your summary, what is the main point?

What are the major areas of support?

_____

Should you include an example for each area?

_____

Read the summary and notice how closely it fit your own ideas.

Political Authority

Weber describes the three command sources as traditional, charismatic, and legal authority. Traditional authority is not written but based on long-standing customs such as the power of queens or tribal chiefs. Charismatic authority is based on the charm and vision of a leader such as Gandhi. Legal authority, such as that of American presidents, comes from written laws and is vested in the office rather than the person.

Exercise 6   SUMMARIZING

Read the following passages and mark the key terms. Begin your summary with a statement of the main point and add the appropriate supporting details. Use your markings to help you write the summary. Be brief but include the essential elements.

Passage A. Leaves to the Defense

A plant's leaves are the parts most exposed to the environment. Here they spread out and absorb sunlight and carbon dioxide for photosynthesis. And here they also catch the attention of hungry herbivores. It is not surprising, therefore, that many plants have evolved leaves with protective mechanisms.

The most obvious defense is having sharp prickles. Leaves of many hollies have several sharp projections along the edges, and thistle leaves carry this motif over the whole leaf surface. In cacti, the entire leaf has become a sharp spine, with the stem taking over the role of photosynthesis completely. Some grasses grow their weapons in miniature, producing saws rather than swords.

Many leaves have more subtle defenses, such as specialized epidermal hairs. The itchy juice secreted by the hairs of tomato plants, for instance, deters some animals from brushing against them, much less eating them. The hook-shaped hairs of beans entangle small insects, and the insect stops feeding on the plant while it struggles to free itself. The nettle leaf has hairs of both these types. Epidermal hairs of other kinds of plants release glue, which traps small insects and immobilizes the feet and mouthparts of larger ones.

Some leaves' defenses are not external but internal. For example, leaf cells may contain sharp, needle-like crystals of calcium oxalate, called raphides, which ensure that animals will not take a second mouthful of leaves from the plant.

Other plants produce toxic chemicals. For example, milkweed leaves contain cardiac glycosides, chemicals that cause the heart to beat faster, sometimes leading to death of the animal.

In some plants, leaves produce their defenses only when needed. For example, tannins are defensive chemicals that precipitate the digestive enzymes of many herbivores; unable to digest its food, the animal starves. Sugar maples produce leaves with little tannin in the spring. In years when this first set of leaves is eaten by a heavy infestation of insects, the tree grows a set of replacement leaves containing more tannins.

A plant must fend off not only hungry herbivores but also other plants that compete with it for sunlight and water. Many plants produce chemicals that inhibit the growth of near neighbors, and what better way to deploy them into a "no trespassing" zone than by washing off the leaves? This is how shrubs of the chaparral in California inhibit the germination of seeds in the surrounding soil. Similarly, it is notoriously difficult to grow anything under a walnut tree because of a substance called juglone, which washes onto the ground and inhibits the growth of other plants.

Karen Arms and Pamela S. Camp, A Journey into Life

Use your marked text to write a summary.

Passage B. Suicide Among College Students

Compared to nonstudents of the same age, the suicide rate among college students is somewhat higher. Why is this so? For one thing, among the younger college students who commit suicide (ages 18–22), a common thread is the inability to separate themselves from their family and to solve problems on their own. College presents many of these younger students with the challenge of having to be independent in many ways while remaining dependent on family in other ways, such as financially and emotionally.

Several other characteristics of the college experience may relate to suicide. A great emphasis is put on attaining high grades and the significance of grades may be blown out of proportion. A student may come to perceive grades as a measurement of his or her total worth as a person, rather than just one of many ways a person can be evaluated. If a student is unable to achieve expected grades, there may be a total loss of self-esteem and loss of hope for any success in life.

In the college setting, where self-esteem can be tenuous, the end of a relationship can also be devastating. A student who has recently lost a close friend or lover can become so deeply depressed that suicide becomes an attractive alternative. The problem can be compounded when depression interferes with coursework and grades slip.

Curtis O. Byer and Louis W. Shainberg, Living Well

Use your marked text to write a summary.

Passage C. Making a Healthy Choice When It Comes to New Products

According to Charles M. Harper, chairman of ConAgra, Incorporated, the Healthy Choice line of frozen dinners, began with his own heart attack, which had been brought on by years of "eating anything I could get my hands on." As he lay in the hospital recuperating, Harper imagined a line of healthy frozen foods that tasted good.

The Healthy Choice product line was carefully tested with consumers before being introduced to the general population. ConAgra's research and development staff spent a year working under the directive, "whatever the cost, don't sacrifice taste." The first test market results surprised even the ConAgra team. The low-sodium, low-fat, low-cholesterol frozen entrees sold much better than expected. According to the firm's vice president of marketing and sales, "We benefited from low expectations, [the products] were much better than people thought [they] would be." This finding supported ConAgra's decision to position the product against other high-quality frozen dinners rather than as a diet or health food.

The new product's brand name and packaging were an important part of the development process. The name *Healthy Choice* was chosen for the positive connotation it held for consumers. Because ConAgra felt the product would be an impulse purchase, it was important to make the items stand out in the freezer case. This was accomplished through the dark green packaging that not only differed from the competition but also suggested freshness and nutritive value.

Thomas C. Kinner et al., Principles of Marketing

Use your marked text to write a summary.

SUMMARY POINTS

- Getting the main idea the author is trying to convey is the single most important reading comprehension skill. To do this the reader must first determine the topic, a general term that forms an umbrella for the specific ideas presented.
- The main idea is the point the author is trying to convey about the topic. In some passages the main idea is stated in a sentence, and in others it is unstated.
- Details support, develop, and explain the main idea; some are major and some are minor.
- Organizational patterns for presenting details and developing ideas can vary, and anticipating the pattern can help the reader.
- Summaries condense material and include the main ideas and major details.

SELECTION 1

PSYCHOLOGY

Stage 1: Skill Development

Preview

The author's main purpose is to describe the infant-mother love relationship.

agree ☐   disagree ☐

After reading this selection, I will need to know the meaning of contact comfort.

agree ☐   disagree ☐

Activate Schema

Do parents who were abused as children later abuse their own children?

Learning Strategy

Be able to explain the needs of the infant monkey and the effect that deprivation of those needs can have on the whole pattern of psychological development. Relate these findings to human behavior.

Word Knowledge

Are you familiar with the following words in this selection?

surrogate	desensitized
functional	ingenious
anatomy	deprived
tentatively	persisted
novel	deficient

Your instructor may ask ten true-false questions from the Instructor's Manual to stimulate your thinking using these words.

Stage 2: Integrate Knowledge While Reading

Use thinking strategies as you read:

1. Predict   2. Picture   3. Relate   4. Monitor   5. Fix up

© 1997 Addison-Wesley Educational Publishers Inc.

Monkey Love
From James V. McConnell, *Understanding Human Behavior*

The scientist who has conducted the best long-term laboratory experiments on love is surely Harry Harlow, a psychologist at the University of Wisconsin. Professor Harlow did not set out to study love—it happened by accident. Like many other psychologists, he was at first primarily
5   interested in how organisms learn. Rather than working with rats, Harlow chose to work with monkeys.

Since he needed a place to house and raise the monkeys, he built the Primate Laboratory at Wisconsin. Then he began to study the effects of brain lesions on monkey learning. But he soon found that young animals
10   reacted somewhat differently to brain damage than did older monkeys, so he and his wife Margaret devised a breeding program and tried various ways of raising monkeys in the laboratory. They rapidly discovered that monkey infants raised by their mothers often caught diseases from their parents, so the Harlows began taking the infants away from their mothers at birth and
15   tried raising them by hand. The baby monkeys had been given cheesecloth diapers to serve as baby blankets. Almost from the start, it became obvious to the Harlows that their little animals developed such strong attachments to the blankets that, in the Harlows' own terms, it was often hard to tell where the diaper ended and the baby began. Not only this, but if the
20   Harlows removed the "security" blanket in order to clean it, the infant monkey often became greatly disturbed—just as if its own mother had deserted it.

Harry Harlow found a surrogate mother for the monkey

The search to find a surrogate mother

The Surrogate Mother

25

What the baby monkeys obviously needed was an artificial or *surrogate* mother—something they could cling to as tightly as they typically clung to their own mother's chest. The Harlows sketched out many different designs, but none really appealed to them. Then, in 1957, while enjoying a champagne flight high over the city of Detroit, Harry Harlow glanced out of the airplane window and "saw" an image of an artificial monkey mother. It

30

was a hollow wire cylinder, wrapped with a terry-cloth bath towel, with a silly wooden head at the top. The tiny monkey could cling to this "model mother" as closely as to its real mother's body hair. This surrogate mother could be provided with a functional breast simply by placing a milk bottle so that the nipple stuck through the cloth at an appropriate place on the

35

surrogate's anatomy. The cloth mother could be heated or cooled; it could be rocked mechanically or made to stand still; and, most important, it could be removed at will.

While still sipping his champagne, Harlow mentally outlined much of the research that kept him, his wife, and their associates occupied for many

40

years to come. And without realizing it, Harlow had shifted from studying monkey learning to monkey love.

Infant-Mother Love

Warm surrogate mother

The chimpanzee or monkey infant is much more developed at birth than the human infant, and apes develop or mature much faster than we

45

do. Almost from the moment it is born, the monkey infant can move around and hold tightly to its mother. During the first few days of its life the infant will approach and cling to almost any large, warm, and soft object in its environment, particularly if that object also gives it milk. After a week or so, however, the monkey infant begins to avoid newcomers and

50

focuses its attentions on "mother"—real or surrogate.

During the first two weeks of its life warmth is perhaps the most important psychological thing that a monkey mother has to give to its baby. The Harlows discovered this fact by offering infant monkeys a choice of two types of mother-substitutes—one wrapped in terry cloth and one that was

55

made of bare wire. If the two artificial mothers were both the same temperature, the little monkeys always preferred the cloth mother. However, if the wire model was heated, while the cloth model was cool, for the first two weeks after birth the baby primates picked the warm wire mother-substitutes as their favorites. Thereafter they switched and spent

60

most of their time on the more comfortable cloth mother.

Why is cloth preferable to bare wire? Something that the Harlows called *contact comfort* seems to be the answer, and a most powerful influence it is. Infant monkeys (and chimps too) spend much of their time rubbing against their mothers' skins, putting themselves in as close contact with the parent

65 as they can. Whenever the young animal is frightened, disturbed, or annoyed, it typically rushes to its mother and rubs itself against her body. Wire doesn't "rub" as well as does soft cloth. Prolonged "contact comfort" with a surrogate cloth mother appears to instill confidence in baby monkeys and is much more rewarding to them than is either warmth or milk. Infant
70 monkeys also prefer a "rocking" surrogate to one that is stationary.

     According to the Harlows, the basic quality of an infant's love for its mother is *trust.* If the infant is put into an unfamiliar playroom without its mother, the infant ignores the toys no matter how interesting they might be. It screeches in terror and curls up into a furry little ball. If its cloth mother
75 is now introduced into the playroom, the infant rushes to the surrogate and clings to it for dear life. After a few minutes of contact comfort, it apparently begins to feel more secure. It then climbs down from the mother-substitute and begins tentatively to explore the toys, but often rushes back for a deep embrace as if to reassure itself that its mother is still
80 there and that all is well. Bit by bit its fears of the novel environment are "desensitized" and it spends more and more time playing with the toys and less and less time clinging to its "mother."

Good Mothers and Bad

     The Harlows found that, once a baby monkey has come to accept its
85 mother (real or surrogate), the mother can do almost no wrong. In one of their studies, the Harlows tried to create "monster mothers" whose behavior would be so abnormal that the infants would desert the mothers. Their purpose was to determine whether maternal rejection might cause abnormal behavior patterns in the infant monkeys similar to those
90 responses found in human babies whose mothers ignore or punish their children severely. The problem was—how can you get a terry-cloth mother to reject or punish its baby? Their solutions were ingenious—but most of them failed in their main purpose. Four types of "monster mothers" were tried, but none of them was apparently "evil" enough to impart fear or
95 loathing to the infant monkeys. One such "monster" occasionally blasted its babies with compressed air; a second shook so violently that the baby often fell off; a third contained a catapult that frequently flung the infant away from it. The most evil-appearing of all had a set of metal spikes buried beneath the terry cloth; from time to time the spikes would poke through
100 the cloth making it impossible for the infant to cling to the surrogate.

     The baby monkeys brought up on the "monster mothers" did show a brief period of emotional disturbance when the "wicked" temperament of the surrogates first showed up. The infants would cry for a time when displaced from their mothers, but as soon as the surrogates returned to
105 normal, the infant would return to the surrogate and continue clinging, as if all were forgiven. As the Harlows tell the story, the only prolonged distress

created by the experiment seemed to be that felt by the experimenters!

There was, however, one type of surrogate that uniformly "turned off"
the infant monkeys. S. J. Suomi, working with the Harlows, built a terry-cloth
mother with ice water in its veins. Newborn monkeys would attach
themselves to this "cool momma" for a brief period of time, but then
retreated to a corner of the cage and rejected her forever.

From their many brilliant studies, the Harlows conclude that the love of
an infant for its mother is *primarily a response to certain stimuli the mother offers.*
Warmth is the most important stimulus for the first two weeks of the
monkey's life, then contact comfort becomes paramount. Contact comfort
is determined by the softness and "rub-ability" of the surface of the mother's
body—terry cloth is better than are satin and silk, but all such materials are
more effective in creative love and trust than bare metal is. Food and mild
"shaking" or "rocking" are important too, but less so than warmth and
contact comfort. These needs—and the rather primitive responses the
infant makes in order to obtain their satisfaction—are programmed into the
monkey's genetic blueprint. The growing infant's requirement for social
and intellectual stimulation becomes critical only later in a monkey's life.
And yet, if the baby primate is deprived of contact with other young of its
own species, its whole pattern of development can be profoundly disturbed.

Mother-Infant Love

The Harlows were eventually able to find ways of getting female isolates
pregnant, usually by confining them in a small cage for long periods of time
with a patient and highly experienced normal male. At times, however, the
Harlows were forced to help matters along by strapping the female to a
piece of apparatus. When these isolated females gave birth to their first
monkey baby, they turned out to be the "monster mothers" the Harlows
had tried to create with mechanical surrogates. Having had no contact with
other animals as they grew up, they simply did not know what to do with
the furry little strangers that suddenly appeared on the scene. These
motherless mothers at first totally ignored their children, although if the
infant persisted, the mothers occasionally gave in and provided the baby
with some of the contact and comfort it demanded.

Surprisingly enough, once these mothers learned how to handle a baby,
they did reasonably well. Then, when they were again impregnated and gave
birth to a second infant, they took care of this next baby fairly adequately.

Maternal affection was totally lacking in a few of the motherless
monkeys, however. To them the newborn monkey was little more than an
object to be abused the way a human child might abuse a doll or a toy train.
These motherless mothers stepped on their babies, crushed the infant's face
into the floor of the cage, and once or twice chewed off their baby's feet and

fingers before they could be stopped. The most terrible mother of all
popped her infant's head into her mouth and crunched it like a potato chip.

150   We tend to think of most mothers—no matter what their species—as
having some kind of almost divine "maternal instinct" that makes them
love their children and take care of them no matter what the cost or
circumstance. While it is true that most females have built into their genetic
blueprint the tendency to be interested in (and to care for) their offspring,
155   this inborn tendency is always expressed in a given environment. The
"maternal instinct" is strongly influenced by the mother's past experiences.
Humans seem to have weaker instincts of all kinds than do other animals—
since our behavior patterns are more affected by learning than by our
genes, we have greater flexibility in what we do and become. But we pay a
160   sometimes severe price for this freedom from genetic control.

Normal monkey and chimpanzee mothers seldom appear to inflict real
physical harm on their children; human mothers and fathers often do.
Serapio R. Zalba, writing in a journal called *Trans-action,* estimated in 1971
that in the United States alone, perhaps 250,000 children suffer physical
165   abuse by their parents each year. Of these "battered babies," almost 40,000
may be very badly injured. The number of young boys and girls killed by
their parents annually is not known, but Zalba suggests that the figure may
run into the thousands. Parents have locked their children in tiny cages,
raised them in dark closets, burned them, boiled them, slashed them with
170   knives, shot them, and broken almost every bone in their bodies. How can
we reconcile these facts with the much-discussed maternal and paternal
"instincts"?

The research by the Harlows on the "motherless mothers" perhaps
gives us a clue. Mother monkeys who were themselves socially deprived or
175   isolated when young seemed singularly lacking in affection for their infants.
Zalba states that most of the abusive human parents that were studied
turned out to have been abused and neglected *themselves* as children. Like
the isolated monkeys who seemed unable to control their aggressive
impulses when put in contact with normal animals, the abusive parents
180   seem to be greatly deficient in what psychologists call "impulse control."
Most of these parents also were described as being socially isolated, as
having troubles adjusting to marriage, often deeply in debt, and as being
unable to build up warm and loving relationships with other people—
including their own children. Since they did not learn how to love from
185   their own parents, these mothers and fathers simply did not acquire the
social skills necessary for bringing up their own infants in a healthy fashion.

Stage 3: Recall

Stop to self-test and relate to issues. Your instructor may ask ten true-false
questions to stimulate your recall.

main idea major subject of the pease

SKILL DEVELOPMENT: SUMMARIZING

Using this selection as a source, summarize on index cards the information that you might want to include in a research paper entitled "Animal Rights: Do Scientists Go Too Far?"

SKILL DEVELOPMENT: MAIN IDEA

Answer with *T* (true) or *F* (false).

_T_ 1. The main point of the first four paragraphs is that Harlow's shift to studying monkey love occurred by accident.

_T_ 2. In the second section titled "Infant-Mother Love," the main point is that an infant monkey needs the "contact comfort" of the mother to give it a feeling of security while interacting with the environment.

_F_ 3. In the beginning of the section titled "Good Mothers and Bad," the main point is that baby monkeys will reject monster mothers.

_T_ 4. In the beginning of the section titled "Mother-Infant Love," the main point is that the maternal instinct is not influenced by the mother's past experiences.

_F_ 5. The author's overall pattern of organization for this selection is comparison and effect. *cause*

COMPREHENSION QUESTIONS

1. Who or what is the topic? *infant money behavior*

What is the main idea the author is trying to convey about the topic? *Monkey rather be wid real parent.*

After reading the selection, answer the following questions with *a, b, c,* or *d.*

_c_ 2. When Harry Harlow originally started his experiments with monkeys, his purpose was to study
   a. love.
   b. breeding.
   c. learning.
   d. disease.

_d_ 3. The reason that the author mentions Harry Harlow's revelations on the airplane is to show
   a. that he had extrasensory perception.
   b. that he liked to travel.
   c. that he was always thinking of his work.
   d. in what an unexpected way brilliant work often starts.

_b_   4. In his experiments Harlow used all of the following in designing his surrogate mothers except
    a. a terry-cloth bath towel.
    b. real body hair.
    c. a rocking movement.
    d. temperature controls.

_A_   5. Harlow manipulated his experiments to show the early significance of warmth by
    a. heating wire.
    b. changing from satin to terry cloth.
    c. equalizing temperature.
    d. creating "monster mothers."

_C_   6. Harlow feels that for contact comfort the cloth mother was preferable to the wire mother for all of the following reasons except
    a. the cloth mother instilled confidence.
    b. the wire mother doesn't "rub" as well.
    c. the wire mother was stationary.
    d. with the cloth mother, the infant feels a greater sense of security when upset.

_C_   7. Harlow's studies show that when abused by its mother, the infant will
    a. leave the mother.
    b. seek a new mother.
    c. return to the mother.
    d. fight with the mother.

_b_   8. For an infant to love its mother, Harlow's studies show that in the first two weeks the most important element is
    a. milk.
    b. warmth.
    c. contact comfort.
    d. love expressed by the mother.

_b_   9. In Harlow's studies with motherless monkeys, he showed that the techniques of mothering are
    a. instinctive.
    b. learned.
    c. inborn.
    d. natural.

_d_   10. The Harlows feel that child abuse is caused by all of the following problems except
    a. parents who were abused as children.
    b. socially isolated parents.
    c. parents who cannot control their impulses.
    d. parents who are instinctively evil.

Answer the following with *T* (true) or *F* (false).

__T__ 11. The author feels that love in infant monkeys has a great deal of similarity to love in human children.

__T__ 12. The author implies that isolated monkeys have difficulty engaging in normal peer relationships.

__T__ 13. After learning how to handle the first baby, many motherless mothers became better parents with the second infant.

__T__ 14. Zalba's studies support many of the findings of the Harlow studies.

__F__ 15. Harlow had initially planned to perform drug experiments on the monkeys.

VOCABULARY

According to the way the italicized word was used in the selection, indicate *a*, *b*, *c*, or *d* for the word or phrase that gives the best definition.

__d__ 1. "the *surrogate* mother" (24)
 a. mean
 b. thoughtless
 c. loving
 d. substitute

__b__ 2. "a *functional* breast" (33)
 a. mechanical
 b. operational
 c. wholesome
 d. imitation

__a__ 3. "on the surrogate's *anatomy*" (35)
 a. body
 b. head
 c. offspring
 d. personality

__b__ 4. "begins *tentatively* to explore" (78)
 a. rapidly
 b. hesitantly
 c. aggressively
 d. readily

__d__ 5. "fears of the *novel* environment" (80)
 a. hostile
 b. literary
 c. dangerous
 d. new

__a__ 6. "fears . . . are *desensitized*" (81)
 a. made less sensitive
 b. made more sensitive
 c. electrified
 d. communicated

__c__ 7. "solutions were *ingenious*" (92)
 a. incorrect
 b. noble
 c. clever
 d. honest

__b__ 8. "*deprived of* contact" (125)
 a. encouraged
 b. denied
 c. assured
 d. ordered into

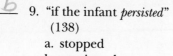 9. "if the infant *persisted*"
(138)
   a. stopped
   b. continued
   c. fought
   d. relaxed

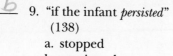 10. "to be greatly *deficient*"
(180)
   a. lacking
   b. supplied
   c. overwhelmed
   d. secretive

WRITTEN RESPONSE

Use information from the text to answer the following question:

How does a trusting relationship with a mother give an infant the confidence to explore the environment and the ability to love?

Response Strategy: Describe the elements necessary in the development of the trusting relationship needed for confidence and for love. Use Harlow's experiments to support your statements. (Use your own paper for this response.)

SELECTION 2

HISTORY

Stage 1: Skill Development

Preview

Who are some of the heroes mentioned?

When did the Civil Rights Movement begin?

Activate Schemata

How did Martin Luther King, Jr. die?

Who was Cesar Chavez?

Learning Strategy

Read to learn the significance of each leader's contribution to the Civil Rights Movement.

Word Knowledge

Are you familiar with the following words in this selection?

ensuing	revived
sprawling	massive
acrimony	futile
scathing	protracted
pacifists	filibuster

Your instructor may ask ten true-false questions from the *Instructor's Manual* to stimulate your thinking using these words.

Stage 2: Integrate Knowledge While Reading

Use the thinking strategies as you read:

1. Predict   2. Picture   3. Relate   4. Monitor   5. Fix up

Heroes for Civil Rights
From James Martin et al., *America and Its People*

On a cold afternoon in Montgomery, Alabama, Rosa Parks, a well-respected black seamstress, who was active in the NAACP, took a significant stride toward equality. She boarded a bus and sat in the first row of the "colored" section. The white section of the bus quickly filled, and according to Jim Crow rules, blacks were expected to give up their seats rather than force whites—male or female—to stand. The time came for Mrs. Parks to give up her seat. She stayed seated. When told by the bus driver to get up or he would call the police, she said, "You may do that." Later she recalled that the act of defiance was "just something I had to do." The bus stopped, the driver summoned the police, and Rosa Parks was arrested.

Black Montgomery rallied to Mrs. Parks's side. Like her, they were tired of riding in the back of the bus, tired of giving up their seats to whites, tired of having their lives restricted by Jim Crow. Local black leaders decided to organize a boycott of Montgomery's white-owned and white-operated bus system. They hoped that economic pressure would force changes which court decisions could not. For the next 381 days, more than ninety percent of Montgomery's black citizens participated in an heroic and successful demonstration against racial segregation. The common black attitude toward the protest was voiced by an elderly black woman when a black leader offered her a ride. "No," she replied, "my feets is tired, but my soul is rested."

© 1997 Addison-Wesley Educational Publishers Inc.

To lead the boycott, Montgomery blacks turned to the new minister of the Dexter Avenue Baptist Church, a young man named Martin Luther King, Jr. Reared in Atlanta, the son of a respected and financially secure

25 minister, King had been educated at Morehouse College, Crozier Seminary, and Boston University, from which he earned a doctorate in theology. King was an intellectual, excited by ideas and deeply influenced by the philosophical writings of Henry David Thoreau and Mahatma Gandhi as well as the teachings of Christ. They believed in the power of nonviolent,

30 direct action.

King's words as well as his ideas stirred people's souls. At the start of the Montgomery boycott he told his followers:

There comes a time when people get tired. We are here this evening to say to those who have mistreated us so long that we are tired—tired of

35 being segregated and humiliated, tired of being kicked about by the brutal feet of oppression. . . . We've come here tonight to be saved from the patience that makes us patient with anything less than freedom and justice. . . . If you protest courageously and yet with dignity and Christian love, in the history books that are written in future generations, historians

40 will have to pause and say "there lived a great people—a black people— who injected a new meaning and dignity into the veins of civilization."

Dr. Martin Luther King, Jr., gave voice to the new mood: "We're through with tokenism and gradualism and see-how-far-you've-comeism. We're through with we've-done-more-for-your-people-than-anyone-else-ism.

45 We can't wait any longer. Now is the time."

Sit-ins

On Monday, February 1, 1960, four black freshmen at North Carolina Agricultural and Technical College—Ezell Blair, Jr., Franklin McClain, Joseph McNeill, and David Richmond—walked into the F. W. Woolworth

50 store in Greensboro, North Carolina, and sat down at the lunch counter. They asked for a cup of coffee. A waitress told them that she would only serve them if they stood.

Instead of walking away, the four college freshmen stayed in their seats until the lunch counter closed. The next morning, the four college students

55 reappeared at Woolworth's accompanied by twenty-five fellow students. On Wednesday, student protesters filled sixty-three of the lunch counter's sixty-six seats. The sit-in movement had begun.

In April, 142 student sit-in leaders from eleven states met in Raleigh, North Carolina, and voted to set up a new group to coordinate the sin-ins,

60 the Student Non-Violent Coordinating Committee (SNCC). Martin Luther King told the students that their willingness to go to jail would "be the thing to awaken the dozing conscience of many of our white brothers." The president of Fisk University echoed King's judgment: "This is no student panty raid. It is a dedicated universal effort, and it has cemented the Negro

65 community as it has never been cemented before."

College Registration

Civil rights activists' next major aim was to open state universities to black students. Although many southern states opened their universities to black students without incident, others were stiff-backed in their opposition
70   to integration. A major breakthrough occurred in September 1962, when a federal court ordered the state of Mississippi to admit James Meredith—a nine-year veteran of the Air Force—to the University of Mississippi in Oxford. Ross Barnett, the state's governor, promised on statewide television that he would "not surrender to the evil and illegal forces of tyranny" and
75   would go to jail rather than permit Meredith to register for classes. Barnett flew into Oxford, named himself special registrar of the university, and ordered the arrest of federal officials who tried to enforce the court order.

James Meredith refused to back down. A "man with a mission and a nervous stomach," Meredith was determined to get a higher education. "I
80   want to go to the university," he said. "This is the life I want. Just to live and breathe—that isn't life to me. There's got to be something more." Meredith arrived at the campus in the company of police officers, federal marshals, and lawyers. Angry white students waited, chanting, "Two, four, six, eight— we don't want to integrate."

85   Four times James Meredith tried unsuccessfully to register. He finally succeeded on the fifth try, escorted by several hundred federal marshals. The ensuing riot left two people dead and 375 injured, including 166 marshals. Ultimately, President Kennedy sent 16,000 troops to put down the violence.

90   ## "Boomingham"

It was in Birmingham, Alabama, that civil rights activists faced the most determined resistance. A sprawling steel town of 340,000 known as the "Pittsburgh of the South," Birmingham had a long history of racial acrimony.

95   Day after day, well dressed and neatly groomed men, women and children marched against segregation—only to be jailed for demonstrating without a permit. On April 12, King himself was arrested—and while in jail wrote a scathing attack on those who asked black Americans to wait patiently for equal rights. A group of white clergymen had publicly
100   criticized King for staging "unwise and untimely" demonstrations.

For two weeks, all was quiet, but in early May demonstrations resumed with renewed vigor. On May 2 and again on May 3, more than a thousand of Birmingham's black children marched for equal rights. In response, Birmingham's police chief, Theophilus Eugene "Bull" Connor, unleashed
105   police dogs on the children and sprayed them with 700 pounds of water pressure—shocking the nation's conscience. Tension mounted as police arrested 2,543 blacks and whites between May 2 and May 7, 1963. Under intense criticism, the Birmingham Chamber of Commerce reached an agreement on May 9 with black leaders to desegregate public facilities in

110 ninety days, hire blacks as clerks and salespersons in sixty days, and release
demonstrators without bail in return for an end to the protests.

The March on Washington

The violence that erupted in Birmingham and elsewhere in 1961 and
1962 alarmed many veteran civil rights leaders. In December 1962, two
115 veteran fighters for civil rights—A. Philip Randolph and Bayard Rustin—
met at the office of the Brotherhood of Sleeping Car Porters in Harlem.
Both men were pacifists, eager to rededicate the civil rights movement to
the principle of nonviolence. Both men wanted to promote passage of
Kennedy's civil rights bill, school desegregation, federal job training
120 programs, and a ban on job discrimination. Thirty-two years before,
Randolph had threatened to lead a march on Washington unless the
federal government ended job discrimination against black workers in war
industries. Now Rustin revived the idea of a massive march for civil rights
and jobs.

125 On August 28, 1963, more than 200,000 people gathered around the
Washington Monument and marched eight-tenths of a mile to the Lincoln
Memorial. As they walked, the marchers carried placards reading: "Effective
Civil Rights Laws—Now! Integrated Schools—Now! Decent Housing—
Now!" and sang the civil rights anthem, "We Shall Overcome."

130 ### The Civil Rights Act of 1964

For seven months, debate raged in the halls of Congress. In a futile
effort to delay the Civil Rights Bill's passage, opponents proposed more than
500 amendments and staged a protracted filibuster in the Senate. On July 2,
1964—a year and a day after President Kennedy had sent it to Congress—
135 the Civil Rights Act was enacted into law. As finally passed, the act
prohibited discrimination in voting, employment, and public facilities such
as hotels and restaurants, and it established the Equal Employment
Opportunity Commission (EEOC) to prevent discrimination in
employment on the basis of race, religion, or sex. Ironically, the provision
140 barring sex discrimination had been added by opponents of the civil rights
act in an attempt to kill the bill.

Stage 3: Recall

Stop to self-test and relate to issues. Your instructor may ask ten true-false
questions to stimulate your recall.

SKILL DEVELOPMENT: ORGANIZATION

Answer the following with *T* (true) or *F* (false).

_____ 1. The overall pattern or organization is comparison-contrast.

_I_____ 2. The main point of the section titled "Sit-ins" is that college students became involved in the integration of lunch counters.

_I_____ 3. By beginning the first paragraph with Rosa Parks, the author suggests that her actions precipitated the sequence of events.

_I_____ 4. The passage creates a cause-and-effect relationship for the Civil Rights Act of 1964.

_F_____ 5. Boomingham was more likely the name of the Alabama city before 1963.

Timeline: Starting with Rosa Parks, make a time line of the major events and heroes leading to the Civil Rights Act.

COMPREHENSION QUESTIONS

After reading the selection, answer the following questions with _a, b, c,_ or _d._

_b_____ 1. The best statement of the main idea of this selection is
   a. Rosa Parks began the Civil Rights movement.
   b. Many heroes protested discrimination and fought for equality and civil rights.
   c. The Civil Rights Act was passed by Congress in 1964.
   d. Martin Luther King, Jr., began his career by leading the boycott in Montgomery, Alabama.

_c_____ 2. Rosa Parks's protest was that
   a. she would not get off the bus.
   b. she sat in the section reserved for whites.
   c. she would not give up her seat to a white.
   d. she refused to sit down on the bus.

_a_____ 3. The force designed to make the boycott of the Montgomery bus system successful was
   a. economic pressure.
   b. religious fervor.
   c. the good will of the people of Alabama.
   d. violence against oppressors.

_b_____ 4. The purpose of the words quoted from the speech made by Martin Luther King at the beginning of the Montgomery boycott was
   a. to explain the nonviolent tactics of Gandhi.
   b. to inspire the protesters with pride.
   c. to honor Rosa Parks and other brave protesters.
   d. to call for Congress to pass the Civil Rights Act.

_d_____ 5. All of the following are true of the "sit-ins" except
   a. they started in Greensboro, North Carolina.

b. the protesters were primarily students.

c. the protesters needed to be willing to go to jail.

d. the first protesters were freshmen at Fisk University.

_d_ 6. To prevent James Meredith from enrolling in the University of Mississippi,
   a. the President sent troops.
   b. several hundred federal marshals escorted Meredith.
   c. a federal court order was issued.
   d. the state governor became registrar of the university.

_b_ 7. In Birmingham, civil rights activists were typically jailed for
   a. disorderly conduct.
   b. demonstrating without a permit.
   c. trespassing on private property.
   d. aggression against police.

_a_ 8. The author suggests that the protest that most shocked the nation and ignited national support for civil rights was
   a. the children's march in Birmingham.
   b. the Woolworth's sit-in.
   c. James Meredith's college registration.
   d. the Montgomery bus boycott.

_d_ 9. The Civil Rights Act of 1964 contained all of the following except
   a. equal employment opportunities for women.
   b. integration of hotels.
   c. prohibitions on voting discrimination.
   d. higher wage guarantees for black workers.

_c_ 10. The author suggests that the 1963 march on Washington
   a. was a long and arduous walk through many southern cities.
   b. turned violent as the crowds swelled.
   c. put pressure on Congress to pass civil rights legislation.
   d. was attended by more whites than blacks.

Answer the following with *T* (true) or *F* (false).

_F_ 11. James Meredith was the first black student to attend a southern university.

_T_ 12. The Montgomery bus boycott lasted for over a year.

_F_ 13. Bull Connor was governor of Alabama.

_F_ 14. The author suggests that Kennedy was against the Civil Rights Act.

_F_ 15. The author suggests that Randolph and Rustin were southerners who had previously participated in sit-in demonstrations.

VOCABULARY

According to the way the italicized word was used in the selection, select *a, b, c,* or *d* for the word or phrase that gives the best definition.

___C___ 1. "The *ensuing* riot" (87)
   a. brutal
   b. speedy
   c. resulting
   d. dangerous

___a___ 2. "A *sprawling* town" (92)
   a. spread out
   b. ugly
   c. growing
   d. unfriendly

___d___ 3. "racial *acrimony*" (94)
   a. incidents
   b. alliances
   c. allegations
   d. animosity

___b___ 4. "a *scathing* attack" (98)
   a. timely
   b. stinging
   c. lengthy
   d. publicized

___a___ 5. "men were *pacifists*" (117)
   a. opponents of violence
   b. militants
   c. advocates for arms
   d. religious dissidents

___b___ 6. "*revived* the idea" (123)
   a. created
   b. rekindled
   c. argued
   d. verified

___a___ 7. "a *massive* march" (123)
   a. enormous
   b. forceful
   c. uncontrolled
   d. spontaneous

___d___ 8. "In a *futile* effort" (131)
   a. last chance
   b. angry
   c. hopeful
   d. ineffectual

___b___ 9. "a *protracted* filibuster" (133)
   a. short
   b. prolonged
   c. relentless
   d. merciless

___C___ 10. "a protracted *filibuster*" (133)
   a. sit-in demonstration
   b. drama
   c. legislative delay tactic
   d. committee meeting

WRITTEN RESPONSE

Use the information from the text to answer this question:
People and events in history are important for their cause-and-effect relationship to other people and other events. Explain the importance of three of

the people or events in this selection in terms of historical cause-and-effect significance.

© 1997 Addison-Wesley Educational Publishers Inc.

SELECTION 3

GEOGRAPHY

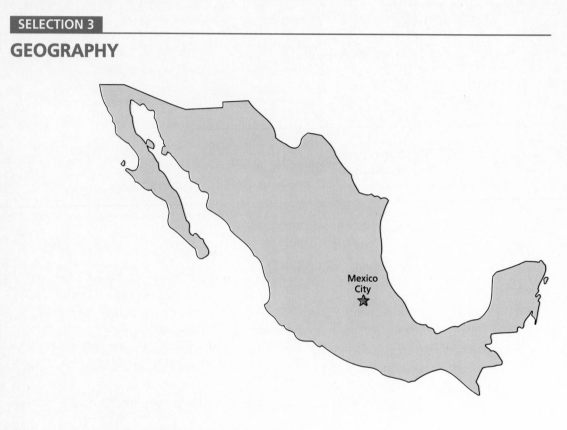

Mexico
City

Stage 1: Skill Development

Preview

The author's main purpose is to tell the history of Mexico.

agree ☐   disagree ☐

After reading this selection, I will need to know the problems facing Mexico.

agree ☐   disagree ☐

Activate Schema

Why do many Mexicans seek to leave Mexico and immigrate to the United States?

Learning Strategy

Be able to explain the problems created by the large and rapidly expanding Mexican population.

Word Knowledge

Are you familiar with the following words in this selection?

colossus	augmented
legacy	appalling
arable	vibrant
expropriation	burgeoning
dwindling	sustained

Your instructor may ask ten true-false questions from the *Instructor's Manual* to stimulate your thinking using these words.

Stage 2: Integrate Knowledge While Reading

Use the thinking strategies as you read:

1. Predict   2. Picture   3. Relate   4. Monitor   5. Fix up

Mexico: Land of Promise
From H. J. De Blij and Peter O. Muller, *Geography,* 7th ed.

Mexico is the colossus of Middle America, with a 1994 population of 91.8 million—exceeding the combined total of all the other countries and islands of the realm by 24 million—and a territory more than twice as large. Indeed, in all of Spanish-influenced Middle and South America, no country
5   has even half as large a population as Mexico (Colombia and Argentina are next). Moreover, Mexico has grown so rapidly that its population has *doubled* since the early 1970s.

How does Mexico do in terms of territory and population?

The United Mexican States—the country's official name—consists of 31
10 States and the Federal District of Mexico City, the capital. Urbanization has rapidly expanded in the developing world, and no less than 71 percent of the Mexican people now reside in towns and cities.

How many states are in Mexico?

Revolution and Redistribution
15 After achieving independence from Spain in the early 1800s, Mexico failed for nearly a century to come to grips with the problems of land distribution, which were a legacy of the colonial period. By the opening of the twentieth century, the situation had worsened to the point where 8,245 haciendas covered nearly 40 percent of Mexico's entire area; moreover,
20 about 96 percent of all rural families owned no land whatsoever and worked as *peones* (landless, constantly indebted serfs) on the haciendas. There was

deprivation and hunger, and the few remaining Amerindian lands and
small holdings owned by mestizos or whites could not produce enough food
to satisfy the country's needs. Meanwhile, thousands of acres of arable land
25 lay idle on the haciendas, which blanketed just about all the good farmland
in Mexico.

Why did the large haciendas create a problem?

Not surprisingly, a revolution began in 1910 and set into motion a
sequence of events that is still unfolding today. One of its major objectives
30 was the redistribution of Mexico's land, and a program of expropriation
and parceling out of the haciendas was made law by the Constitution of
1917. Since then, about half the cultivated land of Mexico has been
redistributed, mostly to peasant communities consisting of 20 families or
more. Such lands are called *ejidos*; the government holds title to the land,
35 and use rights are parceled out to villages and then individuals for
cultivation. Most of the *ejido* lands carved out of haciendas lie in central and
southern Mexico, where Amerindian traditions of landownership and
cultivation survived and where the adjustments were most successfully made.

How did the revolution change land ownership?

40 With such a far-reaching program, it is understandable that
agricultural productivity temporarily declined. The miracle is that land
reform has been carried off without a major death toll and that the power
of the wealthy landowning aristocracy could be broken without ruin to the
state. Mexico alone among the region's countries with large Amerindian
45 populations has made major strides toward solving the land of question,
although there is still widespread malnutrition and poverty in the
countryside. But the revolution that began in 1910 did more than that; it
also resurrected the Amerindian contribution to Mexican life and blended
Spanish and Amerind heritages in the country's social and cultural spheres.
50 It brought to Mexico the distinctiveness that it alone possesses in Middle
and South America.

How do you think hacienda owners viewed redistribution?

Farming

The revolution could change the distribution of land, but it could not
55 change the land itself or the methods by which it was farmed. Corn (maize),
beans, and squash continue to form the subsistence food of most Mexicans,
with corn the chief staple (still occupying over half the cultivated land). Yet
corn is grown all too often where the conditions are not right for it, so that
yields are low; wheat might do better, but the people's preference, not soil
60 suitability, determines the crop. And if the people's preference has not

changed a great deal, neither have farming methods over much of the country.

What causes the low crop yield in Mexico?

Teeming Mexico City

65   The Mexico City conurbation[7] has borne the brunt of the recent migratory surge toward urban areas. With a total population of 22.4 million (second in the world in 1994), it is already home to nearly one out of every four Mexicans, and it continues to grow at an astonishing rate. Each day, about 1,000 people move to Mexico City; when added to the 1,000 or so
70   babies born there daily, that produces a truly staggering addition of approximately 750,000 people every year. However, birth rates in urban Mexico are higher than the national level; with half its population 18 years of age or younger, some demographers have forecast an astounding total of between *40 and 50 million* residents for greater Mexico City by 2010! In any
75   case, by 2000 Mexico City will have become the world's largest single population agglomeration,[8] surpassing metropolitan Tokyo.

Why is Mexico City called a conurbation and an agglomeration?

[7]**Conurbation**   General term used to identify large multi-metropolitan complexes formed by the coalescence of two or more major urban areas. The Boston-Washington **Megalopolis** along the U.S. northeastern seaboard is an outstanding example.

[8]**Agglomeration**   Process involving the clustering or concentrating of people or activities. Often refers to manufacturing plants and businesses that benefit from close proximity because they share skilled-labor pools and technological and financial amenities.

Environmental Hazards

80 Even in a well-endowed natural environment, such an enormous cluster of humanity would severely strain local resources. But Mexico City is hardly located in a favorable habitat; in fact, it lies squarely within one of the most hazardous surroundings of any city on earth—and human abuses of the immediate environment are constantly aggravating the potential for disaster. The conurbation may be located in the heart of the scenic Valley of
85 Mexico, whose situational virtues led to the building of Tenochtitlán by the Aztecs, but serious geologic problems loom: the vulnerability of the basin to major volcanic and seismic activity (such as the devastating earthquake of 1985), and the overall instability resulting from the weak, dry-lakebed surface that underlies much of the metropolis (aggravated by land
90 subsidence as groundwater supplies are pumped out in vast quantities). Water availability presents another problem in this semiarid climate: dwindling local supplies must be augmented by increases in the long-distance transportation of drinking water from across the mountains, an enormously expensive undertaking that requires the accompanying growth
95 of a parallel network to pipe sewage out of the waste-choked basin.

What are the environmental difficulties of Mexico City?

Air Pollution

Mexico City's appalling air pollution, however, poses the greatest health hazard and is conceded to be the world's most serious, exacerbated by the
100 thin air that contains 30 percent less oxygen than at sea level (the city's elevation is 7,350 feet/2,240 m). The conurbation's 3-million-plus cars and 7,500 diesel buses produce about 75 percent of the smog, with the remainder caused by the daily spewing of 15,000 tons of chemical pollutants into the atmosphere by the area's 37,000 factories. Despite new legislation
105 aimed at improving air quality, on any given day the pollution of Mexico City's air can approach *100 times* the acceptable level.

What causes poor air quality?

Urbanization

For the affluent and tourists, Mexico City is undoubtedly one of the
110 hemisphere's most spectacular primate cities, with its grand boulevards, magnificent palaces and museums, vibrant cultural activities and night life, and luxury shops. But most of its residents dwell in a world apart from the glitter of the *Paseo de la Reforma*. An increasing majority of them are forced to live in the miserable poverty and squalor of the conurbation's 500 slums
115 as well as the innumerable squatter shacktowns that form the burgeoning metropolitan fringe (the notorious *ciudades perdidas,* or "lost cities"). This is the domain of the newcomers, the peasant families who have abandoned

the hard life of the difficult countryside, lured to the urban giant in search of a better life. With Mexico's underemployment rate hovering above 30
120 percent in recent years, decent jobs and upward mobility quickly become elusive goals for most of the new arrivals.

What are the difficulties of rapid urbanization?

Informal Sector

Despite the overwhelming odds, a surprising number of migrants
125 eventually do enjoy some economic success by becoming part of the so-called *informal sector*. This is a primitive form of capitalism that is now common in many developing countries; it takes place beyond the control—and especially the taxation—of the government. Participants are unlicensed sellers of homemade goods (such as arts and crafts, clothing, food
130 specialties) and services (auto repair, odd jobs, and the like), and their willingness to engage in this hard work has transformed many a slum into a beehive of activity that can propel resourceful residents toward a middle-class existence. For its part, although officially discouraging the growth of squatter settlements, the government has recently made life on the Mexico
135 City outskirts more comfortable by improving schools, roads, and other municipal services; moreover, it still permits squatters who settle on public lands to gain free title to those properties after a period of five years.

What activities in the United States would compare with Mexico's informal sector?

140 ## Population

The ongoing growth of Mexico City (and its problems of overcrowding and environmental degradation) is not a unique phenomenon. According to the United Nations, in 1992 there were 37 metropolitan areas worldwide whose populations exceeded 5 million; by 2010, that total is predicted to
145 rise to 60. Of these 23 additions to the 5-million-plus category, all are located in developing realms. Moreover, 15 of these "megacities" will contain at least 15 million people by 2010: Mexico City; Tokyo, Japan; São Paulo, Brazil; Bombay, India; Shanghai, China; Lagos, Nigeria; Beijing, China; Dhaka, Bangladesh; Jakarta, Indonesia; New York, U.S.A.; Karachi,
150 Pakistan; Manila, the Philippines; Calcutta, India; Tianjin, China; and Delhi, India. These growth leaders, of course, are simply the tip of the iceberg, because urbanization rates are skyrocketing throughout the developing world.

What is happening to populations worldwide?

155   Mexico has made impressive gains in industrialization, it is addressing itself with new determination to agrarian reform, and it seeks to integrate all sectors of the population into a truly Mexican nation. After a century of struggle and oppression, this country has lately taken long strides toward overcoming its chronic problems. However, meaningful further progress is

160   threatened by a final challenge: the rapid growth of its huge population. Ultimately, no amount of reform can keep pace with a growth rate (now 2.3 percent yearly) that will, if sustained, produce a Mexican population of twice the size (184 million) of today's 92 million by the year 2025. No political or economic system in the developing world could long withstand

165   the impact of such population growth. Today, there are indications that the annual rate of natural increase may be slowing, but until it is checked and stabilized, Mexico's latest accomplishments remain under a demographic cloud.

How is the promise of Mexico threatened?

Stage 3: Recall

Stop to self-test and relate to issues. Your instructor may ask ten true-false questions to stimulate your recall.

SKILL DEVELOPMENT: SUMMARIZING

Using this selection as a source, summarize on your paper the information that you might want to include in a research paper entitled "The Threat of Global Overpopulation."

COMPREHENSION QUESTIONS

After reading the selection, answer the following questions with *a, b, c,* or *d.*

_A_ 1. The best statement of the main idea of this selection is
  a. Mexico is a rapidly developing country threatened by overpopulation.
  b. the revolution in Mexico did not bring economic freedom to its people.
  c. Mexico City is the urban center of Mexico.
  d. Mexico is the economic heart of Middle America.

_b_ 2. In 1994 the population of Mexico was
  a. equal to the combined populations of Columbia and Argentina.
  b. millions greater than all other countries in Middle America.
  c. double that of all Middle American countries.
  d. half as large as the population of South America.

d 3. Mexico was previously conquered and ruled by
   a. Portugal.
   b. Brazil.
   c. South America.
   d. Spain.

b 4. After the revolution, land redistribution became a priority because
   a. the serfs would not work on the land.
   b. the land was owned by a relative few rather than many.
   c. the land was dry and could not be farmed.
   d. the *mestizos* wanted the Amerindian holdings.

a 5. In the redistribution, the *ejido* lands are owned by
   a. the government.
   b. twenty families collectively.
   c. the individuals who cultivate them.
   d. Amerindians with a tradition of landownership.

c 6. The author suggests that
   a. wheat is more nutritious than maize.
   b. corn is changing as the chief staple.
   c. wheat might produce a greater yield than corn.
   d. the people prefer the crop with the highest yield.

d 7. The reader can conclude that the city with the largest population in 1994 was
   a. Mexico City.
   b. New York.
   c. Bombay.
   d. Tokyo.

d 8. Mexico City has all of the following geologic problems except
   a. it is built on a dry lake bed.
   b. the climate is semiarid and water is scarce.
   c. the area is vulnerable to earthquakes.
   d. the Aztecs started the city in a valley.

a 9. The author suggests that the migrants who become sellers and part of the informal sector
   a. illegally avoid taxes.
   b. are licensed by the government.
   c. are officially encouraged by the government.
   d. gradually move to the United States.

c 10. The author feels that the future of Mexico is most severely threatened by
   a. poor farm land.
   b. government policies.
   c. overpopulation.
   d. lack of jobs.

Answer the following with *T* (true) or *F* (false).

_T_ 11. The United Mexican States consists of thirty-one states and one district.

_F_ 12. The author suggests that the population of Mexico City is increasing by over 2,000 people per day.

_F_ 13. The air pollution in Mexico City is the second worst in the world after that in Tokyo.

_T_ 14. The author suggests that the Paseo de la Reforma is one of the main tourist streets of Mexico City.

_T_ 15. In Mexico City a squatter can get public land free by living on it for five years.

VOCABULARY

According to the way the italicized word was used in the selection, select *a*, *b*, *c*, or *d* for the word or phrase that gives the best definition.

_a_ 1. "*colossus* of Middle America" (1)
    a. giant
    b. heart
    c. center
    d. leader

_a_ 2. "*legacy* of the colonial power" (17)
    a. legality
    b. inheritance
    c. requirement
    d. authority

_d_ 3. "acres of *arable* land" (24)
    a. dry
    b. unreachable
    c. tillable
    d. remote

_b_ 4. "program of *expropriation*" (30)
    a. moving people onto property
    b. taxing property owners
    c. government taking property
    d. government buying property

_a_ 5. "*dwindling* local supplies" (92)
    a. lessening
    b. reusable
    c. much needed
    d. inaccessible

_A_ 6. "*augmented* by increases" (92)
    a. mixed
    b. filtered
    c. intercepted
    d. enlarged

_c_ 7. "*appalling* air pollution"
(98)
   a. apparent
   b. disease-producing
   c. dreadful
   d. disruptive

_b_ 8. "*vibrant* cultural activities"
(111)
   a. central
   b. lively
   c. ongoing
   d. worthy

_c_ 9. "*burgeoning* metropolitan
fringe" (115)
   a. polluted
   b. illicit
   c. growing
   d. poor

_b_ 10. "that will, if *sustained*"
(162)
   a. subsided
   b. upheld
   c. magnified
   d. disregarded

WRITTEN RESPONSE

Use the information from the text to respond to the following:
What are the causes of the critical problems facing Mexico?
Response Strategy: Describe several problems and give examples from the text for each. (Use your own paper for this response.)

COLLABORATIVE CRITICAL THINKING

Population Explosion

Many experts feel that the world is threatened by overwhelming population growth, particularly in developing countries. Interpret the following graph to understand the enormity of the problem.

Pretend that you have been selected to be a member of a presidential advisory board to offer recommendations for curbing both national and worldwide population growth. You begin by working on a small subcommittee with two other board members to brainstorm solutions. Your group understands that the population problem has many aspects and no simple solutions, but the task of your subcommittee is to make two lists of suggestions for the full committee to review. The first should be a list of five suggestions for addressing the population problem in the United States, and the second should be a list of five suggestions for advising or influencing world population growth.

Your committee realizes that for each government action, there can be an unpredictable reaction. Thus, for each of the ten suggestions, the com-

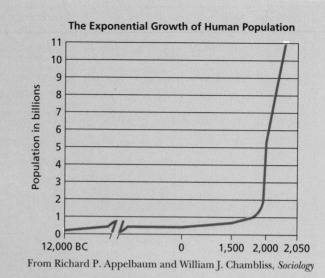

The Exponential Growth of Human Population

From Richard P. Appelbaum and William J. Chambliss, *Sociology*

mittee must describe possible positive and negative reactions. Outline these suggestions on paper and include the predicted reactions. Conclude your paper by listing ways in which the world population problems can become problems for the United States. Read the following passage to stimulate your thinking and to emphasize that there are no simple solutions.

Population Control

In the early 1970s, India forced government employees who had more than two children to undergo sterilization. With the encouragement of the central government, some states in India also forced men to be sterilized after their second child was born. If the men refused, they could be fined $250 and imprisoned for up to a year. In some villages, overzealous government officials rounded up and sterilized all the men, without checking how many children they had. The program stirred up widespread opposition. Demographer Frank Notestein had predicted in 1971 that if a developing country tried to force its people to practice birth control, it "would be more likely to bring down the government than the birth rate." Indeed, the sterilization program apparently contributed to the fall of Prime Minister Indira Gandhi's government in 1977. Since then, India has returned to a voluntary program, which, however, has failed to control the relentless population growth because of low literacy and a dearth of sustained family planning information and services. India now has a fertility rate of 4.3 children per woman (compared with 1.9 in the United States), and it will become the world's most populous nation by about 2045.

China has had more success with its program of combining rewards and punishments. For a couple with only one child, rewards are substantial. The parents get a salary bonus, and the child receives free schooling, priority in medical care, admission to the best schools and universities, and preference in employment. In contrast, multichild parents are severely penalized. They must pay all costs for each additional child, are taxed about 10 percent of their income, and are often denied promotion for two years. Since it started this "one-child family" campaign in 1979, China has halved its birth rate, a record unmatched by any other developing nation.

Beginning in 1986, though, the birth rate began to rise again because the government relaxed its one-child policy—by allowing rural couples to have a second baby if their firstborn was a girl. One reason for the relaxation has been the increasing prosperity among the Chinese, many of whom are willing to pay the fines for having more than one child. Another reason is the international criticism that China has received for pressuring women to abort fetuses even late in pregnancy. A third reason is that the one-child policy has encouraged, albeit unintentionally, the killing of female infants by parents who hope to have sons. Nevertheless, China continues to exhort couples to have only one child, though it now focuses on persuasion, education, and publicity campaigns rather than coercion and penalties. All this has been quite successful with urban couples, though it tends to fall on deaf ears in the countryside. Recently, in 1990, more than half of all births in China were of first children, and an additional 25 to 30 percent were of second children. Only 15 percent were of third children.

From Alex Thio, *Sociology*

1. Give five suggestions for reducing United States population growth (with predicted reactions).
2. Give five suggestions for curbing world population growth (with predicted reactions).
3. How can world population problems become problems for the United States?

WORD BRIDGE

Structure

What is the longest word in the English language and what does it mean? Maxwell Nurnberg and Morris Rosenblum in *How to Build a Better Vocabulary* (Prentice-Hall, Inc. 1949) say that at one time the longest word in Webster's *New International Dictionary* was

pneumonoultramicroscopicsilicovolcanokoniosis

Look at the word again and notice the smaller and more familiar word parts. Do you know enough of the smaller parts to figure out the meaning of the word? Nurnberg and Rosenblum unlock the meaning as follows:

pneumono: pertaining to the lungs, as in *pneu*monia

ultra: beyond, as in *ultra*violet rays

micro: small, as in *micro*scope

scopic: from the root of Greek verb *skopein,* to view or look at

silico: from the element *silicon,* found in quartz, flint, and sand

volcano: the meaning of this is obvious

koni: the principal root, from a Greek word for dust

osis: a suffix indicating illness, as trichin*osis*

Now, putting the parts together again, we deduce that *pneumonoultramicroscopic-silicovolcanokoniosis* is a disease of the lungs caused by extremely small particles of volcanic ash and dust.

This dramatic example demonstrates how an extremely long and technical word can become more manageable by breaking it into smaller parts. The same is true with many of the smaller words that we use every day. A knowledge of word parts will help you unlock the meaning of literally thousands of words. One vocabulary expert identified a list of thirty prefixes, roots, and suffixes and claims that knowing these thirty word parts will help unlock the meaning to 14,000 words.

Words, like people, have families and, in some cases, an abundance of close relations. Clusters, or what might be called *word families,* are comprised of words with the same base or root. For example, *bio* is a root meaning *life.* If you know that *biology* means *the study of life,* it becomes easy to figure out the definition of a word like *biochemistry.* Word parts form new words as follows:

prefix + root   root + suffix   prefix + root + suffix

Prefixes and suffixes are added to root words to change the meaning. A prefix is added to the beginning of a word and a suffix is added to the end. For example, the prefix *il* means *not.* When added to the word *legal,* the resulting word, *illegal,* becomes the opposite of the original. Suffixes can change the meaning or change the way the word can be used in a sentence. The suffix *cide* means to *kill.* When added to *frater,* which means *brother,* the resulting word, *fratricide,* means to *kill one's brother.* Adding *ity* or *ize* to *frater* changes both the meaning and the way the word can be used grammatically in a sentence.

To demonstrate how prefixes, roots, and suffixes overlap and make families, start with the root *gamy,* meaning *marriage,* and ask some questions.

1. What is the state of having only one wife called? _____
(*mono* means *one*)

2. What is a man who has two wives called? _____
   (*bi* means *two* and *ist* means *one who*)
3. What is a man who has many wives called? _____
   (*poly* means *many*)
4. What is a woman who has many husbands called? _____
   (*andry* means *man*)
5. What is a hater of marriage called? _____
   (*miso* means *hater of*)

In several of the *gamy* examples, the letters change slightly to accommodate language sounds. Such variations of a letter or two are typical when working with word parts. Letters are often dropped or added to maintain the rhythm of the language, but the meaning of the word part remains the same regardless of the change in spelling. For example, the prefix *con* means *with* or *together* as in *conduct*. This same prefix is used with variations in many other words:

> *cooperate   collection   correlate   communicate   connect*

Thus, *con, co, col, cor,* and *com* are all forms of the prefix that means *with* or *together*.

Exercise 7   WORD FAMILIES

Create your own word families from the word parts that are supplied. For each of the following definitions, supply a prefix, root, or suffix to make the appropriate word.

Prefix: *bi* means *two*

1. able to speak two languages: bi _____

2. having two feet, like humans: bi _____

3. representing two political parties: bi _____

4. occurs at two-year intervals: bi _____

5. having two lenses on one glass: bi _____

6. cut into two parts: bi _____

7. mathematics expression with two terms: bi _____

8. instrument with two eyes: bi _____

9. tooth with two points: bi _____

10. coming twice a year: bi _____

Root: *vert* means *to turn*

1. to change one's beliefs: _____ vert

2. to go back to old ways again: _____ vert

3. a car with a removable top: _____ vert _____

4. to change the direction of a stream: _____ vert

5. activities intended to undermine or destroy: _____ vers _____

6. an outgoing, gregarious person: _____ vert

7. a quiet, introspective, shy person: _____ vert

8. conditions that are turned against you; misfortune: _____ vers _____

9. one who deviates from normal behavior, especially sexual: _____ vert

10. one who is sometimes introspective and sometimes gregarious: _____ vert

Suffix: *ism* means *doctrine, condition,* or *characteristic.*

1. addiction to alcoholic drink: _____ ism

2. a brave and courageous manner of acting: _____ ism

3. doctrine of the fascists of Germany: _____ ism

4. doctrine concerned only with fact and reality: _____ ism

5. system using terror to intimidate: _____ ism

6. using someone's words as your own: _____ ism

7. driving out an evil spirit: _____ ism

8. purification to join the church: _____ ism

9. informal style of speech using slang: _____ ism

10. characteristic of one region of the country: _____ ism

Exercise 8   PREFIXES, ROOTS, AND SUFFIXES

Using the prefix, root, or suffix provided, write the words that best fit the following definitions.

1. *con* means *with*

infectious or catching: con _____

2. *contra* means *against*

   to speak against another's statement: contra _____

3. *post* means *after*

   to delay or set back: post _____

4. *psych* means *mind*

   a physician who studies the mind: psych _____

5. *pel* means *drive* or *push*

   to push out of school: _____ pell

6. *thermo* means *heat*

   device for regulating furnace heat: therm _____

7. *ven* means *come*

   a meeting for people to come together: _____ ven _____

8. *rupt* means *break* or *burst*

   a volcanic explosion: _____ rupt _____

9. *meter* means *measure*

   instrument to measure pressure: _____ meter

10. *naut* means *voyager*

    voyager in the sea: _____ naut

Answer the following questions to learn about your own learning and reflect on your progress. Your instructor may collect your responses.

When trying to determine the author's point, why is it important to determine the topic first?

_____

Why is prior knowledge important in stating the main idea?

_____

Why should the main idea be stated in a complete sentence?

_____

Which pattern of organization do you find most difficult to recognize? Why?

_____

When you write a term paper, where do you usually state the main idea? Why?

_____

What pattern of organization do you most frequently use in your papers?

_____

For what purpose have you written a summary as part of your school work? What was difficult about writing it?

_____

Reflect on the Longer Selections

Total your short-answer responses for the three longer selections.

Comprehension scores:
completed = _____   # correct = _____   # incorrect = _____ accuracy = _____ %

How would you categorize the questions you missed?

_____

How are your errors similar to or different from the errors in the last chapter?

_____

Which was your least favorite selection? Why?

_____

Do you like to read selections about people? Why or why not?

_____

_____

_____

Clip out and explain three questions that you missed. Attach these questions and your analysis to the Learning Log for your instructor.

Reflect on the Vocabulary

Total your vocabulary responses for the longer selections.

completed = ﹘﹘﹘   # correct = ﹘﹘﹘   # incorrect = ﹘﹘﹘   accuracy = ﹘﹘﹘ %

List the words that you missed.

_____

_____

How many vocabulary items in this chapter were totally new words for you?

_____

Describe a situation in which you could use a new word from this chapter.

_____

_____

_____

_____

_____

Using the perforations, tear out the Learning Log for your instructor.

CHAPTER 4

Organizing Textbook Information

What is a knowledge network?

What is annotating?

What is notetaking?

What is outlining?

What is mapping?

THE DEMANDS OF COLLEGE STUDY

Your first assignment in most college courses will be to read Chapter 1 of the appointed textbook, at which time you will immediately discover that a textbook chapter contains an amazing amount of information. Your instructor will continue to make similar assignments designating the remaining chapters in rapid succession. Your task is to select the information that needs to be remembered, try to learn it, and organize it for future study which might be a midterm or final exam that is weeks or months away.

In a recent study, three college professors investigated the question, "What are the demands on students in introductory college history courses?"[1] They observed classes for a ten-week period and analyzed the actual reading demands, finding that students were asked to read an average of 825 pages in each class over the ten-week period. The average length of weekly assignments was over 80 pages, but the amount varied both with the professor and the topic. In one class, students had to read 287 pages in only ten days.

The college history professors expected students to be able to see relationships between parts and wholes, to place people and events into a historical context, and to retain facts. Professors spent 85 percent of the class time lecturing and 6 percent of the time testing. Interaction was surprisingly limited. Student-student exchanges occurred 4 percent of the time in the only class that broke into groups, and student-instructor exchanges occurred a meager 2.5 percent of the average class time. In short, the demands were high and students were expected to work independently to organize textbook material efficiently and effectively to prepare for that crucial 6 percent of test-taking time.

BUILDING KNOWLEDGE NETWORKS

The old notion of studying and learning is that studying is an information-gathering activity. Knowledge is the "product" and the student acquires "it" by transferring information from the text to memory. With this view, good learners locate important information, review it, and then transfer the information into long-term memory. The problem with this model is that review does not always guarantee recall, and rehearsal is not always enough to ensure that information is encoded into long-term memory.

More recent theories of studying and learning reflect the thinking of cognitive psychologists and focus on schemata, prior knowledge, and the learner's own goals. To understand and remember, the learner hooks new information to already existing schemata, or networks of knowledge. As the reader's personal knowledge expands, new networks are created. The learner, not the professor, decides how much effort should be expended and adjusts studying according to

[1]J. G. Carson, N. D. Chase, S. U. Gibson, and M. F. Hargrove. Literacy demands of the undergraduate curriculum. *Reading, Research, and Instruction* 31, (1992); 25–30.

the answers to questions such as "How much do I need to know?" "Will the test be multiple-choice or essay?" and "Do I want to remember this forever?" The learner makes judgments and selects the material to be remembered and integrated into knowledge networks.

METHODS OF ORGANIZING TEXTBOOK INFORMATION

This chapter will discuss four methods of organizing textbook information for future study: annotating, notetaking, outlining, and mapping. In a recent review of more than five hundred research studies on organizing textbook information, two college developmental reading professors concluded that "no one study strategy is appropriate for all students in all study situations."[2] They encourage students to develop a repertoire of skills. They feel that students need to know, for example, that underlining takes less time than notetaking, but notetaking or outlining produces better test results.

Your selection of a study strategy for organizing textbook material will vary according to the announced testing demands, the nature of the material, the amount of time you have to devote to study, and your preference for a particular strategy. Being familiar with all four strategies affords a repertoire of choices.

The following comments on organizing textbook and lecture materials come from college freshmen taking an introductory course in American History. These history students were coenrolled in a Learning Strategies for History course that focused on how to be a successful student. Their comments probably address some of your experiences in trying to rapidly organize large amounts of textbook material.

> Organization of my class notes is very important. The notes can be very easy to refer to if they are organized. This enables me to go back and fill in information and it also helps me to understand the cycle of events that is taking place. I generally try to outline my notes by creating sections. Sections help me to understand the main idea or add a description of a singular activity. I usually go back and number the sections to make them easy for reference.
>
> Taking notes can be very difficult sometimes. In class, if my mind strays just a few times, I can easily lose track of where my notes were going. Then again, when I am reading my textbook, I may read without even realizing what I just read. The difference in class and the textbook is that I can go back and reread the text.
>
> It is very easy to overdo the notes that I take from the text. Originally, I tended to take too much information from the book, but now, as I read more, I can better grasp the main idea. Underlining also makes a big difference. When I underline, I can go back and reread the book. The underlined parts aid me in grasping the most important ideas from the paragraphs. These underlined parts can contain descriptive information that might otherwise not need to be written down. This helps me to cut down on my notetaking from the text.

(Student made an A in History)

[2]D. Caverly and V. Orlando, *Textbook Strategies in Teaching Reading and Study Strategies at the College Level* (Newark, N.J.: International Reading Association, 1991), 86–165.

Reading related chapters in the text before going to class and highlighting important events are definitely conducive to good notetaking. Although I am not quite perfect yet, I do not write down as much irrelevant information as I used to.

(Student made a B in History)

In starting college, I have made a few changes in how I take notes. For instance, I am leaving a lot more space in taking notes. I find that they are easier to read when they are spread out. I have also been using a highlighter and marking topics and definitions and people's names. I make checks near notes that will definitely be on a test so I can go over it.

When I am reading, I have begun to do a lot of underlining in the book, which I would never do before because my school would not take back books if they were marked. I have also started to note important parts with a little star and confusing parts with a question mark.

(Student made a C in History)

Taking notes is no longer something that you can just do and expect to have good and complete notes. I have learned that taking notes is a process of learning within itself.

(Student made a B in History)

Generally, I think that I take good notes. I use the outline format to organize the notes that I take down. When we had our second history reading assignment, I tried making questions out of the material I read over, but that tended to go very slowly. For our reading assignment for today's class, I tried to take notes while I read. The result of that was that I stopped taking notes on the assignment just so I could complete reading it all. I think that the best way to do it is to completely read the assignment and then go back over it to clear up any confusion. I would also recommend going over your lecture notes before starting your reading assignment which is something I didn't do this past week. I also try to key in on words like "two significant changes" or "major factors." Sometimes you may go three or four pages without seeing anything like that. My question is, "What do you do then?" I think that you should write down the point or points that were repeated the most or stressed the most.

(Student made an A in History)

All of these students were successful in history, although the final grades vary. Each student's reflection offers sincere and sound advice. However you organize material—by annotating, notetaking, outlining, or mapping—seek to make meaning by making connections.

ANNOTATING

Which of the following would seem to indicate the most effective use of the textbook as a learning tool?

1. A text without a single mark—not even the owner's name has spoiled the sacred pages
2. A text ablaze with color—almost every line is adorned with a red, blue, yellow, and/or green magic marker

3. A text with a scattered variety of markings—underlines, numbers, and stars are interspersed with circles, arrows, and short, written notes

Naturally number three is the best, but unfortunately the first two are not just silly examples; they are commonplace in every classroom. The student's rationale for the first is probably for resale of the book at the end of the course. The reason for the second is procrastination in decision making, which is a result of reading without thinking. In other words, the student underlines everything and relies on coming back later to figure out what is *really* important and worth remembering. Both of these extremes are inefficient and ineffective methods of using a college textbook.

Why Annotate?

The textbook is a learning tool and should be used as such; it should not be preserved as a treasure. A college professor requires a particular text because it contains information vital to your understanding of the course material. The text places a vast body of knowledge in your hands, much more material than the professor could possibly give in class. It is your job to wade through this information, to make some sense out of it, and to select the important points that need to be remembered.

Annotating is a method of highlighting main ideas, significant supporting details, and key terms. The word *annotate* means to add marks. By using a system of symbols and notation and not just magic markers, you mark the text after the first reading so that a complete rereading will not be necessary. The markings indicate pertinent points to review for an exam.

Marking in the textbook itself is frequently faster than summarizing, outlining, or notetaking. In addition, since your material and personal reactions are all in one place, you can view them at a glance for later study rather than referring to separate notebooks. Your textbook has become a workbook.

Students who annotate, however, will probably want to make a list of key terms and ideas on their own paper in order to have a reduced form of the information for review and self-testing.

When to Annotate

Annotating ideas as they are first read is a mistake. The annotations should be done after a unit of thought has been presented and the information can be viewed as a whole. This may mean marking after a single paragraph or after three pages; marking varies with the material. When you are first reading, every sentence seems of major importance as each new idea unfolds, and the tendency is to annotate too much. Overmarking serves no useful purpose and wastes both reading and review time. If you wait until a complete thought has been developed, the significant points will emerge from a background of lesser details. You will then have all the facts, and you can decide what you want to remember. At the end of the course your textbook should have that worn, but well-organized look.

How to Annotate

Develop a System of Notations. Highlighting material is not underlining; it is circling and starring and numbering and generally making an effort to put the material into perspective visually. Notations vary with the individual, and each student develops a number of original techniques. **Anything that makes sense to you is a correct notation.** Here is an example of a marking system:

Main idea ( )

Supporting material _____

Major trend or possible essay exam question ✳

Important smaller point to know for multiple-choice item ✔

Word that you must be able to define ◯

Section of material to reread for review { }

Numbering of important details under a major issue (1), (2), (3)

Didn't understand and must seek advice ?

Notes in the margin Ex., Def., , Topic

Questions in the margin why signif.?

Indicating relationships ⌒

Related issue or idea ← R

Examples of Annotating. The following passage is taken from a biology textbook. Notice how the notations have been used to highlight main ideas and significant supporting details. This same passage will be used throughout this chapter to demonstrate each of the five methods of organizing textbook material.

Circulatory Systems

When we examine the systems by which blood reaches all the cells of an animal, we find two general types, known as open and closed circulatory systems.

Def. I

Open Circulatory Systems

The essential feature of the **open circulatory system** is that the blood moves through a body cavity—such as the abdominal cavity—and bathes the cells directly. The open circulatory system is particularly characteristic of insects and other arthropods, although it is also found in some other organisms.

In most insects the blood does not take a major part in oxygen transport. <u>Oxygen</u> *3* enters the animal's body through a separate <u>network of branching tubes that open</u> to the <u>atmosphere</u> on the <u>outside</u> of the animal. (This type of respiratory system will be discussed in more detail in the next chapter.) <u>Blood</u> *4* in an open circulatory system <u>moves</u> somewhat <u>more slowly</u> than in the average closed system. The slower system is adequate for insects because it does <u>not</u> have to <u>supply the cells</u> with <u>oxygen.</u>

Def. II

Closed Circulatory Systems

In a **closed circulatory system,** the <u>blood flows</u> through a well-defined system of <u>vessels with many branches.</u> *1* In the majority of closed systems the blood is responsible for oxygen transport. To supply all the body cells with <u>sufficient oxygen,</u> the blood must <u>move quickly through</u> *2* the blood vessels. A closed circulatory system must therefore have an efficient <u>pumping</u> *3* mechanism, or heart, to set the blood in motion and keep it moving briskly through the body.

Ex. 4 <u>All vertebrates</u> possess closed circulatory systems. Simple closed systems are also found in some invertebrates, including the annelid worms. A good example of such a simple closed circulatory system can be seen in the <u>earthworm.</u> *5*   *Ex. R → regeneration?*

Victor A. Greulach and Vincent J. Chiapetta, eds., *Biology*

Exercise 1   ANNOTATING

Using a variety of notations, annotate the following passage as if you were preparing for a quiz on the material. Remember, do not underscore as you read, but wait until you finish a paragraph or a section and then mark the important points.

Stress Management

Each of us has our own optimum stress level, which is influenced by heredity and other factors. <u>Some people thrive at stress levels that would quickly lead others to the state of exhaustion.</u> How can we tell if we are stressed beyond our optimum level? Sometimes it is obvious; but, more often we fail to associate the symptoms we experience with their cause. Different people respond to stress differently. For example, one person might gorge him- or herself with food while another might lose his or her appetite. One person might have trouble falling asleep at night while another person might sleep most of the time.

General Guidelines for Stress Management

Adopt a new way of looking at life. Stress management begins with adopting the philosophy that you, as an individual, are basically responsible for your own emotional and physical well-being. You can no longer allow other people to determine whether or not you are happy. You have little control over the behavior of anyone but yourself, and your emotional well-being is too important to trust to anyone but yourself. Your goal should be to develop such positive emotional wellness that nobody can ruin your day.

A positive outlook on life. This is absolutely essential to successful stress management. Your perception of events, not the events themselves, is what causes stress. Almost any life situation can be perceived as either stressful or nonstressful, depending on your interpretation. A negative view of life guarantees a high stress level. People who habitually view life negatively can recondition themselves to be more positive. One way is by applying a thought-stopping technique: Whenever you catch yourself thinking negatively, force yourself to think about the positive aspects of your situation. Eventually you will just automatically begin to see life more positively.

A regular exercise program. Exercise is an excellent tension reliever. In addition to the physical benefits, exercise is also good for the mind. Participating in at least three aerobic exercise sessions a week for at least 20 minutes each can greatly reduce stress. Daily stretching exercises provide relaxation and improve flexibility and posture. Participate in leisure activities that keep you physically active.

Be reasonably organized. Disorganization, sloppiness, chaos, and procrastination may seem very relaxed, but they are stressful. Set short-term, intermediate-term, and long-term goals for yourself. Every morning list the things you want and need to accomplish that day.

Learn to say no. Some people accept too many responsibilities. If you spread yourself too thin, not only will you be highly stressed, but important things will be done poorly or not at all. Know your limits and be assertive. If you don't have time to do something or simply don't want to do it, don't. Practice saying no effectively. Try, "I'm flattered that you've asked me, but given my commitments at this time, I won't be able to. . . ."

Learn to enjoy the process. Our culture is extremely goal oriented. Many of the things we do are directed toward achieving a goal, with no thought or expectation of enjoying the process. You may go to college for a degree, but you should enjoy the process of obtaining that degree. You may go to work for a paycheck, but you should enjoy your work. Happiness can seldom be achieved when pursued as a goal. It is usually a by-product of other activities. In whatever you do, focus on and enjoy the activity itself, rather than on how well you perform the activity or what the activity will bring you.

✓ *Don't be a perfectionist.* Perfectionists set impossible goals for themselves, because perfection is unattainable. Learn to tolerate and forgive both yourself and others. Intolerance of your own imperfections leads to stress and low self-esteem. Intolerance of others leads to anger, blame, and poor relationships, all of which increase stress.

✓ *Look for the humor in life.* Humor can be an effective part of stress management. Humor results in both psychological and physical changes. Its psychological effects include relief from anxiety, stress, and tension, an escape from reality, and a means of tolerating difficult life situations. Physically, laughter increases muscle activity, breathing rate, heart rate, and release of brain chemicals such as catecholamines and endorphins.

✓ *Practice altruism.* **Altruism** is unselfishness, placing the well-being of others ahead of one's own. Altruism is one of the best roads to happiness, emotional health, and stress management. As soon as you start feeling concern for the needs of others, you immediately feel less stressed over the frustration of your own needs. Invariably, the most selfish people are the most highly stressed as they focus their attention on the complete fulfillment of their own needs, which can never happen.

✓ *Let go of the past.* Everyone can list things in the past that he or she might have done differently. Other than learning through experience and trying not to make the same mistakes again, there is nothing to be gained by worrying about what you did or didn't do in the past. To focus on the past is nonproductive, stressful, and robs the present of its joy and vitality.

✓ *Eat a proper diet.* How you eat affects your emotions and your ability to cope. When your diet is good you feel better and deal better with difficult situations. Try eating more carefully for two weeks and feel the difference it makes.

✓ There is no unique stress-reduction diet, despite many claims to the contrary. The same diet that helps prevent heart disease, cancer, obesity, and diabetes (low in sugar, salt, fat, and total calories; adequate in vitamins, minerals, and protein) will also reduce stress.

✓ *Get adequate sleep.* Sleep is essential for successfully managing stress and maintaining your health. People have varying sleep requirements, but most people function best with seven to eight hours of sleep per day. Some people simply don't allot enough time to sleep, while others find that stress makes it difficult for them to sleep.

✓ *Avoid alcohol and other drugs.* The use of alcohol and other drugs in an effort to reduce stress levels actually contributes to stress in several ways. In the first place, it does *not* reduce the stress from a regularly occurring stressor such as an unpleasant job or relationship problems. Further, as alcohol and other drugs wear off, the rebound effect makes the user feel very uncomfortable and more stressed than before.

Don't overlook the possibility that excess caffeine intake is contributing to your stress. Caffeine is a powerful stimulant that, by itself, produces many of the physiological manifestations of stress. Plus, its effect of increased "nervous" energy contributes to more stressful, rushed behavior patterns. Remember that not only coffee and tea, but chocolate and many soft drinks contain caffeine.

Checkpoint

1. Why might two people in the same situation experience very different stress levels?
2. What is meant by "learn to enjoy the process"?
3. In what ways can being other-centered help reduce stress?

Curtis O. Boyer and Louis W. Shainberg, *Living Well*

Review your annotations. Have you sufficiently highlighted the main idea and the significant supporting details?

NOTETAKING

What Is Notetaking?

Many students prefer to jot down on their own paper brief sentence summaries of important textbook information. Margin space to the left of the summaries can be used to identify topics. Thus, topics of importance and explanations are side-by-side on notepaper for later study. In order to reduce notes for review, key terms can be further highlighted with a yellow marker to trigger thoughts for self-testing.

Why Take Textbook Notes?

Students who prefer this method say that working with a pencil and paper while reading keeps them involved with the material and thus improves concentration. Notetaking takes longer than annotating, but sometimes a student who has already annotated the text may feel the need, based on later testing demands, time, and the complexity of the material, to organize the information further into notes.

Although the following notetaking system recommends sentence summaries, writing short phrases can sometimes be more efficient and still adequately communicate the message for later study.

How to Take Notes

One of the most popular systems of notetaking is called the Cornell Method. The steps are as follows:

1. Draw a line down your paper two and one-half inches from the left side to create a two-and-one-half-inch margin for noting key words and a six-inch area on the right for sentence summaries.

2. After you have finished reading a section, tell yourself what you have read and jot down sentence summaries in the six-inch area on the right side of your paper. Use your own words and make sure you have included the main ideas and significant supporting details. Be brief, but use complete sentences.

3. Review your summary sentences and underline key words. Write these key words in the column on the left side of your paper. These words can be used to stimulate your memory of the material for later study.

The Cornell Method can be used for taking notes on classroom lectures. The chart shown on the following page, developed by Norman Stahl and James King, both explains the procedure and gives a visual display of the results. The example on page 186 applies the Cornell Method of notetaking to the biology passage on the circulatory system which you have already read.

Exercise 2   NOTETAKING

In college courses, you will usually take notes on lengthy chapters or entire books. For practice with notetaking here, use the passage, "Stress Management," which you have already annotated. Prepare a two-columned sheet and take notes using the Cornell Method.

OUTLINING

What Is an Outline?

An outline organizes and highlights major points and subordinates items of lesser importance. In a glance the indentations, Roman numerals, numbers, and letters quickly show how one idea relates to another and how all aspects relate to the whole. The layout of the outline is simply a graphic display of main ideas and significant supporting details.

The following example is the picture-perfect version of the basic outline form. In practice your "working outline" would probably not be as detailed or as regular as this.

Use the tools of the outline format, *especially the indentations and numbers,* to devise your own system for organizing information.

Title

I. First main idea
   A. Supporting idea
      1. Detail
      2. Detail
      3. Detail
        a. Minor detail
        b. Minor detail

Taking Class Notes: The Cornell Method

← 2½ INCHES →	← 6 INCHES →
REDUCE IDEAS TO CONCISE JOTTINGS AND SUMMARIES AS CUES FOR RECITING.	*RECORD THE LECTURE AS FULLY AND AS MEANINGFULLY AS POSSIBLE.*
Cornell Method	This sheet demonstrates the Cornell Method of taking classroom notes. It is recommended by experts from the Learning Center at Cornell University.
Line drawn down paper	You should draw a line down your notepage about 2½ inches from the left side. On the right side of the line simply record your classroom notes as you usually do. Be sure that you write legibly.
After the lecture	After the lecture you should read the notes, fill in materials that you missed, make your writing legible, and underline any important materials. Ask another classmate for help if you missed something during lecture.
Use the recall column for key phrases	The recall column on the left will help you when you study for your tests. Jot down any important words or key phrases in the recall column. This activity forces you to rethink and summarize your notes. The key words should stick in your mind.
Five Rs	The Five Rs will help you take better notes based on the Cornell Method.
Record	1. Record any information given during the lecture which you believe will be important.
Reduce	2. When you reduce your information you are summarizing and listing key words/phrases in the recall column.
Recite	3. Cover the notes you took for your class. Test yourself on the words in the recall section. This is what we mean by recite.
Reflect	4. You should reflect on the information you received during the lecture. Determine how your ideas fit in with the information.
Review	5. If you review your notes you will remember a great deal more when you take your midterm.
Binder & paper	Remember it is a good idea to keep your notes in a standard-sized binder. Also you should use only full-sized binder paper. You will be able to add mimeographed materials easily to your binder.
Hints	Abbreviations and symbols should be used when possible. Abbrev. & sym. give you time when used auto.

From N. A. Stahl and J. King, "A Language Experience Model for Teaching College Reading, Study and Survival" (Paper delivered at the twenty-fifth College Reading Association Annual Conference, Louisville, Ky., 30 October 1981).

Circulatory System

Two types Open and closed	There are <u>two types</u>, the <u>open</u> and the <u>closed</u>, by which blood reaches all the cells of an animal.
Open	In the <u>open system</u>, found mostly in insects and other arthropods, <u>blood moves</u> through the body and
Bathes cells	<u>bathes the cells directly</u>. The blood moves slower than in the closed system, and
Oxygen from outside	<u>oxygen</u> is <u>supplied from</u> <u>outside</u> air through tubes.
Closed	In the <u>closed system</u>, blood <u>flows through</u> a system of
Blood vessels Blood carries oxygen Heart pumps	<u>vessels</u>, <u>oxygen is carried</u> by the <u>blood</u> so it must move quickly, and the <u>heart</u> serves as a <u>pumping</u> mechanism. All vertebrates, as well as earthworms, have closed systems.

    B. Supporting Idea
       1. Detail
       2. Detail
    C. Supporting idea
 II. Second main idea
    A. Supporting idea
    B. Supporting idea

Why Outline?

    Students who outline usually drop the preciseness of picture-perfect outlines, but make good use of the numbers, letters, indentations, and mixture of topics and phrases from the system to take notes and show levels of importance. A quick look to the far left of an outline indicates the topic with subordinate ideas indented underneath. The letters, numbers, and indentations form a visual display of the significance of the parts that make up the whole. Good outliners use plenty of paper so the levels of importance are evident at a glance.

Another use of the outline is to organize notes from class lectures. During class most professors try to add to the material in the textbook and put it into perspective for students. Since the notes taken in class represent a large percentage of the material you need to know in order to pass the course, they are extremely important. While listening to a class lecture, you must almost instantly receive, synthesize, and select material and, at the same time, record something on paper for future reference. The difficulty of the task demands order and decision making. Do not be so eager to copy down every detail that you miss the big picture. One of the most efficient methods of taking lecture notes is to use a modified outline form, a version with the addition of stars, circles, and underlines to emphasize further the levels of importance.

How to Outline

Professors say that they can walk around a classroom and look at the notes students have taken from the text or from a lecture and tell how well each has understood the lesson. The errors most frequently observed fall into the following categories:

1. Poor organization
2. Failure to show importance
3. Writing too much
4. Writing too little

To avoid these pitfalls the most important thing to remember in outlining is *"What is my purpose?"* You don't need to include everything and you don't need a picture-perfect version for study notes. Include only what you feel you will need to remember later, and use the numbering system and the indentations to show how one thing relates to another. Several other important guidelines to remember are as follows:

1. Get a general overview before you start.
   (How many main topics do there seem to be?)
2. Use phrases rather than sentences.
   (Can you state it in a few short words?)
3. Put it in your own words.
   (If you cannot paraphrase it, do you really understand it?)
4. Be selective.
   (Are you highlighting or completely rewriting?)

After outlining, indicate key terms with a yellow marker so that they will be highly visible for later review and self-testing.

Take a careful look at the following outline of the biology passage on the circulatory system on pp. 180–181. Notice how the numbers and letters, as well as the distance from the left side of the paper, show levels of importance.

I. Open circulatory system
   A. Blood moves through the body and bathes cells directly
   B. Examples-insects and other arthropods
   C. Oxygen supplied from outside air through tubes
   D. Slower blood movement since not supplying cells with oxygen
II. Closed circulatory system
   A. Blood flows through system of vessels
   B. Oxygen carried by blood so it must move quickly
   C. Heart serves as pumping mechanism
   D. Example-all vertebrates
   E. Example-earthworms

Exercise 3   OUTLINING

Outline the key ideas in the following selection as if you were planning to use your notes to study for a quiz. You may want to annotate before you outline.

Reacting to Stress with Defense Mechanisms

Stress may occasionally promote positive outcomes. Motivated to overcome stress and the situations that produce it, we may learn new and adaptive responses. It is also clear, however, that stress involves a very unpleasant emotional component. **Anxiety** is a general feeling of tension or apprehension that often accompanies a perceived threat to one's well-being. It is this unpleasant emotional component that often prompts us to learn new responses to rid ourselves of stress.

There are a number of techniques, essentially self-deception, that we may employ to keep from feeling the unpleasantness associated with stress. These techniques, or tricks we play on ourselves, are not adaptive in the sense of helping us to get rid of anxiety by getting rid of the source of stress. Rather, they are mechanisms that we can and do use to defend ourselves against the *feelings* of stress. They are called **defense mechanisms.** Freud believed defense mechanisms to be the work of the unconscious mind. He claimed that they are ploys that our unconscious mind uses to protect us (our *self* or *ego*) from stress and anxiety. Many psychologists take issue with Freud's interpretation of defense mechanisms and consider defense mechanisms in more general terms than did Freud, but few will deny that defense mechanisms exist. It *is* true that they are generally ineffective if consciously or purposively employed. The list of defense mechanisms is a long one. Here, we'll review some of the more common defense mechanisms, providing an example of each, to give you an idea of how they might serve as a reaction to stress.

Repression. The notion of **repression** came up earlier in our discussion of memory. In a way, it is the most basic of all the defense mechanisms. It is sometimes referred to as *motivated forgetting,* which gives us a good idea of what is involved. Repression is a matter of conveniently forgetting about some stressful, anxiety-producing event, conflict, or frustration. Paul had a teacher in high school he did not get along with at all. After spending an entire semester trying his best to do whatever was asked, Paul failed the course. The following summer, while walking with his girlfriend, Paul encountered this teacher. When he tried to introduce his girlfriend, Paul could not remember his teacher's name. He had repressed it. As a long-term reaction to stress, repressing the names of people we don't like or that we associate with unpleasant, stressful experiences is certainly not a very adaptive reaction. But at least it can protect us from dwelling on such unpleasantness.

Denial. **Denial** is a very basic mechanism of defense against stress. In denial, a person simply refuses to acknowledge the realities of a stressful situation. When a physician first tells a patient that he or she has a terminal illness, a common reaction is denial; the patient refuses to believe that there is anything seriously wrong.

Other less stressful events than serious illness sometimes evoke denial. Many smokers are intelligent individuals who are well aware of the data and the statistics that can readily convince them that they are slowly (or rapidly) killing themselves by continuing to smoke. But they deny the evidence. Somehow they are able to convince themselves that they aren't going to die from smoking; that's something that happens to other people, and besides, they *could* stop whenever they wanted.

Rationalization. **Rationalization** amounts to making excuses for our behaviors when facing the real reasons for our behaviors would be stressful. The real reason Kevin failed his psychology midterm is that he didn't study for it and has missed a number of classes. Kevin hates to admit, even to himself, that he could have been so stupid as to flunk that exam because of his own actions. As a result, he rationalizes: "It wasn't really *my* fault. I had a lousy instructor. We used a rotten text. The tests were grossly unfair. I've been fighting the darn flu all semester. And Marjorie had that big party the night before the exam." Now Susan, on the other hand, really did want to go to Marjorie's party, but she decided that she wouldn't go unless somebody asked her. As it happens, no one did. In short order, Susan rationalized that she "didn't want to go to that dumb party anyway"; she needed to "stay home and study."

Compensation. We might best think of **compensation** in the context of personal frustration. This defense mechanism is a matter of overemphasizing some positive trait or ability to counterbalance a shortcoming in some other trait or ability. If some particular goal-directed behavior becomes blocked, a person may compensate by putting extra effort and attention into some other aspect of behavior. For example, Karen, a seventh grader, wants to be popular. She's a reasonably bright and pleasant teenager, but isn't—in the judgment of her classmates—very pretty. Karen *may* compensate for her lack of good looks by studying very hard to be a good student, or by memorizing jokes and funny stories, or by becoming a good musician. Compensation is not just an attempt to be a well-rounded individual. It is a matter of expending *extra* energy and resources in one direction to offset shortcomings in other directions.

Fantasy. **Fantasy** is one of the more common defense mechanisms used by college students. It is often quite useful. Particularly after a hard day when stress levels are high, isn't it pleasant to sit in a comfortable chair, kick off your shoes, lie back, close your eyes, and daydream, perhaps about graduation day, picturing yourself walking across the stage to pick up your diploma—with honors.

When things are not going well for us, we may retreat into a world of fantasy where everything always goes well. Remember that to engage from time to time in fantasizing is a normal and acceptable response to stress. You should not get worried if you fantasize occasionally. On the other hand, you should realize that there are some potential dangers here. You need to be able to keep separate those activities that are real and those that occur in your fantasies. And you should realize that fantasy in itself will not solve whatever problem is causing you stress. Fantasizing about academic successes may help you feel better for a while, but it is not likely to make you a better student.

Projection. **Projection** is a matter of seeing in others those very traits and motives that cause us stress when we see them in ourselves. Under pressure to do well on an exam, Mark may want to cheat, but his conscience won't let him. Because of projection, he may think he sees cheating going on all around him.

Projection is a mechanism that is often used in conjunction with hostility and aggression. When people begin to feel uncomfortable about their own levels of hostility, they often project their aggressiveness onto others, coming to believe that others are "out to do me harm," and "I'm only defending myself."

Regression. To employ **regression** is to return to earlier, even childish, levels of behavior that were once productive or reinforced. Curiously enough, we often find regression in children. Imagine a four year old who until very recently was an only child. Now Mommy has returned from the hospital with a new baby sister. The four year old is no longer "the center of the universe," as her new little sister now gets parental attention. The four year old reverts to earlier behaviors and starts wetting the bed, screaming for a bottle of her own, and crawling on all fours in an attempt to get attention. She is regressing.

Many defense mechanisms can be seen on the golf course, including regression. After Doug knocks three golf balls into the lake, he throws a temper tantrum, stamps his feet, and tosses his three-iron in the lake. His childish regressive behavior won't help his score, but it may act as a release from the tension of his stress at the moment.

Displacement. The defense mechanism of **displacement** is usually discussed in the context of aggression. Your goal-directed behavior becomes blocked or thwarted. You are frustrated, under stress, and somewhat aggressive. You cannot vent your aggression directly at the source of the frustration, so you displace it to a safer outlet. Dorothy expects to get promoted at work, but someone else gets the new job she wanted. Her goal-directed behavior has been frustrated. She's upset and angry at her boss, but feels (perhaps correctly) that blowing her top at her boss will do more harm than good. She's still frustrated, so she displaces her hostility toward her husband, children, and/or the family cat.

Displacement doesn't have to involve hostility and aggression. A young couple discovers that having children is not going to be as easy as they thought. They want children badly, but there's an infertility problem that is causing considerable stress. Their motivation for love, sharing, and caring may be displaced toward a pet, nephews and nieces, or some neighborhood children—at least until their own goals can be realized with children of their own.

The list of defense mechanisms provided above is not an exhaustive one. These are among the most common, and this list gives you an idea of what defense mechanisms are like.

Josh Gerow, *Psychology: An Introduction*

© 1997 Addison-Wesley Educational Publishers Inc.

Exercise 4   OUTLINING

For additional practice outline the previous passage on "Stress Management" beginning on p. 181. Use your annotations and notes to help.

MAPPING

What Is Mapping?

Mapping is a visual system of condensing material to show relationships and importance. A map is a diagram of the major points, with their significant subpoints, that support a topic. The purpose of mapping as an organizing strategy is to improve memory by grouping material in a highly visual way.

Why Map?

Proponents of popular learning style theories would say that mapping offers a visual organization that appeals to learners with a preference for spatial representation, as opposed to the linear mode offered by outlining and notetaking. A map provides a quick reference to overviewing an article or a chapter and can be used to reduce notes for later study.

How to Map

Use the following steps for mapping.

1. Draw a circle or a box in the middle of a page and in it write the subject or topic of the material.
2. Determine the main ideas that support the subject and write them on lines radiating from the central circle or box.
3. Determine the significant details and write them on lines attached to each main idea. The number of details you include will depend on the material and your purpose.

Maps are not restricted to any one pattern, but can be formed in a variety of creative shapes, as the following diagrams illustrate:

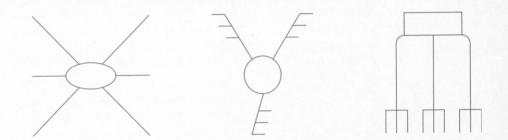

The following map highlights the biology passage on the circulatory system. Notice how the visual display emphasizes the groups of ideas supporting the topic.

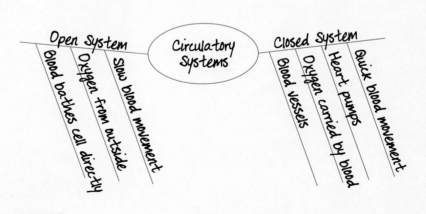

Exercise 5   MAPPING

Refer to Exercise 3 and design a map for the passage entitled, "Reacting to Stress with Defense Mechanisms," which you previously outlined. Use your outline to help you in making the map. Experiment with several different shapes for your map patterns on notebook or unlined paper.

Exercise 6   MAPPING

For additional practice design a map for the passage entitled "Stress Management."

SUMMARY POINTS

- Textbook reading is study reading. It is reading to learn and involves establishing knowledge networks. Students must select which textbook information to remember and organize it to facilitate further study.
- Annotating is a method of using symbols and notations to highlight main ideas, significant supporting details, and key terms.
- The Cornell Method of notetaking includes writing summary sentences and marginal notes.
- The layout of the outline is a graphic presentation of main ideas and significant supporting details.
- Mapping is a visual system of condensing material to show relationships and importance.

SELECTION 1

BIOLOGY

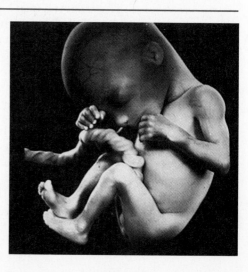

Stage 1: Skill Development
Preview

This selection is divided into how many sections?_____

After reading this selection, I will need to know

How to Annotate

Activate Schema

What hour of which day were you born? _Afternoon_

How much did you weigh? _8 lt_

Learning Strategy

Be able to describe fetal growth in each trimester.

Stage 2: Integrate Knowledge While Reading

As you read, use the thinking strategies discussed in Chapter 2.

1. Predict   2. Picture   3. Relate   4. Monitor   5. Fix up

Skill Development: Outlining

Outline or map the key ideas in each section as if you were planning to use your notes to study for a quiz.

Pregnancy and Birth

From Robert Wallace, _Biology: The World of Life_[3]

Descriptions in bus-station novels notwithstanding, fertilization occurs with the mother-to-be totally unaware of the event. If there are sperm cells thrashing around in the genital tract at any time within forty-eight hours before ovulation to about twelve hours after, the odds are very good that
5   pregnancy will occur. As soon as the egg is touched by the head of a sperm, it undergoes violent pulsating movements which unite the twenty-three chromosomes of the sperm with its own genetic complement. From this single cell, about 1/175 of an inch in diameter, a baby weighing several pounds and composed of trillions of cells will be delivered about 266
10   days later.

For convenience, we will divide the 266 days, or nine months, into three periods of three months each. We can consider these _trimesters_ separately, since each is characterized by different sorts of events.

---

[3]From _Biology: The World of Life,_ 3rd Edition, by Robert A. Wallace. Copyright © 1981 by Scott, Foresman and Company, HarperCollins College Publishers.

The First Trimester

15   In the first trimester the embryo begins the delicate structural differentiations that will lead to its final form. It is therefore particularly susceptible during this period to any number of factors that might influence its development. In fact the embryo often fails to survive this stage.

The first cell divisions result in cells that all look about alike and have
20   roughly the same potentials. In other words, at this stage the cells are, theoretically anyway, interchangeable. Seventy-two hours after fertilization the embryo will consist of sixteen such cells. (So, how many divisions will have taken place?) Each cell will divide before it reaches the size of the cell that has produced it; hence the cells will become progressively smaller with
25   each division. By the end of the first month the embryo will have reached a length of only 1/8 inch, but it will consist of millions of cells.

In the second month the features of the embryo become more recognizable. Bone begins to form throughout the body, primarily in the jaw and shoulder areas. The head and brain are developing at a much faster
30   rate than the rest of the body, so that at this point the ears appear and open, lidless eyes stare blankly into the amniotic fluid. The circulatory system is developing and blood is pumped through the umbilical cord out to the chorion, where it receives life-sustaining nutrients and deposits the poisons it has removed from the developing embryo. The nitrogenous
35   wastes and carbon dioxide filter into the mother's bloodstream, where they will be circulated to her own kidneys and lungs for removal. At about day 46 the primordial reproductive organs begin to form, either as testes or ovaries, and it is now, for the first time, that the sex of the embryo becomes apparent. Near the end of the second month fingers and toes begin to
40   appear on the flattened paddles which have formed from the limb buds. By this time the embryo is about two inches long and is more or less human in appearance; it is now called a *fetus*. Growth and differentiation continue during the third month, but now the fetus begins to move. It breathes the amniotic fluid in and out of bulblike lungs and swallowing motions become
45   distinct. At this point individual differences can be distinguished in the behavior of fetuses. The clearest differences are in their facial expressions. Some frown a lot; others smile or grimace. It would be interesting to correlate this early behavior with the personality traits that develop after birth.

50   ### The Second Trimester

In the second trimester the fetus grows rapidly, and by the end of the sixth month it may be about a foot long, although it will weigh only about a pound and a half. Whereas the predominant growth of the fetus during the first trimester was in the head and brain areas, during the second trimester
55   the body grows at a much faster relative rate than the brain and begins to catch up in size with the head.

The fetus is by this time behaving more vigorously. It is able to move freely within its sea of amniotic fluid and the delighted mother can feel it kicking and thrashing about. Interestingly, the fetus must sleep now, so there are periods when it is inactive. It is capable of reacting to more types of stimuli as time passes. For example, by the fifth month the eyes are sensitive to light, although there is still no sensitivity to sound. Other organs seem to be complete, but remain nonfunctional. For example, the lungs are developed, but they cannot exchange oxygen. The digestive organs are present, but they cannot digest food. Even the skin is not prepared to cope with the temperature changes in the outside world. In fact, at the end of the fifth month the skin is covered by a protective cheesy paste consisting of wax and sweatlike secretions mixed with loosened skin cells (*vernix caseosa*). The fetus is still incapable in nearly all instances of surviving alone.

By the sixth month the fetus is kicking and turning so constantly that the mother often must time her own sleep periods to coincide with her baby's. The distracting effect has been described as similar to being continually tapped on the shoulder, but not exactly. The fetus moves with such vigor that its movements are not only felt from the inside, but can be seen clearly from the outside. To add to the mother's distraction, the fetus may even have periods of hiccups. By this stage it is so large and demanding that it places a tremendous drain on the mother's reserves.

At the end of the second trimester the fetus has the unmistakable appearance of a human baby (or a very old person, since its skin is loose and wrinkled at this stage). In the event of a premature birth around the end of this trimester, the fetus may be able to survive.

The Third Trimester

During the third trimester the fetus grows until it is no longer floating free in its amniotic pool. It now fills the abdominal area of the mother. The fetus is crowded so tightly into the greatly enlarged uterus that its movement is restricted. In these last three months the mother's abdomen becomes greatly distended and heavy, and her posture and gait may be noticeably altered in response to the shift in her center of gravity. The mass of tissue and amniotic fluid that accompanies the fetus ordinarily weighs almost twice as much as the fetus itself. Toward the end of this period, milk begins to form in the mother's mammary glands, which in the previous trimester have undergone a sudden surge of growth.

At this time, the mother is at a great disadvantage in several ways in terms of her physical well-being. About 85 percent of the calcium she eats goes to the fetal skeleton, and about the same percentage of her iron intake goes to the fetal blood cells. Of the protein she eats, much of the nitrogen goes to the brain and other nerve tissues of the fetus.

Some interesting questions arise here. If a woman is unable to afford expensive protein-rich foods during the third trimester, what is the probability of a lowered I.Q. in her offspring? On the average the poorer people in this country show lower I.Q. scores. Are they poor because their I.Q.'s are low, or are I.Q.'s low because they are poor? Is there a self-perpetuating nature about either of these alternatives?

In the third trimester, the fetus is large. It requires increasingly greater amounts of food, and each day it produces more poisonous wastes for the mother's body to carry away. Her heart must work harder to provide food and oxygen for two bodies. She must breathe, now, for two individuals. Her blood pressure and heart rate rise. The fetus and the tissues maintaining it form a large mass that crowds the internal organs of the mother. In fact, the crowding of the fetus against the mother's diaphragm may make breathing difficult for her in these months. Several weeks before delivery, however, the fetus will change its position, dropping lower in the pelvis (called "*lightening*") and thus relieve the pressure against the mother's lungs.

There are important changes occurring in the fetus in these last three months, and some of these are not very well understood. The effects of these changes, however, are reflected in the survival rate of babies delivered by Caesarian section (an incision through the mother's side). In the seventh month, only 10 percent survive; in the eighth month, 70 percent; and in the ninth, 95 percent survive.

Interestingly, there is another change in the relationship of the fetus and mother at this time. Whereas measles and certain other infectious diseases would have affected the embryo during the first trimester of pregnancy, at this stage the mother's antibodies confer an immunity to the fetus, a protection that may last through the first few weeks of infancy.

At some point about 255 to 265 days from the time of conception the life-sustaining placenta begins to break down. Certain parts shrink, the tissue structure begins changing, and the capillaries begin to disintegrate. The result is a less hospitable environment for the fetus, and premature births at this time are not unusual. At about this time the fetus slows its growth, and drops into position with its head toward the bottom of the uterus. Meanwhile, the internal organs undergo the final changes that will enable the newborn to survive in an entirely different kind of world. Its home has been warm, rather constant in its qualities, protected, and confining. It is not likely to encounter anything quite so secure again.

Birth

The signal that there will soon be a new member of the earth's most dominant species is the onset of *labor,* a series of uterine contractions that usually begin at about half-hour intervals and gradually increase in frequency. Meanwhile, the sphincter muscle around the cervix dilates, and as the periodic contractions become stronger, the baby's head pushes through the extended cervical canal to the opening of the vagina. The

145 infant is finally about to emerge into its new environment, one that, in time, may give it the chance to propel its own genes into the gene pool of the species.

Once the baby's head emerges, the pattern of uterine contractions changes. The contractions become milder and more frequent. After the

150 head gradually emerges through the vaginal opening, the smaller shoulders and the body appear. Then with a rush the baby slips into a new world. As soon as the baby has emerged, the umbilicus by which it is attached to the placenta is tied off and cut. The placenta is expelled by further contractions as the *afterbirth.* The mother recovers surprisingly rapidly. In other species,

155 which deliver their young unaided, the mother immediately chews through the umbilicus and eats the afterbirth so that it will not advertise to predators the presence of a helpless newborn. Fortunately, the behavior never became popular in our own species.

The cutting of the umbilicus stops the only source of oxygen the infant

160 has known. There is a resulting rapid buildup of carbon dioxide in the blood, which affects a breathing center in the brain. An impulse is fired to the diaphragm, and the baby gasps its first breath. Its exhaling cry signals that it is breathing on its own.

In American hospitals the newborn is then given the first series of the

165 many tests it will encounter during its lifetime. This one is called the *Apgar test series,* in which muscle tone, breathing, reflexes, and heart rate are evaluated. The obstetrician then checks for skin lesions and evidence of hernias. If the infant is a boy, it is checked to see whether the testes have properly descended into the scrotum. A footprint is then recorded as a

170 means of identification, since the new individual, despite the protestations of proud parents, does not yet have many other distinctive features that would be apparent to the casual observer. And there have been more than a few cases of accidental baby-switching.

Stage 3: Recall

Review to self-test. Your instructor may ask ten true-false questions to stimulate your recall.

SKILL DEVELOPMENT: OUTLINING

Review your outline or map without referring to the text before answering the comprehension questions.

Your instructor may ask ten true-false questions to stimulate your recall.

COMPREHENSION QUESTIONS

Mark each statement with *T* for true or *F* for false.

_I_   1. Babies are footprinted as a means of identification.

_F_   2. The fetus is most susceptible to measles during the last trimester.

_F_   3. During fertilization, the mother can feel the sperm and the egg touch.

_F_   4. During the first trimester, changes in the facial expression of the fetus occur.

_I_   5. During the second trimester, the fetus can have the hiccups.

_I_   6. During the third trimester, the fetus floats freely with room to move in the uterus.

_T_   7. The author implies that the mother's body works the hardest during the third trimester.

_F_   8. The baby is forced to breathe when the cervix dilates.

_I_   9. Sperm can live for several hours in the genital tract.

_I_   10. During the third trimester, the mother's antibodies confer immunity to the fetus.

SELECTION 2

HISTORY

Stage 1: Skill Development

Preview

The pattern of organization in the first part of the selection is

After reading this selection, I will need to know Sojourner Truth's feelings on the weakness of women.

agree ☑   disagree ☐

Activate Schema

Why did the Civil War throw women into many leadership roles?

Learning Strategy

Look at the historical trend toward altering the image of women and note the contributions to this change made by individuals and groups.

Word Knowledge

Are you familiar with the following words in this selection?

restrictive	pursue
detriment	hygiene
defiant	incessant
communal	convalescent
hecklers	naive

Your instructor may ask ten true-false questions from the *Instructor's Manual* to stimulate your thinking using these words.

Stage 2: Integrate Knowledge While Reading

As you read, use the thinking strategies discussed in Chapter 2.
1. Predict   2. Picture   3. Relate   4. Monitor   5. Fix up

Skill Development: Notetaking

Use the Cornell Method of notetaking to organize material in this selection for future study.

Women in History
From Leonard Pitt, *We Americans*[4]

Three Radical Women

Amelia Bloomer (1818–1894) published the first newspaper issued expressly for women. She called it *The Lily*. Her fame, however, rests chiefly in dress reform. For six or eight years she wore an outfit composed of a knee-length skirt over full pants gathered at the ankle, which were soon
5   known everywhere as "bloomers." Wherever she went, this style created great excitement and brought her enormous audiences—including hecklers. She was trying to make the serious point that women's fashions,

[4]From Pitt, *We Americans*. Copyright © 1987 Kendall/Hunt Publishing Company. Reprinted with permission.

often designed by men to suit their own tastes, were too restrictive, often to the detriment of the health of those who wore them. Still, some of her
10 contemporaries thought she did the feminist movement as much harm as good.

Very few feminists hoped to destroy marriage as such. Most of them had husbands and lived conventional, if hectic, lives. And many of the husbands supported their cause. Yet the feminists did challenge certain marital
15 customs. When Lucy Stone married Henry Blackwell, she insisted on being called "Mrs. Stone," a defiant gesture that brought her a lifetime of ridicule. Both she and her husband signed a marriage contract, vowing "to recognize the wife as an independent, rational being." They agreed to break any law which brought the husband "an injurious and unnatural superiority." But
20 few of the radical feminists indulged in "free love" or joined communal marriage experiments. The movement was intended mainly to help women gain control over their own property and earnings and gain better legal guardianship over their children. Voting also interested them, but women's suffrage did not become a central issue until later in the century.
25 Many black women were part of the movement, including the legendary Sojourner Truth (1797–1883). Born a slave in New York and forced to marry a man approved by her owner, Sojourner Truth was freed when the state abolished slavery. After participating in religious revivals, she became an active abolitionist and feminist. In 1851 she saved the day at a
30 women's rights convention in Ohio, silencing hecklers and replying to a man who had belittled the weakness of women:

The man over there says women need to be helped into carriages and lifted over ditches, and to have the best place everywhere. Nobody ever helps me into carriages or over puddles, or gives me the best place—and
35 ain't I a woman? . . . Look at my arm! I have ploughed and planted and gathered into barns, and no man could head me—and ain't I a woman? I could work as much and eat as much as a man—when I could get it—and bear the lash as well! And ain't I a woman? I have borne thirteen children, and seen most of 'em sold into slavery, and when I cried out my mother's
40 grief, none but Jesus heard me—and ain't I a woman?

Changing the Image and the Reality

The accomplishments of a few women who dared pursue professional careers had somewhat altered the image of the submissive and brainless child-woman. Maria Mitchell of Nantucket, whose father was an astronomer,
45 discovered a comet at the age of twenty-eight. She became the first woman professor of astronomy in the U.S. (at Vassar in 1865). Mitchell was also the first woman elected to the American Academy of Arts and Sciences and a founder of the Association for the Advancement of Women. Elizabeth Blackwell applied to twenty-nine medical schools before she was accepted.
50 She attended all classes, even anatomy class, despite the sneers of some

male students. As a physician, she went on to make important contributions in sanitation and hygiene.

By about 1860 women had effected notable improvements in their status. Organized feminists had eliminated some of the worst legal
55   disadvantages in fifteen states. The Civil War altered the role—and the image—of women even more drastically than the feminist movement did. As men went off to fight, women flocked into government clerical jobs. And they were accepted in teaching jobs as never before. Tens of thousands of women ran farms and businesses while the men were gone. Anna Howard
60   Shaw, whose mother ran a pioneer farm, recalled:

> It was an incessant struggle to keep our land, to pay our taxes, and to live. Calico was selling at fifty cents a yard. Coffee was one dollar a pound. There were no men left to grind our corn, to get in our crops, or to care for our livestock; and all around us we saw our struggle reflected in the
65   lives of our neighbors.

Women took part in crucial relief efforts. The Sanitary Commission, the Union's volunteer nursing program and a forerunner of the Red Cross, owed much of its success to women. They raised millions of dollars for medicine, bandages, food, hospitals, relief camps, and convalescent homes.
70   North and South, black and white, many women served as nurses, some as spies and even as soldiers. Dorothea Dix, already famous as a reformer of prisons and insane asylums, became head of the Union army nurse corps. Clara Barton and "Mother" Bickerdyke saved thousands of lives by working close behind the front lines at Antietam, Chancellorsville, and
75   Fredericksburg. Harriet Tubman led a party up the Combahee River to rescue 756 slaves. Late in life she was recognized for her heroic act by being granted a government pension of twenty dollars per month.

Southern white women suffered more from the disruptions of the Civil War than did their northern sisters. The proportion of men who went to
80   war or were killed in battle was greater in the South. This made many women self-sufficient during the war. Still, there was hardly a whisper of feminism in the South.

The Civil War also brought women into the political limelight. Anna Dickson skyrocketed to fame as a Republican speaker, climaxing her career
85   with an address to the House of Representatives on abolition. Stanton and Anthony formed the National Woman's Loyal League to press for a constitutional amendment banning slavery. With Anthony's genius for organization, the League in one year collected 400,000 signatures in favor of the Thirteenth Amendment.
90   Once abolition was finally assured in 1865, most feminists felt certain that suffrage would follow quickly. They believed that women had earned the vote by their patriotic wartime efforts. Besides, it appeared certain that black men would soon be allowed to vote. And once black men had the

95 ballot in hand, how could anyone justify keeping it from white women—or black women? Any feminist who had predicted in 1865 that women would have to wait another fifty-five years for suffrage would have been called politically naive.

Stage 3: Recall for Self-Testing

Stop and self-test. Recall what you have read. Do not allow gaps of knowledge to exist. Review your use of the thinking strategies. Did you use all five? Your instructor may ask ten true-false questions to stimulate your recall.

SKILL DEVELOPMENT: NOTETAKING

Review your notes before answering the following comprehension questions.

COMPREHENSION QUESTIONS

After reading the selection, answer the following questions with *a, b, c,* or *d.*

c 1. The best statement of the main point of this selection is that
   a. women made impressive gains because of their work during the Civil War.
   b. many women made early contributions toward changing the stereotypical image of the female role.
   c. Bloomer, Stone, and Truth changed a radical image into a reality.
   d. women were slow to get the right to vote despite their efforts.

b 2. In originating "bloomers," Amelia Bloomer's greatest concern was
   a. fashion.
   b. principle.
   c. expense.
   d. good taste.

c 3. The major purpose of Sojourner Truth's quoted speech was to
   a. prove that women are stronger than men.
   b. reprimand men for social courtesy.
   c. dramatize the strengths of women.
   d. praise childbearing as a womanly virtue.

d 4. Lucy Stone's major motive in retaining the name "Mrs. Stone" after marriage as to
   a. condone "free love" without marriage.
   b. de-emphasize the responsibilities of marriage.
   c. purchase property in her own name.
   d. be recognized as an independent person equal to her husband.

_c_ 5. The article explicitly states that women worked during the Civil War in all of the following except
   a. farms and businesses.
   b. the military.
   c. government clerical jobs.
   d. the Red Cross.

_a_ 6. The author implies that the eventual assumption of responsible roles by large numbers of women was primarily due to
   a. the feminist movement.
   b. the determination and accomplishments of female professionals.
   c. a desire to give women a chance.
   d. economic necessity.

_c_ 7. The author believes that the Civil War showed southern women to be
   a. as capable but less vocal than northern women.
   b. more capable than their northern sisters.
   c. capable workers and eager feminists
   d. less able to assume responsible roles than northern women.

_c_ 8. The author's main purpose in mentioning the accomplishments of Maria Mitchell is to point out that
   a. she discovered a comet.
   b. her professional achievements in astronomy were exceptional and thus somewhat improved the image of women.
   c. she was the first woman professor of astronomy in the United States.
   d. she was a founder of the Association for the Advancement of Women.

_a_ 9. The article states or implies that all of the following women worked to abolish slavery except
   a. Anna Howard Shaw.
   b. Harriet Tubman.
   c. Anna Dickson.
   d. Stanton and Anthony.

_a_ 10. In the author's opinion, the long wait by women after the Civil War for suffrage
   a. was predictable in 1865.
   b. would not have been expected in 1865.
   c. was due to the vote of black men.
   d. was justified.

Answer the following with *T* (true) or *F* (false).

_T_ 11. Women were granted the right to vote in 1920.

_F_ 12. Sojourner Truth had been a southern slave.

_T_ 13. The author implies that feminist leaders were more concerned with their own right to vote than with the abolition of slavery.

_F_ 14. From the very beginning, the right to vote was the focal point of the women's movement.

_T_ 14. Sojourner Truth had thirteen children.

VOCABULARY

According to the way the italicized word was used in the selection, indicate *a, b, c,* or *d* for the word or phrase that gives the best definition.

_d_ 1. "were too *restrictive*" (8)
   a. showy
   b. expensive
   c. complicated
   d. confining

_a_ 2. "to the *detriment of*" (9)
   a. harm
   b. anger
   c. apology
   d. objection

_c_ 3. "a *defiant* gesture" (16)
   a. unlucky
   b. resistive
   c. admirable
   d. ignorant

_a_ 4. "*communal* marriage experiments" (20)
   a. permanent
   b. living together in groups
   c. illegal
   d. uncommon

_b_ 5. "silencing *hecklers*" (30)
   a. soldiers
   b. rioters
   c. disciples
   d. verbal harassers

_a_ 6. "*pursue* professional careers" (42)
   a. strive for
   b. abandon
   c. acknowledge
   d. indicate

_c_ 7. "sanitation and *hygiene*" (52)
   a. garbage disposal
   b. biology
   c. health care
   d. mental disorders

_b_ 8. "an *incessant* struggle" (61)
   a. earlier
   b. final
   c. novel
   d. unceasing

_d_ 9. "*convalescent* homes" (69)
   a. sanitary
   b. government
   c. reclaimed
   d. recuperating

_b_ 10. "called politically *naive*" (97)
   a. unsophisticated
   b. well informed
   c. dishonest
   d. unfortunate

WRITTEN RESPONSE

Use information from the text to answer the following question:

How did the actions of many early women "somewhat alter the image of the submissive and brainless child-woman"?

Writing Suggestion: List the women mentioned in the text and discuss how each changed stereotypical thinking. (Use your own paper.)

COLLABORATIVE
CRITICAL
THINKING

Electing a Female President

Form a collaborative group with two other classmates to discuss possible female candidates for president of the United States. The road to the presidency has typically been through service in the Congress or through the vice presidency. Which women in public life today would have a chance of winning a presidential election?

The task of the group is to name three women who have the leadership skill, the vision, the political clout, and the public appeal to become president. For each of the women, list the following:

1. Credentials

2. Political party

3. Base of political support

4. Position on important issues

5. Negative aspects that will cost votes

Read the following excerpt from a political science textbook concerning gender and politics for insight. In order to win the election, your female candidate will have to appeal to both men and women.

Gender

Women and men are moderately different in certain political respects. The "gender gap" in party loyalties widened at the beginning of the 1990s; in 1993, 41 percent of women, but only 29 percent of men, considered themselves Democrats.

Women were prevented from participating in politics for a large part of our history; they only got the vote, by constitutional amendment, in 1920. Not all of them immediately took advantage of this new opportunity. For many years, women voted and participated at lower rates than men—about 10 or 15 percent lower in the elections of the 1950s, for example—and only after the women's movement gained force during the 1970s did substantial numbers of female candidates begin to run for high offices. Though an office-holding gap remains, the participation gap virtually disappeared.

Women do differ somewhat from men in certain policy preferences. Women tend to be more opposed to violence, whether by criminals or by the state. More of them oppose capital punishment and the use of military force abroad. More favor arms control and peace agreements. Women also tend to be somewhat more supportive of protective policies to care for the weak and the helpless.

Contrary to common impression, women have not been particularly more supportive than men of women's rights or abortion. This is another case, like that of Catholic Americans and the Catholic church, in which the opinions of ordinary members of social groups are not necessarily the same as those of organizations that claim to represent them. Women do differ among themselves, however; professionals and others working outside the home are much more liberal on these issues than are homemakers.

From Edward S. Greenberg and Benjamin I. Page, *The Struggle for Democracy*

SELECTION 3

BIOLOGY

Stage 1: Skill Development

Preview

The pattern of organization in the first paragraph is definition and example.

agree ☐   disagree ☐

After reading this selection, I will need to know how honeybees communicate information about the location of a supply of nectar.

agree ☐   disagree ☐

Activate Schema

How do cats establish a territory?

How do humans establish a territory?

Why do bears hibernate?

Learning Strategy

Be able to define the boldfaced words and to explain reasons for the animal behaviors.

Word Knowledge

Are you familiar with the following words in this selection?

sufficient	stash
exclusive	crevices
venture	foraging
diverse	duration
scarcity	correlated

Your instructor may ask ten true-false questions from the *Instructor's Manual* to stimulate your thinking using these words.

Stage 2: Integrate Knowledge While Reading

Use the thinking strategies as you read:
1. Predict   2. Picture   3. Relate   4. Monitor   5. Fix up

Skill Development: Annotating and Notetaking

Annotate the important points in the selection and then organize the material that you want to remember for future study into notes.

Animal Behavior for Successful Resource Allocation
From Eldon D. Enger, J. Richard Kormelink, Frederick C. Ross, and Rodney J. Smith, *Concepts in Biology*, 7th ed.

Territoriality

For an animal to be successful, it must receive sufficient resources to live and reproduce. Therefore, we find many kinds of behaviors that divide the available resources so that the species as a whole is benefited, even
5 though some individuals may be harmed. One kind of behavior pattern that is often tied to successful reproduction is territoriality. **Territoriality** consists of the setting aside of space for the exclusive use of an animal for food, mating, or other purposes. A **territory** is the space an animal defends against others of the same species. This territory has great importance
10 because it reserves exclusive rights to the use of a specific piece of space. When territories are first being established, there is much conflict between individuals. This eventually gives way to the use of a series of signals that

define the territory and communicate to others that the territory is occupied. The male redwing blackbird has red shoulder patches, but the
15 female does not. The male will perch on a high spot, flash his red shoulder patches, and sing to other male redwing blackbirds that happen to venture into his territory. Most other males get the message and leave his territory; those that do not leave, he attacks. He will also attack a stuffed, dead male redwing blackbird in his territory, or even a small piece of red cloth. Clearly,
20 the spot of red is the characteristic that stimulates the male to defend his territory. Such key characteristics that trigger specific behavior patterns are called **sign stimuli.**

How do dogs show territoriality?

Dominance Hierarchy

25   Another way of allocating resources is by the establishment of a **dominance hierarchy,** in which a relatively stable, mutually understood order of priority within the group is maintained. A dominance hierarchy is often established in animals that form social groups. One individual in the group dominates all others. A second-ranking individual dominates all but
30 the highest-ranking individual, and so forth, until the lowest-ranking individual must give way to all others within the group. This kind of behavior is seen in barnyard chickens, where it is known as a *pecking order.*

A dominance hierarchy allows certain individuals to get preferential treatment when resources are scarce. The dominant individual will have
35 first choice of food, mates, shelter, water, and other resources because of the position occupied. Animals low in the hierarchy may fail to mate or be malnourished in times of scarcity. In many social animals, like wolves, only the dominant males and females reproduce. This ensures that the most favorable genes will be passed to the next generation. Poorly adapted
40 animals with low rank may never reproduce.

How do herd animals show dominance hierarchy?

Periods of Scarcity

Resource allocation becomes most critical during periods of scarcity. In some areas, the dry part of the year is most stressful. In temperate areas,
45 winter reduces many sources of food and forces organisms to adjust. Animals have several ways of coping with seasonal stress.

Some animals simply avoid the stress by hibernating. Hibernation is a physiological slowing of all body processes that allows an animal to survive on food it has stored within its body. Hibernation is typical of many insects,
50 bats, marmots, and some squirrels. Other animals have built-in behavior patterns that cause them to store food during seasons of plenty for periods of scarcity. These behaviors are instinctive and are seen in a variety of

animals. Squirrels bury nuts, acorns, and other seeds. (They also plant trees because they never find all the seeds they bury.) Chickadees stash seeds in
55   cracks and crevices when seeds are plentiful and spend many hours during the winter exploring similar places for food. Some of the food they find is food they stored. Honeybees store honey, which allows them to live through the winter when nectar is not available. This requires a rather complicated set of behaviors that coordinates the activities of thousands of bees in the
60   hive.

What do other creatures such as fish, birds, and wildebeests do during periods of scarcity?

Honey Navigation to Nectar

The activities of honeybees involve communication among the various
65   individuals that are foraging for nectar. The bees are able to communicate information about the direction and distance of the nectar source from the hive. If the source of nectar is some distance from the hive, the scout bee performs a "wagging dance" in the hive. The bee walks in a straight line for a short distance, wagging its rear end from side to side. It then circles
70   around back to its starting position and walks the same path as before. This dance is repeated many times. The direction of the straight-path portion of the dance indicates the direction of the nectar relative to the position of the sun. For instance, if the bee walks straight upward on a vertical surface in the hive, that tells the other bees to fly directly toward the sun. If the path is
75   thirty degrees to the right of vertical, the source of the nectar is thirty degrees to the right of the sun's position.

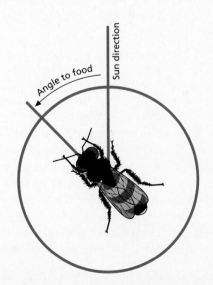

The duration of the entire dance and the number of waggles in the straight-path portion of the dance are positively correlated with the time the bee must fly to get to the nectar source. So the dance is able to
80 communicate the duration of flight as well as the direction. Since the recruited bees have picked up the scent of the nectar source from the dancer, they also have information about the kind of flower to visit when they arrive at the correct spot. Since the sun is not stationary in the sky, the bee must constantly adjust to its angle to the sun. It appears that they do
85 this with some kind of internal clock. Bees that are prevented from going to the source of nectar or from seeing the sun will still fly in the proper direction sometime later, even though the position of the sun is different.

How do the honeybees find the nectar?

Signals from Time Changes
90 The ability to sense changes in time is often used by animals to prepare for seasonal changes. In areas away from the equator, the length of the day changes as the seasons change. The length of the day is called the **photoperiod.** Many birds prepare for migration and have their migration direction determined by the changing photoperiod. For example, in the fall
95 of the year many birds instinctively change their behavior, store up fat, and begin to migrate from northern areas to areas closer to the equator. This seasonal migration allows them to avoid the harsh winter conditions signaled by the shortening of days. The return migration in the spring is triggered by the lengthening photoperiod. This migration certainly requires
100 a lot of energy, but it allows many birds to exploit temporary food resources in the north during the summer months.

What is a photoperiod?

Like honeybees, some daytime-migrating birds use the sun to guide them. We need two instruments to navigate by the sun—an accurate clock
105 and a sextant for measuring the angle between the sun and the horizon. Can a bird perform such measurements without instruments when we, with our much bigger brains, need these instruments to help us? It is unquestionably true! For nighttime migration, some birds use the stars to help them find their way. In one interesting experiment, warblers, which
110 migrate at night, were placed in a planetarium. The pattern of stars as they appear at any season could be projected onto a large domed ceiling. During autumn, when these birds would normally migrate southward, the stars of the autumn sky were shown on the ceiling.

How do birds find their way back home?

115   The birds responded with much fluttering activity at the south side of the cage, as if they were trying to migrate southward. Then the experimenters tried projecting the stars of the spring sky, even though it was autumn. Now the birds tended to try to fly northward, although there was less unity in their efforts to head north; the birds seemed somewhat

120 confused. Nevertheless, the experiment showed that the birds recognized star patterns and were influenced by them.

    In the animal world, mating is the most obviously timed event. In the Pacific Ocean, off some of the tropical islands, lives a marine worm known as the *palolo worm*. Its habit of making a well-timed brief appearance in

125 enormous swarms is a striking example of a biological-clock phenomenon. At mating time, these worms swarm into the shallows of the islands and discharge sperm and eggs. There are so many worms that the sea looks like noodle soup. The people of the islands find this an excellent time to change their diet. They dip up the worms much as North Americans dip up smelt.

Social Behavior

130   Many species of animals are characterized by interacting groups called societies, in which there is division of labor.

    Honeybees, for example, have an elaborate communication system and are specialized for specific functions. A few individuals known as *queens* and

135 *drones* specialize in reproduction, while large numbers of *worker* honeybees are involved in collecting food, defending the hive, and eating for the larvae. These roles are quite rigidly determined by inherited behavior patterns. Each worker honeybee has a specific task, and all tasks must be fulfilled for the group to survive and prosper.

140   Some societies show little specialization of individuals other than that determined by sexual differences or differences in physical size and endurance. The African wild dog illustrates such a flexible social organization. These animals are nomadic and hunt in packs. Although an individual wild dog can kill prey about its own size, groups are able to kill

145 fairly large animals if they cooperate in the chase and the kill, which often involves a chase of several kilometers. When the dogs are young, they do not follow the pack. When adults return from a successful hunt, they regurgitate food if the proper begging signal is presented to them. Therefore, the young and adults that remained behind to guard the young are fed by the hunters.

150 The young are the responsibility of the entire pack, which cooperates in their feeding and protection. During the time that the young are at the den site, the pack must give up its nomadic way of life. Therefore, the young are born during the time of year when prey are most abundant.

Stage 3: Recall

    Stop to self-test and relate. Your instructor may ask ten true-false questions to stimulate your recall.

SKILL DEVELOPMENT: NOTETAKING

Review your notes before answering the following comprehension questions.

COMPREHENSION QUESTIONS

After reading the selection, answer the following questions with *a, b, c,* or *d.*

a 1. The best statement of the main idea of this selection is that
   a. animals have a specific territory and pecking order for mating.
   b. animals engage in a variety of behavior patterns for the benefit and successful reproduction of the species.
   c. resource allocations are critical during periods of scarcity.
   d. the comparison of animal societies has led to a search for processes that shape all societies.

c 2. In the example of the male redwing blackbird, the specific trigger for territorial behavior is
   a. a red spot.
   b. a blackbird.
   c. aggressive behavior.
   d. all of the above.

c 3. A dominance hierarchy in an animal species implies all of the following except
   a. social grouping
   b. equality among workers
   c. ranking from highest to lowest
   d. mutually understood order

c 4. During hibernation animals survive on food that is
   a. growing in the wild.
   b. stored in their bodies.
   c. taken from lower-ranking animals.
   d. found by migration to areas of less seasonal stress.

c 5. In the "wagging dance" of the bee, the straight path portion of the dance indicates
   a. the direction of the nectar relative to the hive.
   b. the direction of the sun.
   c. the direction of the nectar relative to the sun's position.
   d. the distance of the hive to the nectar.

a 6. The photoperiod for a bird
   a. changes with the seasons.
   b. remains the same throughout the year.
   c. is affected by climatic changes.
   d. is longer in the northern winter than summer.

_b_ 7. Birds use all of the following to aid in migration except
   a. sun.
   b. stars.
   c. internal clock.
   d. sextant.

_b_ 8. In a honeybee society the "wagging dance" to indicate the direction of food is done by
   a. the queen.
   b. the drone.
   c. the scout bees.
   d. all members of the society.

_c_ 9. In animal species organized into societies,
   a. the parts are greater than the whole.
   b. all members reproduce.
   c. the individual is subordinated for the advantage of the group.
   d. labor is not divided or specialized.

_c_ 10. African wild dogs do all of the following except
   a. regurgitate food for the young.
   b. give up a short period of nomadic life for the young
   c. prefer individually to kill prey their own size.
   d. feed and protect the young of other dogs.

Answer the following with *T* (true) or *F* (false).

_F_ 11. Photoperiods signal birds to migrate.

_F_ 12. Pacific islanders eat the palolo worm during a certain time of the year.

_F_ 13. In a honeybee's "wagging dance," the number of waggles indicates the direction of the flower.

_T_ 14. Worker honeybees clean the cells, feed the larvae, bear the young, and build new nests.

_T_ 15. The possession of territory affects reproductive success.

VOCABULARY

According to the way the italicized word was used in the selection, select *a*, *b*, *c*, or *d* for the word or phrase that gives the best definition.

_a_ 1. "receive *sufficient* resources" (2)
   a. excessive
   b. unlimited
   c. adequate
   d. needed

_b_ 2. "reserves *exclusive* rights" (10)
   a. restricted
   b. necessary
   c. mandatory
   d. purposeful

c 3. "happen to *venture*" (16)
a. sing
b. fight
c. wander
d. hurry

b 4. "get *preferential* treatment" (33)
a. related
b. more favorable
c. hostile
d. valuable

c 5. "times of *scarcity*" (37)
a. terror
b. choice
c. flight
d. sparseness

d 6. "Chickadees *stash* seeds" (54)
a. eat
b. hide
c. supply
d. crack

a 7. "in cracks and *crevices*" (55)
a. splits in rocks
b. mountains
c. rivers
d. bluffs

d 8. "*foraging* for nectar" (65)
a. fighting
b. sucking
c. hunting
d. digging

a 9. "The *duration* of the entire dance" (77)
a. ending
b. span
c. beginning
d. organization

b 10. "are positively *correlated*" (78)
a. intersected
b. united
c. fabricated
d. related

WRITTEN RESPONSE

Use information from the text to respond to the following:
Explain and give examples of three animal behavior patterns that are tied to successful resource allocation.

Response Strategy: Define three terms, relate each to resource allocation, and give examples both in and beyond the text.

WORD BRIDGE

Dictionary

Do you have an excellent collegiate dictionary such as *Webster's New Collegiate Dictionary*? Every college student needs two dictionaries: a small one for class and a large one to keep at home. In class you may use a small paperback dictionary for quick spelling or word meaning checks. The paperback is easy to carry but does not provide the depth of information needed for college study and found in the larger collegiate editions. Good dictionaries contain not only the definitions of words, but also provide the following additional information for each word:

Guide Words. The two words at the top of each dictionary page are the first and last entries on the page. They help guide your search for a particular entry by indicating what is covered on that page.

Flagrante delicto is the first entry on the page of the dictionary on which *flamingo* appears, and *flappy* is the last entry.

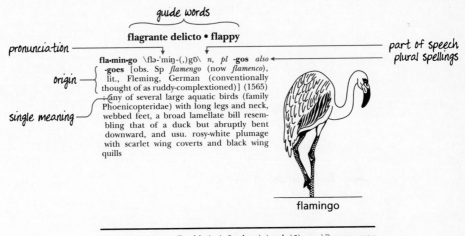

flamingo

\ə\ **abut** \ᵊ\ **kitten,** F **table** \ər\ **further** \a\ **ash** \ā\ **ace** \ä\ m**op, ma**r
\aù\ **out** \ch\ **chin** \e\ **bet** \ē\ **easy** \g\ **go** \i\ **hit** \ī\ **ice** \j\ **job**
\ŋ\ **sing** \ō\ **go** \ò\ **law** \òi\ **boy** \th\ **thin** \t̲h̲\ **the** \ü\ **loot** \ù\ **foot**
\y\ **yet** \zh\ **vision** \à, k̲, ⁿ, œ , œ̄ , ᵫ , ᵫ̄ , ᵋ\ *see* Guide to Pronunciation

By permission. From *Webster's Tenth New Collegiate Dictionary;* © 1993 by Merriam-Webster Inc., publisher of the Merriam-Webster® Dictionaries.

Pronunciation. The boldface main entry divides the word into sounds, using a dot between each syllable. In parentheses after the entry, letters and symbols show the pronunciation. A diacritical mark (') at the end of a syllable indicates stress on that syllable. A heavy mark means major stress; a lighter one shows minor stress.

A key explaining the symbols and letters appears at the bottom of the dictionary page. For example, a word like *ragweed* (rag' wēd) would be pronounced with a short *a* as in *ash* and a long *e* as in *easy.*

The *a* in *flamingo* sounds like the *a* in *abut,* and the final *o* has a long sound as in *go.* The stress is on the first syllable.

Parts of Speech. The part of speech is indicated in an abbreviation for each meaning of a word. A single word, for example, may be a noun with one definition and a verb with another. The noun *flamingo* can be used as only one part of speech, but *sideline* can be both a noun and a verb.

Spellings. Spellings are given for the plural of the word and for special forms. This is particularly useful in determining whether letters are added or

²**lemma** *n* [Gk, husk, fr. *lepein* to peel — more at LEPER] (1906) : the lower of the two bracts enclosing the flower in the spikelet of grasses

lem·ming \'le-miŋ\ *n* [Norw] (1713) : any of various small short-tailed furry-footed rodents (as genera *Lemmus* and *Dicrostonyx*) of circumpolar distribution that are notable for the recurrent mass migrations of a European form (*L. lemmus*) which often continue into the sea where vast numbers are drowned — **lem·ming·like** \-,lik\ *adj*

lem·nis·cate \lem-'nis-kət\ *n* [NL *lemniscata*, fr. fem. of L *lemniscatus* with hanging ribbons, fr. *lemniscus*] (ca. 1781) : a figure-eight shaped curve whose equation in polar coordinates is $\rho^2 = a^2 \cos 2\theta$ or $\rho^2 = a^2 \sin 2\theta$

lem·nis·cus \lem-'nis-kəs\ *n, pl* **-nis·ci** \-'nis-,ki, -,kē; -'ni-,sī\ [NL, fr. L, ribbon, fr. Gk *lēmniskos*] (ca. 1905) : a band of fibers and esp. nerve fibers — **lem·nis·cal** \-kəl\ *adj*

¹**lem·on** \'le-mən\ *n* [ME *lymon*, fr. MF *limon*, fr. ML *limon-*, *limo*, fr. Ar *laymūn*] (15c) **1 a :** an acid fruit that is botanically a many-seeded pale yellow oblong berry and is produced by a small thorny tree (*Citrus limon*) **b :** a tree that bears lemons **2 :** one (as an automobile) that is unsatisfactory or defective — **lem·ony** \'le-mə-nē\ *adj*

lemon 1: branch with fruit and flowers

²**lemon** *adj* (1598) **1 :** of the color lemon yellow **2 a :** containing lemon **b :** having the flavor or scent of lemon

lem·on·ade \,le-mə-'nād\ *n* (1604) : a beverage of sweetened lemon juice mixed with water

lemon balm *n* (ca. 1888) : a bushy perennial Old World mint (*Melissa officinalis*) often cultivated for its fragrant lemon-flavored leaves

lem·on·grass \'le-mən-,gras\ *n* (1801) : a grass (*Cymbopogon citratus*) of robust habit that grows in tropical regions, is used as an herb, and is the source of an essential oil with an odor of lemon or verbena

lemon law *n* (1982) : a law offering car buyers relief (as by repair, replacement, or refund) for defects detected during a specified period after purchase

lemon shark *n* (1942) : a medium-sized requiem shark (*Negaprion brevirostris*) of the warm Atlantic that is yellowish brown to gray above with yellow or greenish sides

lemon sole *n* (1876) : any of several flatfishes and esp. flounders: as **a :** a bottom-dwelling flounder (*Microstomus kitt*) of the northeastern Atlantic that is an important food fish **b :** WINTER FLOUNDER

lemon yellow *n* (1807) : a brilliant greenish yellow color

lem·pi·ra \lem-'pir-ə\ *n* [AmerSp, fr. *Lempira*, 16th cent. Indian chief] (ca. 1934) — see MONEY table

le·mur \'lē-mər\ *n* [NL, fr. L *lemures*, pl., ghosts] (1795) : any of various arboreal chiefly nocturnal mammals that were formerly widespread but are now largely confined to Madagascar, are related to the monkeys but are usu. regarded as constituting a distinct superfamily (Lemuroidea), and usu. have a muzzle like a fox, large eyes, very soft woolly fur, and a long furry tail

lemur

le·mu·res \'le-mə-,rās, 'lem-yə-,rēz\ *n pl* [L] (1555) : spirits of the unburied dead exorcised from homes in early Roman religious rites

lend \'lend\ *vb* **lent** \'lent\; **lend·ing** [ME *lenen*, *lenden*, fr. OE *lǣnan*, fr. *lǣn* loan — more at LOAN] *vt* (bef. 12c) **1 a :** to give for temporary use on condition that the same or its equivalent be returned **b :** to let out (money) for temporary use on condition of repayment with interest **2 a :** to give the assistance or support of : AFFORD, FURNISH ⟨a dispassionate and scholarly manner which ~*s* great force to his criticisms —*Times Lit. Supp.*⟩ **b :** to adapt or apply (oneself) readily : ACCOMMODATE ⟨a topic that ~*s* itself admirably to class discussion⟩ ~ *vi* : to make a loan ***usage*** see LOAN — **lend·able** \'len-də-bəl\ *adj* — **lend·er** *n*

lending library *n* (1708) : a library from which materials are lent; *esp* : RENTAL LIBRARY

lend–lease \'lend-'lēs\ *n* [U.S. *Lend-Lease* Act (1941)] (1941) : the transfer of goods and services to an ally to aid in a common cause with payment made by a return of the original items or their use in the cause or by a similar transfer of other goods and services — **lend–lease** *vt*

length \'leŋ(k)th, 'len(t)th\ *n, pl* **lengths** \'leŋ(k)ths, 'len(t)ths, 'leŋ(k)s\ [ME *lengthe*, fr. OE *lengthu*, fr. *lang* long] (bef. 12c) **1 a :** the longer or longest dimension of an object **b :** a measured distance or dimension ⟨10 feet in ~⟩ — see METRIC SYSTEM table, WEIGHT table **c :** the quality or state of being long **2 a :** duration or extent in time **b :** relative duration or stress of a sound **3 a :** distance or extent in space **b :** the length of something taken as a unit of measure ⟨his horse led by a ~⟩ **4 :** the degree to which something (as a course of action or a line of thought) is carried — often used in pl. ⟨went to great ~*s* to learn the truth⟩ **5 a :** a long expanse or stretch **b :** a piece constituting or usable as part of a whole or of a connected series : SECTION ⟨a ~ of pipe⟩ **6 :** a vertical dimension of an article of clothing — **at length 1 :** FULLY, COMPREHENSIVELY **2 :** at last : FINALLY

length·en \'leŋ(k)-thən, 'len(t)-\ *vb* **length·ened; length·en·ing** \'leŋ(k)th-niŋ, 'len(t)th-; 'leŋ(k)-thə-, 'len(t)-\ *vt* (14c) : to make longer ~ *vi* : to grow longer ***syn*** see EXTEND — **length·en·er** \'leŋ(k)th-nər, 'len(t)th-; 'leŋ(k)-thə-, 'len(t)-\ *n*

length·ways \'leŋ(k)th-,wāz, 'len(t)th-\ *adv* (1599) : LENGTHWISE

length·wise \-,wiz\ *adv* (ca. 1580) : in the direction of the length : LONGITUDINALLY — **lengthwise** *adj*

lengthy \'leŋ(k)-thē, 'len(t)-\ *adj* **length·i·er; -est** (1689) **1 :** protracted excessively : OVERLONG **2 :** EXTENDED, LONG — **length·i·ly** \-thə-lē\ *adv* — **length·i·ness** \-thē-nəs\ *n*

le·nience \'lē-nyən(t)s, -nē-ən(t)s\ *n* (1796) : LENIENCY

le·nien·cy \'lē-nē-ən(t)-sē, -nyən(t)-sē\ *n, pl* **-cies** (1780) **1 :** the quality or state of being lenient **2 :** a lenient disposition or practice ***syn*** see MERCY

le·nient \'lē-nē-ənt, -nyənt\ *adj* [L *lenient-*, *leniens*, prp. of *lenire* to soften, soothe, fr. *lenis* soft, mild; prob. akin to Lith *lėnas* tranquil — more at LET] (1652) **1 :** exerting a soothing or easing influence : relieving pain or stress **2 :** of mild and tolerant disposition; *esp* : INDULGENT — **le·nient·ly** *adv*

Leni–Len·a·pe *or* **Len·ni–Len·a·pe** \,le-nē-'le-nə-pē, -lə-'nä-pē\ *n* [Delaware (Unami dialects) *lə̄ni-lə̄ná·pe*] (ca. 1782) : DELAWARE 1

Le·nin·ism \'le-nə-,ni-zəm\ *n* (1918) : the political, economic, and social principles and policies advocated by Lenin; *esp* : the theory and practice of communism developed by or associated with Lenin — **Le·nin·ist** \-nist\ *n or adj* — **Le·nin·ite** \-,nit\ *n or adj*

le·nis \'lē-nəs, 'lā-\ *adj* [NL, fr. L, mild, smooth] (ca. 1897) : produced with an articulation that is lax in relation to another speech sound ⟨\t\ in *gutter* is ~, \t\ in *toe* is fortis⟩

len·i·tion \lə-'ni-shən\ *n* [L *lenire*] (1912) : the change from fortis to lenis articulation

len·i·tive \'le-nə-tiv\ *adj* [ME *lenitif*, fr. MF, fr. ML *lenitivus*, fr. L *lenitus*, pp. of *lenire*] (15c) : alleviating pain or harshness : SOOTHING — **lenitive** *n* — **len·i·tive·ly** *adv*

len·i·ty \'le-nə-tē\ *n* (1548) : the quality or state of being lenient : CLEMENCY

le·no \'lē-(,)nō\ *n* [perh. fr. F *linon* linen fabric, lawn, fr. MF *lin* flax, linen, fr. L *linum* flax] (1821) **1 :** an open weave in which pairs of warp yarns cross one another and thereby lock the filling yarn in position **2 :** a fabric made with a leno weave

¹**lens** *also* **lense** \'lenz\ *n* [NL *lent-*, *lens*, fr. L, lentil; fr. its shape] (1693) **1 a :** a piece of transparent material (as glass) that has two opposite regular surfaces either both curved or one curved and the other plane and that is used either singly or combined in an optical instrument for forming an image by focusing rays of light **b :** a combination of two or more simple lenses **c :** a piece of glass or plastic used (as in safety goggles or sunglasses) to protect the eye **2 :** a device for directing or focusing radiation other than light (as sound waves, radio microwaves, or electrons) **3 :** something shaped like a double-convex optical lens ⟨~ of sandstone⟩ **4 :** a highly transparent biconvex lens-shaped or nearly spherical body in the eye that focuses light rays (as upon the retina) — see EYE illustration **5 :** something that facilitates and influences perception, comprehension, or evaluation ⟨the author's own ~ seems blurred by bias —Seymour Topping⟩ — **lensed** \'lenzd\ *adj* — **lens·less** \'lenz-ləs\ *adj*

²**lens** *vt* (1942) : to make a motion picture of : FILM

lens·man \-mən, -,man\ *n* (1938) : PHOTOGRAPHER

Lent \'lent\ *n* [ME *lente* springtime, Lent, fr. OE *lencten*; akin to OHG *lenzin* spring] (13c) : the 40 weekdays from Ash Wednesday to Easter observed by the Roman Catholic, Eastern, and some Protestant churches as a period of penitence and fasting

len·ta·men·te \,len-tə-'men-(,)tā\ *adv or adj* [It, fr. *lento* slow] (1724) : LENTO

len·tan·do \len-'tän-(,)dō\ *adv or adj* [It] (ca. 1847) : becoming slower — used as a direction in music

Lent·en \'len-tᵊn\ *adj* (bef. 12c) : of, relating to, or suitable for Lent; *esp* : MEAGER ⟨~ fare⟩

len·tic \'len-tik\ *adj* [L *lentus* sluggish] (ca. 1938) : of, relating to, or living in still waters (as lakes, ponds, or swamps) — compare LOTIC

len·ti·cel \'len-tə-,sel\ *n* [NL *lenticella*, dim. of L *lent-*, *lens* lentil] (ca. 1864) : a loose aggregation of cells which penetrates the surface (as of a stem) of a woody plant and through which gases are exchanged between the atmosphere and the underlying tissues

len·tic·u·lar \len-'ti-kyə-lər\ *adj* [ME, fr. L *lenticularis* lentil-shaped, fr. *lenticula* lentil] (15c) **1 :** having the shape of a double-convex lens **2 :** of or relating to a lens **3 :** provided with or utilizing lenticules ⟨a ~ screen⟩

len·ti·cule \'len-tə-,kyü(ə)l\ *n* [L *lenticula*] (1942) **1 :** any of the minute lenses on the base side of a film used in stereoscopic or color photography **2 :** any of the tiny corrugations or grooves molded or embossed into the surface of a projection screen

len·til \'len-tᵊl\ *n* [ME, fr. OF *lentille*, fr. L *lenticula*, dim. of *lent-*, *lens*] (13c) **1 :** a widely cultivated Eurasian annual leguminous plant (*Lens culinaris*) with flattened edible seeds and leafy stalks used as fodder **2 :** the seed of the lentil

len·tis·si·mo \len-'ti-sə-,mō\ *adv or adj* [It, superl. of *lento*] (ca. 1903) : at a very slow tempo — used as a direction in music

len·ti·vi·rus \,len-tə-'vi-rəs\ *n* [NL, fr. L *lentus* slow + NL *virus*] (1982) : any of a group of retroviruses that cause slowly progressive often fatal animal diseases

len·to \'len-(,)tō\ *adv or adj* [It, fr. *lento*, adj., slow, fr. L *lentus* pliant, sluggish, slow — more at LITHE] (ca. 1724) : at a slow tempo — used esp. as a direction in music

Leo \'lē-(,)ō\ *n* [L (gen. *Leonis*), lit., lion — more at LION] **1 :** a northern constellation east of Cancer **2 a :** the 5th sign of the zodiac in astrology — see ZODIAC table **b :** one born under this sign — **Le·o·nine** \'lē-ə-,nin\ *adj*

le·one \lē-'ōn\ *n, pl* **leones** *or* **leone** [*Sierra Leone*] (1964) — see MONEY table

Le·o·nid \'lē-ə-nid\ *n, pl* **Leonids** *or* **Le·on·i·des** \lē-'ä-nə-,dēz\ [L *Leon-*, *Leo*; fr. their appearing to radiate from a point in Leo] (1876) : any of the meteors in a meteor shower occurring every year about November 14

le·o·nine \'lē-ə-,nin\ *adj* [ME, fr. L *leoninus*, fr. *leon-*, *leo*] (14c) : of, relating to, suggestive of, or resembling a lion

leop·ard \'le-pərd\ *n* [ME, fr. OF *leupart*, fr. LL *leopardus*, fr. Gk *leopardos*, fr. *leōn* lion + *pardos* leopard] (13c) **1 :** a large strong cat (*Panthera pardus*) of southern Asia and Africa that is adept at climbing and is usu. tawny or buff with black spots arranged in rosettes — called also *panther* **2 :** a heraldic representation of a lion passant guardant — **leop·ard·ess** \-pər-dəs\ *n*

leopard frog *n* (1839) : a common No. American frog (*Rana pipiens*) that is bright green or brown with large black white-margined blotches on the back; *also* : a similar frog (*R. sphenocephala*) of the southeastern U.S.

dropped to form the new words. The plural of *flamingo* can be spelled correctly in two different ways. Both *flamingos* and *flamingoes* are acceptable.

Origin. For many entries, the foreign word and language from which the word was derived will appear after the pronunciation. For example, *L* stands for a Latin origin and *G* for Greek. A key for the many dictionary abbreviations usually appears at the beginning of the book.

The word *flamingo* has a rich history. It is Portuguese (*Pg*) and comes from the Spanish (*fr Sp*) word *flamenco*. It is derived ultimately from the Old Provençal (*fr OProv*) *flamenc*, from *flama* for *flame*, which comes from the Latin (*fr L*) word *flamma*.

Multiple Meanings. A single word can have many shades of meaning or several completely different meanings. Different meanings are numbered.

The word *flamingo* has only one meaning. The word *sideline*, however, has several, as shown in the entry.

A sideline can be a business, a product, or a designated area. In addition, it can mean to move something out of the action.

> ¹**side·line** \-,lin\ *n* (1862) **1** : a line at right angles to a goal line or end line and marking a side of a court or field of play for athletic games **2 a** : a line of goods sold in addition to one's principal line **b** : a business or activity pursued in addition to one's regular occupation **3 a** : the space immediately outside the lines along either side of an athletic field or court **b** : a sphere of little or no participation or activity — usu. used in pl.
> ²**sideline** *vt* (1943) : to put out of action : put on the sidelines

By permission. From *Webster's Tenth New Collegiate Dictionary;* © 1993 by Merriam-Webster Inc., publisher of the Merriam-Webster® Dictionaries.

Exercise 7 USING THE DICTIONARY

Answer the following questions, using page 666 from *Webster's Tenth New Collegiate Dictionary*, with *T* (true), *F* (false), and *CT* (can't tell).

_F_   1. *Lent* is eight weekends before Easter.

_F_   2. *Lentils* can be eaten.

_T_   3. The word *lemming* is derived from the Greek word *lemmus*, which means to drown.

_T_   4. A convex *lens* lets in more light than a concave lens.

_T_   5. *Lenient* can be both an adjective and a noun.

_T_   6. The plural of *leone* can be either *leones* or *leone*.

_T_   7. One of the origins of *lemur* is the Latin word *lemures*, meaning *ghosts*.

_F_   8. The word *lemures* can be correctly pronounced in two different ways.

___T___ 9. When the words *lend* and *lease* are used together to mean a transfer of goods, no hyphen is required.

___F___ 10. A legitimate word can be formed by adding the suffix *-esque* to the first part of Leonardo da Vinci's name.

Exercise 8   USING YOUR DICTIONARY

Many students purchase small paperback abridged dictionaries and then are frustrated because they cannot find the words they want in them. Small dictionaries are very limited. College students need the range of information that appears in the following collegiate dictionaries:

The Random House Dictionary of the English Language

The American Heritage Dictionary of the English Language

Webster's New World Dictionary

Merriam Webster's Collegiate Dictionary

The Oxford American Dictionary

The Dictionary of Cultural Literacy, 2nd edition

Use your own dictionary to answer the following questions about words in this chapter.

1. *Naive* is derived from what language?

2. What is the meaning of the root word in *convalescent*?

3. Give three synonyms for *zeal*.

4. How is *flamboyant* connected with architecture?

5. What is *spontaneous combustion*?

LEARNING LOG
CHAPTER 4

Name _____

Answer the following to learn about your own learning and reflect on your progress. Your instructor may collect your responses.

Why would you tend to learn more from notetaking than from annotating?

Notetaking is in your own words annotating is not

Why is it important to indent outlined notes?

outline notes are not your main ideas

Do you prefer the Cornell notetaking system or outlining? Why?

I like Cornell notetaking because it is easier to read

When taking notes from a text, why do most students tend to write too much?

because they don't understand

When you take lecture notes, do you tend to write too much or too little? Why?

to little because when you are writing the instructor is still talking and you can miss something

Reflect on the Longer Selections

Total your short-answer responses for the three longer selections.

Comprehension scores:

completed = ⟋   # correct = ___   # incorrect = ___   accuracy = ___%

Do you continue to miss the same types of questions or different ones? Explain.

yes because it is a lot that I don't understand

Did you answer the main idea items correctly? If not, what was the problem?

I'm not sure

Did you feel that any of the questions were unclear? Explain.

no it's me not trying to get into a study habit

Did you collaborate with a classmate in answering the question? Why or why not?

no I got to busy.

Clip out and explain three questions that you missed. Attach these questions and your analysis to the Learning Log for your instructor.

Reflect on the Vocabulary

Total your vocabulary responses for the longer selections.

completed = _____   # correct = ___   # incorrect = ___   accuracy = ___%

List the words that you missed.

_____

_____

For two of the vocabulary items, list recognizable roots.

_____

_____

How many of the vocabulary items in this chapter did you already know?

_not that many_____

_____

List a word that you find difficult to remember. Explain.

_Schemata_____

_____

© 1997 Addison-Wesley Educational Publishers Inc.

Using the perforations, tear out the Learning Log for your instructor.

CHAPTER 5

Inference

What is an inference?
What is the connotation of a word?
What is figurative language?
How do you draw conclusions?

WHAT IS AN INFERENCE?

The first and most basic level of reading is the literal level, that is, what are the facts? In reacting to a literal question, you can actually point to the words on the page that answer the question. Reading, however, progresses beyond this initial stage. A second and more sophisticated level of reading deals with motives, feelings, and judgments; this is the **inferential level.** At this level you no longer can point to the answer, but instead must form the answer from suggestions within the selection. In a manner of speaking, the reader must read **between the lines** for the implied meaning.

Rather than directly stating a fact, authors often subtly suggest and thus manipulate the reader. Suggestion can be a more effective method of getting the message across than a direct statement. Suggestion requires greater writing skill, and it is also usually more artistic, creative, and entertaining. The responsible reader searches beyond the printed word for insights into what was left unsaid.

For example, in cigarette advertisements the public is enticed through suggestion, not facts, into spending millions of dollars on a product that is stated to be unhealthful. Depending on the brand, smoking offers the refreshment of a mountain stream or the sophisticated elegance of the rich and famous. Never in the ads is smoking directly praised or pleasure promised; instead, the positive aspects are *implied.* A lawsuit for false advertising is avoided because nothing tangible has been put into print. The emotionalism of the full-page advertisement is so overwhelming that the consumer hardly notices the warning peeking from the bottom of the page—"Warning: The Surgeon General Has Determined That Cigarette Smoking Is Dangerous to Your Health."

Exercise 1   IMPLIED MEANING IN ADVERTISEMENTS

Look through magazines and newspapers to locate advertisements for (1) cigarettes, (2) alcoholic beverages, and (3) fragrances. What characteristics do all three types of advertisements have in common? Select one advertisement for each product and answer the following questions about each of your three selections:

1. What is directly stated about the product?
2. What does the advertisement say about the product?
3. Who seems to be the potential customer for the product?

Authors and advertisers have not invented a new comprehension skill; they are merely capitalizing on an already highly developed skill of daily life. When asked by a coworker, "How do you like your boss?" the employee might answer, "I think she wears nice suits," rather than "I don't like my boss." A lack of approval has been suggested, whereas the employee has avoided making a direct negative statement. In everyday life, we make inferences about people by examining what people say, what they do, and what others say about them. The intuition of everyday life applied to the printed word is the inferential level of reading.

CONNOTATION OF WORDS

Notice the power of suggested meaning in responding to the following questions:

1. If you read an author's description of classmates, which student would you assume is smartest?
   a. A student annotating items on a computer printout
   b. A student with earphones listening to the radio
   c. A student talking with classmates about soap operas
2. Which would you find in a small town?
   a. Movies
   b. Cinema
   c. Picture shows
3. Who probably earns the most money?
   a. A businessperson in a dark suit, white shirt, and tie
   b. A businessperson in slacks and a sport shirt
   c. A businessperson in a pale blue uniform

Can you prove your answers? It's not the same as proving when the Declaration of Independence was signed, yet you still have a feeling for how each question should be answered. Even though a right or wrong answer is difficult to explain in this type of question, certain answers can still be defended as most accurate—they are *a, c,* and *a.* The answers are based on feelings, attitudes, and knowledge commonly shared by society.

A seemingly innocent tool, word choice is the first key to implied meaning. For example, if a person is skinny, he is unattractive, but if he is slender or slim he must be attractive. All three words might refer to the same underweight person, but *skinny* communicates a negative feeling while *slender* or *slim* communicates a positive one. This feeling or emotionalism surrounding a word is called **connotation. Denotation** is the specific meaning of a word, but the connotative meaning goes beyond this to reflect certain attitudes and prejudices of society. Even though it may not seem premeditated, writers select words, just as advertisers select symbols and models, to manipulate the reader's opinions.

Exercise 2   CONNOTATION OF WORDS

In each of the following word pairs, write the letter of the word that connotes the more positive feeling:

_____ 1. (a) guest   (b) boarder

_____ 2. (a) surplus   (b) waste

_____ 3. (a) conceited   (b) proud

_____ 4. (a) buzzard   (b) robin

_____ 5. (a) heavyset   (b) obese

_____ 6. (a) explain   (b) brag

_____ 7. (a) house   (b) mansion

_____ 8. (a) song   (b) serenade

_____ 9. (a) calculating   (b) clever

_____ 10. (a) neglected   (b) deteriorated

_____ 11. (a) colleague   (b) accomplice

_____ 12. (a) ambition   (b) greed

_____ 13. (a) kitten   (b) cat

_____ 14. (a) courageous   (b) audacious

_____ 15. (a) contrived   (b) designed

_____ 16. (a) flower   (b) orchid

_____ 17. (a) distinctive   (b) peculiar

_____ 18. (a) baby   (b) kid

_____ 19. (a) persuasion   (b) propaganda

_____ 20. (a) gold   (b) tin

_____ 21. (a) slump   (b) decline

_____ 22. (a) lie   (b) misrepresentation

_____ 23. (a) janitor   (b) custodian

_____ 24. (a) offering   (b) collection

_____ 25. (a) soldiers   (b) mercenaries

Exercise 3   CONNOTATION IN TEXTBOOKS

For each of the underlined words in the following sentences, indicate the meaning of the word and reasons why the connotation is positive or negative. Note the example.

While the unions fought mainly for better wages and hours, they also <u>championed</u> various social reforms.

Leonard Pitt, *We Americans*

championed: *Means "supported"; suggests heroes and thus a positive cause*

1. The ad was part of the oil companies' program to sell their image rather than their product to the public. In the ad they <u>boasted</u> that they were re-seeding all the disrupted areas with a newly developed grass that grows five times faster than the grass that normally occurs there.

   Robert Wallace, *Biology: The World of Life*

   boasted: _____

2. John Adams won the election, despite <u>backstage maneuvering</u> by Alexander Hamilton against him.

   James Kirby Martin et al., *America and Its People*

   backstage maneuvering: _____

3. Tinbergen, like Lorenz and von Frisch, entered retirement by continuing to work. Tinbergen was a hyperactive child who, at school, was allowed to periodically dance on his desk to let off steam. So in "<u>retirement</u>" he entered a new arena, stimulating the use of ethological methods in autism.

   Robert Wallace, *Biology: The World of Life*

   "retirement": _____

4. The nation's capital is <u>crawling</u> with lawyers, lobbyists, registered foreign agents, public relations consultants, and others—more than 14,000 individuals representing nearly 12,000 organizations at last count—all seeking to influence Congress.

   Robert Lineberry et al., *Government in America*

   crawling: _____

5. Not since Wilson had tried to <u>ram</u> the League of Nations through the Senate had any president put more on the line.

   Leonard Pitt, *We Americans*

   ram: _____

FIGURATIVE LANGUAGE

Figurative language requires readers to make inferences about comparisons that are not literally true and sometimes not logically related. What does it mean to say, "She worked like a dog"? To most readers it means that she worked hard, but since few dogs work, the comparison is not literally true or particularly logical. **Figurative language** is, in a sense, another language because it is a different way of using "regular language" words so that they take on new meaning. For example, "It was raining buckets" or "raining cats and dogs" are lively, figurative ways of describing a heavy rain. New speakers of English, however, who comprehend on a literal level, might look up in the sky for the descending pails or animals. The two expressions create an exaggerated, humorous effect, but, on the literal level, they do not make sense.

When first used, "works like a dog" and "raining cats and dogs" were probably very clever. Now the phrases have lost their freshness, but still convey meaning for those who are "in the know." Such phrases are called **idioms,** or expressions that do not make literal sense but have taken on a new generally accepted meaning over many years of use.

Examples:

She tried to *keep a stiff upper lip* during the ordeal.

His eyes were *bigger than his stomach.*

What do the following idioms mean?

make up your mind? _Don't have all day_

give me five? _hand shake_

hold a job? _go to work_

catch a cold? _put on a coat_

fitting like a glove? _tight fit_

Authors using figurative language try to move beyond familiar idioms and create original expressions. They use devices called similes, metaphors, personifications, and verbal irony to paint vivid images and to add zest, surprise, and beauty to our language. Readers may be caught off guard because such expressions are not literally true. Sophisticated readers use clues within the passage, as well as prior knowledge, to figure out meaning for these imaginative uses of language.

A **simile** is a comparison of two unlike things using the words *like* or *as*.

Examples:

The spring flower pushed up its bloom *like a lighthouse* beckoning on a gloomy night.

> And every soul, it passed me by,
> *Like the whizz* of my crossbow!
>
> Samuel Coleridge, *The Ancient Mariner*

A **metaphor** is a direct comparison of two unlike things (without using *like* or *as*).

Examples:

The corporate accountant is a computer from nine to five.

Miss Rosie was a wet brown bag of a woman who used to be the best looking gal in Georgia.

Lucille Clifton, Good Times

Personification is attributing human characteristics to nonhuman things.

Examples:

The *birds speak* from the forest.

Time marches on.

Verbal irony[1] is the use of words to express a meaning that is the opposite of what is literally said. If the intent is to hurt, the irony is called **sarcasm.**

Examples:

"What a great looking corporate outfit!" (said to someone wearing torn jeans)

"There is nothing like a sunny day for a picnic." (said to pouring rain)

Exercise 4   FIGURATIVE LANGUAGE IN TEXTBOOKS

The figurative expressions in the following sentences are underlined. Identify the figurative type, define each expression, and suggest, if possible, the reason for its use.

Example:

As a trained nurse working in the immigrant slums of New York, she knew that <u>table-top</u> abortions were common among poor women, and she had seen some of the tragic results.

Leonard Pitt, We Americans

It is a metaphor, which may now be an idiom, and means illegal. The connection suggests the reality of where the operations probably occurred.

1. The War of 1812 was Tecumseh's final test. Although his alliance was incomplete, he recognized that the war was his last chance to prevail against the

---

[1]In situational irony, events occur contrary to what is expected, as if in a cruel twist of fate. For example, Juliet awakens and finds that Romeo has killed himself because he thought she was dead.

"Long Knives," as the Americans were called. He <u>cast his lot</u> with the British, who at one point gave him command over <u>a red coat army.</u>

Leonard Pitt, We Americans

cast his lot: _____

red coat army: _____

2. Parker's wife was sitting on the front porch floor, snapping beans. Parker was sitting on the step, some distance away, watching her sullenly. She was plain, plain. The skin on her face was thin and drawn as tight <u>as the skin on an onion</u> and her eyes were grey and sharp <u>like the points of two icepicks.</u>

Flannery O'Connor, "Parker's Back"

as the skin on an onion: _____

like the points of two icepicks: _____

3. Americans "<u>discovered</u>" the Spanish Southwest in the 1820s. Yankee settlers Moses and Stephen Austin took a party of settlers into Texas in 1821.

Leonard Pitt, We Americans

"discovered": _____

4. Then she screamed an extremely fierce "I said, preach it" and stepped up on the altar. The Reverend kept on throwing out phrases <u>like home-run balls</u> and Sister Monroe made a quick break and grasped for him. For just a second, everything and everyone in the church except Reverend Taylor and Sister Monroe hung loose <u>like stockings on a washline.</u>

Maya Angelou, "Sister Monroe"

like home-run balls: _S_____

like stockings on a washline: _S_____

5. The <u>Moving Finger</u> writes; and, having writ,
Moves on; nor all <u>your Piety nor Wit</u>
Shall lure it back <u>to cancel half a Line,</u>
Nor all your <u>Tears wash out a Word of it.</u>

The Rubáiyát of Omar Khayyám

Moving Finger: _m_____

your Piety nor Wit: ————————————————————

to cancel half a Line: ————————————————————

Tears wash out a Word of it: ————————————————————

IMPLIED MEANING

Reading would be rather dull if the author stated every idea, never giving you a chance to figure things out for yourself. For example, in a mystery novel you carefully weigh each word, each action, each conversation, each description, and each fact in an effort to identify the villain and solve the crime before it is revealed at the end. Although textbook material may not have the Sherlock Holmes spirit of high adventure, authors use the same techniques to imply meaning.

Note the inferences in the following example:

Johnson in Action

Lyndon Johnson suffered from the inevitable comparison with his young and stylish predecessor. LBJ was acutely aware of his own lack of polish; he sought to surround himself with Kennedy advisers and insiders, hoping that their learning and sophistication would rub off on him. Johnson's assets were very real—an intimate knowledge of Congress, an incredible energy and determination to succeed, and a fierce ego. When a young marine officer tried to direct him to the proper helicopter, saying, "This one is yours," Johnson replied, "Son, they are all my helicopters."

LBJ's height and intensity gave him a powerful presence; he dominated any room he entered, and he delighted in using his physical power of persuasion. One Texas politician explained why he had given in to Johnson: "Lyndon got me by the lapels and put his face on top of mine and he talked and talked and talked. I figured it was either getting drowned or joining."

Robert A. Divine et al., *America Past and Present*

Answer the following with *T* (true) or *F* (false).

_____ 1. Johnson was haunted by the style and sophistication of John F. Kennedy. (True. He "suffered from the inevitable comparison," and he went so far as to maintain the Kennedy advisors.)

_____ 2. Johnson could be both egotistical and arrogant about his presidential power. (True. The anecdote about the helicopters proves that.)

_____ 3. Even if he did not mentally persuade, Johnson could physically overwhelm people into agreement.
(True. His delight in "using his physical power of persuasion" and the anecdote about the Texas politician support that.)

The following examples show how authors use suggestion. From the clues given, you can deduce the facts.

Exercise 5 INFERENCE FROM DESCRIPTION

Looking back on the Revolutionary War, one cannot say enough about Washington's leadership. While his military skills proved less than brilliant and he and his generals lost many battles, George Washington was the single most important figure of the colonial war effort. His original appointment was partly political, for the rebellion that had started in Massachusetts needed a commander from the South to give geographic balance to the cause. The choice fell to Washington, a wealthy and respectable Virginia planter with military experience dating back to the French and Indian War. He had been denied a commission in the English army and had never forgiven the English for the insult. During the war he shared the physical suffering of his men, rarely wavered on important questions, and always used his officers to good advantage. His correspondence with Congress to ask for sorely needed supplies was tireless and forceful. He recruited several new armies in a row, as short-term enlistments gave out.

Leonard Pitt, *We Americans*[2]

Answer the following with *T* (true) or *F* (false).

___F___ 1. The author regards George Washington as the most brilliant military genius in American history.

___T___ 2. A prime factor in Washington's becoming president of the United States was a need for geographic balance.

___T___ 3. Washington resented the British for a past injustice.

___T___ 4. The Revolutionary War started as a rebellion in the Northeast.

___T___ 5. The author feels that Washington's leadership was courageous and persistent even though not infallible.

Exercise 6 INFERENCE FROM ACTION

When he came to the surface he was conscious of little but the noisy water. Afterward he saw his companions in the sea. The oiler was ahead in the race. He was swimming strongly and rapidly. Off to the correspondent's left, the cook's great white and corked back bulged out of the water, and in the rear the captain was hanging with his one good hand to the keel of the overturned dinghy.

There is a certain immovable quality to a shore, and the correspondent wondered at it amid the confusion of the sea.

Stephen Crane, *The Open Boat*

[2]From Pitt, *We Americans*. Copyright © 1987 by Kendall/Hunt Publishing Company. Reprinted with permission.

Answer the following with *a, b, c,* or *d.* Draw a map indicating the shore and the positions of the four people in the water to help you visualize the scene.

____ 1. The reason that the people are in the water is because of
   a. a swimming race.
   b. an airplane crash.
   c. a capsized boat.
   d. a group decision.

____ 2. In relation to his companions, the correspondent is
   a. closest to the shore.
   b. the second or third closest to the shore.
   c. farthest from the shore.
   d. in a position that is impossible to determine.

____ 3. The member of the group that had probably suffered a previous injury is the
   a. oiler.
   b. correspondent.
   c. cook.
   d. captain.

____ 4. The member of the group that the author seems to stereotype negatively as least physically fit is the
   a. oiler.
   b. correspondent.
   c. cook.
   d. captain.

____ 5. The story is being told through the eyes of the
   a. oiler.
   b. correspondent.
   c. cook.
   d. captain.

Exercise 7   INFERENCE FROM FACTUAL MATERIAL

Except for some minor internal disturbances in the nineteenth century, Switzerland has been at peace inside stable boundaries since 1815. The basic factors underlying this long period of peace seem to have been (1) Switzerland's position as a buffer between larger powers, (2) the comparative defensibility of much of the country's terrain, (3) the relatively small value of Swiss economic production to an aggressive state, (4) the country's value as an intermediary between belligerents in wartime, and (5) Switzerland's own policy of strict and heavily armed neutrality. The difficulties which a great power might encounter in attempting to conquer Switzerland have often been popularly exaggerated since the Swiss Plateau, the heart of the country, lies open to Germany and France, and even the Alps have frequently been traversed by strong military forces in past times. On the other hand, resistance in the mountains might well be hard to thoroughly extinguish. In World War II Switzerland was able to hold a club over the head of Germany by mining the tunnels through which Swiss rail lines avoid the crests of Alpine passes. Destruction of these tunnels would have been very costly to Germany, as well as to its military partner, Italy.

Jesse H. Wheeler et al., Regional Geography of the World

Answer the following with *T* (true) or *F* (false).

_F_ 1. The author implies that Switzerland is rich with raw materials for economic production.

_F_ 2. The most important economic area of Switzerland is protected from its neighbors by the Alps.

_F_ 3. In World War II Germany did not invade Switzerland primarily because of the fear of the strong Swiss army.

_T_ 4. The maintenance of a neutral Swiss position in World War II was due in part to a kind of international blackmail.

_I_ 5. The Swiss have avoided international war on their soil for over one hundred years.

PRIOR KNOWLEDGE AND IMPLIED MEANING

Have you ever considered what makes a joke funny? Why is it no longer funny when you have to explain the meaning of a joke to someone who didn't understand it? The answer is that jokes are funny because of implied connections. The meaning that you may have to reluctantly explain is the inference or **implied meaning.** If the listener does not share the background knowledge to which the joke refers, your hilarious comic attempt will fall flat because the listener cannot understand the implied meaning. Listeners cannot connect with something they don't know, so you must choose the right joke for the right audience.

College reading may not be filled with comedy, but **prior knowledge** is expected and specifics are frequently implied rather than directly spelled out. For example, if a sentence began, "Previously wealthy investors were leaping from buildings in the financial district," you would know that the author was referring to the Stock Market Crash of 1929 on Wall Street in New York City. Although the specifics are not directly stated, you have used prior knowledge and have "added up" the details that are meaningful to you to infer time and place.

Exercise 8   INFERRING TIME AND PLACE

Read the following passages and indicate *a, b,* or *c* for the suggested time or place. Use your prior knowledge of "anchor" dates in history to logically think about the possible responses. Underline the clues that helped you arrive at your answer.

Passage A

As women strove to maintain a semblance of home on the trail, they often experienced a profound sense of loss. The Sabbath, which had been ladies' day back home and an emblem of women's moral authority, was often spent working or traveling, especially once the going got rough. "Oh dear me I did not think we would have abused the sabbath in such a manner," wrote one guilt-stricken female emigrant. Women also felt the lack of close companions, to whom they could turn for comfort. One woman, whose husband separated their wagon from the train after a dispute, sadly watched the other wagons pull away: "I felt that indeed I had left all my friends to journey over the dreaded plains without one female acquaintance even for a companion—of course I wept and grieved about it but to no purpose."

James Davidson et al., Nation of Nations

   C   1. The time when this takes place is probably in the
  a. 1920s.
  b. 1710s.
  c. 1840s.

   a   2. The section of the United States is most likely the
  a. west.
  b. south.
  c. north.

3. Underline the clues to your answers.

Passage B

There was an average of fifty storms a year. Cities kept their street lights on for twenty-four hours a day. Dust covered everything from food to bedspreads and piled up in dunes in city streets and barnyards. Thousands died of "dust pneumonia." One woman remembered what it was like at night: "A trip for water to rinse the grit from our lips, and then back to bed with washclothes over our noses, we try to lie still, because every turn stirs the dust on the blankets."

By the end of the decade three and a half million people had abandoned their farms and joined a massive migration to find a better life. Not all were forced out by the dust storms; some fell victim to large-scale agriculture, and many tenant farmers and hired hands were expendable during the depression. In most cases they not only lost their jobs, but they also were evicted from their houses.

Gary B. Nash et al., The American People

_b_____ 4. The time is probably in the
        a. 1690s.
        b. 1770s.
        c. 1930s.

_c_____ 5. The place is most likely
        a. New England.
        b. the Great Plains.
        c. the Deep South.

        6. Underline the clues to your answer.

Passage C

If natives struck whites as starkly underdressed, Europeans seemed, by the Indians' standards, grotesquely overdressed. Indeed, European fashion was ill-suited to the environment between the Chesapeake and the Caribbean. Elizabethan gentlemen strutted in silk stockings attached with garters to padded, puffed knee breeches, topped by long-sleeved shirts and tight quilted jackets called "doublets." Men of lesser status wore coarse woolen hose, canvas breeches, shirts, and fitted vests known as "jerkins"; when at work, they donned aprons of dressed leather. Women wore gowns with long, full skirts, low-cut bodices, aprons, and hosiery held up by garters. Both sexes favored long hair, and men sported mustaches and beards. Such fashions complicated life in the American environment, especially since heavy clothing and even shoes rotted rapidly from sweat and humidity. The pungent aroma of Europeans also compounded the discomfort of natives who came in contact with them. For despite sweltering heat, the whites who swaddled themselves in woolens and brocades also disdained regular bathing and regarded Indian devotion to daily washing as another uncivilized oddity.

It would have been natural for Indians to wonder why the barbaric newcomers did not adapt their dress to a new setting. The answer may be that for Europeans—entering an alien environment inhabited by peoples whom they identified as "naked savages"—the psychological risk of shedding familiar apparel was simply too great. However inappropriate or even unhealthy, heavy, elaborate dress afforded the comfort of familiarity and distinguished the "civilized" newcomer from "savage" native in America.

James Davidson et al., *Nation of Nations*

_a_____ 7. The time is probably in the early
        a. 1600s.
        b. 1200s.
        c. 1400s.

8. The place is most likely
   a. Massachusetts.
   b. Virginia.
   c. Indiana.

9. Underline the clues to your answers.

Expanding Prior Knowledge

Your responses on these passages depends on your previous knowledge of history and your general knowledge. If you did not understand many of the inferences, you might ask, "How can I expand my prior knowledge?" The answer is not an easy formula or a quick fix. The answer is part of the reason that you are in college; it is a combination of broadening your horizons, reading more widely, and being an active participant in your own life. Expanding prior knowledge is a slow and steady daily process.

DRAWING CONCLUSIONS

To arrive at a conclusion, the reader must make a logical deduction from both stated and unstated ideas. Using the hints as well as the facts, the reader relies on prior knowledge and experience to interpret motives, actions, and outcomes. Conclusions are drawn on the basis of perceived evidence, and because perceptions differ, conclusions can vary from reader to reader. Generally, however, the author attempts to direct the reader to a preconceived conclusion. Read the following example and look for a basis for the stated conclusion.

Underground Conductor

Harriet Tubman was on a northbound train when she overheard her name spoken by a white passenger. He was reading aloud an ad which accused her of stealing $50,000 worth of property in slaves, and which offered a $5000 reward for her capture. She lowered her head so that the sunbonnet she was wearing hid her face. At the next station she slipped off the train and boarded another that was headed south, reasoning that no one would pay attention to a black woman traveling in that direction. She deserted the second train near her hometown in Maryland and bought two chickens as pat of her disguise. With her back hunched over in imitation of an old woman, she drove the chickens down the dusty road, calling angrily and chasing them with her stick whenever she sensed danger. In this manner Harriet Tubman was passed by her former owner who did not even notice her. The reward continued to mount until it reached $40,000.

Leonard Pitt, *We Americans*

Conclusion: Harriet Tubman was a clever woman who became a severe irritant to white slave owners.

What is the basis for this conclusion?

That now matter who you are you cane overcome anythiy or anyone.

(Her disguise and subsequent escape from the train station provide evidence for her intelligence. The escalating amount of the reward, finally $40,000, proves the severity of the sentiment against her.)

Exercise 9   DRAWING CONCLUSIONS

Read the following passages. For the first two passages indicate evidence for the conclusions that have been drawn. For the latter passages, write your own conclusion, as well as indicate evidence.

Passage A

A tragic counterpoint to the voluntary movement of American workers in search of jobs was the forced relocation of 120,000 Japanese-Americans from the West Coast. Responding to racial fears in California after Pearl Harbor, President Roosevelt approved an army order in February 1942 to move both the Issei (Japanese-Americans who had emigrated from Japan) and the Nisei (people of Japanese ancestry born in the United States and therefore American citizens) to concentration camps in the interior. Forced to sell their farms and businesses at distress prices, the Japanese-Americans lost not only their liberty but also most of their worldly goods. Herded into ten hastily built detention centers in seven western states, they lived as prisoners in tar-papered barracks behind barbed wire, guarded by armed troops.

Robert Divine et al., *America Past and Present*

Conclusion: After Pearl Harbor many Japanese-Americans were treated unfairly by the American government.

What is the basis for this conclusion?

Pearl Harbor will go down in history

Passage B

Pesticides are biologically rather interesting substances. They have no known counterpart in the natural world, and most of them didn't even exist thirty years ago. Today, however, a metabolic product of DDT, called DDE, may be the most common and widely distributed man-made chemical on earth. It has been found in the tissues of living things from the polar regions to the remotest parts of the oceans, forests, and mountains. Although the permissible level of DDT in cow's milk, set by the U.S. Food and Drug Administration, is 0.05 parts per million, it often occurs in human milk in concentrations as high as 5 parts per million and in human fat at levels of more than 12 parts per million.

Robert Wallace, Biology: The World of Life

Conclusion: DDT accumulates in the environment far beyond the areas where it was directly applied.

What is the basis for this conclusion?

_____

_____

Passage C

Reagan had a pleasing manner and a special skill as a media communicator. Relying on lessons learned in his acting days, he used television as Franklin Roosevelt had used radio in the 1930s. In prepared television speeches, or when chatting with reporters, he appeared like a trusted uncle who talked in soothing terms about concerns everyone shared. He was a gifted storyteller, who loved using anecdotes or one-liners to make his point.

For much of his presidency, Reagan enjoyed enormous popularity. People talked about a "Teflon" presidency—criticisms fell way, and disagreements over policy never diminished his personal approval ratings. As he left office, 68 percent of the American public approved of his performance over the past eight years, the highest rating for any president at the end of his term since World War II.

Gary B. Nash et al., The American People

Conclusion: _____

_____

What is the basis for this conclusion?

_____

Passage D

Panic attacks are not common, but they can be very debilitating for those who suffer them. They consist of sudden, irrational feelings of doom, sometimes accompanied by choking, sweating, and heart palpitations.

In an experiment conducted at NIMH laboratories in Maryland, a group of people who had previously suffered panic attacks were given 480 mg caffeine, equivalent to about 5 cups of brewed coffee. Panic attacks were precipitated in almost half of those people. In a group of 14 people who had never before experienced a panic attack, two suffered an attack after receiving 720 mg caffeine.

Oakley Ray and Charles Ksir, Drugs, Society, & Human Behavior

Conclusion: _____

_____

What is the basis for this conclusion? _____

_____

Exercise 10 BUILDING A STORY WITH INFERENCES

The following story unfolds as the reader uses the clues to predict and make inferences. To make sense out of the story, the reader is never told—but must figure out—who the main character is, what he is doing, and why he is doing it. Like a mystery, the story is fun to read because you are actively involved. Use your inferential skills to figure it out.

Caged

Emphatically, Mr. Purcell did not believe in ghosts. Nevertheless, the man who bought the two doves, and his strange act immediately thereafter, left him with a distinct sense of the eerie.

Purcell was a small, fussy man; red cheeks and a tight, melon stomach. He owned a pet shop. He sold cats and dogs and monkeys; he dealt in fish food and bird seed, and prescribed remedies for ailing canaries. He considered himself something of a professional man.

There was a bell over the door that jangled whenever a customer entered. This morning, however, for the first time Mr. Purcell could recall, it failed to ring. Simply he glanced up, and there was the stranger, standing just inside the door, as if he had materialized out of thin air.

The storekeeper slid off his stool. From the first instant he knew instinctively, unreasonably, that the man hated him; but out of habit he rubbed his hands briskly together, smiled and nodded.

"Good morning," he beamed. "What can I do for you?"

The man's shiny shoes squeaked forward. His suit was cheap, ill-fitting, but obviously new. A gray pallor deadened his pinched features. He had a shuttling glance and close-cropped hair. He stared closely at Purcell and said, "I want something in a cage."

"Something in a cage?" Mr. Purcell was a bit confused. "You mean—some kind of pet?"

"I mean what I said!" snapped the man. "Something alive that's in a cage."

"I see," hastened the storekeeper, not at all certain that he did. "Now let me think. A white rat, perhaps."

"No!" said the man. "Not rats. Something with wings. Something that flies."

"A bird!" exclaimed Mr. Purcell.

"A bird's all right." The customer pointed suddenly to a suspended cage which contained two snowy birds. "Doves? How much for those?"

"Five-fifty. And a very reasonable price."

"Five-fifty?" The sallow man was obviously crestfallen. He hesitantly produced a five-dollar bill. "I'd like to have those birds. But this is all I got. Just five dollars."

Mentally, Mr. Purcell made a quick calculation, which told him that at a fifty-cent reduction he could still reap a tidy profit. He smiled magnanimously. "My dear man, if you want them that badly, you can certainly have them for five dollars."

"I'll take them." He laid his five dollars on the counter. Mr. Purcell teetered on tiptoe, unhooked the cage, and handed it to his customer. The man cocked his head to one side, listening to the constant chittering, the rushing scurry of the shop. "That noise?" he blurted. "Doesn't it get you? I mean all this caged stuff. Drives you crazy, doesn't it?"

Purcell drew back. Either the man was insane, or drunk.

"Listen." The staring eyes came closer. "How long d'you think it took me to make that five dollars?"

The merchant wanted to order him out of the shop. But he heard himself dutifully asking, "Why—why, how long *did* it take you?"

The other laughed. "Ten years! At hard labor. Ten years to earn five dollars. Fifty cents a year."

It was best, Purcell decided, to humor him. "My, my! Ten years—"

"They give you five dollars," laughed the man, "and a cheap suit, and tell you not to get caught again."

Mr. Purcell mopped his sweating brow. "Now, about the care and feeding of—"

"Bah!" The sallow man swung around, and stalked abruptly from the store.

Purcell sighed with sudden relief. He waddled to the window and stared out. Just outside, his peculiar customer had halted. He was holding the cage shoulder-high, staring at his purchase. Then, opening the cage, he reached inside and drew out one of the doves. He tossed it into the air. He drew out the second and tossed it after the first. They rose like wind-blown balls of fluff and were lost in the smoky grey of the wintry city. For an instant the liberator's silent and lifted gaze watched after them. Then he dropped the cage. A futile, suddenly forlorn figure, he shoved both hands deep in his trouser pockets, hunched down his head and shuffled away. . . .

The merchant's brow was puckered with perplexity. "Now why," Mr. Purcell muttered, "did he do that?" He felt vaguely insulted.

Lloyd Eric Reeve, *Household Magazine*

1. Where had the man been?

2. How do you know for sure? Underline the clues.

3. When did you figure it out? Circle the clincher.

4. Why does he want to set the birds free? *Because he just became free*

5. Why should the shopkeeper feel insulted? *Because he thought the stranger was insane. But he just released from prison.*

6. After freeing the birds, why is the stranger "a futile, suddenly forlorn figure," rather than happy and excited? *because he had to go back*

SUMMARY POINTS

- The inferential level of reading deals with motives, feelings, and judgments. The reader must read between the lines and look for the implied meaning in words and actions.
- The author's choice of words can manipulate the reader. The feeling or emotionalism surrounding a word is its connotation. The connotation of a word reflects certain attitudes and prejudices of society that can be positive or negative.
- Figurative language creates images to suggest attitudes. It is a different way of using "regular language" words so that the words take on a new meaning.
- A simile is a comparison of two unlike things using the words *like* or *as*, whereas a metaphor is a directly stated comparison.
- Personification attributes human characteristics to nonhuman things.
- Verbal irony expresses a meaning the opposite of what is literally said.
- Readers use implied meaning to draw conclusions.
- Based on hints, facts, and prior knowledge, readers interpret motives, actions, and outcomes.
- Suggested meaning is powerful and can be a more effective method of getting the message across than a direct statement.

SELECTION 1

LITERATURE

Stage 1: Skill Development

Preview

The author's main purpose is to tell a story.

agree ☑   disagree ☐

This selection is narrative rather than expository.

agree ☑   disagree ☐

After reading this, I will need to explain a theory.

agree ☑   disagree ☐

Activate Schema

Have you read another short story by de Maupassant entitled "The Necklace"? no

Learning Strategy

Use the action and the characters to develop a conclusion or a theme about human qualities.

Word Knowledge

Are you familiar with the following words in this selection?

cherish	prerogative
unappeased	atrocious
foraging	bellicose
wiry	devoured
ferocious	reprisal

Your instructor may ask ten true-false questions from the *Instructor's Manual* to stimulate your thinking using these words.

Stage 2: Integrate Knowledge While Reading

Use the thinking strategies as you read.
1. Predict   2. Picture   3. Relate   4. Monitor   5. Fix up

Mother Savage

From Guy de Maupassant, *Mademoiselle Fifi and Other Stories*

I had not been back to Virelogne for fifteen years. I returned there to do some shooting in the autumn, staying with my friend Serval, who had finally rebuilt his château, which had been destroyed by the Prussians.

I was terribly fond of that part of the country. There are some
5   delightful places in this world which have a sensual charm for the eyes. One loves them with a physical love. We people who are attracted by the countryside cherish fond memories of certain springs, certain woods,

certain ponds, certain hills, which have become familiar sights and can
touch our hearts like happy events. Sometimes indeed the memory goes
10   back towards a forest glade, or a spot on a river bank, or an orchard in
blossom, glimpsed only once on a happy day, but preserved in our heart like
those pictures of women seen in the street on a spring morning, wearing
gay, flimsy dresses, and which leave in our soul and flesh an unappeased,
unforgettable desire, the feeling that happiness has passed us by.

15   At Virelogne I loved the whole region, scattered with little woods and
crossed by streams which ran through the ground like veins carrying blood
to the earth. We fished in them for crayfish, trout and eels. What heavenly
happiness we knew there! There were certain places where we could bathe,
and we often found snipe in the tall grass which grew on the banks of those
20   narrow brooks.

I walked along, as light-footed as a goat, watching my two dogs foraging
ahead of me. Serval, a hundred yards to my right, was beating a field of
lucerne. I went round the bushes which mark the edge of Saudres woods,
and I noticed a cottage in ruins.

25   All of a sudden I remembered it as it had been the last time I had seen
it, in 1869, neat, covered with vines, with chickens outside the door. What is
sadder than a dead house, with nothing left standing but its skeleton, a
sinister ruin?

I remembered too that a woman had given me a glass of wine inside the
30   house, one day when I was very tired, and that afterwards Serval had told
me the story of the occupants. The father, an old poacher, had been killed
by the gendarmes. The son, whom I had seen before, was a tall, wiry fellow
who was likewise supposed to be a ferocious killer of game. People called
the family the Savages.

35   Was it a name or a nickname?

I called out to Serval. He came over to me with his long lanky stride. I
asked him: 'What has become of the people who lived here?'

And he told me this story.

'When war was declared, the younger Savage, who was then thirty-three
40   years old, enlisted, leaving his mother alone at home. People didn't feel too
sorry for the old woman, though, because they knew she had money.

'So she stayed all alone in this isolated house, far away from the village,
on the edge of the woods. But she wasn't afraid, because she was made of
the same stuff as her men, a tough, tall, thin old woman, who didn't laugh
45   very often and whom nobody joked with. Country women don't laugh much
anyway. That's the men's business! They have sad, narrow souls, because they
lead dull, dreary lives. The peasant learns a little noisy gaiety in the tavern,
but his wife remains serious, forever wearing a stern expression. The muscles
of her face have never learnt the motions of laughter.

50   'Mother Savage continued to lead her usual life in her cottage, which
was soon covered with snow. She came to the village once a week to get

bread and a little meat; then she returned to her cottage. As there was talk of wolves in the region, she went out with a gun slung over her shoulder, her son's gun, which was rusty, with the butt worn down by the rubbing of
55 the hand. She was a strange sight, the Savage woman, tall, rather bent, striding slowly through the snow, with the barrel of the gun showing above the tight black head-dress which imprisoned the white hair nobody had ever seen.

'One day the Prussians arrived. They were distributed among the local
60 inhabitants according to the means and resources of each. The old woman, who was known to be well off, had four soldiers billeted on her.

'They were four big young fellows with fair skins, fair beards and blue eyes, who had remained quite plump in spite of the hardships they had already endured, and good-natured even though they were in conquered
65 territory. Alone with that old woman, they showed her every consideration, sparing her fatigue and expense as best they could. All four were to be seen washing at the well every morning in their shirt-sleeves, splashing water, in the cold glare of the snow, over their pink and white flesh, the flesh of men of the north, while Mother Savage went to and fro, cooking their soup.
70 They could then be seen cleaning the kitchen, polishing the floor, chopping wood, peeling potatoes, washing the linen, and doing all the household jobs, just like four good sons helping their mother.

'But the old woman kept thinking all the time about her own son, her tall thin boy with his hooked nose, his brown eyes, and the bushy moustache
75 which covered his upper lip with a roll of black hair. Every day she asked each of the soldiers sitting around her hearth: "Do you know where the French regiment has gone—the Twenty-third Infantry? My boy is in it."

'They would reply: "No, we don't know. We have no idea."

'And, understanding her grief and anxiety, they, who had mothers of
80 their own at home, performed countless little services for her. She for her part was quite fond of her four enemies, for peasants scarcely ever feel patriotic hatred: that is the prerogative of the upper classes. The humble, those who pay the most because they are poor and because every new burden weighs heavily on them, those who are killed in droves, who form
85 the real cannon-fodder because they are the most numerous, who, in a word, suffer the most from the atrocious hardships of war because they are the weakest and most vulnerable, find it hard to understand those bellicose impulses, those touchy points of honour and those so-called political manoeuvres which exhaust two nations within six months, the victor as well
90 as the vanquished.

'The people around here, speaking of Mother Savage's Germans, used to say: "Those four have found a cosy billet, and no mistake."

'Now, one morning, when the old woman was alone in the house, she caught sight of a man a long way off on the plain coming towards her home.
95 Soon she recognized him: it was the man whose job it was to deliver letters.

He handed her a folded piece of paper, and she took the spectacles she used for sewing out of their case. Then she read:

> Madame Savage, this is to give you some sad news. Your son Victor was killed yesterday by a cannon-ball which pretty well cut him in two. I was very close, seeing as we were side by side in the company, and he had asked me to let you know if anything happened to him.
>
> I took his watch out of his pocket to bring it back to you when the war is over.
>
> Best regards.
>
> CÉSAIRE RIVOT,
> Private in the 23rd Infantry.

'The letter was dated three weeks earlier.

'She didn't cry. She stood stock still, so shocked and dazed that she didn't even feel any grief yet. She thought to herself: "Now it's Victor who's gone and got killed." Then, little by little, the tears came into her eyes and grief flooded into her heart. Ideas occurred to her one by one, horrible, agonizing ideas. She would never kiss him again, her big boy, never! The gendarmes had killed the father, the Prussians had killed the son. He had been cut in two by a cannon-ball. And it seemed to her that she could see the horrible thing happening: the head falling, the eyes wide open, while he was chewing the end of his bushy moustache as he always did when he was angry.

'What had they done with his body afterwards? If only they had sent her boy back to her, as they had sent back her husband, with the bullet in the middle of his forehead!

'But then she heard the sound of voices. It was the Prussians coming back from the village. She quickly hid the letter in her pocket and, having had time to wipe her eyes, greeted them calmly, looking her usual self.

'All four of them were laughing with delight, for they had brought back a fine rabbit, which had probably been stolen, and they made signs to the old woman that they were going to eat something good.

'She set to work straight away getting dinner ready, but when it came to killing the rabbit, her heart failed her. And it wasn't the first by any means! One of the soldiers had to kill it with a punch behind the ears.

'Once the animal was dead she stripped the skin from the red body; but the sight of the blood which she was touching, which covered her hands, the warm blood which she could feel growing cold and congealing, made her tremble from head to foot; and she kept seeing her big boy cut in two and red all over, like the animal still quivering in her hands.

'She sat down to table with her Prussians, but she couldn't eat, not so much as a mouthful. They devoured the rabbit without bothering about her. She watched them on the sly, without speaking, thinking over an idea, her face so expressionless that they noticed nothing.

140 'Suddenly she said: "We've been together a whole month now and I don't even know your names."

'They understood, not without some difficulty, what she wanted, and gave her their names. But that wasn't enough: she got them to write them down for her on a piece of paper, with the addresses of their families; and,

145 setting her spectacles on her big nose, she inspected the unfamiliar script and then folded the sheet of paper and put it in her pocket, with the letter which had told her of the death of her son.

'When the meal was over, she said to the men: "I'm going to do some work for you."

'And she started taking straw up to the loft in which they slept.

150 'They were puzzled by what she was doing. She explained to them that the straw would keep them warmer, and they gave her a helping hand. They piled the bundles of straw up to the roof and thus made themselves a sort of big, warm, sweet-smelling room with four walls of forage, where they would sleep wonderfully well.

155 'At supper one of them was upset to see that Mother Savage didn't eat anything again. She said that she was suffering from cramps. Then she lit a good fire to warm herself, and the four Germans climbed up to their room by the ladder which they used every evening.

'As soon as the trap-door was closed, the old woman took away the

160 ladder. Then she quietly opened the outside door and went out to fetch some more bundles of straw with which she filled the kitchen. She walked barefoot in the snow, moving so quietly that the men heard nothing. Every now and then she listened to the loud, uneven snores of the four sleeping soldiers.

165 'When she decided her preparations were sufficient, she threw one of the bundles of straw into the hearth, and when it had caught fire she scattered it over the others. Then she went outside and watched.

'Within a few seconds a blinding glare lit up the whole inside of the cottage. Then it became a fearful brazier, a gigantic furnace, the light of

170 which shone through the narrow window and fell on the snow in a dazzling ray.

'Then a great cry came from the top of the house, followed by a clamour of human screams, of heartrending shrieks of anguish and terror. Then, as the trap-door collapsed inside the cottage, a whirlwind of fire shot

175 into the loft, pierced the thatched roof, and rose into the sky like the flame of a huge torch; and the whole cottage went up in flames.

'Nothing more could be heard inside but the crackling of the flames, the crumbling of the walls and the crashing of the beams. All of a sudden the roof fell in, and the glowing carcass of the house was hurled up into the

180 air amid a cloud of smoke, a great fountain of sparks.

'The white countryside, lit up by fire, glistened like a cloth of silver tinted with red.

'In the distance a bell began ringing.

'Old Mother Savage remained standing in front of her burnt-out home, armed with her gun, her son's gun, for fear that one of the men should escape.

'When she saw that it was all over, she threw the weapon in the fire. An explosion rang out.

'People came running up, peasants and Prussians.

'They found the woman sitting on a tree trunk, calm and satisfied.

'A German officer, who spoke French like a Frenchman, asked her: "Where are your soldiers?"

'She stretched out her thin arm towards the red heap of the dying fire, and replied in a loud voice: "In there!"

'They crowded around her. The Prussian asked: "How did the fire break out?"

'"I started it," she said.

'They didn't believe her, thinking that the disaster had driven her mad all of a sudden. So, as everyone gathered around her to listen to her, she told the story from beginning to end, from the arrival of the letter to the last screams of the men who had been burnt with her house. She didn't leave out a single detail of what she had felt or of what she had done.

'When she had finished, she took two pieces of paper out of her pocket, and, in order to tell them apart, put on her spectacles again. Then, showing one of them, she said: "This one is Victor's death."

'Showing the other, and nodding in the direction of the red ruins, she added: "This one is their names so as you can write to their families."

'She calmly held out the white sheet of paper to the officer, who was holding her by the shoulders, and went on: "You must write to say what happened, and tell their parents that it was me that did it. Victoire Simon, the Savage woman! Don't forget."

'The officer shouted out some orders in German. She was seized and pushed against the walls of the house, which were still warm. Then twelve men lined up quickly facing her, at a distance of twenty yards. She didn't budge. She had understood, and stood there waiting.

'An order rang out, followed straight away by a long volley. A late shot went off by itself, after the others.

'The old woman didn't fall. She collapsed as if her legs had been chopped off.

'The Prussian officer came over to her. She had been practically cut in two, and in her hand she was clutching her letter soaked in blood.'

My friend Serval added: 'It was by way of a reprisal that the Germans destroyed the local château, which belonged to me.'

I for my part was thinking of the mothers of the four gentle boys burnt

225   in there, and of the fearful heroism of that other mother, shot against that wall.

And I picked up a little stone, still blackened by the fire.

Stage 3: Recall

Stop to self-test and relate. Your instructor may ask five true-false questions to stimulate your recall.

SKILL DEVELOPMENT: IMPLIED MEANING

According to the implied meaning in the selection answer the following with *T* (true) or *F* (false).

  _T_   1. The author begins the story by painting a picture to appeal to the reader's senses.

  _T_   2. The story suggests that the pain of war spreads beyond the battle-ground.

  _T_   3. The phrase, "fond memories . . . which have become familiar sights and can touch our hearts like happy events," contains personification.

  _F_   4. The phrase, "streams which ran through the ground like veins carrying blood to the earth," contains a simile.

  _T_   5. Mother Savage treated the soldiers kindly in the beginning because she knew she would kill them in the end.

COMPREHENSION QUESTIONS

After reading the selection, answer the following questions with *a, b, c,* or *d.*

  _a_   1. The best statement of the main idea of this selection is
      a. soldiers pillage the land during war.
      b. family members must become soldiers during war.
      c. a mother takes revenge over the loss of her son.
      d. a mother's love is stronger than a patriotic bond.

  _a_   2. The reader can conclude that the setting for this story is
      a. England.
      b. France.
      c. Spain.
      d. Prussia.

___q___ 3. Serval had to rebuild his house because of
   a. Prussian revenge.
   b. a military battle.
   c. an accidental fire.
   d. smoke and fire damage from the Savage house.

___q___ 4. Serval feels that "country women"
   a. work too hard.
   b. never learn to laugh.
   c. are better at business than men.
   d. spend more time in pubs than men.

___a___ 5. The author suggests that Mother Savage's treatment of the soldiers before the fire was regarded by her neighbors as
   a. comfortable.
   b. insensitive.
   c. cruel.
   d. humorous.

___b___ 6. The author suggests that the ones who suffer the most hardships from war are
   a. the upper class.
   b. the peasants.
   c. politicians.
   d. those who feel the most patriotic hatred.

___c___ 7. The author suggests that the four soldiers treated Mother Savage with
   a. hatred.
   b. ridicule.
   c. respect.
   d. laughter.

___d___ 8. The author suggests that Mother Savage put the straw in the loft in order to
   a. make the soldiers more comfortable.
   b. turn suspicion away from her actions.
   c. fuel the fire.
   d. make them warmer.

___a___ 9. The author suggests that Mother Savage
   a. was the first person the soldiers suspected of setting the fire.
   b. might have gone free if she had remained silent.
   c. wanted to lie about the fire.
   d. did not understand the consequences of what she had done.

___b___ 10. Mother Savage wanted the addresses of the soldiers primarily because
   a. she wanted to show the police that she had planned the murders.
   b. they had been kind to her.
   c. the commander did not know the names of the soldiers.
   d. she wanted their mothers to feel the same pain she had felt.

Answer the following with *T* (true) or *F* (false).

T 11. The "I" in the story remembers Mother Savage for her kindness to him.

T 12. Mother Savage's husband had been killed in a previous war.

F 13. Mother Savage was forced to house more soldiers than others because of her money.

F 14. The soldiers did little to help Mother Savage with the daily chores.

T 15. The rabbit reminded Mother Savage of her son.

VOCABULARY

According to the way the italicized word was used in the selection, select *a, b, c,* or *d* for the word or phrase that gives the best definition.

d 1. "*cherish* fond memories" (7)
   a. choose
   b. relive
   c. glorify
   d. treasure

b 2. "*unappeased,* unforgettable desire" (13)
   a. sick
   b. unsatisfied
   c. selfish
   d. unnatural

b 3. "*foraging* ahead of me" (21)
   a. searching
   b. walking
   c. running
   d. barking

d 4. "tall, *wiry* fellow" (32)
   a. angry
   b. evil
   c. tense
   d. lanky

a 5. "*ferocious* killer of game" (33)
   a. fierce
   b. steady
   c. untrustworthy
   d. sneaky

c 6. "*prerogative* of the upper class" (82)
   a. curse
   b. fate
   c. privilege
   d. feeling

b 7. "*atrocious* hardships of war" (86)
   a. real
   b. horrible
   c. unavoidable
   d. shared

d 8. "*bellicose* impulses" (87)
   a. sudden
   b. quick
   c. calculated
   d. warlike

_a_   9. "*devoured* the rabbit" (136)
      a. removed
      b. gobbled
      c. cooked
      d. cut

_b_   10. "by way of a *reprisal*" (222)
      a. retaliation
      b. excuse
      c. resolution
      d. solution

WRITTEN RESPONSE

Use the information from the text and your own ideas to answer the following question:

Why did Mother Savage treat the soldiers as she did, both in the beginning and in the end?

ESSAY

Stage 1: Skill Development

Preview

The author's main purpose is to change the school system.

      agree ☑   disagree ☐

The overall pattern of organization is definition-example.

      agree ☑   disagree ☐

After reading this selection, I will need to explain how to teach Spanish.

      agree ☐   disagree ☐

Activate Schema

How do parents who speak English as a second language keep their first language alive for their children?

What is the national debate about English Only or English Plus?

Learning Strategy

Read to understand what the author means by a public and a private language.

Word Knowledge

Are you familiar with the following words in this selection?

congruity   profound   garbled

tact   pried   menial

accentuated   effusive   —myth

—trivial

Your instructor may ask ten true-false questions from the *Instructor's Manual* to stimulate your thinking using these words.

Stage 2: Integrate Knowledge While Reading

Use the thinking strategies as you read:
1. **Predict**   2. **Picture**   3. **Relate**   4. **Monitor**   5. **Fix up**

Bilingual Education
From Richard Rodriguez, *Hunger of Memory*

I remember, to start with, that day in Sacramento, in a California now nearly thirty years past, when I first entered a classroom—able to understand about fifty stray English words. The third of four children, I had been preceded by my older brother and sister to a neighborhood Roman
5   Catholic school. But neither of them had revealed very much about their classroom experiences. They left each morning and returned each afternoon, always together, speaking Spanish as they climbed the five steps to the porch. And their mysterious books, wrapped in brown shopping-bag paper, remained on the table next to the door, closed firmly behind them.
10   An accident of geography sent me to a school where all my classmates were white and many were the children of doctors and lawyers and business executives. On that first day of school, my classmates must certainly have been uneasy to find themselves apart from their families, in the first institution of their lives. But I was astonished. I was fated to be the "problem
15   student" in class.
The nun said, in a friendly but oddly impersonal voice: "Boys and girls, this is Richard Rodriguez." (I heard her sound it out: *Rich-heard Road-ree-guess.*) It was the first time I had heard anyone say my name in English. "Richard," the nun repeated more slowly, writing my name down in her
20   book. Quickly I turned to see my mother's face dissolve in a watery blur behind the pebbled-glass door.

Supporters of Bilingual Education

Now, many years later, I hear of something called "bilingual education"—a scheme proposed in the late 1960s by Hispanic-American social activists, later endorsed by a congressional vote. It is a program that seeks to permit non–English-speaking children (many from lower class homes) to use their "family language" as the language of school. Such, at least, is the aim its supporters announce. I hear them, and am forced to say no: It is not possible for a child, any child, ever to use his family's language in school. Not to understand this is to misunderstand the public uses of schooling and to trivialize the nature of intimate life.

Supporters of bilingual education today imply that students like me miss a great deal by not being taught in their family's language. What they seem not to recognize is that, as a socially disadvantaged child, I considered Spanish to be a private language. What I needed to learn in school was that I had the right—and the obligation—to speak the public language of *los gringos*.

My Education

Without question, it would have pleased me to hear my teachers address me in Spanish when I entered the classroom. I would have felt much less afraid. I would have trusted them and responded with ease. But I would have delayed—for how long postponed?—having to learn the language of public society. I would have evaded—and for how long could I have afforded to delay?—learning the great lesson of school, that I had a public identity.

Fortunately, my teachers were unsentimental about their responsibility. What they understood was that I needed to speak a public language. So their voices would search me out, asking me questions. Each time I'd hear them, I'd look up in surprise to see a nun's face frowning at me. I'd mumble, not really meaning to answer. The nun would persist, "Richard, stand up. Don't look at the floor. Speak up. Speak to the entire class, not just to me!" But I couldn't believe that the English language was mine to use.

Three months. Five. Half a year passed. Unsmiling, ever watchful, my teachers noted my silence. They began to connect my behavior with the difficult progress my older sister and brother were making. Until one Saturday morning three nuns arrived at the house to talk to our parents. Stiffly, they sat on the blue living room sofa. From the doorway of another room, spying the visitors, I noted the incongruity—the clash of two worlds, the faces and voices of school intruding upon the familiar setting of home. I overheard one voice gently wondering, "Do your children speak only Spanish at home, Mrs. Rodriguez?" While another voice added, "That Richard especially seems so timid and shy."

That Rich-heard!

With great tact the visitors continued, "Is it possible for you and your

© 1997 Addison-Wesley Educational Publishers Inc.

65 husband to encourage your children to practice their English when they are home?" Of course, my parents complied. What would they not do for their children's well-being? And how could they have questioned the Church's authority which those women represented? In an instant, they agreed to give up the language (the sounds) that had revealed and accentuated our

70 family's closeness. The moment after the visitors left, the change was observed. "*Ahora,* speak to us *en inglés,*" my father and mother united to tell us.

English at Home

At first, it seemed a kind of game. After dinner each night, the family

75 gathered to practice "our" English. (It was still then *inglés,* a language foreign to us, so we felt drawn as strangers to it.) Laughing, we would try to define words we could not pronounce. We played with strange English sounds, often overanglicizing our pronunciations. And we filled the smiling gaps of our sentences with familiar Spanish sounds. But that was cheating,

80 somebody shouted. Everyone laughed. In school, meanwhile, like my brother and sister, I was required to attend a daily tutoring session. I needed a full year of special attention. I also needed my teachers to keep my attention from straying in class by calling out, *Rich-heard*—their English voices slowly prying loose my ties to my other name, its three notes, *Ri-car-*

85 *do.* Most of all I needed to hear my mother and father speak to me in a moment of seriousness in broken—suddenly heartbreaking—English. The scene was inevitable: One Saturday morning I entered the kitchen where my parents were talking in Spanish. I did not realize that they were talking in Spanish however until, at the moment they saw me, I heard their voices

90 change to speak English. Those *gringo* sounds they uttered startled me. Pushed me away. In that moment of trivial misunderstanding and profound insight, I felt my throat twisted by unsounded grief. I turned quickly and left the room. But I had no place to escape to with Spanish. (The spell was broken.) My brother and sisters were speaking English in another part of

95 the house.

Again and again in the days following, increasingly angry, I was obliged to hear my mother and father: "Speak to us *en inglé.*" (*Speak.*) Only then did I determine to learn classroom English. Weeks after, it happened: One day in school I raised my hand to volunteer an answer. I spoke out in a loud

100 voice. And I did not think it remarkable when the entire class understood. That day, I moved very far from the disadvantaged child I had been only days earlier. The belief, the calming assurance that I belonged in public, had at last taken hold. Shortly after, I stopped hearing the high and loud sounds of *los gringos.* A more and more confident speaker of English, I

105 didn't trouble to listen to *how* strangers sounded, speaking to me. And there simply were too many English-speaking people in my day for me to hear American accents anymore.

The Gain and the Loss

110   At last, seven years old, I came to believe what had been technically true since my birth: I was an American citizen.

But the special feeling of closeness at home was diminished by then. Gone was the desperate, urgent, intense feeling of being at home; rare was the experience of feeling myself individualized by family intimates. We remained a loving family, but one greatly changed. No longer so
115   close; no longer bound tight by the pleasing and troubling knowledge of our public separateness. Neither my older brother nor sister rushed home after school anymore. Nor did I. When I arrived home there would often be neighborhood kids in the house. Or the house would be empty of sounds.

120   Following the dramatic Americanization of their children, even my parents grew more publicly confident. Especially my mother. She learned the names of all the people on our block. And she decided we needed to have a telephone installed in the house. My father continued to use the word *gringo*. But it was no longer charged with the old bitterness or distrust.
125   (Stripped of any emotional content, the word simply became a name for those Americans not of Hispanic descent.) Hearing him, sometimes, I wasn't sure if he was pronouncing the Spanish word *gringo* or saying gringo in English.

Matching the silence I started hearing in public was a new quiet at
130   home. The family's quiet was partly due to the fact that, as we children learned more and more English, we shared fewer and fewer words with our parents. Sentences needed to be spoken slowly when a child addressed his mother or father. (Often the parent wouldn't understand.) The child would need to repeat himself. (Still the parent misunderstood.) The young voice,
135   frustrated, would end up saying, "Never mind"—the subject was closed. Dinners would be noisy with the clinking of knives and forks against dishes. My mother would smile softly between her remarks; my father at the other end of the table would chew and chew at his food, while he stared over the heads of his children.

140   My *mother!* My *father!* After English became my primary language, I no longer knew what words to use in addressing my parents. The old Spanish words (those tender accents of sound) I had used earlier—*mamá* and *papá*—I couldn't use anymore. They would have been too painful reminders of how much had changed in my life. On the other hand, the words I heard
145   neighborhood kids call *their* parents seemed equally unsatisfactory. *Mother* and *Father, Ma, Papa, Pa, Dad, Pop* (how I hated the all-American sound of that last word especially)—all these terms I felt were unsuitable, not really terms of address for *my* parents. As a result, I never used them at home. Whenever I'd speak to my parents, I would try to get their attention with eye
150   contact alone. In public conversations, I'd refer to "my parents" or "my mother and father."

My mother and father, for their part, responded differently, as their children spoke to them less. She grew restless, seemed troubled and anxious at the scarcity of words exchanged in the house. It was she who would

155 question me about my day when I came home from school. She smiled at small talk. She pried at the edges of my sentences to get me to say something more. (What?) She'd join conversations she overheard, but her intrusions often stopped her children's talking. By contrast, my father seemed reconciled to the new quiet. Though his English improved

160 somewhat, he retired into silence. At dinner he spoke very little. One night his children and even his wife helplessly giggled at his garbled English pronunciation of the Catholic Grace before Meals. Thereafter he made his wife recite the prayer at the start of each meal, even on formal occasions, when there were guests in the house. Hers became the public voice of the

165 family. On official business, it was she, not my father, one would usually hear on the phone or in stores, talking to strangers. His children grew so accustomed to his silence that, years later, they would speak routinely of his shyness. (My mother would often try to explain: Both his parents died when he was eight. He was raised by an uncle who treated him like little more

170 than a menial servant. He was never encouraged to speak. He grew up alone. A man of few words.) But my father was not shy, I realized, when I'd watch him speaking Spanish with relatives. Using Spanish, he was quickly effusive. Especially when talking with other men, his voice would spark, flicker, flare alive with sounds. In Spanish, he expressed ideas and feelings

175 he rarely revealed in English. With firm Spanish sounds, he conveyed confidence and authority English would never allow him.

I would have been happier about my public success had I not sometimes recalled what it had been like earlier, when my family had conveyed its intimacy through a set of conveniently private sounds.

180 Sometimes in public, hearing a stranger, I'd hark back to my past. A Mexican farmworker approached me downtown to ask directions to somewhere. "¿*Hijito* . . . ?" he said. And his voice summoned deep longing. Another time, standing beside my mother in the visiting room of a Carmelite convent, before the dense screen which rendered the nuns

185 shadowy figures, I heard several Spanish-speaking nuns—their busy, singsong overlapping voices—assure us that yes, yes, we were remembered, all our family was remembered in their prayers. (Their voices echoed faraway family sounds.)

A Private and a Public Individuality

190 Today I hear bilingual educators say that children lose a degree of "individuality" by becoming assimilated into public society. (Bilingual schooling was popularized in the seventies, that decade when middle-class ethnics began to resist the process of assimilation—the American melting pot.) But the bilingualists simplistically scorn the value and necessity of

195 assimilation. They do not seem to realize that there are *two* ways a person is individualized. So they do not realize that while one suffers a diminished sense of *private* individuality by becoming assimilated into public society, such assimilation makes possible the achievements of *public* individuality.

The bilingualists insist that a student should be reminded of his 200 difference from others in mass society, his heritage. But they equate mere separateness with individuality. The fact is that only in private—with intimates—is separateness from the crowd a prerequisite for individuality. (An intimate draws me apart, tells me that I am unique, unlike all others.) In public, by contrast, full individuality is achieved, paradoxically, by those 205 who are able to consider themselves members of the crowd. Thus it happened for me: Only when I was able to think of myself as an American, no longer an alien in *gringo* society, could I seek the rights and opportunities necessary for full public individuality. The social and political advantages I enjoy as a man result from the day that I came to believe that 210 my name, indeed, is *Rich-heard Road-ree-guess.*

I celebrate the day I acquired my new name.

My awkward childhood does not prove the necessity of bilingual education. My story discloses instead an essential myth of childhood— inevitable pain. If I rehearse here the changes in my private life after my 215 Americanization, it is finally to emphasize the public gain. The loss implies the gain: The house I returned to each afternoon was quiet. Intimate sounds no longer rushed to the door to greet me. There were other noises inside. The telephone rang. Neighborhood kids ran past the door of the bedroom where I was reading my schoolbooks—covered with shopping-bag 220 paper. Once I learned public language, it would never again be easy for me to hear intimate family voices. More and more of my day was spent hearing words. But that may only be a way of saying that the day I raised my hand in class and spoke loudly to an entire roomful of faces, my childhood started to end.

Stage 3: Recall

Stop to self-test and relate. Your instructor may ask five true-false questions to stimulate your recall.

SKILL DEVELOPMENT: IMPLIED MEANING

According to the implied meaning in the selection, answer the following with *T* (true) or *F* (false).

 1. The author feels a sense of loss along with the gain in his final victory over the English language.

 2. The author suggests that constant happiness is a myth of childhood.

© 1997 Addison-Wesley Educational Publishers Inc.

_I_ 3. The author could understand spoken English before he could speak it himself.

_T_ 4. The author believes that assimilation is necessary for success.

_R_ 5. The author views the proponents of bilingual education as unrealistic.

COMPREHENSION QUESTIONS

Answer the following with _a, b, c,_ or _d._

_d_ 1. The best statement of the main point of this selection is
   a. children who speak another language are often mistreated by teachers.
   b. bilingual education promotes self-confidence and family unity.
   c. school children should be taught in the language of the school and not in the language of the family.
   d. supporters of bilingual education fail to recognize the needs of the family.

_a_ 2. The author is addressing the issue of bilingual education in American schools and is taking a position against
   a. learning two languages.
   b. speaking two languages at school.
   c. using only English to teach Spanish-speaking students.
   d. using only Spanish to teach Spanish-speaking students.

_d_ 3. In looking back the author believes that his teachers
   a. should have taught him in Spanish.
   b. were afraid to speak to him in Spanish.
   c. did not know how to speak in Spanish.
   d. were correct in not speaking to him in Spanish.

_b_ 4. The author's view of the nuns who came to his house is that
   a. they were wrong to intrude upon his family life.
   b. they were kind and ultimately changed his language perspective.
   c. they did not care about him or his family.
   d. they were too strict and demanding.

_c_ 5. When the author says, "I celebrate the day I acquired my new name," that "day" probably refers to
   a. the day the nuns came to his house.
   b. the day he started school.
   c. the day he first volunteered to answer a question in class.
   d. the day he felt the loss of Spanish in his home.

b　　6. After he learned to speak English in public, the author
　　　　a. focused more on what was said rather than how it was said.
　　　　b. listened to sounds to distinguish among different American accents.
　　　　c. listened for the tone of voice that went with the words.
　　　　d. noticed the high and low sounds of English as well as Spanish.

c　　7. Before his family began speaking English at home, the author believed the family shared a closeness that
　　　　a. was a result of a separation they all felt in public.
　　　　b. gave each of them a public identity.
　　　　c. encouraged them to assimilate into the melting pot.
　　　　d. eventually made him ashamed of his childhood.

b　　8. The author feels that his father was silent because
　　　　a. his father was raised by an uncle after his parents died.
　　　　b. his father lacked confidence with the English language.
　　　　c. the children were frustrated at having to speak slowly to the parents.
　　　　d. his mother became more assertive and dominated conversations.

b　　9. The author feels that those who support bilingual education
　　　　a. do not realize the ultimate danger of the social isolation of language.
　　　　b. do not sympathize with the disadvantaged.
　　　　c. are not willing to resist the process of assimilation.
　　　　d. do not recognize differences in heritage in a mass society.

d　10. The author believes that in order to achieve "full individuality," a person must
　　　　a. resist the characteristics that are common to the crowd.
　　　　b. focus on differences rather than similarities.
　　　　c. be comfortable as a member of the crowd.
　　　　d. have a private rather than a public language.

Answer the following with *T* (true) or *F* (false).

F　11. The author was born in Mexico.

F　12. The author's father had been orphaned at an early age.

F　13. The author did not speak English as his public language until he was in fifth grade.

F　14. The author began to view English as a predominately public language because it was used in class to make oneself understood by others.

T　15. The author suggests that the authentic sounds of the Spanish language bring back warm memories of childhood.

VOCABULARY

According to the way the italicized word was used in the selection, indicate *a, b, c,* or *d* for the word or phrase that gives the best definition.

a 1. "noted the *incongruity*" (58)
    a. emotions
    b. lack of fit
    c. anger
    d. argument

a 2. "With great *tact*" (64)
    a. force
    b. conviction
    c. courage
    d. diplomacy

b 3. "*accentuated* our family's closeness" (69)
    a. emphasized
    b. denied
    c. aggravated
    d. controlled

c 4. "*trivial* misunderstanding" (91)
    a. honest
    b. petty
    c. important
    d. conflicting

a 5. "*profound* insight" (91)
    a. unhappy
    b. false
    c. deeply felt
    d. quick

  6. "*pried* at the edges" (156)
    a. laughed
    b. stopped
    c. asked questions
    d. listened

  7. "was quickly *effusive*" (173)
    a. conservative
    b. bubbling
    c. aware
    d. nervous

  8. "his *garbled* English" (161)
    a. slow
    b. confused
    c. confident
    d. abundant

  9. "*menial* servant" (170)
    a. helpful
    b. loyal
    c. lowly
    d. honest

  10. "essential *myth* of childhood" (213)
    a. truth
    b. fictitious story
    c. concern
    d. difficult limitation

WRITTEN RESPONSE

Use the information from the text to answer the following question:
Why is Rodriguez opposed to using the family language of school children for teaching them in school?

COLLABORATIVE CRITICAL THINKING

The Bilingual Challenge

A culturally diverse population that is highly mobile presents both challenges and opportunities to public education. In the United States, students who must learn English as a second language enter public schools in which instruction is given only in English. Many students thus feel lost and intimidated. Teachers, on the other hand, are overloaded and frustrated. What can be done to help these new students make this difficult transition?

Collaborate in a small group to discuss the needs of elementary school students who speak English as a second language. Look at the situation from the perspective of the student, the teacher, and the school system. For each of the three perspectives, list the difficulties and the opportunities. Given the limited resources that are typical in the schools, what practical recommendations would your group suggest for easing the language transition of the new student? For each of the three perspectives—student, teacher, and school system—record at least three practical suggestions. Explain why you think each is workable and important. Read the following passage to gain additional insight into the problem.

The Misery of Silence

When I went to kindergarten and had to speak English for the first time, I became silent. A dumbness—a shame—still cracks my voice in two, even when I want to say "hello" casually, or ask an easy question in front of the check-out counter, or ask directions of a bus driver. I stand frozen, or I hold up the line with the complete, grammatical sentence that comes squeaking out at impossible length. "What did you say?" says the cab driver, or "Speak up," so I have to perform again, only weaker the second time. A telephone call makes my throat bleed and takes up that day's courage. It spoils my day with self-disgust when I hear my broken voice come skittering out into the open. It makes people wince to hear it. I'm getting better, though.

During the first silent year I spoke to no one at school, did not ask before going to the lavatory, and flunked kindergarten. My sister also said nothing for three years, silent in the playground and silent at lunch. There were other quiet Chinese girls not of our family, but most of them got over it sooner than we did. I enjoyed the silence. At first it did not occur to me I was supposed to talk or to pass kindergarten. I talked at home and to one or two of the Chinese kids in class. I made motions and even made some jokes. I drank out of a toy saucer when the water spilled out of the cup, and everybody laughed, pointing at me, so I did it some more. I didn't know that Americans don't drink out of saucers.

It was when I found out I had to talk that school became a misery, that the silence became a misery. I did not speak and felt bad each time that I did not speak. I read aloud in first grade, though, and heard the barest whisper with little squeaks come out of my throat. "Louder," said the teacher, who scared the voice away again. The other Chinese girls did not talk either, so I knew the silence had to do with being a Chinese girl.

From Maxine Hong Kingston, *The Noman Warrior: Memoirs of a Girlhood among Ghosts*

	Student	Teacher	School System
Difficulties	*Speaking*	*Helping with homework*	
Opportunities			
Suggestions			

WORD BRIDGE

Glossary

The first shock in a new subject area, like sociology or geology, is the vocabulary. Each subject seems to have a language, or jargon, of its own. Words like *sociocultural* or *socioeconomic* crop up again and again in a sociology text. In truth, these words are somewhat unique to the subject-matter area—they are made-up words to describe sociological phenomena. The best explanation of such words and their relation to the subject area can usually be found in the textbook itself rather than in the dictionary. Often, textbooks have definitions inserted in a corner or at the bottom of a page, or more frequently, in a glossary of terms at the end of the book or at the end of a chapter. The glossary defines the words as they are used in the textbook.

Notice the following examples from the glossary of a psychology text. The terms using "learning" are part of the jargon of psychology and would probably not be found in the dictionary.

latent learning   hidden learning that is not demonstrated in performance until that performance is reinforced

learned helplessness   a condition in which a subject does not attempt to escape from a painful or noxious situation after learning in a previous, similar situation that escape is not possible.

learning   demonstrated by a relatively permanent change in behavior that occurs as the result of practice or experience

learning set   an acquired strategy for learning or problem solving; learning to learn

Exercise 11   USING YOUR GLOSSARY

Turn to the glossary at the end of this text for help in defining the following terms. Write a definition for each in your own words.

1. schema

   not knowing to much about a subject

2. bias

   An opinion based on the author point of view

3. context clues

   words hidden in a meaning

4. metacognition

   Understanding the direct process of reading

5. inference

   reading though the lines

Answer the following to learn about your own learning and reflect on your progress. Your instructor may collect your responses.

Why is it interesting to read material with many inferences?

to get the author point of view

Describe the inference of a "clean" joke that you know.

How do you avoid ticks on your pet don't let them wear a watch.

Why would literature tend to contain more inferences than a biology text?

because biology have deep details

"Reading between the lines" is an idiom. What does it mean?

expressions that don't make a lot of sense.

Describe the inference in an advertisement that you like.

Things go better with cake a cola.

Reflect on the Longer Selections

Total your short-answer responses for the two longer selections.

Comprehension scores:

completed = _/_   # correct = ___   # incorrect = ___   accuracy = ___%

How do the types of inferences in the two selections differ?

What did you learn about life from the two selections in this chapter?

Be Kind

Do you prefer to read fiction or nonfiction? Why?

nonfiction I like true stories

Why are there no subheadings in fiction?

Because they are not true stories

Why did you like or dislike the story about Mother Savage?

I like the mother Savage story because

Clip out and explain two questions that you missed. Attach these questions and your analysis to the Learning Log for your instructor.

of her strength.

Reflect on the Vocabulary

Total your vocabulary responses for the longer selections.

Vocabulary scores:

completed = _/_   # correct = ___   # incorrect = ___   accuracy = ___%

List the words that you missed.

_____

_____

_____

Which vocabulary items seem dated or old-fashioned?

_____

_____

_____

What vocabulary item would you probably never use? Why?

_____

_____

_____

Describe one technique that you are using successfully to remember words.

When I Get into deep study I will

use connotaion fwords.

_____

Using the perforations, tear out the Learning Log for your instructor.

Point of View

Are textbooks influenced by the author's point of view?

What is the author's point of view?

What is the reader's point of view?

What is a fact?

What is the author's purpose?

What is the author's tone?

ARE TEXTBOOKS INFLUENCED BY THE AUTHOR'S POINT OF VIEW?

How many of the following statements are true?

_T___ 1. Textbooks contain facts rather than opinions.

_T___ 2. The historical account of an incident is based on fact and thus does not vary from one author to another.

_F___ 3. Except for the style of the author, freshman biology textbooks do not vary in their informational content.

_F___ 4. Textbooks are supposed to be free from an author's interpretation.

Unfortunately, too many students tend to answer *"true"* to all of the above. Paying big money for a thick history book with lots of facts and an authoritative title does not mean, contrary to student belief, that the text is a cleansed chronicle of the nation's past. No purity rule applies to textbook writing. In the case of history, the author portrays the past from a personal and unique perspective. The name of the first president of the United States does not vary from one text to another, but, depending on the point of view of the author, the emphasis on the importance of Washington's administration might vary.

Everything read is affected by the author's point of view, purpose, tone, and presentation of facts and opinions.

WHAT IS THE AUTHOR'S POINT OF VIEW?

Authors of factual material, like authors of fiction, have opinions and theories that influence their presentation of the subject matter. For example, would a British professor's account of American history during the Revolutionary period be the same as the version written by a United States-born scholar from Philadelphia? Because of national loyalties, the two scholars might look at the events from two different angles—the first as a colonial uprising on a distant continent and the second as a struggle for personal freedom and survival. The two authors would write from different **points of view** and express particular opinions because they have different ways of looking at the subject.

Recognizing the author's point of view is part of understanding what you read. Sophisticated readers seek to identify the beliefs of the author in order to "know where he or she is coming from." When the point of view is not directly stated, the author's choice of words and information provide clues for the reader.

The terms **point of view** and **bias** are very similar and are sometimes used interchangeably. When facts are slanted, though not necessarily distorted, toward the author's personal beliefs, the written material is said to reflect the author's bias. Thus, a **bias** is simply an opinion or position on a subject. As commonly used, however, *bias has a negative connotation* suggesting narrow-mindedness and prejudice, whereas *point of view* seems more thoughtful and open. Perhaps you would like to refer to your own opinion as point of view and to those of others, particularly if they disagree with you, as biases!

Read the following passage and use the choice of information and words to identify the author's point of view on whaling.

> Our own species is providing us with clear examples of how density-dependent regulation can fail. The great whales have been hunted to the brink of oblivion over the past few decades as modern whaling methods have reduced personal risk while increasing profits. Although there is nothing that whales provide that can't be obtained elsewhere, the demand for whale products (and their price) hasn't diminished, especially in Japan. Thus, instead of the human predators relaxing their pressure and allowing the whale population to recover, whaling fleets continue to exert their depressing effect on populations of the great mammals. . . . Then, as whales decrease in number, the price of whale products goes up, and the hunt becomes still more avid. If humans actually starved when they couldn't catch whales (which might once have been the case among the Eskimos) both populations might eventually stabilize (or cycle). But the current decline in whale numbers has had no effect on the growth of the human population.
>
> Robert Wallace et al., *Biology: Science of Life*

What is the author's point of view? Underline clues that suggest your answer.

_____

_____

(The author is against commercial whaling because the whale population is severely declining. Whaling is for profit and seemingly unlimited greed and not for products that cannot be obtained elsewhere.)

Exercise 1   COMPARING AUTHORS' POINTS OF VIEW

Read the following two descriptions of Mary of Scotland from two different history books. While both include positive and negative comments, the second author obviously finds the subject more engaging and has chosen to include more positive details.

Passage A

Mary Stuart returned to Scotland in 1561 after her husband's death. She was a far more charming and romantic figure than her cousin Elizabeth, but she was no stateswoman. A convinced Catholic, she soon ran head-on into the granitelike opposition of Knox and the Kirk. In 1567 she was forced to abdicate, and in the following year she fled from Scotland and sought protection in England from Elizabeth. No visitor could have been more unwelcome.

Joseph R. Strayer et al., *The Mainstream of Civilization*

Passage B

Mary Stuart was an altogether remarkable young woman, about whom it is almost impossible to remain objectively impartial. Even when one discounts the flattery that crept into descriptions of her, one is inclined to accept the contemporary evidence that Mary was extraordinarily beautiful, though tall for a girl—perhaps over six feet. In addition to beauty, she had almost every other attractive attribute in high degree: courage, wit, resourcefulness, loyalty, and responsiveness, in short everything needful for worldly greatness save discretion in her relations with men and a willingness to compromise, if need be, on matters of religion. She was a thoroughgoing Roman Catholic, a good lover, and a magnificent hater.

Shepard B. Clough et al., *A History of the Western World*

1. How are the two descriptions alike?

_____

_____

2. How do the two descriptions differ?

1 left the century

2'st in controlle

3. Which do you like better, and why?

B. Because the author is more

passfive

4. What clues signal that the author of the second description is more biased than the first?

_____

_____

5. What is the suggested meaning in the following phrases:

_____

a. "no stateswoman"

_____

b. "A convinced Catholic"

_____

strong/silent

c. "granitelike opposition"

_____

d. "more unwelcomed"

_____

Except one

e. "save discretion in her relations with men"

was not carefull with relations

f. "thoroughgoing Roman Catholic"

_____

g. "magnificent hater"

_____

_____

WHAT IS THE READER'S POINT OF VIEW?

To recognize a point of view, you have to know enough about the subject to realize that there is another opinion beyond the one being expressed. Thus, prior knowledge and a slightly suspicious nature open the mind to countless other views and alternative arguments.

On the other hand, prior knowledge can also lead to a closed mind and rigid thinking. Our existing opinions affect how much we accept or reject of what we read. If our beliefs are particularly strong, sometimes we refuse to hear what is said or we hear something that is not said. Research has shown that readers will actually "tune out" new material that is drastically different from their own views. For example, if you were reading that the AIDS virus should not be a concern for most middle-class Americans, would you be "tuned in" or "tuned out"?

Read the following passage on smoking first from the point of view of a non-smoker and second from the point of view of a smoker, and then answer the questions.

Smoke can permanently paralyze the tiny cilia that sweep the breathing passages clean and can cause the lining of the respiratory tract to thicken irregularly. The body's attempt to rid itself of the smoking toxins may produce a deep, hacking cough in the person next to you at the lunch counter. Console yourself with the knowledge that these hackers are only trying to rid their bodies of nicotines, "tars," formaldehyde, hydrogen sulfide, resins, and who knows what. Just enjoy your meal.

Robert Wallace, *Biology: The World of Life*

1. Is the author a smoker? Underline the clues suggesting your answer.

   No yes

2. What is your view on smoking? *just don't smoke*

Organize something else going on

3. Reading this passage in the guise of a nonsmoker, what message is conveyed to you? _____

4. Assuming the role of a smoker, what message is conveyed to you from reading in this passage? _____

5. What is the main point the author is trying to convey?

_____

(While it is possible that both the smoker and nonsmoker would get exactly the same message, it is more likely that the nonsmoker would be disgusted by the health risks, whereas the smoker would claim exaggeration and discrimination. Smoking causes permanent physical damage.)

Exercise 2   IDENTIFYING POINTS OF VIEW

Read the following passages and answer the questions about point of view.

Passage A. Columbus

On August 3, 1492, Columbus and some ninety mariners set sail from Palos, Spain, in the *Niña, Pinta,* and *Santa Maria.* Based on faulty calculations, the Admiral estimated Asia to be no more than 4500 miles to the west (the actual distance is closer to 12,000 miles). Some 3000 miles out, his crew became fearful and wanted to return home. But he convinced them to keep sailing west. Just two days later, on October 12, they landed on a small island in the Bahamas, which Columbus named San Salvador (holy savior).

A fearless explorer, Columbus turned out to be an ineffective administrator and a poor geographer. He ended up in debtor's prison, and to his dying day in 1506 he never admitted to locating a world unknown to Europeans. Geographers overlooked his contribution and named the Western continents after another mariner, Amerigo Vespucci, a merchant from Florence who participated in a Portuguese expedition to South America in 1501. In a widely reprinted letter, Vespucci claimed that a new world had been found, and it was his name that caught on.

James Martin et al., *America and Its People*

1. Which paragraph sounds more like the Columbus you learned about in elementary school? _____

2. What is the author's position on Columbus? Underline clues for your answer?

_____

3. What is your view of Columbus? What has influenced your view?

_____

_____

4. What is the main point the author is trying to convey? _____

_____

Passage B. Mexican Cession

The tragedy of the Mexican cession is that most Anglo-Americans have not accepted the fact that the United States committed an act of violence against the Mexican people when it took Mexico's northwestern territory. Violence was not limited to the taking of the land; Mexico's territory was invaded, her people murdered, her land raped, and her possessions plundered. Memory of this destruction generated a distrust and dislike that is still vivid in the minds of many Mexicans, for the violence of the United States left deep scars. And for Chicanos—Mexicans remaining within the boundaries of the new United States territories—aggression was even more insidious, for the outcome of the Texas and Mexican-American wars made them a conquered people. Anglo-Americans were the conquerors, and they evinced all the arrogance of military victors.

In material terms, in exchange for 12,000 lives and more than $100,000,000 the United States acquired a colony two and a half times as large as France, containing rich farm lands and natural resources such as gold, silver, zinc, copper, oil, and uranium which would make possible its unprecedented industrial boom. It acquired ports on the Pacific which generated further economic expansion across that ocean. Mexico was left with its shrunken resources to face the continued advances of the expanding capitalist force on its border.

Rodolfo Acuña, *Occupied America: A History of Chicanos*

1. What is the author's point of view? Underline clues. _____

_____

2. How does this author's view differ from what you would expect in most

American history texts? _____

_____

3. What is your point of view on the subject? _____

_____

4. What is the main point the author is trying to convey? _____

_____

Passage C. Surviving in Vietnam

Vietnam ranks after World War II as America's second most expensive war. Between 1950 and 1975, the United States spent $123 billion on combat in Southeast Asia. More importantly, Vietnam ranks—after our Civil War and World Wars I and II—as the nation's fourth deadliest war, with 57,661 Americans killed in action.

Yet, when the last U.S. helicopter left Saigon, Americans suffered what historian George Herring terms "collective amnesia." Everyone, even those who had fought in 'Nam, seemed to want to forget Southeast Asia. It took nearly ten years for the government to erect a national monument to honor those who died in Vietnam.

Few who served in Vietnam survived unscathed, whether psychologically or physically. One of the 303,600 Americans wounded during the long war was 101st Airborne platoon leader James Bombard, first shot and then blown up by a mortar round during the bitter Tet fighting at Hue in February 1968. He describes his traumatic experience as

> *feeling the bullet rip into your flesh, the shrapnel tear the flesh from your bones and the blood run down your leg. . . . To put your hand on your chest and to come away with your hand red with your own blood, and to feel it running out of your eyes and out of your mouth, and seeing it spurt out of your guts, realizing you were dying. . . . I was ripped open from the top of my head to the tip of my toes. I had forty-five holes in me.*

Somehow Bombard survived Vietnam.

Withdrawing U.S. forces from Vietnam ended only the combat. Returning veterans fought government disclaimers concerning the toxicity of the defoliant Agent Orange. VA hospitals across the nation still contain thousands of para- and quadriplegic Vietnam veterans, as well as the maimed from earlier wars. Throughout America the "walking wounded" find themselves still embroiled in the psychological aftermath of Vietnam.

James Divine et al., America: Past and Present

1. What is the author's own view of the war? Underline clues for your answer.

_____

2. What is your own position on the Vietnam War?

_____

3. What is the purpose of Bombard's quotation?

_____

4. How do your feel about war after reading this passage?

_____

5. What is the main point the author is trying to convey?

_____

WHAT IS A FACT AND WHAT IS AN OPINION?

For both the reader and the writer, a point of view is a position or belief that logically evolves through time with knowledge and experience and is usually based on both facts and opinions. For example, what is your position on city curfews for youth, on helping the homeless, on abortion? Are your views on these is-sues supported solely by facts? Do you recognize the difference between the facts and the opinions employed in your thinking?

Both fact and opinion are used persuasively to support positions. You have to determine which is which and then judge the issue accordingly. On the one hand, a fact is a statement based on actual evidence or personal observation. It can be checked objectively with empirical data and proved to be either true or false. On the other hand, an opinion is a statement of personal feeling or a judg-ment. It reflects a belief or an interpretation rather than an accumulation of evi-dence, and it cannot be proved true or false. Adding the quoted opinion of a well-known authority to a few bits of evidence does not improve the data, yet this is an effective persuasive technique. Even though you may feel an opinion is valid, it is still an opinion.

Authors mix facts and opinions, sometimes in the same sentence, in order to win you over to a particular point of view. Persuasive tricks include factually quoting sources who then voice opinions or hedging a statement with "It is a fact that" and attaching a disguised opinion. Recognize that both facts and opinions are valuable but be able to distinguish between the two.

Examples

Fact: Freud developed a theory of personality.

Fact. Freud believed that the personality is divided into three parts.

Opinion: Freud constructed the most complete theory of personality development.

Opinion: The personality is divided into three parts: the id, the ego, and the superego.

Exercise 3   FACT OR OPINION

Read each of the following and indicate *F* for fact and *O* for opinion.

_O_ 1. For women locked into socioeconomic situations that cannot promise financial independence, liberation is relatively meaningless and some-times suggests the denial of femininity as a goal.

Reece McGee et al., *Sociology: An Introduction*

_F_ 2. The territorial base from which Soviet ambitions proceed is the largest country area on the globe.

Jesse H. Wheeler, Jr., et al., *Regional Geography of the World*

_O_ 3. Company sources attribute Coors' success to product quality, boasting that it "is the most expensively brewed beer in the world."

Louis Boone and David L. Kurtz, *Contemporary Business*

O _____ 4. If you wish to "break the hunger habit" in order to gain better control over your own food intake, you might be wise to do so slowly—by putting yourself on a very irregular eating schedule.

> James V. McConnell, *Understanding Human Behavior*

F _____ 5. The first step in running for the nomination is to build a personal organization, because the party organization is supposed to stay neutral until the nomination is decided.

> James M. Burns et al., *Government by the People*

F _____ 6. It is true that American politics often rewards with power those who have proved that they can direct the large institutions of commerce and business, of banking, and of law, education, and philanthropy.

> Kenneth Prewitt and Sidney Verba, *An Introduction to American Government*

O _____ 7. Precipitation is not uniform, and neither is the distribution of population.

> Robert J. Foster, *Physical Geology*

O _____ 8. Massively built, with eyes so piercing they seemed like the headlights of an onrushing train, J. P. Morgan was the most powerful figure in American finance.

> Robert Divine et al., *American Past and Present*

F _____ 9. At least 10 percent of the world's available food is destroyed by pests, waste, and spoilage somewhere between the marketplace and the stomach of the consumer.

> Robert Wallace, *Biology: The World of Life*

F _____ 10. Woman, young girls, and even mere children were tortured by driving needles under their nails, roasting their feet in the fire, or crushing their legs under heavy weights until the marrow spurted from their bones, in order to force them to confess to filthy orgies with demons.

> Edward M. Burns, *Western Civilization*

Exercise 4   FACT AND OPINION IN TEXTBOOKS

The following passage from a history text describes Franklin D. Roosevelt. Notice the mixture of facts and opinions in developing a view of Roosevelt. Mark the items that follow as fact (*F*) or opinion (*O*).

Franklin D. Roosevelt won the Democratic nomination in June 1932. At first glance he did not look like someone who could relate to suffering people; he had spent his entire life in the lap of luxury.

Handsome and outgoing, Roosevelt had a bright political future. Then disaster struck. In 1921, he developed polio. The disease left him paralyzed from the waist down and confined to a wheelchair for the rest of his life. Instead of retiring, however, Roosevelt threw himself into a rehabilitation program and labored diligently to return to the public life. "If you had spent two years in bed trying to wiggle your toe," he later observed, "after that anything would seem easy."

Few intellectuals had a high opinion of him. Walter Lippmann described Roosevelt as "a pleasant man who, without any important qualifications for the office, would very much like to be President."

The people saw Roosevelt differently. During the campaign, he calmed their fears and gave them hope. Even a member of Hoover's administration had to admit: "The people seem to be lifting eager faces to Franklin Roosevelt, having the impression that he is talking intimately to them." Charismatic and utterly charming, Roosevelt radiated confidence. He even managed to turn his lack of a blueprint into an asset. Instead of offering plans, he advocated the experimental method. "It is common sense to take a method and try it," he declared, "if it fails, admit it frankly and try another."

James Martin et al., America and Its People

_F_____ 1. Roosevelt won the Democratic nomination in June 1932.

_O_____ 2. He was handsome and outgoing.

_O_____ 3. He developed polio in 1921.

_O_____ 4. Few intellectuals thought highly of him.

_P_____ 5. Roosevelt radiated confidence.

WHAT IS THE AUTHOR'S PURPOSE?

Be aware that a textbook author can shift from an objective and factual explanation of a topic to a subjective and opinionated treatment of the facts. Recognizing the author's purpose does not mean that you won't buy the product; it just means that you are a more cautious, well-informed consumer.

An author always has a purpose in mind when putting words on paper. The reader of a textbook expects that the author's purpose will be to inform or explain and, in general, this is true. At times, however, texts can slip from factual explanation to persuasion. The sophisticated reader recognizes this shift in purpose and thus is more critical in evaluating the content. A persuasive paragraph for or against birth control alerts the reader to be more skeptical and less accepting than a paragraph explaining how birth control methods work.

The purpose of the author can be a single one or a combination of the following:

to inform	to argue	to entertain
to explain	to persuade	to narrate

| to describe | to condemn | to describe |
| to enlighten | to ridicule | to shock |

Read the following passage to determine the author's purpose.

love, *n.* A temporary insanity curable by marriage or by removal of the patient from the influences under which he incurred the disorder. This disease, like caries and many other ailments, is prevalent only among civilized races living under artificial conditions; barbarous nations breathing pure air and eating simple food enjoy immunity from its ravages. It is sometimes fatal, but more frequently to the physician than to the patient.

Ambrose Bierce, The Devil's Dictionary

(The author defines love in a humorous and exaggerated manner for the purpose of entertaining the reader.)

Exercise 5   DETERMINING THE AUTHOR'S PURPOSE

Read the following passage and answer the questions about the author's purpose.

Isabella Katz and the Holocaust: A Living Testimony

No statistics can adequately render the enormity of the Holocaust, and its human meaning can perhaps only be understood through the experience of a single human being who was cast into the nightmare of the Final Solution. Isabella Katz was the eldest of six children—Isabella, brother Philip, and sisters Rachel, Chicha, Cipi, and baby Potyo—from a family of Hungarian Jews. She lived in the ghetto of Kisvarda, a provincial town of 20,000 people, where hers was a typical Jewish family of the region—middle-class, attached to Orthodox traditions, and imbued with a love of learning.

In 1938 and 1939 Hitler pressured Hungary's regent, Miklós Horthy, into adopting anti-Jewish laws. By 1941 Hungary had become a German ally, and deportations and massacres were added to the restrictions. Isabella's father left for the United States, where he hoped to obtain entry papers for his family, but after Pearl Harbor, Hungary was at war with America and the family was trapped. In the spring of 1944, when Hitler occupied Hungary, the horror of the Final Solution struck Isabella. On March 19 Adolf Eichmann, as SS officer in charge of deportation, ordered the roundup of Jews in Hungary, who numbered some 650,000. On May 28, Isabella's nineteenth birthday, the Jews in Kisvarda were told to prepare for transportation to Auschwitz on the following morning. Isabella recalled:

> And now an SS man is here, spick-and-span, with a dog, a silver pistol, and a whip. And he is all of sixteen years old. On his list appears the name of every Jew in the ghetto. . . . "Teresa Kata," he calls—my mother. She steps forward. . . . Now the SS man moves toward my mother. He raises his whip and, for no apparent reason at all, lashes out at her.

En route to Auschwitz, crammed into hot, airless boxcars, Isabella's mother told her children to "stay alive":

> Out there, when it's all over, a world's waiting for you to give it all I gave you. Despite what you see here. . . . believe me, there is humanity out there, there is dignity. . . . And when this is all over, you must add to it, because sometimes it is a little short, a little skimpy.

Isabella and her family were among more than 437,000 Jews sent to Auschwitz from Hungary.

When they arrived at Auschwitz, the SS and camp guards divided the prisoners into groups, often separating family members. Amid the screams and confusion, Isabella remembered:

> We had just spotted the back of my mother's head when Mengele, the notorious Dr. Josef Mengele, points to my sister and me and says, "Die Zwei" [those two]. This trim, very good-looking German, with a flick of his thumb and a whistle, is selecting who is to live and who is to die.

Isabella's mother and her baby sister perished within a few days.

> The day we arrived in Auschwitz, there were so many people to be burned that the four crematoriums couldn't handle the task. So the Germans built big open fires to throw the children in. Alive? I do not know. I saw the flames. I heard the shrieks.

Isabella was to endure the hell of Auschwitz for nine months.

The inmates were stripped, the hair on their heads and bodies was shaved, and they were herded into crude, overcrowded barracks. As if starvation, forced labor, and disease were not enough, they were subjected to unspeakable torture, humiliation, and terror, a mass of living skeletons for whom the difference between life and death could be measured only in an occasional flicker of spirit that determined to resist against impossible odds. Isabella put it this way:

> Have you ever weighed 120 pounds and gone down to 40? Something like that—not quite alive, yet not quite dead. Can anyone, can even I, picture it? . . . Our eyes sank deeper. Our skin rotted. Our bones screamed out of our bodies. Indeed, there was barely a body to house the mind, yet the mind was still working, sending out the messages "Live! Live!"

In November, just as Isabella and her family were lined up outside a crematorium, they were suddenly moved to Birnbäumel, in eastern Germany—the Russians were getting nearer and the Nazis were closing down their death camps and moving the human evidence of their barbarism out of reach of the enemy. In January, as the Russians and the frigid weather closed in, the prisoners were forced to march through the snows deeper into Germany, heading toward the camp at Bergen-Belsen. Those who could not endure the trial fell by the side, shot or frozen to death. On January 23, while stumbling through a blizzard with the sound of

Russian guns in the distance, Isabella, Rachel, and Chicha made a successful dash from the death march and hid in an abandoned house. Two days later Russian soldiers found them. Philip has been sent to a labor camp, and Cipi made it to Bergen-Belsen, where she died.

Isabella later married and had two children of her own, making a new life in America. Yet the images of the Holocaust remain forever in her memory. "Now I am older," she says, "and I don't remember all the pain. . . . That is not happiness, only relief, and relief is blessed. . . . And children someday will plant flowers in Auschwitz, where the sun couldn't crack through the smoke of burning flesh."

Richard L. Greaves et al., Civilizations of the World

1. What is the author's purpose for including this story in the history textbook?

2. What does the author mean by "its human meaning can perhaps only be understood through the experience of a single human being"?

3. Why does the author include Isabella's quote?

4. Why does the author include Isabella's quote about the SS man?

5. What is Isabella's purpose in relating her story?

6. Is the passage predominately developed through facts or opinions? Give an example of each.

7. How does the passage influence your thinking about the Holocaust?

WHAT IS THE AUTHOR'S TONE?

The tone of an author's writing is similar to the tone of a speaker's voice. For listeners, it is fairly easy to tell the difference between an angry tone and a romantic tone by noticing the speaker's voice. Distinguishing among humor, sarcasm, and irony, however, may be more difficult. **Humorous** remarks are designed to be comical and amusing, while **sarcastic** remarks are designed to cut or give pain. **Ironic** remarks, on the other hand, express something other than the literal meaning and are designed to show the incongruity between the actual and the expected. Making such precise distinctions requires more than just listening to sounds; it requires a careful evaluation of what is said. Because the sound of the voice is not heard in reading, clues to the tone must come from the writer's presentation of the message. The reader's job is to look for clues to answer the question. "What is the author's attitude toward the topic?"

The following is a list of some of the words that can be used to describe the author's tone. Can you imagine an example for each?

angry	hateful	ironic	professional
bitter	hopeful	jovial	respectful

cynical	horrifying	lonely	sarcastic
defensive	hostile	loving	satirical
depressing	humorous	miserable	scornful
enthusiastic	hypocritical	nostalgic	subjective
fearful	hysterical	objective	sincere
gloomy	insulting	optimistic	sympathetic
happy	intellectual	pessimistic	threatening

As an example of tone, pretend that your friend is already a half-hour late for a meeting. You can wait no longer but you can leave a note. On your own paper, write your friend three different notes—one in a sympathetic tone, one in an angry tone, and one in a sarcastic tone. Notice in doing this how your tone reflects your purpose. Which note would you really leave and to which friend?

Read the following passage and note that the overall tone is informative and educational. However, the author sees a certain aspect to the subject matter that brings out another tone. What is that tone?

Some plants depend upon fire to maintain high densities. The most famous example is the giant sequoia (*Sequoiadendron giganteum*) of California. These magnificent trees are replaced by other conifers, but only in the absence of fire. Conservation attempts to protect the sequoia forests by stopping all forest fires have, in effect, almost doomed these trees to disappear, and attempts to restore fire to a useful place in forest management are currently under way in the National Parks Service of the United States.

Large sequoia trees have a thick, fire-resistant bark and so they are not damaged by ground fires that are fatal to many other conifers, such as white fir and sugar pine. Sequoia seedlings also germinate best on bare mineral soil, and ground fires provide a good environment for seedling establishment by removing the litter on the forest floor. Thus organisms as different as blue grouse, moose, and sequoia trees may all depend upon habitat changes brought on by fire in order to keep their numbers high. Good habitats are not necessarily those that are never disturbed.

Charles Krebs, *The Message of Ecology*

(There is an underlying tone of irony as the author points out that fire, which is deadly to most, is essential for the life of the giant sequoias. Irony is the opposite of the expected. In fiction or life, it is the twist or surprise ending that no one anticipates. Irony can make us laugh, but usually it is a bittersweet and somewhat cruel chuckle.)

Exercise 6   DETERMINING THE AUTHOR'S TONE

Read the following passages to determine the author's tone and attitude toward the subject.

Passage A. Water Pollution

In many locales the water is not safe to drink, as evidenced by the recent outbreaks of infectious hepatitis in the United States. Infectious hepatitis is believed to be caused by a virus carried in human waste, usually through a water supply that is contaminated by sewage. There is some disturbing evidence that this virus may be resistant to chlorine, especially in the presence of high levels of organic material. Despite our national pride in indoor plumbing and walk-in bathrooms, sewage treatment for many communities in the United States is grossly inadequate, and waste that has been only partially treated is discharged into waterways. Recently the news services carried a story announcing that the New Orleans water supply may be dangerous to drink. However, we have been assured that there is no cause for alarm—a committee has been appointed to study the problem!

Robert Wallace, *Biology: The World of Life*

1. What is the author's tone? _____

2. Circle the words and phrases that suggest this tone. _____

3. What is the author's point of view? _____

4. What is your own point of view on the subject? _____

5. What is the main point the author is trying to convey?

_____

Passage B. The Redwoods

It is impossible to live in the redwood region without being profoundly affected by the massive destruction of this once-magnificent ecosystem. Miles and miles of clearcuts cover our bleeding hillsides. Ancient forests are being strip-logged to pay off corporate junk bonds. Log trucks fill our roads, heading to the sawmills with loads ranging from 1,000-year-old redwoods, one tree trunk filling an entire logging truck, to six-inch-diameter baby trees that are chipped for pulp.

Judi Bari, "The Feminization of Earth First!" reprinted by permission of *Ms* Magazine, © 1992.

1. What is the author's tone? _____

2. Circle the words and phrases that suggest this tone. _____

3. What is the author's point of view? _____

4. What is your own point of view on the subject? _____

5. What is the main point the author is trying to convey?

_____

Passage C. The Injustice System

It's hard to change 3,000 years of attitudes, but parents and teachers, judges and lawmakers can help. We start by teaching little boys to respect the feelings—and words—of little girls. And what do we teach little girls?

I have two young daughters, and I want to protect them from harm just as my parents wanted to protect me. But the days are long gone when girls went directly from their father's house to their husband's.

I hope I can teach my daughters more than just how to avoid being alone with a man in an elevator. They will study karate as well as ballet. I want them to understand their own strength, the importance of knees and elbows, the power of a well-placed kick.

I'll teach them that the justice system can be unjust. They should use the system, but not trust it, and work to reform it.

Patty Fisher, "The Injustice System." Reprinted with permission of the San Jose Mercury News, March 25, 1992.

1. What is the author's tone? ⎯⎯⎯⎯⎯⎯⎯⎯⎯⎯⎯⎯⎯⎯⎯⎯⎯⎯⎯

2. Circle the words and phrases that suggest this tone.⎯⎯⎯⎯⎯⎯⎯⎯⎯

3. What is the author's point of view? ⎯⎯⎯⎯⎯⎯⎯⎯⎯⎯⎯⎯⎯⎯

4. What is your own point of view on the subject? ⎯⎯⎯⎯⎯⎯⎯⎯

5. What is the main point the author is trying to convey?

⎯⎯⎯⎯⎯⎯⎯⎯⎯⎯⎯⎯⎯⎯⎯⎯⎯⎯⎯⎯⎯⎯⎯⎯⎯⎯⎯⎯⎯⎯⎯⎯

Passage D. The Comma

The commas are the most useful and usable of all the stops. It is highly important to put them in place as you go along. If you try to come back after doing a paragraph and stick them in the various spots that tempt you you will discover that they tend to swarm like minnows into all sorts of crevices whose existence you hadn't realized and before you know it the whole long sentence becomes immobilized and lashed up squirming in commas. Better to use them sparingly, and with affection, precisely when the need for each one arises, nicely, by itself.

Lewis Thomas, "Notes on Punctuation," from *The Medusa and the Snail* by Lewis Thomas. Copyright © 1979 by Lewis Thomas. Reprinted by permission of Viking Penguin, a division of Penguin Books USA Inc.

1. What is the author's tone? ⎯⎯⎯⎯⎯⎯⎯⎯⎯⎯⎯⎯⎯⎯⎯⎯⎯⎯⎯

2. Circle the words and phrases that suggest this tone. ⎯⎯⎯⎯⎯⎯⎯

3. What is the author's point of view? ⎯⎯⎯⎯⎯⎯⎯⎯⎯⎯⎯⎯⎯⎯

4. What is your own point of view on the subject? ⎯⎯⎯⎯⎯⎯⎯⎯

5. What is the main point the author is trying to convey?

_____

Passage E. Only Daughter

I went upstairs to my father's room. One of my stories had just been translated into Spanish and published in an anthology of Chicano writing, and I wanted to show it to him. Ever since he recovered from a stroke two years ago, my father likes to spend his leisure hours horizontally.

I'm not sure if it was because my story was translated into Spanish, or because it was published in Mexico, or perhaps because the story dealt with Tepeyac, the *colonia* my father was raised in and the house he grew up in, but at any rate, my father punched the mute button on his remote control and read my story.

I sat on the bed next to my father and waited. He read it very slowly. As if he were reading each line over and over. He laughed at all the right places and read lines he liked out loud. He pointed and asked questions: "Is this So-and-so?" "Yes," I said. He kept reading.

When he was finally finished, after what seemed like hours, my father looked up and asked: "Where can we get more copies of this for the relatives?"

Of all the wonderful things that happened to me last year, that was the most wonderful.

1. What is the author's tone? _____

2. Circle the words and phrases that suggest this tone. _____

3. What is the author's point of view? _____

4. What is your own point of view on the subject? _____

5. What is the main point the author is trying to convey?

_____

POLITICAL CARTOONS

Political cartoons vividly illustrate how an author or an artist can effectively communicate point of view without making a direct verbal statement. Through their drawings, cartoonists have great freedom to be extremely harsh and judgmental. For example, they take positions on local and national news events and frequently depict politicians as crooks, thieves, or even murderers. Because the accusations are implied rather than directly stated, the cartoonist communicates a point of view but is still safe from libel charges.

To illustrate, study the cartoon on poorly paid labor (below) to determine what the cartoonist feels and is saying about the subject. Use the following steps to help you analyze the implied meaning and point of view.

1. Glance at the cartoon for an overview and then read the dialogue.
2. Answer the question, "What is this about?" to determine the general topic.
3. Study the details for symbolism. Who is the man? Who is the woman? What did Betsy Ross do?
4. What does "Made in America" mean? Where is it used?
5. What is a sweatshop? Who works in sweatshops?
6. With all the information in mind, answer the question, "What is the main point the cartoonist is trying to get across?"
7. Taking the message into consideration, answer "What is the cartoonist's purpose?"
8. What is the tone of the cartoon?
9. What is the cartoonist's point of view or position on the subject? What is your point of view?

To summarize, the cartoonist feels that "Made in America" now means "made within the physical boundaries of America," but made by poorly paid, forced labor. The workers in sweatshops, usually new and desperate immigrants, do not share the rights of Americans that the flag and the colonial leaders symbolize. The tone is both sarcastic and sad. The purpose is to heighten awareness and to ridicule the hypocrisy of the misleading slogan and those who use it as a

The Atlanta Journal, August 10, 1995

shield. The point of view of the cartoonist is against sweatshops and our failure to recognize their existence.

Exercise 7   POLITICAL CARTOONS

Use the same steps to analyze the message and answer the questions on the next cartoon.

1. What is the general topic of this cartoon?

2. What do the people and objects represent?

3. Why is the newspaper included?

4. What is the main point the cartoonist is trying to convey?

5. What is the cartoonist's purpose?

6. What is the tone of the cartoon?

7. What is the cartoonist's point of view?

8. What is your point of view on the subject?

Cartoons are fun but challenging, because they require prior knowledge for interpretation. For current news cartoons, you have to be familiar with the latest happenings in order to make connections and understand the message. Look on the editorial page of your newspaper to enjoy world events from a cartoonist's point of view.

As stated in the beginning of the chapter, even in college textbooks the au-

USA Today, September 21, 1995

thor's attitudes and biases slip through. It is the reader's responsibility to be alert for signs of manipulation and to be ready to question interpretations and conclusions. Sophisticated readers are aware and draw their own conclusions based on their own interpretation of the facts.

SUMMARY POINTS

- Authors have opinions, theories, and prejudices that influence their presentation of material. When facts are slanted, though not necessarily distorted, the material is biased toward the author's beliefs.
- A bias is a prejudice, a mental leaning, or an inclination. The bias, in a sense, creates the point of view, the particular angle from which the author views the material.
- Students should not let their own viewpoints impede their understanding of the author's opinions and ideas.
- Both facts and opinions are used persuasively to support positions. A fact is a statement that can be proved to be either true or false. An opinion is a statement of feeling or a judgment. An author always has a purpose in mind, and a sophisticated reader should recognize that purpose in order to be a well-informed consumer.
- The tone of an author's writing is similar to the tone of a speaker's voice. The reader's job is to look for clues to determine the author's attitude about the subject.

SELECTION 1

ESSAY

Stage 1: Skill Development

Preview

This selection is probably excerpted from a history textbook.

agree ☐   disagree ☐

Activate Schema

What do you believe was the main cause of the Civil War?
Who was Harry Truman?

What was the Louisiana Purchase?

Why are discussion questions and definitions usually inserted within the body of textbook material?

Learning Strategy

Be able to explain the author's point of view on the study of history and identify the elements that identify tone.

Stage 2: Integrate Knowledge While Reading

Use thinking strategies as you read:

1. Predict   2. Picture   3. Relate   4. Monitor   5. Fix up

The Lesson of History
From Dave Barry, *Dave Barry's Greatest Hits*

The difficult thing about studying history is that, except for Harold Stassen, everybody who knows anything about it firsthand is dead. This means that our only source of historical information is historians, who are useless because they keep changing everything around.

5   For example, I distinctly remember learning in fifth grade that the Civil War was caused by slavery. So did you, I bet. As far as I was concerned, this was an excellent explanation for the Civil War, the kind you could remember and pass along as an important historical lesson to your grandchildren. ("Gather 'round boys and girls, while Grandpa tells you what caused the

10   Civil War. Slavery. Now go fetch Grandpa some more bourbon.")

Then one day in high school, out of the blue, a history teacher named Anthony Sabella told me that the Civil War was caused by economic factors. I still think this was a lie, and not just because Anthony Sabella once picked me up by my neck. I mean, today we have more economic factors than ever

15   before, such as the Dow Jones Industrial Average, but you don't see the North and the South fighting each other, do you? Which is good, because the South has 96 percent of the nation's armed pickup trucks, whereas the North mainly has Fitness Centers, so it would be over in minutes.

What kind of a name is "Dow" Jones? *Explain.*

20   Nevertheless, I had to pretend I thought the Civil War was caused by economic factors, or I never would have escaped from Mr. Sabella's class and got into college, where the history professors sneered openly at the primitive high-school-teacher notion that the Civil War had been caused by anything so obvious as economic factors. No, they said, the Civil War was

25   caused by acculturalized regionalism. Or maybe it was romantic transcendentalism, or behavioristic naturalism, or structuralized functionalism. I learned hundreds of terms like these in college, and I no longer even vaguely remember what they mean. As far as I know, any one of them could have caused the Civil War. Maybe we should lock them all in a

30   small room and deny them food and water until one of them confesses.

Was the author "just kidding" when he made that last "off-the-wall" suggestion? Cite specific examples.

What is the cause of all this disagreement among the experts over basic historical issues? Economic factors. If you're a historian and you want to
35   write a best-selling book, you have to come up with a new wrinkle. If you go to a publisher and say you want to write that Harry Truman was a blunt-spoken Missourian who made some unpopular decisions but was vindicated by history, the publisher will pick you up by your neck and toss you into the street, because there are already bales of such books on the market. But if
40   you claim to have uncovered evidence that Harry Truman was a Soviet ballerina, before long you'll be on national morning television, answering earnest questions from David Hartman in a simulated living room.

Don't you think David Hartman is just a little *too* avuncular? Why?

45   So I propose that we laypersons forget about historians and agree among ourselves to believe in a permanent set of historical facts once and for all. Specifically, I propose we use the facts contained in a book I found in my basement recently, called *Civilization Past and Present,* which was apparently one of my wife's high-school textbooks.

50   **Did she steal it? Or what?**

Civilization Past and Present combines the advantage of having a snappy title with the advantage of ending in 1962, just before history starts to get really depressing. It's easy to understand, because my wife has underlined all the important words and phrases (<u>Germany</u>, for example). And it doesn't
55   beat around the bush. For example, on page 599 it makes the following statement in plain black and white: "The causes of the American Civil War are complex."

Since some of you laypersons out there may not have *Civilization Past and Present* in your basements, here's a brief summary to tide you over until
60   you get your own copies:

HISTORY

5,000,000,000 B.C.–1962

After the Earth cooled, it formed an extremely fertile crescent containing primitive people such as the Hittites who believed in just the
65   stupidest things you ever heard of. Then came Greece and Rome, followed by Asia. All of this came to a halt during the Middle Ages, which were caused by the Jutes and featured the following terms underlined by my wife: <u>the steward, the bailiff,</u> and <u>the reeve</u>. Next the Turks got way the hell over into France, after which there were towns. And the Magna Carta. Then

70 France and England fought many wars that involved dates such as 1739 and were settled by the Treaty of Utrecht, which also was used to harness water power. By then the seeds had been sown for several World Wars and the Louisiana Purchase, but fortunately we now have a fairly peaceful atom. Now go fetch Grandpa some more bourbon.

75   Define the following: "Avuncular."

COMPREHENSION QUESTIONS

Answer the following the *T* (true) or *F* (false).

_____ 1. The author feels that historians change their point of view on the truth of the past.

_____ 2. The author's tone is serious.

_____ 3. The author's purpose is to teach history.

_____ 4. The statement that the South has 96 percent of the nation's armed pickup trucks is false.

_____ 5. The author suggests that college professors criticize how history was taught in high school.

_____ 6. The author believes that the Dow Jones contributed to the Civil War.

_____ 7. The author believes that publishers do not welcome historical books without a fresh point of view.

_____ 8. The dates in the author's brief summary of the history text are probably accurate.

_____ 9. The Treaty of Utrecht was not used to harness water power.

_____ 10. The author includes fetching Grandpa's bourbon to show that Grandpa was an alcoholic.

VOCABULARY

Write a response to the following items.

1. What does *avuncular* mean? _____

2. Why is it mentioned twice in the selection? _____

3. What mnemonic technique could you use for remembering this word?

_____

WRITTEN RESPONSE

How does the author make this selection humorous? **Explain and give examples of at least four ways in which Barry adds humor.**

© 1997 Addison-Wesley Educational Publishers Inc.

POLITICAL SCIENCE

Stage 1: Skill Development

Preview

The author describes the influence of the media on the political system.

agree ☐   disagree ☐

Activate Schema

How much of the daily news do you get from television, radio, or newspapers?

Would you consider yourself a liberal or a conservative? Why?

Learning Strategy

Be able to describe how the media influence the news.

Begin to decide if you think this influence is positive or negative.

Word Knowledge

Are you familiar with the following words in this selection?

crucial	crafty	ferreting	peripheral
clout	wrath	epitomized	inherent
ally	chastised		

Your instructor may ask ten true-false questions from the *Instructor's Manual* to stimulate your thinking using these words.

Stage 2: Integrate Knowledge While Reading

Use thinking strategies as you read:

1. Predict   2. Picture   3. Relate   4. Monitor   5. Fix up

The Mass Media
From Robert L. Lineberry, George C. Edwards III, and Martin P. Wattenberg, *Government in America*

In today's technological world, the media—like computers, atomic power, aircraft, and automobiles—are everywhere. The American political system has entered a new period of **high-tech politics,** a politics in which the behavior of citizens and policymakers, as well as the political agenda itself, is
5   increasingly shaped by technology. The **mass media** are a key part of this technology. Television, radio, newspapers, magazines, and other means of popular communication are called mass media because they reach and profoundly influence not only the elites but the masses.

The Mass Media Today
10   These days, the news media often make the news as well as report it. Television news anchors are paid Hollywood-style salaries and sometimes behave in Hollywood style (as Dan Rather did when he stalked off the set of the evening news one night, and as Diane Sawyer did when she modeled for *Vanity Fair*). At the 1992 political party conventions, Tom Brokaw not only
15   reported the news but also appeared on the "Tonight Show," trading jokes with Jay Leno. Secure in their jobs as long as their ratings remain high, TV anchors have taken their place beside presidents, senators, and others who shape public opinion and policy.

An effective media strategy is thus crucial to any presidential campaign.
20   Candidates have learned that the secret to controlling the media's focus is limiting what they can report on to carefully scripted events. These are known as media events. A **media event** is staged primarily for the purpose of being covered. If the media are not there, the event would probably not happen or would have no significance. For example, on the eve of the 1992
25   New Hampshire primary, Bill and Hillary Clinton went door-to-door in a middle-class neighborhood with TV crews in tow. The few dozen people the Clintons met could scarcely have made a difference, but they were not really there to win votes by personal contact. Rather, the point was to get pictures on TV of the Clintons reaching out to ordinary people.
30   Getting the right image on TV news for just 30 seconds can easily have a greater payoff than a whole day's worth of handshaking. Whereas once a candidate's G.O.T.V. program stood for "Get Out the Vote," today it is more likely to mean "Get on TV."

Yet image making doesn't stop with the campaign—it is also a critical
35 element in day-to-day governing. Politicians' images in the press are seen as
good indicators of their clout. This is especially true of presidents, who in
recent years have devoted major attention to maintaining a well-honed
public image. As President Nixon wrote in an internal White House memo
in 1969:

40   When I think of the millions of dollars that go into one lousy 30-
second television spot advertising a deodorant, it seems to me unbelievable
that we don't do a better job in seeing that Presidential appearances always
have the very best professional advice whenever they are to be covered on
TV. . . . The President should never be without the very best professional
45 advice for making a television appearance.

The Development of the Mass Media

We clearly live in a mass media age today, but it was not always this way.
There was virtually no daily press when the First Amendment was written
during Washington's presidency. The daily newspaper is largely a product of
50 the late nineteenth century; radio and television have been around only
since the first half of the twentieth. As recently as the presidency of Herbert
Hoover (1929–1933), reporters submitted their questions to the president
in writing, and he responded in writing—if at all. As Hoover put it, "The
President of the United States will not stand and be questioned like a
55 chicken thief by men whose names he does not even know."

Hoover's successor, Franklin D. Roosevelt (1933–1945), practically
invented media politics. To Roosevelt, the media were a potential ally.
Power radiated from Washington under him—and so did news. Roosevelt
promised reporters **two press conferences**—presidential meetings with
60 reporters—a week, and he delivered them. He held 337 press conferences
in his first term, 374 in his second, and 279 in his third. Roosevelt was *the*
newsmaker. Stories and leads flowed from the White House like a flood; the
United Press news syndicate carried four times as much Washington news
under FDR as it had under Hoover. FDR was also the first president to use
65 radio, broadcasting a series of reassuring "fireside chats" to the Depression-
ridden nation. Roosevelt's crafty use of radio helped him win four
presidential elections. Theodore White tells the story of the time in 1944
when FDR found out that his opponent, Thomas E. Dewey, had purchased
15 minutes of air time on NBC immediately following his own address.
70 Roosevelt spoke for 14 minutes and then left one minute silent. Thinking
that the network had experienced technical difficulties, many changed their
dials before Dewey came on the air.

Another Roosevelt talent was knowing how to feed the right story to the
right reporter. He used presidential wrath to warn reporters off material he
75 did not want covered, and chastised news reports he deemed inaccurate.
His wrath was rarely invoked, however, and the press revered him, never
even reporting to the American public that the President was confined to a

wheelchair. The idea that a political leader's private life might be public business was alien to journalists in FDR's day.

80   This relatively cozy relationship between politicians and the press lasted through the early 1960s. As ABC's Sam Donaldson writes, when he first came to Washington in 1961, "many reporters saw themselves as an extension of the government, accepting, with very little skepticism, what government officials told them." The events of the Vietnam War and the

85   Watergate scandal, though, soured the press on government. Today's newspeople work in an environment of cynicism. To them, politicians rarely tell the whole story; the press sees ferreting out the truth as their job. No one epitomized this attitude in the 1980s better than Donaldson, who earned a hard-nosed reputation by regularly shouting unwanted questions

90   at President Reagan. In his book, *Hold On, Mr. President!,* Donaldson says,

> If you send me to cover a pie-baking contest on Mother's Day, I'm going to ask dear old Mom whether she used artificial sweetener in violations of the rules, and while she's at it, could I see the receipt for the apples to prove she didn't steal them. I maintain that if Mom has nothing
>
> 95   to hide, no harm will have been done. But the questions should be asked.

Critics of aggressive reporters like Donaldson believe that the media undermine public confidence in government, as well as discourage people from public service due to the microscopic attention they can expect to receive.

100   **Reporting the News**

Regardless of the medium, it cannot be emphasized enough that news reporting is a business in America. Striving for the bottom line—profits— shapes how journalists define the news, where they get the news, and how they present it. Because some news stories attract more viewers or readers

105   than others, there are certain inherent biases in what the American public sees and reads.

Defining News

As every journalism student will quickly tell you, news is what is timely and different. It is when a man bites a dog as opposed to when a dog bites a

110   man. An oft-repeated speech on foreign policy or a well-worn statement on fighting drug abuse is less newsworthy than an odd episode. The public rarely hears about the routine ceremonies at state dinners, but when President Bush threw up all over the Japanese Prime Minister, the world's media jumped on the story. In its search for the unusual, the news media

115   can give its audience a very peculiar view of events and policymakers.

Millions of new and different events happen every day; journalists must decide which of them are newsworthy. In their pursuit of high ratings, news shows are tailored to a fairly low level of audience sophistication. To a large extent, TV networks define news as what is entertaining to the average

120   viewer.

Presenting the News

Once the news has been "found," it has to be neatly compressed into a
30-second news segment or fit in among the advertisements in a newspaper.
If you had to pick a single word to describe news coverage by the print and
125   broadcast media, it would be *superficial*. "The name of the game," says
former White House press secretary Jody Powell, "is skimming off the
cream, seizing on the most interesting, controversial, and unusual aspects of
an issue." TV news, in particular, is little more than a headline service.

Strangely enough, as technology has enabled the media to pass along
130   information with greater speed, news coverage has become less complete.
Newspapers once routinely reprinted the entire text of important political
speeches; now the *New York Times* is virtually the only paper that does this—
and even they have cut back sharply on this practice. In place of speeches,
Americans now hear **sound bites** of 15 seconds or less on TV. The average
135   length of time that a presidential candidate has been given to talk
uninterrupted on the TV news steadily declined from 1968 to 1988.
Responding to criticism of sound-bite journalism, in 1992 CBS News briefly
vowed it would let a candidate speak for at least 30 seconds at a time.
However, CBS found this to be unworkable, and soon dropped the
140   threshold to 20 seconds, and said that even this was flexible.

Even successful politicians often feel frustrated by this process. A year
after his 1976 election victory Jimmy Carter told a reporter that

it's a strange thing that you can go through your campaign for
president, and you have a basic theme that you express in a 15- or 20-
145   minute standard speech, . . . but the traveling press—sometimes exceeding
100 people—will never report that speech to the public. The peripheral
aspects become the headlines, but the basic essence of what you stand for
and what you hope to accomplish is never reported.

Rather than presenting their audience with the whole chicken, the media
150   typically gives just a McNugget. Why then should politicians work to build a
carefully crafted case for their point of view when a catchy line will do just as
well? Indeed, one major reason that CBS's 1992 plan to provide longer
sound bites failed was that the candidates rarely said anything that lent itself
to lengthy coverage.

Bias in the News
155
Many people believe that the news is biased in favor of one point of
view. During the 1992 presidential campaign, George Bush often charged
that the press was against him. "Annoy the Media—Reelect Bush" became
one of his favorite lines. The charge that the media have a liberal bias has
160   become a familiar one in American politics, and there is some limited
evidence to support it. A lengthy study by the *Los Angeles Times* in the
mid–1980s found that reporters were twice as likely to call themselves liberal
as the general public. And a 1992 survey of 1400 journalists found that 44

percent identified themselves as Democrats, compared to just 16 percent
165   who said they were Republicans.

Ideally the news should mirror reality; in practice there are far too
many possible stories for this to be the case. Journalists must select which
stories to cover and to what degree. Because news reporting is a business,
the overriding bias is toward stories which will draw the largest audience.
170   Surveys show that people are most fascinated by stories with conflict,
violence, disaster, or scandal. Good news is unexciting; bad news has the
drama that brings in big audiences.

Stage 3: Recall

Stop to self-test and relate the issues. Your instructor may ask ten true-false
questions to stimulate your recall.

SKILL DEVELOPMENT: EXPLORING POINTS OF VIEW

Form a small collaborative group to discuss the following questions.

1. In what ways are the nightly network news shows biased?
2. Name a media reporter who seems to be liberal.
3. Name a media reporter who seems to be conservative.
4. Why would some people feel that news anchors should not act like Hollywood celebrities?
5. Does your local newspaper have a liberal or conservative slant?
6. What would this author say about the newspaper, *USA Today?* What is your opinion of the newspaper?

COMPREHENSION QUESTIONS

After reading the selection, answer the following questions with *a, b, c,* or *d.*

_____   1. The best statement of the main idea of this selection is
   a. modern mass media are dominated by celebrity reporters.
   b. mass media define and shape today's news and newsmakers.
   c. mass media no longer compete in a free market because of conglomerate ownership.
   d. mass media are corrupt and create news in order to make money.

_____   2. The author implies that the creation of the term *mass* for media refers to the
   a. scope of the audience.
   b. the depth of reporting.
   c. the quality of the coverage.
   d. the variety of communications.

_____ 3. The author implies that a *media event*
   a. would exist as news without media coverage.
   b. is an important news event.
   c. would not exist without media coverage.
   d. exists to fill time on slow news days.

_____ 4. The quote by President Nixon about television spots suggests that
   a. he was against media events.
   b. he resented deodorant advertisements.
   c. he wanted to be a Hollywood celebrity.
   d. he understood the power of a short television appearance.

_____ 5. The author suggests that the reason for Roosevelt's large number of news conferences was
   a. more news events occurred under Roosevelt than in previous administrations.
   b. Roosevelt knew how to manipulate the press to strengthen his popularity.
   c. the public wanted to hear more news from Washington.
   d. newspapers were less popular because of the advent of radio.

_____ 6. The author would probably agree that
   a. Roosevelt's wheelchair confinement would be reported today.
   b. Roosevelt's wheelchair confinement would not be reported today.
   c. the public had no right to know about Roosevelt's wheelchair confinement.
   d. the public had no desire to know about Roosevelt's wheelchair confinement.

_____ 7. The tone of Sam Donaldson's anecdote about the pie-baking contest is
   a. bitter.
   b. skeptical.
   c. nostalgic.
   d. sympathetic.

_____ 8. The main purpose of the selection is
   a. to shock.
   b. to inform.
   c. to ridicule.
   d. to entertain.

_____ 9. The author suggests that sound bites of political speeches
   a. are much less than the average viewer wants to hear.
   b. give an incorrect impression of politicians.
   c. are necessary because of the technology.
   d. reflect the need of the news to entertain.

_____ 10. The author's presentation of the data suggests that George Bush's accusations against the press were
   a. unfounded.
   b. false.
   c. substantiated.
   d. ridiculous.

Answer the following with *T* (true) or *F* (false).

_____ 11. The author implies that news anchors should not behave like Hollywood celebrities.

_____ 12. The author implies that Bill and Hillary Clinton's door-to-door performance for television was a typical example of how politicians use the media for their own gain.

_____ 13. The reader can infer that Hoover missed a golden opportunity by maintaining a negative attitude toward the press.

_____ 14. In the anecdote by Theodore White, the author suggests that Roosevelt knowingly sabotaged Dewey's plan for a large audience.

_____ 15. The author implies that daily news coverage is influenced by the need to show a profit.

VOCABULARY

According to the way the italicized word was used in the selection, select *a, b, c,* or *d* for the word or phrase that gives the best definition.

_____ 1. "*crucial* to any . . . campaign" (19)
   a. vital
   b. obligated
   c. harmonious
   d. favorable

_____ 2. "indicators of their *clout*" (36)
   a. prestige
   b. eligibility
   c. financing
   d. honor

_____ 3. "potential *ally*" (57)
   a. captive
   b. adversary
   c. source
   d. friend

_____ 4. "*crafty* use of radio" (66)
   a. experienced
   b. self-taught
   c. shrewd
   d. righteous

_____ 5. "presidential *wrath*" (74)
   a. anger
   b. charm
   c. power
   d. diplomacy

_____ 6. "*chastised* news reports" (75)
   a. dismissed
   b. destroyed
   c. ignored
   d. reprimanded

—— 7. *"ferreting* out the truth" (87)
    a. finishing
    b. searching
    c. canceling
    d. calling

—— 8. *"epitomized* this attitude" (88)
    a. deserved
    b. exemplified
    c. earned
    d. promoted

—— 9. *"inherent* biases" (105)
    a. acceptable
    b. unknown
    c. undefined
    d. innate

—— 10. *"peripheral* aspects" (146)
    a. disputed
    b. controversial
    c. auxiliary
    d. unofficial

WRITTEN RESPONSE

Compare and contrast the news coverage in your local daily newspaper and the coverage in *USA Today*. Explain what seems to be the purpose and audience for each.

Response Strategy: In order to compare the newspapers, purchase the same daily copy of your local paper and *USA Today*. Discuss and give examples of the type of news stories that receive front-page coverage, the depth of the news coverage, the variety of sections in each paper, and the obvious attempts of each paper to appeal to a specific audience.

COLLABORATIVE CRITICAL THINKING

Network News

Most television viewers have a regular favorite among the network nightly news anchors. Some people watch the same anchor faithfully every night of the week. What are the reasons that people prefer one network anchor over another? The reasons probably relate to the attitude of the anchor, the selection of the news stories, and the treatment of the news.

Which of the nightly network news programs do you watch most often? Do you prefer ABC, CBS, or NBC? Can you explain why? To answer this question for yourself, collaborate with at least two other classmates to devise a plan and a checklist for watching each of the three nightly news programs. Everyone in the group should take notes on the "performance" of each news anchor and be prepared to participate in a group discussion. This is an activity that requires keen inferential skills. You will be evaluating what is said, how it is said, and what is not said. Consider the following questions when devising a checklist for gathering information:

1. Does the presentation of the news seem to have a liberal slant or a conservative slant?
2. If there is a story about the president, is it treated in a positive or negative manner?
3. If there is a story about social issues, is it given a liberal or conservative slant?
4. How did the choice of news differ on a single night for each of the networks?
5. What negatives were implied about people or events?
6. For a single news event, how did the choice of those who were interviewed differ?
7. Was the program all headline news or were personal-interest segments included?
8. Did the news anchor show a personal response to a news story?

Although all members of the group may not agree on the same choice of anchors, be prepared to share the reasons for your own first choice with the class.

SELECTION 3

POLITICAL SCIENCE

Stage 1: Skill Development

Preview

The author is condemning the Japanese for Pearl Harbor.

agree ☐　　　disagree ☐

Activate Schema

Why is the Japanese language difficult for Americans to learn?

Learning Strategy

Be able to describe ways in which Japanese thinking differs from American thinking and lifestyles.

Word Knowledge

Review the vocabulary items that follow the selection. Seek an understanding of unfamiliar words.

Stage 2: Integrate Knowledge While Reading

Use thinking strategies as you read:
1. Predict   2. Picture   3. Relate   4. Monitor   5. Fix up

Japanese Americans
From Don C. Locke, *Increasing Multicultural Understanding*[1]

As Japan is moving into a position to dominate the world economy in the twenty-first century, it is imperative that we look carefully at how the Japanese and Japanese Americans influence the dominant culture of the United States. An advertiser's recent campaign to buy only products "made
5   in the U.S.A." supports the contention that many in the dominant culture of the United States feel threatened, resentful, and suspicious of the Japanese. Japanese technology has outstripped that of the United States, causing negative feelings to persist. The Japanese economy is highly industrialized and, technologically speaking, is giving industries in the
10   United States fierce competition.

Given this impact on the dominant culture of the United States, we need to be aware of the Japanese not only in economic terms, but in cultural terms as well.

Poverty and Economic Concerns

15   In Japan, schools at the primary and secondary level have assumed such importance in determining an individual's future that chances of acquiring higher status are virtually decided before one is barely out of the teenage years. Schooling is critical because social advancement for most Japanese means joining the ranks of white-collar workers in one of the country's giant
20   corporations. As Nakane (1972) reports, once a person gets such a job— known in Japan as becoming a "salary man"—he can generally count on remaining with the company for life. During his career promotions come regularly; he can usually predict when he will become the head of a department or assistant to a manager. Except during periods of unusual
25   economic turmoil, employees are seldom discharged or laid off.

[1]Don C. Locke, *Increasing Multicultural Understanding*. Newbury Park, California: SAGE Publications, 1993., pp. 62–72.

To obtain a corporate job that will set him up for life, however, the aspirant must be a graduate of one of the better universities. The difficult stage in the individual's career is passing the examinations that qualify him for the limited positions open in the universities. The psychological toll of such early status competition is marked by an alarming number of suicides among children who despair over their academic prospects.

Jenkins (1973) conducted a study on blue- and white-collar democracy in other countries and found that in Japan the man is known by the company that keeps him. Joining a large corporation upon leaving school, the Japanese youth expects to stay with the firm for his entire working life, never to be fired except for criminal acts or on grounds of insanity. In return, he is expected to work loyally, to identify with the corporation, to follow the rules, and to wait his turn for promotion. The Japanese worker derives not only his livelihood and security from his place in the corporation, but also health care, further education, and social life. Every large corporation also has a semiformal system to ensure that the employee's assignments match his personal needs and career desires as much as possible. If he is a young man seeking to marry, the company stands ready to help him find a bride and to provide a priest and a hall for the wedding ceremony.

This kind of lifelong dependency on a single organization clearly does not fit Western traditions of mobility and diversity. In the United States one finds a somewhat different educational and occupational pattern of development among Japanese Americans. Though the "model minority" label often attached to them is considered inaccurate by some experts, Japanese Americans do constitute a group that seems to have "made it" as far as educational attainment is concerned.

History of Oppression

Japanese immigrants began coming to the United States in large numbers around 1890. They were at once subjected to the punishment and harrassment already known to the Chinese.

Sue and Sue (1990) conclude that because Japan was a rising international power, the anti-Japanese feeling did not manifest itself directly in legislation to restrict immigration, but led to a "gentlemen's agreement" to stem the flow of Asians to the United States. To harass the Japanese further, California in 1913 passed the Alien land Law, which forbade aliens to own land. The Alien Land Law was an emotional warning to the public that Japanese farmers were going to take over agricultural land. In fact, the Japanese owned only 12,726 farm acres out of 11 million acres in California in 1912 (Chuman, 1976).

After the devastating attack on Pearl Harbor on December 7, 1941, all Japanese living in the United States came under extreme suspicion. Thousands of Japanese Americans were rounded up and "contraband" such as cameras, flashlights, and hunting rifles were confiscated. These events

70 were reported prominently by the news media, but the fact that none of
those apprehended had done anything to harm the national interest was
largely ignored. A total of 110,000 Japanese Americans were sent to
concentration camps. They accepted their internment with virtually no
resistance; imprisoned for no crime but their race, they met their fate with
75 resignation, a primary characteristic of Japanese culture.

Language and the Arts

Many Japanese-American families still speak Japanese at home but
communicate well in English outside the home. Many other differences in
styles of communication between Japanese culture and the dominant
80 culture in the United States are nonverbal. For instance, there is very little
eye contact among Japanese. Direct eye contact is considered impolite and
even disrespectful toward seniors. Minimal eye contact takes place only
among families and peers.

In Japan, there is a maximum amount of body contact between mother
85 and child, including sleeping together. Young teenagers might hold hands,
but hugging and kissing are considered to be in poor taste. After childhood,
there is no body contact with others except that between husband and wife,
which occurs only in total privacy.

Instead of shaking hands, the Japanese traditionally bow. The depth of
90 the bow indicates the social position of the person being greeted. A
complete bow is made when one is looking at a shrine. Upon encountering
an old friend or relative he or she has not seen in a long time, a Japanese
bows many times.

Since physical space is limited in Japan, the amount of "personal space"
95 individuals are comfortable with around them is smaller than in the United
States. Taking up a large personal space is interpreted as rude and hostile.

For Japanese, earth and heaven meet through people to form art. Art is
elegant and even reverent, yet simple and easily handled. It is usually linear
and nonrepetitive; it has one theme and definite closure. Often, art in the
100 form of paintings, screens, scrolls, and clothing is characterized by bright
colors and subjects of nature and/or people. The cultural emphasis on
silence and reservation of verbal communication can be seen in the classical
dance-drama form known as *Noh,* in which actors wearing masks exchange
little or no verbal dialogue. The martial arts stress relaxation, deflection,
105 and the interaction of mind and body as sources of inner strength in
defending against an outside aggressor. Other important Japanese art forms
that combine spiritual and aesthetic experience are *ikebana* (flower
arranging), gardening, and the intense and highly stylized tea ceremony.

Sociopolitical Factors

110 The Japanese-American social structure has often been described as
vertical rather than horizontal, meaning that relations are clearly defined to

those above or below in the social hierarchy. The lack of political activity among Japanese Americans can be explained through a close examination of these values. Japanese Americans value maintaining low visibility and
115 conformity in order not to bring negative attention to themselves. A model Japanese leader is one who is informed, possesses thorough knowledge, and yet avoids the spotlight.

In general, Japanese Americans have achieved high socioeconomic mobility in spite of discrimination against them. The value system of the
120 Japanese encouraged economic success and educational opportunity and further opened the door to higher occupational status.

Child-Rearing Practices

In Japan, as well as among Japanese Americans, elders are viewed with great respect, and a strong family system is very important. According to
125 Garfinkle (1983), the dominant orientation of the Japanese family begins with the constant interest and pressure that the Japanese mother provides for her children. The Japanese mother devotes herself to the rearing of her children and pushes them to excel academically. The intensely close relationship between mother and child shows the most pervasive values of
130 Japanese society; the work ethic, selflessness, and group endeavor. When it comes to the discipline of children, the Japanese mother is more inclined than the American mother to appeal to feelings as a coercive tool, by simply expressing her displeasure. Japanese writers on child rearing recommend mildness in the direct verbal teaching of children. They believe that
135 children should be admonished in a firm but calm manner, and that adults should not use abusive language or show anger and impatience. A study by Kurokawa (1968) with Japanese-American families showed that the Japanese mother rocks the child more and talks less, while the American mother talks more and touches less.

140 According to anthropologist Ruth Benedict (1945), the Japanese father is less of a disciplinarian than are fathers in almost any Western nation. To the Japanese father, the child may show only respect. The father is the great exemplar to the child, of high hierarchical position, and the child must learn to express the proper respect to him "for training." Sue (1981) and
145 Watanabe (1973) also describe the family system as patriarchal, with the father's authority unquestioned. The primary duty of a son is allegiance to his father, before his obligations to be a good husband and father to his own children. Subservience to males is the female role in the family, along with the performance of domestic duties and education of the children.

150 ### Religious Practices

Japanese churches have played a significant role in the development of community solidarity and cohesion. Most of the first Japanese who came to the United States were Buddhists. Buddhism is closely tied to the family system so revered in Japanese culture. Many sacred rites are performed at a

155 family shrine. Faith is renewed on a day-to-day basis, with observances conducted within the family. Buddhism encourages the awareness of Japanese values and heritage. From Confucianism came the standard of social behavior that dictates respect and obedience for authority and for elders. Henkin (1985) explains how the Buddhist/Confucian/Shintoist

160 background of the Japanese culture in Japan has established a perceptual, conceptual, and behavioral ground of being that advocates inner discipline and encourages people to conceal frustrations and disappointments. Also, they are expected to submerge individual concerns, to recognize filial piety and moral obligations to others as superior to personal desires, and to

165 persist in their tasks in the face of unhappiness despite the probability of failure or defeat.

　　Culture emphases on money, education, and group conformity do not come from religion as much as from the geography and history of Japan. The standard of group cooperation grew out of Japan's being a rice-growing

170 country. During the days of the feudal system and afterwards, the neighborhood had to work together, because survival depended upon it. Even though Japan now has a large urban population, these values are still upheld. Also, because Japan is such a small island, there is fierce competition for jobs. Thus the geography of the land dictates the almost

175 obsessive value the culture places on education and money—not religion. The values of group conformity and social status via education and money are very much a part of the lives of Japanese Americans as well.

Stage 3: Recall

　　Step to self-test and relate the issues. Your instructor may ask ten true-false questions to stimulate your recall.

SKILL DEVELOPMENT: EXPLORING POINT OF VIEW

　　Form a small collaborative group and discuss the following questions to explore your own point of view and the point of view the author describes on issues introduced in the selection.

1. Do you believe Japan will dominate the world economy in the twenty-first century? Why or why not?
2. Do you believe that Japanese technology has outstripped American technology? Why or why not?
3. How would you feel about staying with one firm for your entire working life?
4. What is your opinion on the differences in pressures to succeed and the freedom of choice of youths in the United States and Japan?
5. What is your feeling about eye contact?
6. On a bus or rapid transit vehicle, how much personal space do you need?

7. How do you feel about a culture including flower arranging and a tea ceremony as art forms?

8. How does respect for elders and parents differ in Japan and the United States?

9. How does Buddhism differ from predominant religions found in the United States?

10. How do you think the Japanese culture affects business in Japan?

COMPREHENSION QUESTIONS

After reading the selection, answer the following questions with *a, b, c,* or *d.*

_____ 1. The best statement of the main idea of this selection is
   a. Japanese Americans have greatly influenced the dominant culture of the United States.
   b. Japanese corporations value education for business advancement.
   c. Japanese Americans consider the home the center of their culture.
   d. Japanese Americans are influenced by traditions that affect their cultural and economic values.

_____ 2. The author mentions "made in the U.S.A." to show that
   a. Japanese products are superior to American products.
   b. Americans feel threatened by Japanese competition.
   c. trade tariffs could limit competition in certain industries.
   d. the Japanese have negative feelings about American technology.

_____ 3. The author implies that career promotions in large corporations in Japan are based on
   a. mobility.
   b. aggressiveness.
   c. length of time at the company.
   d. social status.

_____ 4. The author implies that the underlying purpose of the Alien Land Law was
   a. to incite the public against Japanese immigrants.
   b. to motivate Californians to pass restrictions on Japanese immigration.
   c. to punish and harass the Chinese.
   d. to curb Japan's rising international power.

_____ 5. The author puts quotation marks around the word *contraband* to emphasize
   a. the nature of the goods taken.
   b. the economic value of the confiscated goods.
   c. that the goods were not illegal for others.
   d. the threat posed to the national interest.

_____ 6. The Japanese would consider all of the following unacceptable except
    a. a mother and child sleeping in the same bed.
    b. hugging a girl in public.
    c. looking directly into the eyes of an elder.
    d. a student occupying an extra desk for books and clothing.

_____ 7. To the Japanese, art is all of the following except
    a. a combination of the spiritual and aesthetic.
    b. horizontal and repetitive.
    c. a meeting of heaven and earth through people.
    d. simple and reverent.

_____ 8. According to the author, in a Japanese family discipline typically is
    a. swift and severe.
    b. the primary responsibility of the father.
    c. emotional rather than physical.
    d. not needed because of the close bond between mother and child.

_____ 9. According to the author, the dominant role in the Japanese family is
    a. equally shared by the mother and father.
    b. clearly assigned to the father.
    c. held by the mother who is the educator.
    d. dependent on who is the elder in the family.

_____ 10. The author implies that the teachings of Buddhism
    a. mirror the values of the Japanese culture.
    b. focus on the importance of personal desires.
    c. are in conflict with the teachings of Christianity.
    d. conflict with the Japanese emphasis on the group.

Answer the following with _T_ (true) or _F_ (false).

_____ 11. The author implies that the Japanese value conformity over individuality.

_____ 12. The author implies that the Japanese corporate structure promotes independence in workers.

_____ 13. The author implies that some Japanese Americans were involved in Pearl Harbor.

_____ 14. According to the article, a Japanese man should put the needs of his father before those of his wife.

_____ 15. The author believes that the geography of Japan dictates the cultural emphasis on money.

VOCABULARY

According to the way the italicized word was used in the selection, select *a, b, c,* or *d* for the word or phrase that gives the best definition.

—— 1. "*imperative* that we look" (2)
    a. critical
    b. interesting
    c. rewarding
    d. suggested

—— 2. "*aspirant* must be a graduate" (27)
    a. relative
    b. seeker
    c. employer
    d. friend

—— 3. "*derives* not only his livelihood" (39)
    a. drains
    b. requests
    c. requires
    d. gains

—— 4. "rifles were *confiscated*" (69)
    a. seized
    b. issued
    c. hidden
    d. authorized

—— 5. "met their fate with *resignation*" (75)
    a. resistance
    b. grief
    c. dignity
    d. submissiveness

—— 6. "*Minimal* eye contact" (82)
    a. close
    b. minor
    c. distant
    d. forbidden

—— 7. "definite *closure*" (99)
    a. rhythm
    b. conclusion
    c. spirit
    d. clarity

—— 8. "as a *coercive* tool" (132)
    a. emotional
    b. relevant
    c. forceful
    d. helpful

—— 9. "*exemplar* to the child" (143)
    a. substitute
    b. manager
    c. facilitator
    d. model

—— 10. "*allegiance* to his father" (146)
    a. love
    b. favoritism
    c. humility
    d. loyalty

WRITTEN RESPONSE

Explain at least four aspects of the Japanese cultural heritage that contribute to the high achievement of Japan in the marketplace.

Answer the following questions to learn about your own learning and reflect on your progress. Your instructor may collect your responses.

How can your point of view cloud your understanding of material you read?

_____

Select a current and controversial news issue and describe your position.

_____

When you read for pleasure, what type of material do you tend to enjoy? What tends to be the author's main purpose in that material?

_____

Define the following tones and give an example:

sarcastic

_____

skeptical

_____

cynical

_____

Reflect on the Longer Selections

Total your short-answer responses for the three longer selections.

Comprehension scores:
completed = ___   # correct = ___   # incorrect = ___   % accuracy = ___

What did you enjoy most about the humorous Dave Barry selection? How do comics use a different perspective or point of view to make us laugh? Give an example.

_____

What is multiculturalism?

_____

How can education give us greater appreciation for different cultural views?

_____

Name some recent events that you feel have been overcovered by the media in an effort to make the news interesting.

_____

What types of questions did you miss on the comprehension?

_____

_____

Clip out and explain three questions that you missed. Attach these questions and your analysis to the Learning Log for your instructor.

Reflect on the Vocabulary

Total your vocabulary responses for the longer selections.

completed = ___   # correct = ___   # incorrect = ___   accuracy = ___%

List the words that you missed.

_____

_____

How are you remembering *avuncular?*

_____

_____

Use it in a sentence that reflects its meaning.

_____

_____

Vocabulary Review

Begin to review the vocabulary words from previous chapters.

Using the perforations, tear out the Learning Log for your instructor.

CHAPTER

7

Critical Thinking

What is critical thinking?

What are the barriers to critical thinking?

How do you identify issues?

What are the parts of an argument?

What are the types of evidence?

How do you evaluate an argument for relevance, believability, and consistency?

What is creative thinking?

WHAT IS CRITICAL THINKING?

Do you accept the thinking of others or do you think for yourself? Do you examine and judge? Can you identify important questions and systematically search for answers? Can you justify what you believe? If so, you are thinking critically. For example, if each of the following represented a textbook portrayal of Christopher Columbus, which would you tend to accept most readily and why?

Was he a courageous hero?

Was he a despot who enslaved the Indians?

Was he a hapless explorer who failed to find India or gold?

Rather than answer immediately, most students would say, "I need more information. I want to consider the arguments, weigh the facts, and draw my own conclusions."

Definition

Thinking critically means deliberating in a purposeful, organized manner in order to assess the value of information, both old and new. Critical thinkers search, compare, analyze, clarify, evaluate, and conclude. Critical thinkers do not start from scratch; they build on previous knowledge or schemata to forge new relationships. They recognize both sides of an issue and evaluate the reasons and evidence in support of each.

Some professors speak of critical thinking as if it were a special discipline rather than an application of many known skills. Frank Smith, an educator who has written eleven books on thinking, says that thinking critically refers simply to the manner in which thinking is done.[1] It is merely an approach to thinking, in the same sense that thinking impulsively or thinking seriously are approaches, and the approach can be practiced and learned.

College Goals

Many colleges cite the ability to think critically as one of the essential academic outcome goals for students graduating after four years of college work. An educated person is expected to think systematically, to evaluate, and to draw conclusions based on logic. At your college, an emphasis on critical thinking probably crosses the curriculum, and thus becomes a part of every college course. When an instructor returns a paper to you and writes, "Good logic" or "Not enough support," the comments are referring to critical thinking. The same is true if you make a class presentation and are told either that your thesis was very convincing or that you were missing vital support. Critical thinking is thus not a new skill; it is the systematic application of many well-learned skills.

[1]Frank Smith, *To Think* (New York: Teachers' College Press, 1990)

APPLICATION OF FAMILIAR SKILLS

Critical thinking involves the application of many different skills that have already been introduced and practiced in this text. These skills include identifying the main idea, significant supporting details, inferences, and points of view, as well as others. A few new techniques for evaluating the support for an argument or thesis will be introduced in this chapter.

Critical thinking instruction has its own specialized vocabulary, often using seemingly complex terms for simple ideas. As you work through this chapter, you will become familiar with the critical thinking application of the following terminology:

analogy	fallacy
argument	inductive
assertion	premise
conclusion	relevance
consistency	reliability
deductive	

CHARACTERISTICS OF CRITICAL THINKERS

Critical thinkers question, challenge, and evaluate the status quo. In a book titled *Thought and Knowledge*, Diane Halpern lists four characteristics of critical thinkers which are presented in the box below.[2]

CHARACTERISTICS OF CRITICAL THINKERS

1. **Willingness to plan**
   They think first and write later. They refrain from being impulsive and develop a habit of planning.

2. **Flexibility**
   They are open to new ideas and willing to consider new solutions for old problems.

3. **Persistence**
   They keep on working on a difficult task even when they get tired and discouraged. Good thinking is hard work.

4. **Willingness to self-correct**
   They are not defensive about their errors. They figure out what went wrong and learn from their mistakes.

[2]D. Halpern, *Thought and Knowledge*, 2nd ed. (Hillsdale, N.J.: Lawrence Erlbaum Associates, 1989), pp. 29–30.

Barriers to Critical Thinking

Some people will not allow themselves to think critically. They are mired in their own belief system and do not want to change or be challenged. They are gullible and thus easily persuaded by a slick presentation or an illogical argument. In their book *Invitation to Critical Thinking*,[3] Joel Rudinow and Vincent E. Barry identified the following barriers to critical thinking:

1. Frame of Reference

    Each of us has an existing belief system that influences the way we deal with incoming information. We interpret new experiences according to what we already believe. We are culturally conditioned to resist change and feel that our own way is best. We refuse to look at the merits of something our belief system rejects, such as the advantages of legalizing drugs, for example.

2. Wishful Thinking

    We talk ourselves into believing things that we know are not true because we want them to be true. We irrationally deceive ourselves and engage in self-denial. For example, we might refuse to believe well-founded claims of moral corruption leveled at our favored politician or relative.

3. Hasty Moral Judgments

    We tend to evaluate someone or something as good or bad, right or wrong, and remain fixed in this thinking. Such judgments are often prejudiced, intolerant, emotional, and self-righteous. An example of such a barrier to thinking critically would be the statement, "Abortion should never be legal."

4. Reliance on Authority

    An authority such as a clergy member, a doctor, or a teacher is an expert source of information. We give authorities and institutions such as church or government the power to think for us and thus block our own ability to question and reason.

5. Labels

    Labels ignore individual differences and lump people and things into categories. Labels oversimplify, distort the truth, and usually incite anger and rejection. To say, "People who love America and people who do not," forces others to take sides as a knee-jerk reaction.

Exercise 1   IDENTIFY TYPES OF BARRIERS

Read the following statements and identify with *a, b, c,* or *d* the type of barrier the statement best represents.

    a. Wishful thinking
    b. Frame of reference or hasty moral judgments

[3]J. Rudinow and V. E. Barry. *Invitation to Critical Thinking,* New York: Harcourt Brace College Publishers, 1994, pp. 11–19.

c. Reliance on authority

d. Labels

 _____ 1. The new drug will not be helpful because the FDA has not yet approved it.

(The answer is *c,* reliance on authority, which in this case is a government agency. A critical thinker might argue that the FDA is slow to test and respond to new drugs, and that many drugs are used safely and successfully in other countries before the FDA grants approval for Americans.)

_____ 2. My son was not involved in the robbery because my son could not do such a horrible thing.

_____ 3. In some countries people eat horse meat and dog meat, but it is wrong to do so because these animals are friends of humans.

_____ 4. Our country is divided into two groups of people: those who work and those who don't work.

_____ 5. Polygamy and polyandry should be legalized.

POWER OF CRITICAL THINKING

Critical thinkers are willing to hold their own opinions up to scrutiny and to consider over and over again, "Is this position worth holding?" They drive to the heart of issues and assess reasons for opposing views. They solve problems and gain knowledge. They do not feel the need to persuade or to argue for right or wrong, but they are not afraid of questions. As a result of logical thinking and the ability to justify their own positions, critical thinkers gain confidence.

Courtroom Analogy

Jurors use critical thinking in deciding court cases. The judge defines the issue and clever lawyers argue "conflicting versions of the truth" before the jury. Each presents reasons and selected evidence to support the case of the client. Needless to say, in the summation to the jury, each attorney interprets the truth in the client's best interest. The jury is left to weigh the validity of the evidence, to reflect on what might be missing, and to decide between two logical arguments. Through the critical thinking process, the jurors systematically answer the following questions:

1. What is the issue?
2. What are the arguments?
3. What is the evidence?
4. What is the verdict?

College students can adapt the jury's critical thinking approach to textbook reading. The same four questions are as relevant in weighing information about Christopher Columbus, genetic engineering, or manic depression as they are to making life-or-death courtroom decisions.

RECOGNIZE AN ARGUMENT

We often make statements that are not arguments. Assertions such as "I like milk" or "We had a huge overnight snowfall, and my car is covered" are not meant to trigger extensive thought, provoke questions, and lead to analysis. These are nonargumentative statements that are intended to inform or explain. An argument, on the other hand, is an assertion or set of assertions that supports a conclusion and is intended to persuade.

The basic difference between an argument and an nonargumentative statement is the intent or purpose. Nonargumentative statements do not question truth but simply offer information to explain and thereby help us understand. For example, the statement, "The grass is wet because it rained last night" is an explanation, not an argument. To say, however, "You should water the grass tonight because rain is not predicted for several days" constitutes an argument. In the latter case, the conclusion of watering the grass is based on a "fact," the forecast, and the intent is to persuade by appealing to reason. To identify arguments we must use inferential skills and recognize the underlying purpose or intent of the author.

Exercise 2   IDENTIFY THE ARGUMENT

Practice recognizing arguments by identifying each of the following statements with *A* for argument or *N* for a nonargumentative statement of information.

_N_ 1. The foods in salad bars sometimes contain preservatives to keep them looking fresh and appealing.
     (This is not an argument. It is not intended to move you to action. It is a statement of fact similar to "It sometimes snows at night.")

_A_ 2. Food preservatives can cause cancer and thus you should avoid eating food that contains them.

_A_ 3. According to the verification of a famed Nobel laureate, take Vitamin C regularly in order to prevent colds.

_AN_ 4. Contaminated water can cause many serious, life-threatening diseases.

_A_ 5. Parrots talk because people have taught them how to speak and to understand.

STEPS IN CRITICAL THINKING

Analyzing an argument through critical thinking and evaluation combines the use of most of the skills that have been taught in this text. The amount of analysis depends on the complexity of the argument. Some arguments are simple, while others are lengthy and complicated. The following is a four-step procedure that can be used as a format to guide your critical thinking:

1. Identify the issue.
2. Identify the support for the argument.
3. Evaluate the support.
4. Evaluate the argument.

Step 1: Identify the Issue

In the courtroom, the judge instructs the jury on the issue and the lawyers provide the arguments. In reading, however, the issues may not be as obvious or clearly defined. The reader must cut through the verbiage to recognize underlying issue as well as to identify support.

Good readers are "tuned in" to look for issues that have opposing points of view. Writers strive to convince readers but are under no obligation to explain, or even to admit persuasion. Knowledgeable readers, however, sense possible biases; they look for the hidden agendas. Good readers constantly ask, "How am I being manipulated or persuaded?" to detect an argument and then ask "What is the debatable question or central issue in this argument?"

In a college course on critical thinking or logic, the parts of an argument that you would be asked to identify would probably be called the conclusion and the premises. The conclusion is an assertion or position statement. It is what the author is trying to convince you to believe or to do. For example, in the statement, "You should water the grass because rain is not in the forecast," the conclusion is "You should water the grass." The premise, or support, is "because rain is not in the forecast." In the terminology of this textbook, the conclusion also could be viewed as a statement of the main point.

To identify the issue or conclusion in persuasive writing, use your main-idea reading skills. First ask yourself, "What is the passage main about?" to determine the topic. Then ask, "What is the main point the author is trying to convey about the topic?" Your answer will be a statement of the issue that is being argued which could also be called the main point, the thesis, or the conclusion.

Begin by reading the material all the way through. Do not allow your own beliefs to cloud your thinking. Set aside your own urge to agree or disagree, but be alert to the bias of the author. Be aware of the barriers to critical thinking that include limited frame of reference, wishful thinking, hasty moral judgments, reliance on authority, and labeling. Be sensitive to emotional language and the connotation of words. Cut through the rhetoric and get to the heart of the matter.

Read the following passage and identify the issue that is being argued.

The technology for television has far exceeded the programming. Viewers are recipients of crystal clear junk. Network programming appeals to the masses for ratings and advertising money and offers little creative or stimulating entertainment.

Several debatable issues about television are suggested by this passage. They include the abundance of technological advancement, the power of ratings, and the importance of advertising money. The central issue, however, concerns the quality of network programming. Although it is not directly stated, the argument or central issue is "Network television programming is not any good."

Recognizing Analogies as a Familiar Pattern in Issues. Polya, a pioneer in mathematical problem solving, said we cannot imagine or solve a problem that is totally new and absolutely unlike any problem we have ever known.[4] We seek connections and look for similarities to previous experiences. Such comparisons are called **analogies.**

Analogies are most easily made on a personal level. We think about how the issue has affected or could affect us or someone we know. For example, if high school principals were seeking your input on the issue of declining mathematics scores, you would first relate the problem to your own experience. How did you score in math? Why do you think you did or did not do well? What about your friends? From your memory of high school, what would you identify as the key reasons for the declining scores? The problem now has a personal meaning and is linked to prior knowledge.

Linking new knowledge with personal and expanded comparisons applies past experience to new situations. Two researchers tested the importance of analogies by asking students to read technical passages with and without analogies to familiar topics.[5] The students who read the material containing the analogies scored higher on tests of comprehension and recall than students who did not have the benefit of the familiar comparisons.

Referring back to the previous example on television programming, what analogies could you draw from your own personal experience? What television programs do you consider junk? Are they all junk? What network programs do you feel are high-quality entertainment?

Identifying the Issue Through Signal Words. The central issue may be stated as the thesis or main point at the beginning of an argument, it may be imbedded within the passage or it may be stated at the end as a conclusion. The following key words are sometimes used to signal the central issue being argued:

in summary	consequently
therefore	for these reasons

[4]G. Polya, *How to Solve It*, 2nd ed. (Princeton, N.J.: Princeton University Press, 1957).
[5]C. C. Hansen and D. F. Halpern, *Using analogies to improve comprehension and recall of scientific passages.* Paper presented at the 28th Annual Meeting of the Psychonomic Society (Seattle, Wash., 1987).

thus   finally

it follows that   as a result

Example: What is the central issue that is being argued in the following passage?

A year in a United States prison costs more than a year at Harvard; however, almost no one is rehabilitated. Prisoners meet and share information with other hardened criminals to refine their skills. It seems reasonable, therefore, to conclude that prisons in the U.S. are societal failures.

The central issue in this argument is directly stated in the last sentence. Note the inclusion of the signal word *therefore*.

Exercise 3   IDENTIFY THE ISSUE

Read the following passages and underline or state in a sentence the central issue that is being argued in each.

1. Weekly television comedies frequently show parents in an unflattering light. The parents are usually bettered by the kids, who are portrayed as smarter. The kids win laughs with rude and sarcastic comments directed at the parents.

2. The price of oil, gas, and electricity continues to rise for heating and cooling homes. This rise could lead to renewed interest in solar heating. If the price of installing solar heating panels declined, the result could be that more people would use solar energy as a source for home heating and cooling.

3. Shoplifting raises the price of what we purchase by more than 2 percent. Medicare fraud costs the average taxpayer several hundred dollars each year. The costs of exaggerated insurance claims is passed along to all policy holders in increased premiums. For these reasons it follows that when we cheat corporations, we cheat ourselves and our friends.

4. Censorship is difficult to enforce. A major problem concerns who will do the enforcing. A second issue involves what works will be censored. As a result of these complexities, censorship is unacceptable.

5. Multiple-choice questions measure recognition rather than recall. They do not encourage students to study "the big picture," and thus they should not be used in college classes.

Step 2: Identify Support for the Argument

In a college logic course, after identifying the central issue of an argument, you would be asked to identify and number the premises. Premises are reasons or evidence offered in support of the position being argued. In the previous example about watering the grass, only one premise, "because rain is not in the forecast," was offered. Other premises such as "the grass will die without water" and "water is plentiful right now" would have added further evidence in support of the conclusion. In reality, the identification of premises is simply the identification of significant supporting details for the main point.

Identifying Supporting Reasons through Signal Words. Supporting reasons may be directly stated or may be signaled. The key words that signal support for an argument are in some cases the same as those that signal significant supporting details. They include the following:

because	first . . . second . . . finally
since	assuming that
if	given that

Example: The following example of a previous passage shows how signal words can introduce supporting details.

One can conclude that prisons in the United States are failures. First, almost no one is rehabilitated. Second, prisoners meet and share information with other hardened criminals to refine their skills. Taxpayers should also consider that a year in prison costs more than a year at Harvard.

Note: The argument is the same with or without the signal words. In a longer passage the signal words usually make it easier to identify the significant supporting details or reasons.

Exercise 4   IDENTIFY THE PARTS OF AN ARGUMENT

Read the following passages and identify the central issue that is being argued and the supporting reasons. Place the letter *I* before sentences containing the central issue and place the letter *S* before those containing supporting reasons.

1. The shad or any fish that runs upstream is an excellent choice for sea ranching. Such fish use their own energies to swim and grow in open waters and then swim back to be harvested.

2. Major game reserves in Africa such as the Ngorongoro Crater are in protected areas, but many lie adjacent to large tracts of land with no conservation status. Animals who migrate off the reserves compete with humans for food and are endangered. Thus, clear boundaries between areas for animals and people would minimize friction.

3. Advertisements can be misleading. Their major purpose is to sell something. They use suggestion rather than logic to be convincing.

4. A visit to a doctor's office is a lesson in humility for the patient. First, you see the receptionist who tells you to fill out forms and wait your turn. Next, the nurse takes your blood pressure and extracts blood while you look at the diplomas on the wall. Finally, you are led into a bare room to strip down and wait still longer for the doctor to appear for a few expensive minutes of consultation.

5. In most companies, college graduates get higher-paying jobs than those who do not attend college. As the years go by in a company, promotions and their accompanying raises tend to go primarily to the college graduates. Thus, it can be concluded that a college degree is worth money.

Identifying Types of Supporting Reasons. As support for arguments, readers would probably prefer the simplicity of a smoking gun with fingerprints on it, but such conclusive evidence is usually hard to find. Evidence comes in many different forms, and may be tainted with opinion. The box below contains some categories of "evidence" typically used as supporting reasons in an argument. Each type, however, has its pitfalls and should be immediately tested with an evaluative question.

Step 3: Evaluate The Support

As a reader, you will decide to accept or reject the author's conclusion based on the strength and acceptability of the reasons and evidence. Strong arguments are logically supported by well-crafted reasons and evidence, but clever arguments can be supported by the crafty use of reason and evidence.

In evaluating the support for an argument, teachers of logic warn students to beware of *fallacies*. A **fallacy** is an inference that appears to be reasonable at first glance, but closer inspection proves it to be unrelated, unreliable, or illogical. For example, to say that something is right because everybody is

CATEGORIES OF SUPPORT FOR ARGUMENTS

1. Facts: objective truths
   Ask: How were the facts gathered, and are they true?
2. Examples: anecdotes to demonstrate the truth
   Ask: Are the examples true and relevant?
3. Analogies: comparisons to similar cases
   Ask: Are the analogies accurate and relevant?
4. Authority: words from a recognized expert
   Ask: What are the credentials and biases of the expert?
5. Causal relationship: saying one thing caused another
   Ask: Is it an actual cause or merely an association?
6. Common knowledge claim: assertion of wide acceptance
   Ask: Is it relevant and does everyone really believe it?
7. Statistics: numerical data
   Ask: Do the numbers accurately describe the population?
8. Personal experiences: personal anecdotes
   Ask: Is the experience applicable to other situations?

doing it is not a convincing reason for accepting an idea. Such "reasoning," however, can be compelling and is so frequently used that it is labeled a *bandwagon fallacy.*

Logicians have categorized, labeled, and defined over 200 types of fallacies or tricks of persuasion. The emphasis for the critical thinker should not be on memorizing a long list of fallacy types but, rather, on understanding how such irrelevant reasoning techniques can manipulate logical thinking. Fallacies are tools employed in constructing a weak argument that critical thinkers should spot. In a court of law, the opposing attorney would shout "Irrelevant, Your Honor!" to alert the jury to the introduction of fallacious evidence.

Evaluate the support for an argument according to three areas of reasoning: *relevance, believability,* and *consistency.* The following list of fallacies common to each area can sensitize you to the "tools" of constructing a weak argument.

I. Relevance Fallacies: Is the support related to the conclusion?

Testimonials: opinions of agreement from respected celebrities who are not actually experts

Example: A famous actor endorses a headache pill.

Transfer: an association with a positively or negatively regarded person or thing in order to lend the same association to the argument (also guilt or virtue by association)

Example: A local politician quoting President Lincoln in a speech as if Lincoln would have agreed with and voted for the candidate.

Ad Hominem: an attack on the person rather than the issue in hopes that if the person is opposed, the idea will be opposed

Example: Do not listen to Mr. Hite's views on education because he is a banker.

Bandwagon: the idea that everybody is doing it and you will be left out if you do not quickly join the crowd

Example: Everybody around the world is drinking coke so you should too.

Straw person: a setup in which a distorted or exaggerated form of the opponent's argument is introduced and knocked down as if to represent a totally weak opposition

Example: When a teen-aged daughter is told she cannot go out on the weeknight before a test, she replies with "That's unreasonable to say that I can never go out on a weeknight."

Misleading Analogy: a comparison of two things suggesting that they are similar when they are, in fact, distinctly different

Example: College students are just like elementary school students; they need to be taught self discipline.

II. Believability Fallacies: Is the support believable or highly suspicious?

Incomplete facts *or* **card stacking:** omission of factual details in order to misrepresent reality

Example: Buy stock in this particular restaurant chain because it is under new management and people eat out a lot.

Misinterpreted statistics: numerical data misapplied to unrelated populations which they were never intended to represent

Example: Over 20 percent of people exercise daily and thus do not need fitness training.

Overgeneralizations: examples and anecdotes asserted to apply to all cases rather than a select few

Example: High school students do little work during their senior year and thus are overwhelmed at college.

Questionable authority: testimonial suggesting authority from people who are not experts

Example: Dr. Lee, a university sociology professor, testified that the DNA reports were 100 percent accurate.

III. Consistency Fallacies: Does the support hold together or does it fall apart and contradict itself?

Appeals to pity: pleas to support the underdog, the person or issue that needs your help

Example: Please give me an A for the course because I need it to get into law school.

Appeals to emotions: highly charged language used for emotional manipulation

Example: Give money to our organization to help the children who are starving orphans in desperate need of medical attention.

Oversimplification: reduction of an issue to two simple choices, without consideration of other alternatives or "gray areas" in between

Example: The choices are very simple in supporting our foreign-policy decision to send troops. You are either for America or against it.

Begging the question *or* **circular reasoning:** support for the conclusion which is merely a restatement of it

Example: Drugs should not be legalized because it should be against the law to take illegal drugs.

Slippery slope: Objecting to something because it will lead to greater evil and disastrous consequences

Example: Support for assisting the suicide of a terminally ill patient will lead to the ultimate disposal of the marginally sick and elderly.

Exercise 5   IDENTIFY THE FALLACY

Identify the type of fallacy in each of the following statements by indicating *a, b,* or *c.*

 1. Hollywood movie stars and rock musicians are not experts on the environment and should not be dictating our environmental policy.
   a. testimonial
   b. *ad hominem*
   c. bandwagon

 2. Michael Jordan says, "I always wear this brand of athletic shoes. They are the best."
   a. *ad hominem*
   b. misleading analogy
   c. testimonial

 3. The fight for equal rights is designed to force men out of jobs and encourage women to leave their young children alone at home.
   a. bandwagon
   b. questionable authority
   c. straw person

4. People should give blood because it is important to give blood.
   a. begging the question
   b. appeal to pity
   c. appeal to emotion

5. Prayer in the schools is like cereal for breakfast. They both get the morning off to a good start.
   a. circular reasoning
   b. appeal to emotions
   c. misleading analogy

6. The advocate for rezoning of the property concluded by saying, "George Washington was also concerned about land and freedom."
   a. transfer
   b. *ad hominem*
   c. straw person

 7. The explanation for the distribution of grades is simple. College students either study or they do not study.
   a. misinterpreted statistics
   b. oversimplification
   c. appeal to pity

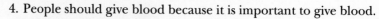

_b_   8. Your written agreement with my position will enable me to keep my job.
   a. misinterpreted statistics
   b. appeal to pity
   c. card stacking

_a_   9. Everyone in the neighborhood has worked on the new park design and agreed to it. Now we need your signature of support.
   a. bandwagon
   b. appeal to emotion
   c. begging the question

_C_   10. Democrats go to Washington to spend money with no regard for the hard-working taxpayer.
   a. circular reasoning
   b. bandwagon
   c. overgeneralization

_A_   11. The suicide rate is highest over the Christmas holidays, which means that Thanksgiving is a safe and happy holiday.
   a. misinterpreted statistics
   b. card stacking
   c. questionable authority

_b_   12. The workers' fingers were swollen and infected, insects walked on their exposed skin, and their red eyes begged for mercy and relief. We all must join their effort.
   a. oversimplification
   b. appeal to emotions
   c. overgeneralization

_a c_   13. Our minister, Dr. Johnson, assured the family that our cousin's cancer was a slow-growing one so that a brief delay in treatment would not be detrimental.
   a. transfer
   b. straw person
   c. questionable authority

_b_   14. Crime in this city has been successfully addressed by increasing the number of police officers, seeking neighborhood support against drug dealers, and keeping teenagers off the streets at night. The city is to be commended.
   a. misleading analogy
   b. incomplete facts
   c. misinterpreted statistics

_a_   15. A biology professor cannot possibly advise the swim coach on the placement of swimmers in the different races.
   a. _ad hominem_
   b. testimonial
   c. transfer

Determining What Support Is Missing. Arguments are written to persuade, and thus include the proponent's version of the convincing reasons. Writers do not usually supply the reader with any more than one or two weak points that could be made by the other side. In analyzing an argument, ask yourself, "What is left out?" Be an advocate for the opposing point of view and guess at the evidence that would be presented. Decide if evidence was consciously omitted because of its adverse effect on the conclusion. For example, a business person arguing for an increased monthly service fee might neglect to mention how much of the cost is administrative overhead and profit.

Step 4: Evaluate The Argument

Important decisions are rarely quick or easy. A span of incubation time is often needed for deliberating among alternatives. Allow yourself time to go over and over arguments, weighing the support, and looking at the issues from different perspectives. Good critical thinkers are persistent in seeking solutions.

Diane Halpern expresses the difficulty of decision making by saying, "There is never just one war fought. Each side has its own version, and rarely do they agree."[6] The reader must consider carefully in seeking the truth. Halpern uses a picture of a table and compares the legs of the table to four different degrees of support.

1. Unrelated reasons give no support.
2. A few weak reasons do not adequately support.
3. Many weak reasons can support.
4. Strong related reasons provide support.

Remember, in critical thinking there is no "I'm right, and you are wrong." There are, however, strong and weak arguments. Strong relevant, believable, and consistent reasons build a good argument.

Exercise 6   EVALUATE YOUR OWN DECISION MAKING

Now that you are familiar with the critical thinking process, analyze your own thinking in making an important recent decision of where to attend college. No college is perfect; many factors must be considered. The issue or conclusion is that you have decided to attend the college where you are now enrolled. List relevant reasons and/or evidence that supported your decision. Evaluate the strength of your reasoning. Are any of your reasons fallacies?

1. _____

2. _____

3. _____

4. _____

[6]Halpern, *Thought and Knowledge,* p. 191.

5. _____

How would you evaluate your own critical thinking in making a choice of colleges? Perhaps you relied heavily on information from others. Were those sources credible?

INDUCTIVE AND DEDUCTIVE REASONING

In choosing a college, did you follow an inductive or deductive reasoning process? Did you collect extensive information on several colleges and then weigh the advantages and disadvantages of each? **Inductive** reasoners start by gathering data, and then, after considering all available material, they formulate a conclusion. Textbooks written in this manner give details first and lead you into the main idea or conclusion. They strive to put the parts into a logical whole and thus reason "up" from particular details to a broad generalization.

Deductive reasoners, on the other hand, follow the opposite pattern. Deductive reasoning starts with the conclusion of a previous experience and applies it to a new situation. Perhaps your college choice is a family tradition, your parents are graduates, and you have always expected to attend. Although your thinking may have begun with this premise for your choice, you may then have discovered many reasons why the college is right for you. When writers use a deductive pattern, they first give a general statement and then enumerate the reasons.

Despite this formal distinction between induction and deductive reasoning, in real life we switch back and forth as we think. Our everyday observations lead to conclusions which we then reuse and modify to form new conclusions.

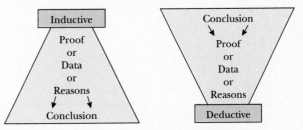

Example of Applying the Critical Thinking Steps 1–4

The following is an example of how the four-step format can be used to evaluate an argument. Read the argument, analyze according to the directions for each step, and then read the explanation of how the critical thinking process was applied.

The Argument: Extraterrestrial Life

Surely life exists elsewhere in the universe. After all, most space scientists today admit the possibility that life has evolved on other planets.

Besides, other planets in our solar system are strikingly like Earth. They revolve around the sun, they borrow light from the sun, and several are known to revolve on their axes, and to be subject to the same laws of gravitation as earth. What's more, aren't those who make light of extraterrestrial life soft-headed fundamentalists clinging to the foolish notion that life is unique to their planet?

Joel Rudinow and Vincent Barry, Invitation to Critical Thinking

Step 1: Identify the Issue

What is the topic of this argument and what is the main point the writer is trying to convey? Although many ideas may be included, what is the central concern that is being discussed and supported? Underline the central issue if it is directly stated or write it above the passage if it is implied.

Step 2: Identify the Support for the Argument

What are the significant supporting details that support the central issue that is being argued? Put brackets at the beginning and end of each assertion of support and number the assertions separately and consecutively. Do not number background information or examples that merely illustrate a point.

Step 3: Evaluate the Support

Examine each supporting assertion separately for relevance, believability, and consistency. Can you identify any as fallacies that are intended to sell a weak argument? Also list the type of supporting information that you feel is missing.

1. _____

2. _____

3. _____

What is missing?_____

Step 4: Evaluate the Argument

What is your overall evaluation of the argument? Is the argument convincing? Does the argument provide good reasons and/or evidence for believing the thesis?

Explanation of the Steps

Step 1: Identify the Issue

The central issue, assertion, thesis, main point, or conclusion is directly stated in the first sentence. Good critical thinkers would note, however, that "life" is not clearly defined as plant, animal, or human.

Step 2: Identify the Support for the Argument

This argument contains the three main premises or significant supporting details that can be numbered as follows:

1. Space scientists admit the possibility that life has evolved from other planets.
2. Other planets in our solar system are strikingly like Earth.
3. Those who make light of extraterrestrial life are soft-headed fundamentalists clinging to the foolish notion that life is unique to this planet.

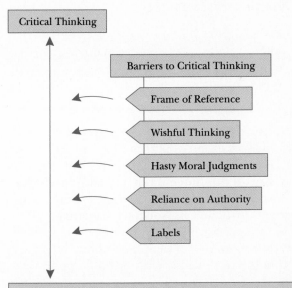

Critical Thinking

Barriers to Critical Thinking

Frame of Reference

Wishful Thinking

Hasty Moral Judgments

Reliance on Authority

Labels

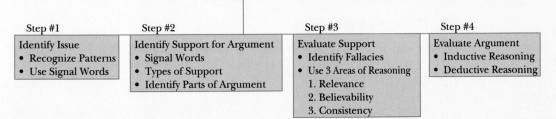

Four–Step Procedure to Guide Critical Thinking

Step #1	Step #2	Step #3	Step #4

Identify Issue
• Recognize Patterns
• Use Signal Words
	Identify Support for Argument
	• Signal Words
	• Types of Support
	• Identify Parts of Argument
		Evaluate Support
		• Identify Fallacies
		• Use 3 Areas of Reasoning
		  1. Relevance
		  2. Believability
		  3. Consistency
			Evaluate Argument
			• Inductive Reasoning
			• Deductive Reasoning

Credit: Professor Helen R. Carr, San Antonio College

Step 3: Evaluate the Support

The first supporting detail is a vague appeal to authority that does not reveal who "most space scientists" are. Do the scientists work for NASA? The second statement is also vague and presented as a misleading comparison. Other planets may be round, but they have different temperatures and different atmospheres. The third statement is an oversimplified, personal attack on those who may not agree with the argument. Scientific support for this argument seems to be missing.

Step 4: Evaluate the Argument

This is not a good argument. There may be good reasons to believe that life exists on other planets, but this argument fails to provide them. The possibility of extraterrestrial life might be argued through statistics from astronomy and a specific definition of "life."

Exercise 7   APPLY THE STEPS

Read the following arguments and apply the four-step format for evaluation. State the issue, state the support, evaluate the support, and evaluate the argument.

Argument 1: School Prayer

In the fury that surrounds the debate about school prayer, it is sometimes forgotten that prayer is an essential part of religion. To permit school prayer is virtually the same as endorsing religion. What can be said, then, for religion? Not much, I'm afraid. Indeed, religion is dangerous. It has spawned numerous wars throughout history. Today it continues to sow the seeds of discontent and destruction in Northern Ireland and the Middle East. It divides people by emphasizing their differences rather than their similarities. It breeds intolerance of people of opposed views. Is there any doubt, therefore, that the responsible citizen should oppose school prayer?

Joel Rudinow and Vincent E. Barry, *Invitation to Critical Thinking*

Step 1: Identify the Issue

State or underline the main point or issue the author is arguing.

Step 2: Identify the Support for the Argument

Put brackets at the beginning and end of each major assertion of support and number the assertions.

Step 3: Evaluate the Support

Examine each supporting assertion for relevance, believability, and consistency. Identify and label any fallacies. List missing support.

_____

_____

_____

_____

_____

Step 4: Evaluate the Argument

What is your overall evaluation and why?

_____

_____

Argument 2: Invasion of Privacy

When you call 911 in an emergency, some police departments have a way of telling your telephone number and address without your saying a word. The chief value of this, say the police, is that if the caller is unable to communicate for any reason, the dispatcher knows where to send help. But don't be duped by such paternalistic explanations. This technology is a despicable invasion of privacy, for callers may be unaware of the insidious device. Even if they are, some persons who wish anonymity may be reluctant to call for emergency help. Remember that the names of complainants and witnesses are recorded in many communities' criminal justice systems. A fairer and more effective system seemingly would include an auxiliary number for callers who wish anonymity.

Joel Rudinow and Vincent E. Barry, *Invitation to Critical Thinking*

Step 1: Identify the Issue

State or underline the main point or issue the author is arguing.

Step 2: Identify the Support for the Argument

Put brackets at the beginning and end of each major assertion of support and number the assertions.

Step 3: Evaluate the Support

Examine each supporting assertion for relevance, believability, and consistency. Identify and label any fallacies. List missing support.

_____

_____

_____

_____

Step 4: Evaluate the Argument
What is your overall evaluation and why?

_____

_____

Argument 3: Against Legalizing Euthanasia

The Karen Ann Quinlan case once again has raised the issue of euthanasia. A number of voices have been heard advocating the legalization of voluntary euthanasia. While the agonizing plight of many of our terminally ill makes this proposal understandable, there are good reasons to resist liberalizing our euthanasia laws.

First of all, no matter how you look at it, euthanasia is killing and thus is wrong. The Bible is clear on that point, and our society has always forbidden it.

Second, it is questionable whether a terminally ill patient can make a voluntary decision to begin with. Those who advocate voluntary euthanasia believe that patients should be allowed to die on request when they've developed a tolerance to narcotics. But exactly when are those patients to decide? When they're drugged? If so, then surely their choices can't be considered voluntary. And if they're to decide after the drugs have been withdrawn, this decision can't be voluntary either. Anyone who's had a simple toothache knows how much pain can distort judgment and leave us almost crazy. Imagine how much more irrational we'd likely be if we were suffering from some dreadful terminal disease and suddenly had our ration of morphine discontinued.

But even if such a decision could be completely voluntary, isn't it really unwise to offer such a choice to the gravely ill? I remember how, before she died of stomach cancer, my mother became obsessed with the idea that she was an emotional an financial burden on her family. She actually kept apologizing to us that she went on living! Had she had the option of euthanasia, she might have taken it—not because she was tired of living but because she felt guilty about living!

I shudder to think of the stress that such a choice would have put on us, her family. Surely we would have been divided. Some of us would have said, "Yes, let mother die," while others would have resisted out of a sense of love or devotion or gratitude, or even guilt.

Then there's the whole question of mistaken diagnoses. Doctors aren't infallible. Even the best of them errs. The story is told of the brilliant diagnostician Richard Cabot who, when he was retiring, was given the complete medical histories and results of careful examinations of two patients. The patients had died and only the pathologist who'd seen the descriptions of their postmortems knew their exact diagnoses. The pathologist asked Cabot for his diagnoses. The eminent Dr. Cabot muffed both of them! If a brilliant diagnostician can make a mistake, what about a less accomplished doctor? Let's face it: There's always the possibility of a wrong diagnosis.

But suppose we could be sure of diagnoses. Even so, there's always the chance that some new pain-relieving drug, or even a cure, is just around the corner. Many years ago, the President of the American Public Health Association made this point forcefully when he said, "No one can say today what will be incurable tomorrow. No one can predict what disease will be fatal or permanently incurable until medicine becomes stationary and sterile."

But what frightens me the most about legalizing voluntary euthanasia is that it will open the door for the legalization of *involuntary* euthanasia. If we allow people to play God and decide when and how they'll die, then it won't be long before society will be deciding when and how defective infants, the old and senile, and the hopelessly insane will die as well.

Joel Rudinow and Vincent E. Barry, Invitation to Critical Thinking

Step 1: Identify the Issue

State or underline the main point or issue the author is arguing.

Step 2: Identify the Support for the Argument

Put brackets at the beginning and end of each major assertion of support and number the assertions.

Step 3: Evaluate the Support

Examine each supporting assertion for relevance, believability, and consistency. Identify and label any fallacies. List missing support.

_____

_____

_____

_____

_____

Step 4: Evaluate the Argument
What is your overall evaluation and why?

_____

_____

CREATIVE AND CRITICAL THINKING

A chapter on critical thinking would not be complete without an appeal for creative thinking. You may ask, "Are critical thinking and creative thinking different?" Creative thinking refers to the ability to generate many possible solutions to a problem, whereas critical thinking refers to the examination of those solutions for the selection of the best of all possibilities. Both ways of thinking are essential for good problem solving.

Diana Halpern uses the following story to illustrate creative thinking:[7]

Many years ago when a person who owed money could be thrown into jail, a merchant in London had the misfortune to owe a huge sum to a money-lender. The money-lender, who was old and ugly, fancied the merchant's beautiful teenage daughter. He proposed a bargain. He said he would cancel the merchant's debt if he could have the girl instead.

Both the merchant and his daughter were horrified at the proposal. So the cunning money-lender proposed that they let Providence decide the matter. He told them that he would put a black pebble and a white pebble into an empty money-bag and then the girl would have to pick out one of the pebbles. If she chose the black pebble she would become his wife and her father's debt would be cancelled. If she chose the white pebble she would stay with her father and the debt would still be cancelled. But if she refused to pick out a pebble her father would be thrown into jail and she would starve.

Reluctantly the merchant agreed. They were standing on a pebble-strewn path in the merchant's garden as they talked and the money-lender stooped down to pick up two pebbles. As he picked up the pebbles the girl, sharp-eyed with fright, noticed that he picked up two black pebbles and put them into the money-bag. He then asked the girl to pick out the pebble that was to decide her fate and that of her father.

If you were the girl, what would you do? Think creatively, and, without evaluating your thoughts, list at least five possible solutions. Next think critically to evaluate and then circle your final choice.

[7]Halpern, _Thought and Knowledge_, p. 408

In discussing the possible solutions to the problem, Halpern talks about two kinds of creative thinking, vertical thinking and lateral thinking. **Vertical thinking** is a straightforward and logical way of thinking that would typically result in a solution like, "Call his hand and expose the money-lender as a crook." The disadvantage of this solution is that the merchant is still in debt so the original problem has still not been solved. **Lateral thinking,** on the other hand, is a way of thinking *around* a problem or even redefining the problem. DeBono[8] suggests that a lateral thinker might redefine the problem from "What happens when I get the black pebble?" to "How can I avoid the black pebble?" Using this new definition of the problem and other seemingly irrelevant information, DeBono's lateral thinker came up with a winning solution. When the girl reaches into the bag, she should fumble and drop one of the stones on the "pebble-strewn path." The color of the pebble she dropped could then be determined by looking at the one left in the bag. Since the remaining pebble is black, the dropped one that is now mingled in the path must have been white. Any other admission would expose the money-lender as a crook. Probably the heroine thought of many alternatives, but thanks to her ability ultimately to generate a novel solution and evaluate its effectiveness, the daughter and the merchant lived happily free of debt.

DeBono[9] defines vertical thinking as "digging the same hole deeper" and lateral thinking as "digging the hole somewhere else. For example, after many years of researching a cure for smallpox, Dr. Edward Jenner stopped focusing on patients who were sick with the disease and instead began studying groups of people who never seemed to get the smallpox. Shortly thereafter, using this different perspective, Dr. Jenner discovered the clues that led him to the smallpox vaccine.

Creative and critical thinking enable us to see new relationships. We blend knowledge and see new similarities and differences, a new sequence of events, or a new solution for an old problem. We create new knowledge by using old learning differently.

[8]E. DeBono, *New Think: The Use of Lateral Thinking in the Generation of New Ideas* (New York: Basic Books, 1968), p. 195.

[9]E. DeBono, "Information Processing and New Ideas—Lateral and Vertical Thinking," in S. J. Parnes, R. B. Noller, and A. M. Biondi, eds., *Guide to Creative Action: Revised Edition of Creative Behavior Guidebook* (New York: Charles Scribner's Sons, 1977).

SUMMARY POINTS

- Thinking critically means deliberating in a purposeful, organized manner in order to assess the value of information, both old and new.
- Critical thinkers are flexible, persistent, and willing to plan and self-correct. Some people do not allow themselves to think critically because of their frame of reference, wishful thinking, hasty moral judgments, reliance on authority, and labeling.
- Critical thinkers have power because they are willing to hold their own opinions up to scrutiny.
- Critical thinkers can use a four-step plan for analyzing an argument: (1) Identify the issue; (2) Identify the support for the argument; (3) Evaluate the support; and (4) Evaluate the argument.
- Inductive reasoners start by gathering data and deductive reasoners start with the conclusion.
- Creative thinkers use both vertical and lateral thinking.

SELECTION 1

ESSAY

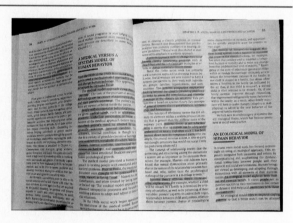

Stage 1: Skill Development

Preview

The author supports the use of highlighters.

agree ☐   disagree ☐

Activate Schema

Do you use highlighters in your textbooks? Why or why not? What do you recall about the meaning of the phrase *laissez-faire* from history or political science?

Learning Strategy

Identify the issue and evaluate the support for the argument.

Word Knowledge

Are you familiar with the following words in this selection?

peripheral　　　　regurgitation

detrimental　　　　laissez-faire

ingesting

Your instructor may ask five true-false questions from the *Instructor's Manual* to stimulate your thinking using these words.

Stage 2: Integrate Knowledge While Reading

Use thinking strategies as you read:
1. Predict　2. Picture　3. Relate　4. Monitor　5. Fix up

The Highlighter Crisis
From Lawrence A. Beyer, *Academic Questions*[10]

The use of highlighters—those marking pens that allow readers to emphasize passages in their books with transparent overlays of bright color—is significantly retarding the education of university students by distorting and cheapening the way many read. Compared to the important
5　issues of academic policy facing education today—government funding, affirmative action, teacher shortages, the role of "the canon" in the humanities—the impact of the humble highlighter might seem trifling. But highlighters, though they appear to be peripheral to educational concerns, are changing the university experience for students in ways that have
10　seriously detrimental consequences.

While some students still read without using any marking implements, and some continue to swear by pens or pencils, most have switched to highlighters. The most common use of highlighters is for simply marking, with a colorful coating over the words, the gist of a text that the student
15　needs to read. While this might seem harmless, such highlighter use in fact encourages passive reading habits in young adults who very much need to learn to read actively, critically, and analytically.

At best, most students who use the highlighter in this fashion are uncritically—almost unthinkingly—ingesting some of the authors'
20　phraseology and gaining sketchy outlines of the texts. At worst, their "reading" consists merely of a skimming sensitivity to those conventional textual indicators that point out which passages are part of the skeletal gists of the texts ("In sum," "The main issue is," etc.). In accenting these passages, students are performing a typographical function that could be

[10]Lawrence A. Beyer. "The Highlighter Crisis." From *Academic Questions*, Summer 1990. Copyright © 1990 by Transaction Publishers.

25 accomplished, with the same absence of understanding, by computers. As if
    seasoning food that will never be eaten, they are coloring pages in vague—
    but never fulfilled—anticipation of a more serious future review of the now-
    edited text.

        It might be objected, with some validity, that a pencil or pen can be
30 misused in the exact same way. It is nevertheless proper to hold the
    highlighter responsible for the deterioration in reading skills. When a
    pencil or pen is used for a highlighting (i.e., underlining) purpose, it is
    ordinarily used also for writing notes in the margins, a process that greatly
    enhances the reader's engagement with the text. The highlighter is virtually
35 useless for this purpose.

        So, while the highlighter seems to be an inexpensive, helpful minor
    item in the everyday world of the university student, its size and price tag
    do not begin to approximate its educational costs. Students, already expert
    at the simplistic regurgitation of ideas, now have an instrument for
40 applying a pretty coating of color that makes texts even easier to ingest
    without thoughtful chewing. Reading becomes a mindless swallowing of
    words that pass through such students without making any lasting
    impression.

        The freedom of inquiry and experimentation that we grant to our
45 university students should not be impeded, but that does not mean
    universities must adopt laissez-faire attitudes about the nonacademic, but
    still educationally important, aspects of university life. There are, in fact,
    participants in the educational process who swim against the laissez-faire
    tide regarding the university's nonacademic responsibilities toward
50 students: for example, those espousing religious, and particularly Christian
    fundamentalist, views. There are campuses where kissing, dancing, and
    drinking are prohibited. Unfortunately, these regulations extend beyond
    the mere protection of the learning process to an enforcement of certain
    particular ideas, attitudes, and ways of living. Yet the religious institutions
55 are on the right track in that they show concern for educational issues
    beyond the narrowly academic. The nature of the *entire* student
    experience—right down to the simple highlighter—must have an
    important place in the educational priorities of university administrators.

SKILL DEVELOPMENT: CRITICAL THINKING

    Apply the four-step format for evaluating the argument. Use the perfora-
    tions to tear out and hand in to your instructor.

Step 1: Identify the Issue

    State the main point or issue the author is arguing.

Step 2: Identify the Support for the Argument

List and number each major assertion of support.

_____

_____

_____

Step 3: Evaluate the Support

Comment on any weaknesses in relevance, believability, and consistency for the assertions listed above.

_____

_____

Identify and label three fallacies in the argument.

_____

_____

_____

What support do you feel is missing?

_____

Step 4: Evaluate the Argument

What is your overall evaluation and why?

_____

_____

What is your opinion on the issue?

_____

COMPREHENSION QUESTIONS

Answer the following item with T (true) or F (false).

_____ 1. The author believes that the highlighter crisis is more important than teacher shortages.

_F_   2. The author believes that most students read without using any mark-ing implements.

_F_   3. The author feels that students mark irrelevant details rather than main ideas.

_T_   4. The author feels that students miss a deeper level of processing when highlighting.

_T_   5. The overall pattern of organization for this passage is cause and effect.

_F_   6. The author is writing primarily to teachers rather than students.

_____   7. The "seasoning food" sentence is an example of a slippery slope fallacy.

_F_   8. The author supports his argument with more facts than opinions.

_F_   9. The author believes that professors should follow a _laissez-faire_ policy regarding the nonacademic activities of students that affect the learn-ing process.

_F_   10. The inclusion of the Christian fundamentalists' views is an _ad hominem_ attack.

VOCABULARY

According to the way the italicized word was used in the selection, indicate _a, b, c,_ or _d_ for the word or phrase that gives the best definition.

_B_   1. "_peripheral_ to educational concerns" (8)
    a. related
    b. unimportant
    c. pertinent
    d. primary

_A_   2. "_detrimental_ conse-quences" (10)
    a. damaging
    b. confusing
    c. unrealistic
    d. fearful

_d_   3. "_ingesting_ some of" (19)
    a. skipping
    b. ignoring
    c. locating
    d. consuming

_C_   4. "_regurgitation_ of ideas" (39)
    a. analysis
    b. paraphrasing
    c. vomiting
    d. swallowing

_a_   5. "_laissez-faire_ attitudes" (46)
    a. leave them alone
    b. conservative
    c. authoritarian
    d. academic

SELECTION 2

SPEECH

Stage 1: Skill Development

Preview

The author believes that businesses should support neighborhoods.

agree ☐   disagree ☐

Activate Schema

How many of your neighbors do you know by name?

Learning Strategy

Identify the issue and evaluate the support for the argument.

Word Knowledge

Are you familiar with the following words in this selection?

veranda   sanitized

stoop   amortizing

eclipsed

Your instructor may ask five true-false questions from the *Instructor's Manual* to stimulate your thinking using these words.

Stage 2: Integrate Knowledge While Reading

Use thinking strategies as you read:

1. Predict   2. Picture   3. Relate   4. Monitor   5. Fix up

A City of Neighborhoods
From a speech by Harvey Milk[11]

Let's make no mistake about this: The American Dream starts with the neighborhoods. If we wish to rebuild our cities, we must first rebuild our neighborhoods. And to do that, we must understand that the quality of life is more important than the standard of living. To sit on the front steps—

5 whether it's a veranda in a small town or a concrete stoop in a big city—and talk to our neighborhoods is infinitely more important than the huddle on the living-room lounger and watch a make-believe world in not-quite living color.

Progress is not America's only business—and certainly not its most

10 important. Isn't it strange that as technology advances, the quality of life so frequently declines? Oh, washing the dishes is easier. Dinner itself is easier—just heat and serve, though it might be more nourishing if we ate the ads and threw the food away. And we no longer fear spots on our glassware when guests come over. But then, of course, the guests don't

15 come, because our friends are too afraid to come to our house and it's not safe to go to theirs.

And I hardly need to tell you that in that 19- or 24-inch view of the world, cleanliness has long since eclipsed godliness. So we'll all smell, look, and actually be laboratory clean, as sterile on the inside as on the out. The

20 perfect consumer, surrounded by the latest appliances. The perfect audience, with a ringside seat to almost any event in the world, without smell, without taste, without feel—alone and unhappy in the vast wasteland of our living rooms. I think that what we actually need, of course, is a little more dirt on the seat of our pants as we sit on the front stoop and talk to

25 our neighbors once again, enjoying the type of summer day where the smell of garlic travels slightly faster than the speed of sound.

There's something missing in the sanitized life we lead. Something that our leaders in Washington can never supply by simple edict, something that the commercials on television never advertise because nobody's yet found a

30 way to bottle it or box it or can it. What's missing is the touch, the warmth, the meaning of life. A four-color spread in *Time* is no substitute for it. Neither is a 30-second commercial or a reassuring Washington press conference.

I spent many years on both Wall Street and Montgomery Street and I

35 fully understand the debt and responsibility that major corporations owe their shareholders. I also fully understand the urban battlefields of New York and Cleveland and Detroit. I see the faces of the unemployed—and the unemployable—of the city. I've seen the faces in Chinatown, Hunters Point, the Mission, and the Tenderloin . . . and I don't like what I see.

[11]Harvey Milk, "A City of Neighborhoods," as excerpted in Diane Ravitch, *The American Reader,* HarperCollins 1991. Copyright © 1978, the Estate of Harvey Milk.

40 Oddly, I'm also reminded of the most successful slogan a business ever coined: The customer is always right.

American business must realize that while the shareholders always come first, the care and feeding of their customer is a close second. They have a debt and a responsibility to that customer and the city in which he or
45 she lives, the cities in which the business itself lives or in which it grew up. To throw away a senior citizen after they've nursed you through childhood is wrong. To treat a city as disposable once your business has prospered is equally wrong and even more short-sighted.

Unfortunately for those who would like to flee them, the problems of
50 the cities don't stop at the city limits. There are no moats around our cities that keep the problems in. What happens in New York or San Francisco will eventually happen in San Jose. It's just a matter of time. And like the flu, it usually gets worse the further it travels. Our cities must not be abandoned. They're worth fighting for, not just by those who live in them, but by
55 industry, commerce, unions, everyone. Not alone because they represent the past, but because they also represent the future. Your children will live there and hopefully, so will your grandchildren. For all practical purposes, the eastern corridor from Boston to Newark will be one vast strip city. So will the area from Milwaukee to Gary, Indiana. In California, it will be that
60 fertile crescent of asphalt and neon that stretches from Santa Barbara to San Diego. Will urban blight travel the arteries of the freeways? Of course it will—unless we stop it.

So the challenge will be to awaken the consciousness of industry and commerce to the part they must play in saving the cities which nourished
65 them. Every company realizes it must constantly invest in its own physical plant to remain healthy and grow. Well, the cities are a part of that plant and the people who live in them are part of the cities. They're all connected; what affects one affects the others.

In short, the cheapest place to manufacture a product may not be the
70 cheapest at all if it results in throwing your customers out of work. There's no sense in making television sets in Japan if the customers in the United States haven't the money to buy them. Industry must actively seek to employ those without work, to train those who have no skills. "Labor intensive" is not a dirty word, not every job is done better by machine. It has become the
75 job of industry not only to create the product, but also to create the customer.

Costly? I don't think so. It's far less expensive than the problem of fully loaded docks and no customers. And there are additional returns: lower rates of crime, smaller welfare loads. And having your friends and neighbors
80 sitting on that well-polished front stoop. . . .

Many companies feel that helping the city is a form of charity. I think it is more accurate to consider it a part of the cost of doing business, that it should be entered on the books as amortizing the future. I would like to see business and industry consider it as such, because I think there's more

85   creativity, more competence perhaps, in business than there is in
      government. I think that business could turn the south of Market Area not
      only into an industrial park but a neighborhood as well. To coin a pun, too
      many of our cities have a complex, in fact, too many complexes. We don't
      need another concrete jungle that dies the moment you turn off the lights
90   in the evening. What we need is a neighborhood where people can walk to
      work, raise their kids, enjoy life. . . .

          The cities will be saved. The cities will be governed. But they won't be
      run from three thousand miles away in Washington, they won't be run from
      the statehouse, and most of all, they won't be run by the carpetbaggers who
95   have fled to the suburbs. You can't run a city by people who don't live there,
      any more than you can have an effective police force made up of people who
      don't live there. In either case, what you've got is an occupying army. . . .

          The cities will not be saved by the people who feel condemned to live in
      them, who can hardly wait to move to Marin or San Jose—or Evanston or
100   Westchester. The cities will not be saved by the people who like it here. The
      people who prefer the neighborhood stores to the shopping mall, who go to
      the plays and eat in the restaurants and go to the discos and worry about
      the education the kids are getting even if they have no kids of their own.

          That's not just the city of the future; it's the city of today. It means new
105   directions, new alliances, new solutions for ancient problems. The typical
      American family with two cars and 2.2 kids doesn't live here anymore. It
      hasn't for years. The demographics are different now and we all know it.
      The city is a city of singles and young marrieds, the city of the retired and
      the poor, a city of many colors who speak in many tongues.
110   The city will run itself, it will create its own solutions.

SKILL DEVELOPMENT: CRITICAL THINKING

Apply the four-step format for evaluating the argument. Use the perforations to tear out and hand in to your instructor.

Step 1: Identify the Issue

State the main point or issue the author is arguing.

_____

Step 2: Identify the Support for the Argument

List and number each major assertion of support.

_____

_____

_____

Step 3: Evaluate the Support

Comment on any weaknesses in relevance, believability, and consistency for the assertions listed above.

_____

_____

Identify and label three fallacies in the argument.

_____

_____

_____

What support do you feel is missing?

_____

Step 4: Evaluate the Argument

What is your overall evaluation and why?

_____

_____

What is your opinion on the issue?

_____

COMPREHENSION QUESTIONS

Answer the following item with _T_ (true) or _F_ (false).

_F_   1. The speaker would consider a dishwashing machine to be a quality-of-life issue.

_T_   2. The speaker would consider sitting on the front stoop to be a standard-of-living issue.

_1_   3. The speaker suggests that people have better access to world events than to their own neighbors.

_1_   4. The speaker probably has a background in finance.

_F_   5. The Tenderloin is probably a wealthy neighborhood in the city.

_F_   6. The speaker rejects the slogan, "The customer is always right."

_1_   7. The speaker probably has no children.

_____   8. The speaker believes that an industrial park should only be a working complex.

_F_   9. The speaker feels that it is a form of charity for businesses to help cities.

_1_   10. This speech is probably being made to business people.

VOCABULARY

According to the way the italicized word was used in the selection, indicate *a, b, c,* or *d* for the word or phrase that gives the best definition.

_A_   1. "*veranda* in a small town" (5)
  a. porch
  b. park
  c. yard
  d. garden

_B_   2. "concrete *stoop*" (5)
  a. square
  b. entrance platform
  c. wall
  d. post

_C_   3. "*eclipsed* godliness" (18)
  a. defined
  b. washed
  c. surpassed
  d. removed

_D_   4. "*sanitized* life we lead" (27)
  a. diverse
  b. unsafe
  c. accelerated
  d. sterilized

_D_   5. "*amortizing* the future" (83)
  a. downsizing
  b. dividing payments for
  c. incorporating ideas for
  d. finding solutions for

SELECTION 3

ESSAY

SHOE

Stage 1: Skill Development

Preview

The author is a police officer.

agree ☐   disagree ☐

Activate Schema

Do you have a handgun in your house?

Learning Strategy

Identify the issue and evaluate the support for the argument.

Word Knowledge

Are you familiar with the following words in this selection?

inadvertently   demented

self-righteousness   mandatory

disgruntled

Your instructor may ask five true-false questions from the *Instructor's Manual* to stimulate your thinking using these words.

Stage 2: Integrate Knowledge While Reading

Use thinking strategies as you read:
1. Predict   2. Picture   3. Relate   4. Monitor   5. Fix up

Why Handguns Must Be Outlawed[12]
Nan Desuka

"Guns don't kill people—criminals do." That's a powerful slogan, much more powerful than its alternate version, "Guns don't kill people—people kill people." But this second version, though less effective, is much nearer to the whole truth. Although accurate statistics are hard to come by, and even

5   harder to interpret, it seems indisputable that large numbers of people, not just criminals, kill, with a handgun, other people. Scarcely a day goes by

[12]From *American Voices,* edited by Dolores la Guardia and Hans P. Guth (Mayfield Publishing: Mountain View California, 1993), pp. 527–531.

without a newspaper in any large city reporting that a child has found a
gun, kept by the child's parents for self-protection, and has, in playing with
this new-found toy, killed himself or a playmate. Or we read of a
storekeeper, trying to protect himself during a robbery, who inadvertently
shoots an innocent customer. These killers are not, in any reasonable sense
of the word, criminals. They are just people who happen to kill people. No
wonder the gun lobby prefers the first version of the slogan, "Guns don't
kill people—criminals do." This version suggests that the only problem is
criminals, not you or me, or our children, and certainly not the members of
the National Rifle Association.

Those of us who want strict control of handguns—for me that means
the outlawing of handguns, except to the police and related service units—
have not been able to come up with a slogan equal in power to "Guns don't
kill people—criminals do." The best we have been able to come up with is a
mildly amusing bumper sticker showing a teddy bear, with the words
"Defend your right to arm bears." Humor can be a powerful weapon (even
in writing *on behalf* of gun control, one slips into using the imagery of
force), and our playful bumper sticker somehow deflates the self-
righteousness of the gun lobby, but doesn't equal the power (again the
imagery of force) of "Guns don't kill people—criminals do." For one thing,
the effective alliteration of "*cr*iminals" and "*k*ill" binds the two words,
making everything so terribly simple. Criminals kill; when there are no
criminals, there will be no deaths from guns.

But this notion won't do. Despite the uncertainty of some statistical
evidence, everyone knows, or should know, that only about 30 percent of
murders are committed by robbers or rapists. For the most part the victims
of handguns know their assailants well. These victims are women killed by
jealous husbands, or they are the women's lovers; or they are drinking
buddies who get into a violent argument; or they are innocent people who
get shot by disgruntled (and probably demented) employees or fellow
workers who have (or imagine) a grudge. Or they are, as I've already said,
bystanders at a robbery, killed by a storekeeper. Or they are children playing
with their father's gun.

Of course this is not the whole story. Hardened criminals also have
guns, and they use them. The murders committed by the robbers and
rapists are what gave credence to Barry Goldwater's quip, "We have a crime
problem in this country, not a gun problem." But here again the half-truth
of a slogan is used to mislead, used to direct attention away from a national
tragedy. Different sources issue different statistics, but a conservative
estimate is that handguns annually murder at least 15,000 Americans,
accidentally kill at least another 3,000, and wound at least another 100,000.
Handguns are easily available, both to criminals and to decent people who
believe they need a gun in order to protect themselves from criminals. The
decent people, unfortunately, have good cause to believe they need
protection. Many parts of many cities are utterly unsafe, and even the tiniest

village may harbor a murderer. Senator Goldwater was right in saying there is a crime problem (that's the truth of his half-truth), but he was wrong in saying there is not also a gun problem.

55   Surely the homicide rate would markedly decrease if handguns were outlawed. The FBI reports that more than 60 percent of all murders are caused by guns, and handguns are involved in more than 70 percent of these. Surely, many, even most, of these handgun killings would not occur if the killer had to use a rifle, club, or knife. Of course violent lovers, angry

60   drunks, and deranged employees would still flail out with knives or baseball bats, but some of their victims would be able to run away, with few or no injuries, and most of those who could not run away would nevertheless survive, badly injured but at least alive. But if handguns are outlawed, we are told, responsible citizens will have no way to protect themselves from

65   criminals. First, one should remember that at least 90 percent of America's burglaries are committed when no one is at home. The householder's gun, if he or she has one, is in a drawer of the bedside table, and the gun gets lifted along with the jewelry, adding one more gun to the estimated 100,000 handguns annually stolen from law-abiding citizens. (See Shields, *Guns*

70   *Don't Die—People Do,* 1981.) Second, if the householder is at home, and attempts to use the gun, he or she is more likely to get killed or wounded than to kill or deter the intruder. Another way of looking at this last point is to recall that for every burglar who is halted by the sight of a handgun, four innocent people are killed by handgun accidents.

75   Because handguns are not accurate beyond ten or fifteen feet, they are not the weapons of sportsmen. Their sole purpose is to kill or at least to disable a person at close range. But only a minority of persons killed with these weapons are criminals. Since handguns chiefly destroy the innocent, they must be outlawed—not simply controlled more strictly, but outlawed—

80   to all except to law-enforcement officials. Attempts to control handguns are costly and ineffective, but even if they were cheap and effective stricter controls would not take handguns out of circulation among criminals, because licensed guns are stolen from homeowners and shopkeepers, and thus fall into criminal hands. According to Wright, Rossi, and Daly (in *Under*

85   *the Gun,* 1983), about 40 percent of the handguns used in crimes are stolen, chiefly from homes that the guns were supposed to protect.

The National Rifle Association is fond of quoting a University of Wisconsin study that says, "gun control laws have no individual or collective effect in reducing the rate of violent crime" (cited in Smith, 1981, p. 17).

90   Agreed—but what if handguns were not available? What if the manufacturer of handguns is severely regulated, and if the guns may be sold only to police officers? True, even if handguns are outlawed, some criminals will manage to get them, but surely fewer petty criminals will have guns. It is simply untrue for the gun lobby to assert that all criminals—since they are

95   by definition lawbreakers—will find ways to get handguns. For the most part, if the sale of handguns is outlawed, guns won't be available, and fewer

criminals will have guns. And if fewer criminals have guns, there is every reason to believe that violent crime will decline. A youth armed only with a knife is less likely to try to rob a store than if he is armed with a gun. This commonsense reasoning does not imply that if handguns are outlawed crime will suddenly disappear, or even that an especially repulsive crime such as rape will decrease markedly. A rapist armed with a knife probably has a sufficient weapon. But *some* violent crime will almost surely decrease. And the decrease will probably be significant if in addition to outlawing handguns, severe mandatory punishments are imposed on a person who is found to possess one, and even severer mandatory punishments are imposed on a person who uses one while committing a crime. Again, none of this activity will solve "the crime problem," but neither will anything else, including the "get tough with criminals" attitude of Senator Goldwater. And of course any attempt to reduce crime (one cannot realistically talk of "solving" the crime problem) will have to pay attention to our systems of bail, plea bargaining, and parole, but outlawing handguns will help.

What will the cost be? First, to take "cost" in its most literal sense, there will be the cost of reimbursing gun owners for the weapons they surrender. Every owner of a handgun ought to be paid the fair market value of the weapon. Since the number of handguns is estimated to be between fifty million and ninety million, the cost will be considerable, but it will be far less than the costs—both in money and in sorrow—that result from deaths due to handguns.

Second, one may well ask if there is another sort of cost, a cost to our liberty, to our constitutional rights. The issue is important, and persons who advocate abolition of handguns are blind or thoughtless if they simply brush it off. On the other hand, opponents of gun control do all of us a disservice by insisting over and over that the Constitution guarantees "the right to bear arms." The Second Amendment in the Bill of Rights says this: "A well-regulated militia being necessary to the security of a free State, the right of the people to keep and bear arms shall not be infringed." It is true that the founding fathers, mindful of the British attempt to disarm the colonists, viewed the presence of "a well-regulated militia" as a safeguard of democracy. Their intention is quite clear, even to one who has not read Stephen P. Halbrook's *That Every Man Be Armed,* an exhaustive argument in favor of the right to bear arms. There can be no doubt that the framers of the Constitution and the Bill of Rights believed that armed insurrection was a justifiable means of countering oppression and tyranny. The Second Amendment may be fairly paraphrased thus: "*Because* an organized militia is necessary to the security of the State, the people have the right to possess weapons." But the owners of handguns are not members of a well-regulated militia. Furthermore, nothing in the proposal to ban handguns would deprive citizens of their rifles or other long-arm guns. All handguns, however, even large ones, should be banned. "Let's face it," Guenther W. Bachmann (a vice president of Smith and Wesson) admits, "they are all

concealable." In any case, it is a fact that when gun control laws have been tested in the courts, they have been found to be constitutional. The constitutional argument was worth making, but the question must now be
145   regarded as settled, not only by the courts but by anyone who reads the Second Amendment.

Still, is it not true that "If guns are outlawed, only outlaws will have guns"? This is yet another powerful slogan, but it is simply not true. First, we are talking not about "guns" but about handguns. Second, the police will
150   have guns—handguns and others—and these trained professionals are the ones on whom we must rely for protection against criminals. Of course the police have not eradicated crime; and of course we must hope that in the future they will be more successful in protecting all citizens. But we must also recognize that the efforts of private citizens to protect themselves with
155   handguns has chiefly taken the lives not of criminals but of innocent people.

SKILL DEVELOPMENT: CRITICAL THINKING

Apply the four-step format for evaluating the argument. Use the perforations to tear out and hand in to your instructor.

Step 1: Identify the Issue

State the main point or issue the author is arguing.

_____

_____

Step 2: Identify the Support for the Argument

List and number each major assertion of support.

_____

_____

_____

Step 3: Evaluate the Support

Comment on any weaknesses in relevance, believability, and consistency for the assertions listed above.

_____

_____

Identify and label three fallacies in the argument.

_____

_____

_____

What support do you feel is missing?

_____

Step 4: Evaluate the Argument

What is your overall evaluation and why?

_____

_____

What is your opinion on the issue?

_____

COMPREHENSION QUESTIONS

Answer the following item with *T* (true) or *F* (false).

F   1. The author believes that the slogan, "Guns don't kill people—people kill people," includes the image of children accidentally killing themselves.

1   2. The author believes that the slogan, "Guns don't kill people—criminals do," is a fallacy of oversimplification.

1   3. The author suggests that 70 percent of the murders are committed by people who are not hardened criminals.

_F_   4. The author implies that Barry Goldwater would most likely support her position.

_F_   5. According to the author, more people are accidently killed with guns each year than are murdered with guns.

_T_   6. With handgun control the author predicts a decrease in murder but not in incidents of domestic violence.

_T_   7. Statistics show that in a home robbery, the burglar is more likely to steal a gun than hear one fired.

_T_   8. According to the passage, about 40 percent of the handguns used in crimes are not purchased by the criminals.

_T_   9. The author believes that the Second Amendment should be interpreted to permit rifles but not handguns.

_T_   10. The author feels that the gun control advocates need a more powerful slogan.

VOCABULARY

According to the way the italicized word was used in the selection, indicate *a, b, c,* or *d* for the word or phrase that gives the best definition.

_B_   1. "*inadvertently* shoots" (10)
  a. surprisingly
  b. unintentionally
  c. remarkably
  d. knowingly

_D_   2. "*self-righteousness* of the gun lobby" (24)
  a. sincerity
  b. blind faith
  c. constant hope
  d. pretended godliness

_A_   3. "*disgruntled* employees" (36)
  a. dissatisfied
  b. clumsy
  c. fearless
  d. disrespectful

_C_   4. "and probably *demented*" (36)
  a. poor
  b. homeless
  c. insane
  d. frightened

_C_   5. "*mandatory* punishments" (105)
  a. lengthy
  b. legal
  c. required
  d. frequent

**COLLABORATIVE
CRITICAL
THINKING**

Gun Control

Gun control is not a simple issue. Regulations are gradually changing as the concerns are hotly debated at the state and federal level. To understand another side of the argument, read the following passage by a famous newspaper columnist. Form a collaborative group with at least two other classmates to discuss and answer the following questions:

1. What is Royko's complete position on gun control?
2. What is his support for the argument?
3. Evaluate the support for strength and for fallacies. Why is his retelling of the news story compelling?
4. On what issues do Desuka and Royko agree?
5. What is the basic disagreement between Desuka and Royko?
6. Which of the two authors did you find more persuasive? Why?
7. In your state what are the regulations regarding the purchase of handguns? Do some research to answer this question.
8. What is the position of the National Rifle Association on gun control? How could the organization affect legislation?
9. What is the position of your group on gun control?
10. Which citizen groups are working toward changing gun control laws?

Shooting Holes In Gun Laws[13]

It was just a short news story, tucked away in the back pages, but it caused me to slightly alter my views on gun control laws.

The story was about a young woman who lives on the South Side of Chicago. A few nights ago, she was waiting for a bus. She had been
5   visiting a friend, and it was after midnight.

Instead of a bus, a car pulled up. A man got out. He was holding a knife. He told the woman to get into the car or he would cut her. She got into the car. The man drove to an alley and spent the next two hours raping her.

10   Then he drove her a few blocks from her home and dumped her out of the car. She began walking home, intending to call the police.

[13]Mike Royko, "Shooting Holes in Gun Laws," November 1989, Reprinted by permission of Tribune Media Services.

But before she got home, another man walked up to her. He, too, had a knife. He walked her to an abandoned building, where he raped her. After he finally let her go, she made it to a friend's house, the police were called, and she was hospitalized.

Now, we've all heard of gang rapes, and of women being held prisoner and raped by whichever two-legged animal happens to wander along.

But this is the first case I've come across of a woman being yanked off the street and raped by two different men within a matter of hours.

So what does this have to do with my views on gun controls?

If that woman had a pistol in her purse or coat pocket, knew how to use it, and was alert to danger, it's doubtful that the first rapist would have been able to get her into his car.

As soon as he got out of his car and approached her with his knife, she could have had the gun out, pointed it at his chest, and said something like: "Go away or die." My guess is that his libido would have quickly cooled. But if it didn't, he would have had a new hole in his anatomy.

Of course, if the woman had a gun in her purse, she would have been violating the law that forbids carrying a concealed weapon. that's a part of the gun laws that I think should be changed.

I still believe all guns should be registered. I'm against the selling of the mini-machine guns that allow deranged people to blow away kids in schoolyards or their former co-workers. I also believe in cooling-off periods before guns are sold and background checks of those who want to buy guns.

But I think the law concerning carrying a concealed weapon should be amended so that a woman who has no serious criminal background or history of mental disorders and lives or works in or near a high-crime area of a city should be able to legally tote a pistol in her purse or pocket.

As long as gun ownership is legal in our society, it doesn't make much sense that I should be able to keep a couple of fully loaded pump-action shotguns in my home, but a woman on a dark street in a dangerous neighborhood is forbidden by law to carry a pistol in her purse.

Who is in greater danger? Me, with my doors double-locked, my dog and my shotguns? Or a woman in a neighborhood where rape and other assaults are almost as common as church pancake parties in small towns?

I'm not saying that a gun in a purse would put an end to all of it. But I don't doubt that after a few mugs suddenly find they have an extra navel, those of similar inclinations might ponder what that lady coming down the street might have in her purse.

Of course, I don't really expect the gun laws to be changed to permit women to protect themselves.

So I have another suggestion for females. Get a gun and carry it in your purse anyway. If you put a hole in some thug who pops out of a doorway or a car with a knife, I doubt if a judge will do more than deliver a lecture.

These days, there's always a good chance that the same judge put the guy with the knife back out on the street in the first place.

Name _____

Answer the following to learn about your own learning and reflect on your progress. Your instructor may collect your responses.

Prior to this chapter, what was your definition of critical thinking?

my idea of critical thinking was judging

How has your definition changed? *I changed my thinking by listening and thinking before I talk.*

Would you like to be a lawyer or to be on a college debating team? Why or why not? *I would like to be a lawyer because it is alot to think about and judge.*

Recall a recent conversation in which a position was supported with fallacious thinking. What was the fallacy that was most used?

_____

_____

How do you think you will use critical thinking when you have graduated from college? Give an example at work and an example in your personal life.

_____

_____

Reflect on the Longer Selections

Critical Thinking Responses:

What difficulties did you experience in identifying and evaluating the arguments?

_____

_____

If you do not agree with a position, why is it difficult to evaluate the argument?

_____

_____

Total your short-answer responses for the three longer selections.

Comprehension scores:
completed = ___   # correct = ___   # incorrect = ___   accuracy = ___%

Do you find true-false responses easier than multiple-choice? Why or why not?

_____

_____

Did you make any careless errors? Why? _____

_____

Clip out and explain three questions that you missed. Attach these questions and your analysis to the Learning Log for your instructor.

Reflect on the Vocabulary

Total your vocabulary responses for the longer selections.
completed = ___ # correct = ___ # incorrect = ___ accuracy = ___%

List the words that you missed.

_____

_____

What is the derivation of the term *laissez-faire?*

_____

_____

Review the vocabulary that you missed in previous chapters.

Using the perforations, tear out the Learning Log for your instructor.

Graphic Illustrations

What do graphics do?

How do you read a diagram?

> *a table?*

> *a map?*

> *a pie graph?*

> *a bar graph?*

> *a line graph?*

> *a flowchart?*

WHAT GRAPHICS DO

If a picture is worth a thousand words, a graphic illustration is worth at least several pages of facts and figures. Graphics express complex interrelationships in simplified form. Instead of plodding through repetitious data, you can glance at a chart, a map, or a graph and immediately see how everything fits together as well as how one part compares with another. Instead of reading several lengthy paragraphs and trying to visualize comparisons, you can study an organized design. The graphic illustration is a logically constructed aid for understanding many small bits of information.

Graphic illustrations are generally used for the following reasons.

1. **To condense.** Pages of repetitious, detailed information can be organized into one explanatory design.
2. **To clarify.** Processes and interrelationships can be more clearly defined through visual representations.
3. **To convince.** Developing trends and gross inequities can be forcefully dramatized.

There are five kinds of graphic illustrations: (1) diagrams, (2) tables, (3) maps, (4) graphs, and (5) flowcharts. All are used in textbooks, and the choice of which is best to use depends on the type of material presented. Study the following explanations of the different graphic forms.

HOW TO READ GRAPHIC MATERIAL

1. Read the title and get an overview. What is it about?
2. Look for footnotes and read italicized introductory material.
   Identify the who, where, and how.
   How and when were the data collected?
   Who collected the data?
   How many persons were included in the survey?
   Do the researchers seem to have been objective or biased?
   Considering the above information, does the study seem valid?
3. Read the labels.
   What do the vertical columns and the horizontal rows represent?
   Are the numbers in thousands or millions?
   What does the legend represent?
4. Notice the trends and find the extremes.
   What are the highest and lowest rates?
   What is the average rate?
   How do the extremes compare with the total?
   What is the percentage of increase or decrease?
5. Draw conclusions and formulate future exam questions.
   What does the information mean?

What needs to be done with the information?
What wasn't included?
Where do we go from here?

This chapter contains explanations and exercises for five types of graphic illustration. Read the explanations, study the illustrations, and respond to the statements as instructed.

Exercise 1   DIAGRAMS

A *diagram* is an outline drawing or picture of an object or a process. It shows the labeled parts of a complicated form such as the muscles of the human body, the organizational makeup of a company's management and production teams, or the directional flow of a natural ecological system.

The following diagrams display the arrangement of teeth in the human mouth and show the anatomy of a single tooth.

Tooth Arrangement and Anatomy

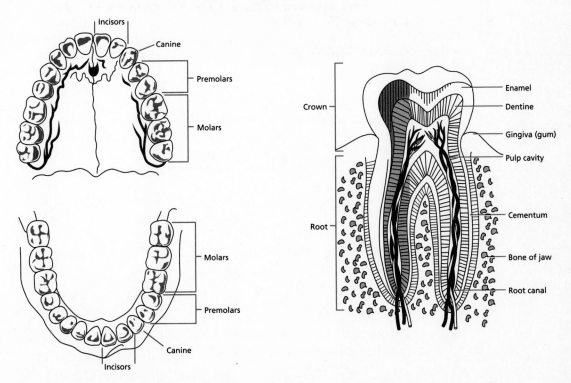

Tooth Arrangement in the Human Mouth   **Anatomy of a Single Tooth**

From Carl E. Rischer and Thomas A. Easton, *Focus on Human Biology*

Refer to the diagram to respond to the following items with *T* (true), *F* (false), or *CT* (can't tell).

_T_   1. The mouth contains eight incisors.

_T_   2. The last three teeth in each jaw are molars.

_CT_   3. Because of overcrowding, many adults have had their molars removed.

_F_   4. The upper jaw contains more premolars than the lower jaw.

_T_   5. The lower jaw contains two canine teeth.

_T_   6. The crown of a tooth extends above the gum.

_F_   7. The outer layer of a tooth is the dentine.

_T_   8. The root of the tooth extends into the bone of the jaw.

_T_   9. The pulp cavity contains the root canal.

_CT_   10. Plaque attacks a tooth and is a precursor of tooth decay.

_____   11. The purpose of each diagram is _the arrangement of the teeth_

Exercise 2   TABLES

A *table* is a listing of facts and figures in columns and rows for quick and easy reference. The information in the columns and rows is usually labeled in two different directions. First read the title for the topic and then read the footnotes to judge the source. Determine what each column represents and how they interact.

In the following tables, note the amounts being compared, the average, and the range.

Refer to the tables on page 363 to respond to the following with *T* (true), *F* (false), or *CT* (can't tell).

_T_   1. Decaffeinated brewed coffee contains no caffeine.

_T_   2. Imported brands of brewed tea can range higher in caffeine than United States brands.

_F_   3. The amount of iced tea measured for caffeine was the same as the amount of brewed tea.

_T_   4. On the average, two ounces of dark chocolate contains more caffeine than two ounces of milk chocolate.

_T_   5. A twelve-ounce serving of Coca-Cola has more caffeine than an equal serving of Pepsi.

Caffeine in Beverages and Foods

Item	Caffeine (mg)	
	Average	Range
Coffee (5-oz. cup)		
Brewed, drip method	115	60–180
Brewed, percolator	80	40–170
Instant	65	30–120
Decaffeinated, brewed	3	2–5
Decaffeinated, instant	2	1–5
Tea (5-oz. cup)		
Brewed, major U.S. brands	40	20–90
Brewed, imported brands	60	25–110
Instant	30	25–50
Iced (12-oz. glass)	70	67–76
Cocoa beverage (5-oz. cup)	4	2–20
Chocolate milk beverage (8-oz. glass)	5	2–7
Milk chocolate (1 oz.)	6	1–15
Dark chocolate, semi-sweet (1 oz.)	20	5–35
Baker's chocolate (1 oz.)	26	26
Chocolate-flavored syrup (1 oz.)	4	4

Caffeine in Popular Soft Drinks

Brand	Caffeine (mg)*
Sugar-Free Mr. Pibb	58.8
Mountain Dew	54.0
Mello Yello	52.8
Tab	46.8
Coca-Cola	45.6
Diet Coke	45.6
Shasta Cola	44.4
Mr. Pibb	40.8
Dr. Pepper	39.6
Big Red	38.4
Pepsi-Cola	38.4
Diet Pepsi	36.0
Pepsi Light	36.0
RC Cola	36.0
Diet Rite	36.0
Canada Dry Jamaica Cola	30.0
Canada Dry Diet Cola	1.2

*Per 12-oz. serving

From Oakley Ray and Charles Ksir, *Drugs, Society, and Human Behavior*

_1_ 6. On the average, iced tea has more caffeine than an equal amount of Coca-Cola.

_1_ 7. In equal amounts, brewed coffee has over twice as much caffeine as a Canada Dry Jamaica Cola.

_C1_ 8. The caffeine is easier to put in dark drinks and food as opposed to lighter ones.

_1_ 9. On the average, instant tea and coffee contain less caffeine than their brewed counterparts.

_1_ 10. Mello Yello is light in color and thus most people assume that is does not contain caffeine.

_____ 11. The purpose of each table is _Caffine drink & food_

Exercise 3 MAPS

A *map* shows a geographic area. It shows differences in physical terrain, direction, or variations over a specified area. The legend of a map, which usually appears in a corner box, explains the meanings of symbols and shading. Use the legend on the following map to help you answer the questions.

Refer to the map on page 365 to respond to the following with *T* (true), *F* (false) or *CT* (can't tell).

_T_ 1. The Nile runs in a north-south direction through Egypt.

_T_ 2. The Sinai blocks the Red Sea from the Mediterranean Sea.

_T_ 3. Nicosia is a city in Cyprus.

_F_ 4. The Saudi Arabian city of Medina has a population of more than 5,000,000 inhabitants.

_T_ 5. Cairo is the largest city shown on this map.

_T_ 6. Egypt's agricultural areas extend along the Nile River.

_F_ 7. Cyprus is an oasis.

_F_ 8. Amman is the largest city in Iraq.

_F_ 9. According to the map, Eritrea contains only two oilfields.

_F_ 10. Damascus is a port city on the Mediterranean Sea.

_____ 11. The purpose of the map is *to show Population, Agriculture*

Geographic Review

Use the map on page 366 to test your knowledge of world geography.

Citizens of the World Show Little Knowledge of Geography

In the spring of 1988, twelve thousand people in ten nations were asked to identify sixteen places on the following world map. The average citizen in the United States could identify barely more than half. Believe it or not, 14 percent of Americans tested could not even find their own country on the map. Despite years of fighting in Vietnam, 68 percent could not locate this Southeast Asian country. Such lack of basic geographic knowledge is quite common throughout the world. Here is the average score for each of the ten countries in which the test was administered.

	Country	Average Score
1	Sweden	11.6
6	United States	8.6
2	West Germany	11.2
7	Great Britain	8.5

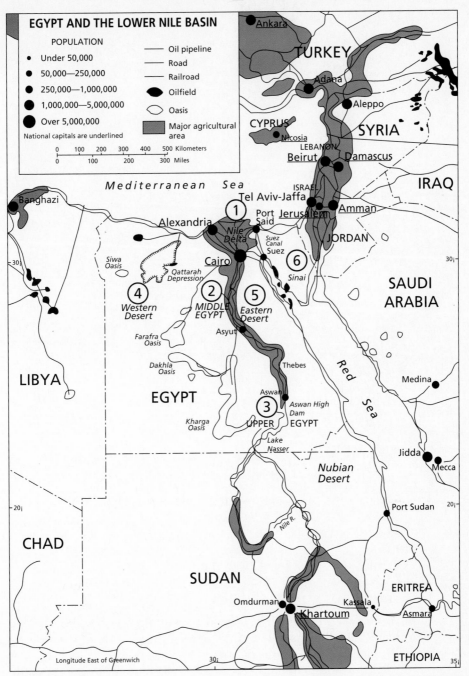

EGYPT AND THE LOWER NILE BASIN

POPULATION

- Under 50,000
- 50,000—250,000
- 250,000—1,000,000
- 1,000,000—5,000,000
- Over 5,000,000

National capitals are underlined

——— Oil pipeline
——— Road
——— Railroad
● Oilfield
○ Oasis
▨ Major agricultural area

| 0 | 100 | 200 | 300 | 400 | 500 Kilometers |
| 0 | | 100 | 200 | | 300 Miles |

From H. J. Deblij and Peter O. Muller, *Geography*.

3	Japan	9.7
8	Italy	7.6
4	France	9.3
9	Mexico	7.4
5	Canada	9.2
10	Soviet Union	7.4

How would you do? To take the test yourself, match the numbers on the map to the places listed.

Robert L. Lineberry et al., *Government in America*

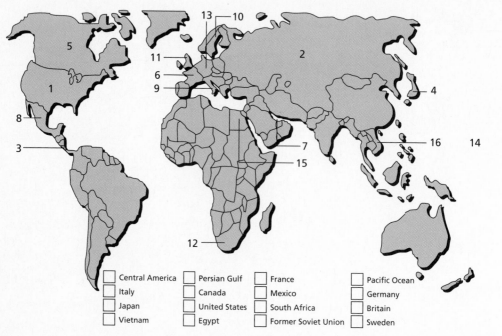

Source: Warren E. Leary, "Two Superpowers' Citizens Do Badly in Geography," *New York Times,* November 9, 1989, A6.

Exercise 4   PIE GRAPHS

A *pie graph* is a circle that is divided into wedge-shaped slices. The complete pie or circle represents a total, or 100 percent. Each slice is a percent or fraction of that whole. Budgets, such as the annual expenditure of the federal or state governments, are frequently illustrated by pie graphs.

Refer to the pie graphs on page 367 to respond to the following with *T* (true), *F* (false), or *CT* (can't tell).

 1. Excise taxes generate 5 percent of the incoming federal budget.

 2. The category contributing the highest percentage of incoming budget money is the category of "individual income taxes."

**The Federal Government Dollar
(Fiscal Year 1994 Estimate)**

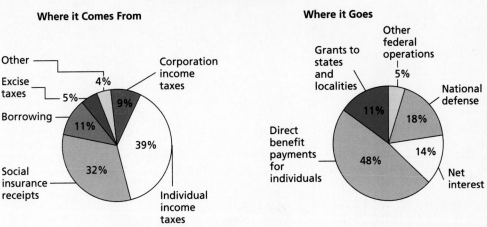

Where it Comes From

Other —
Excise taxes —
Borrowing — 11%
Social insurance receipts — 32%
Corporation income taxes — 4%
5%
9%
39%
Individual income taxes

Where it Goes

Grants to states and localities — 11%
Other federal operations — 5%
National defense — 18%
Direct benefit payments for individuals — 48%
14%
Net interest

Source: *Budget of the United States Government, Fiscal Year 1995* (Washington, D.C.: Government Printing Office, 1994), 12, found in Robert L. Lineberry et al., *Government in America.*

_T_ 3. Federal borrowing accounts for more incoming budget dollars than corporation income taxes.

_T_ 4. More is spent on national defense than on net interest.

_CT_ 5. More is spent on welfare payments than on Medicare.

_T_ 6. The percentage of the budget that comes in from other sources is almost the same (within one point) of the percentage spent on other federal operations.

_CT_ 7. The money for national defense comes from individual income taxes.

_CT_ 8. Social insurance receipts are a rapidly shrinking portion of the incoming budget.

_CT_ 9. In 1994 the federal government spent more on grants to states and localities than was spent in 1993.

_T_ 10. Almost one-half of the federal budget is spent on direct benefit payments for individuals.

_____ 11. The purpose of each pie graph is 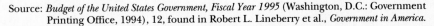 *Where the money go*

Exercise 5   BAR GRAPHS

A *bar graph* is a series of horizontal or vertical bars in which the length of each bar represents a particular amount or number of what is being discussed. A series of different items can be quickly compared by noting the different bar lengths.

Refer to the bar graph on page 368 to respond to the following with *T* (true), *F* (false), or *CT* (can't tell).

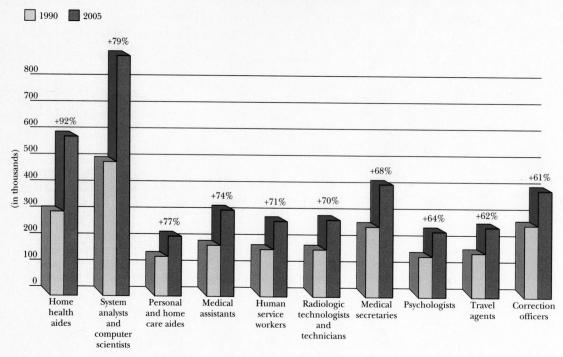

The Ten Fastest-Growing Civilian Ocupations in the United States, 1990–2005*

□ 1990   ■ 2005

(in thousands)

+79%
+92%
+77%
+74%
+71%
+70%
+68%
+64%
+62%
+61%

Home health aides | System analysts and computer scientists | Personal and home care aides | Medical assistants | Human service workers | Radiologic technologists and technicians | Medical secretaries | Psychologists | Travel agents | Correction officers

*Figures for the year 2005 are based on moderate projects from the U.S. Bureau of Labor Statistics
Source: U.S. Bureau of Labor Statistics, *Monthly Labor Review,* November 1991. Found in William E. Thompson and Joseph V. Hickey, *Society in Focus.*

_1_ 1. The highest projected percentage of job increases in the fifteen-year period is in home health aides.

_T_ 2. The projected number of medical assistants needed in 2005 is over 250,000.

_T_ 3. Half of the ten fastest-growing civilian occupations are related to health care fields.

_T_ 4. The greatest number of people projected for any occupation on the chart in the year of 2005 will be needed as systems analysts and computer scientists.

_F_ 5. In 2005, more people are predicted to be working in radiology than as correction officers.

_T_ 6. In 1990, over twice as many people worked as home health aides as were personal and home care aides.

_F_ 7. In 2005, the need projected for travel agents is three times as great as the projection for systems analysts and computer scientists.

_____ 8. Medical assistants are projected to receive higher salaries than human-service workers.

_____ 9. The percentage of increased need for psychologists is projected to be greater than the increased need for personal and home care aides.

_____ 10. Occupations showing less than a 60 percent increase in the fifteen-year period were not shown.

_____ 11. The purpose of the bar graph is _ten fastest going_
Civilian Jobs.

Exercise 6   LINE GRAPHS

A *line graph* is a continuous curve or frequency distribution. The horizontal scale measures one aspect of the data and the vertical line measures another aspect. As the data fluctuate, the line will change direction and, with extreme differences, will become very jagged.

In the graph that follows, notice that the horizontal line measures time and the vertical line measures dollars. This graph shows three different frequency distributions. For Americans the crucial issue is the intersection of these lines.

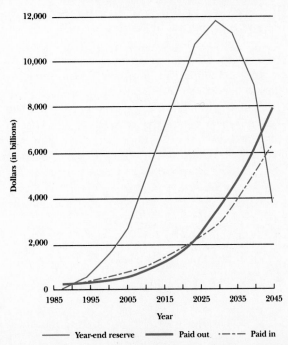

Social Security Receipts, Spending, and Reserves

—— Year-end reserve   ▬▬ Paid out   ·—·— Paid in

Source: U.S. Congress, House Committee on Ways and Means, "1988 Annual Report of the Board of Trustees of the Federal Old-Age and Survivors Insurance and Disability Insurance Trust Funds," 100th Congress, 2nd session, May 5, 1988, pp. 141–142. Found in Edward S. Greeburg and Benjamin I. Page, *The Struggle for Democracy.*

Refer to the line graph to respond to the following with T (true), F (false), or CT (can't tell).

_T___ 1. The budget reserve for Social Security is presently higher than the amount paid out.

_T___ 2. In approximately 2020 the amount paid out in Social Security is projected to be greater than the amount paid in.

_F___ 3. By 2025 the demand for Social Security is projected to outstrip the reserve.

_F___ 4. By 2015 approximately $8,000,000 will be the value of the reserve.

_CT__ 5. The Social Security reserve is used only for Social Security payments.

_____ 6. The purpose of the line graph is _to show what the_ _reserves are._

Exercise 7   FLOWCHARTS

Flowcharts provide a diagram of the relationships and sequence of elements. They were first used in computer programming. Key ideas are stated in boxes, along with supporting ideas that are linked by arrows. In the flowchart on page 371, arrows pointing toward an area indicate money coming into the economy and arrows pointing away from an area indicate money leaving the economy.

In 1993 American companies exported goods worth approximately $448 billion, the European Economic Community nations exported goods worth $731 billion (including trade among EC members), and Japan exported about $340 billion in goods. By comparison, the United States imported $533 billion worth of goods, the EC imported $764 billion worth of goods, and Japan imported $233 billion worth. The difference between the values of a country's exports and imports is called its **balance of trade.** If exports exceed imports, there is a **trade surplus;** if imports exceed exports, there is a **trade deficit.**

Refer to the explanation and the flowchart to respond to the following with T (true), F (false), or CT (can't tell).

_T___ 1. The United States exports more to the European Economic Community than it exports to Japan.

_F___ 2. The United States imports from Japan over twice as much as it exports to Japan.

_F___ 3. The European Economic Community exports to Japan more than ten times as much as it imports.

_CT__ 4. Japanese automobiles make up the highest percentage of goods exported from Japan.

© 1997 Addison-Wesley Educational Publishers Inc.

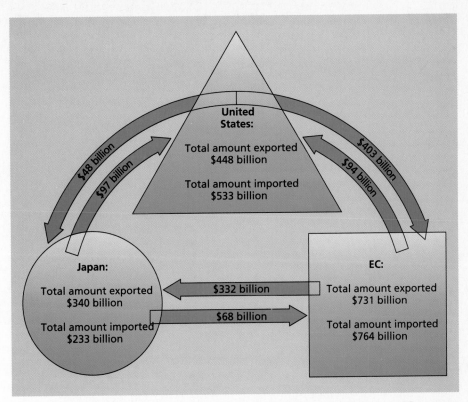

Source: International Financial Statistics, Japan Trade Center, U.S. Department of Commerce, O.E.C.D. data, and Eurostat, External Trade and Balance of Payments, 1993. Found in Thomas C. Kinnear et al., *Principles of Marketing*.

1 _____ 5. Of the three leading world traders, Japan is the only one that exports more than it imports.

_____ 6. The purpose of the flowchart is *to compare the three trades of the world.*

SUMMARY POINTS

Graphic illustrations condense, clarify, and convince. They express complex interrelationships in simplified form. The following kinds of graphic illustrations can be used to present information:

- A *diagram* is an outline drawing or picture of an object or a process.
- A *table* is a listing of facts and figures in columns for quick and easy reference.
- A *map* shows a geographic area.
- A *pie graph* is a circle that is divided into wedge-shaped slices. The whole circle represents 100 percent.

- A *bar graph* is a series of horizontal bars in which the length of each bar represents a particular amount.
- A *line graph* is a continuous curve or frequency distribution.
- *Flowcharts* provide a diagram of the relationships and sequence of elements.

SELECTION 1

ALLIED HEALTH

Stage 1: Skill Development

Preview

The author's main purpose is to condemn alcohol.

agree ☐   disagree ☐

The different sections describe the cause-and-effect relationship of alcohol on the body.

agree ☐   disagree ☐

After reading this selection, I will need to know how alcohol affects the brain.

agree ☐   disagree ☐

Activate Schema

What is the legal limit for driving a car on a breathalyzer test?

Learning Strategy

Trace alcohol through the body and note the effects as it travels.

Word Knowledge

Are you familiar with the following words in this selection?

counterparts   enhanced

diffuse   prudent

sedating   ruefully

lethal   abstinence

toxic   devastates

Your instructor may ask five true-false questions from the *Instructor's Manual* to stimulate your thinking using these words.

Stage 2: Integrate Knowledge While Reading

Use the thinking strategies as you read:

1. Predict   2. Picture   3. Relate   4. Monitor   5. Fix up

Alcohol and Nutrition
From Eva May Nunnelley Hamilton et al., *Nutrition*

People naturally congregate to enjoy conversation and companionship, and it is natural, too, to offer beverages to companions. All beverages ease conversation whether or not they contain alcohol. Still, some people choose alcohol over cola, milk, or coffee, and they should know a few things about
5   alcohol's short term and long term effects on health. One consideration is energy—alcohol yields energy to the body, and many alcoholic drinks are much more fattening than their nonalcoholic counterparts. Additionally, alcohol has a tremendous impact on the overall well-being of the body.

People consume alcohol in servings they call "a drink." However, the
10 serving that some people consider one drink may not be the same as the standard drink that delivers 1/2 ounce pure ethanol:

3 to 4 ounces wine

10 ounces wine cooler

12 ounces beer

15 1 ounce hard liquor (whiskey, gin, brandy, rum, vodka)

The percentage of alcohol in distilled liquor is stated as *proof:* 100-proof liquor is 50 percent alcohol; 90-proof is 45 percent, and so forth. Compared with hard liquor, beer and wine have a relatively low percentage of alcohol.

Alcohol Enters the Body

20 From the moment an alcoholic beverage is swallowed, the body confers special status on it. Unlike foods, which require digestion, the tiny alcohol molecules are all ready to be absorbed; they can diffuse right through the walls of an empty stomach and reach the brain within a minute. A person can become intoxicated almost immediately when drinking, especially if the
25 person's stomach is empty. When the stomach is full of food, molecules of alcohol have less chance of touching the walls and diffusing through, so alcohol affects the brain a little less immediately. (By the time the stomach contents are emptied into the small intestine, it doesn't matter that food is mixed with the alcohol. The alcohol is absorbed rapidly anyway.)

30   A practical pointer derives from this information. If a person wants to drink socially and not become intoxicated, the person should eat the snacks provided by the host (avoid the salty ones; they make you thirstier). Carbohydrate snacks are best suited for slowing alcohol absorption. High-fat snacks help too because they slow peristalsis, keeping the alcohol in the

35 stomach longer.

    If one drinks slowly enough, the alcohol, after absorption, will be collected into the liver and processed without much affecting other parts of the body. If one drinks more rapidly, however, some of the alcohol bypasses the liver and flows for a while through the rest of the body and the brain.

40 **Alcohol Arrives in the Brain**

    People use alcohol today as a kind of social anesthetic to help them relax or to relieve anxiety. One drink relieves inhibitions, and this gives people the impression that alcohol is a stimulant. Actually the way it does this is by sedating *inhibitory* nerves, allowing excitatory nerves to take over.

Figure R-1

Alcohol's Effects on the Brain

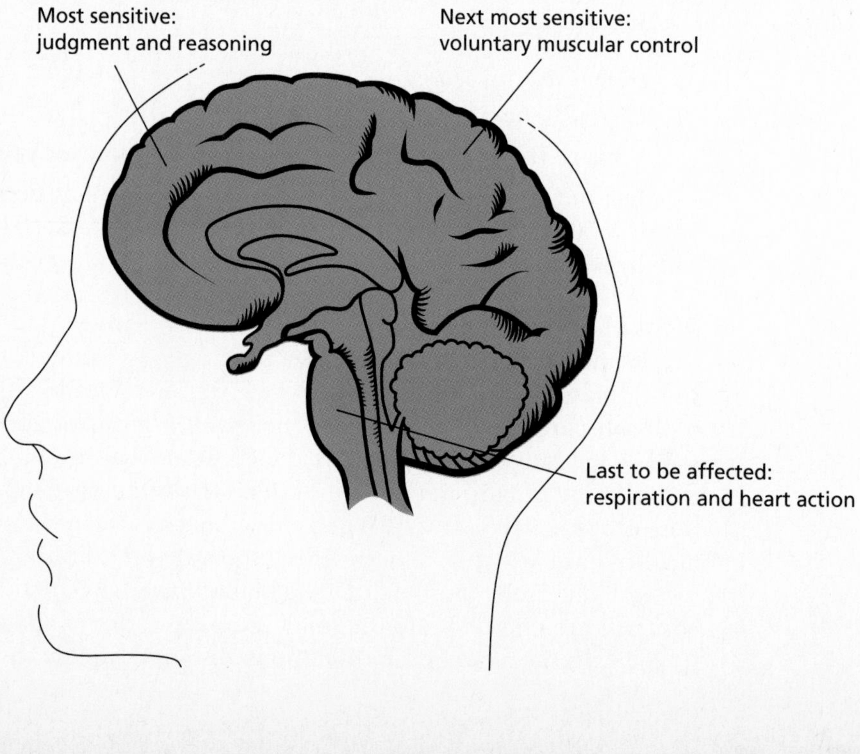

Most sensitive:
judgment and reasoning

Next most sensitive:
voluntary muscular control

Last to be affected:
respiration and heart action

45 This is temporary. Ultimately alcohol acts as a depressant and sedates all the nerve cells. Figure R1 describes alcohol's effects on the brain.

It is lucky that the brain centers respond to elevating blood alcohol in the order described in Figure R1 because a person usually passes out before managing to drink a lethal dose. It is possible, though, for a person to drink 50 fast enough so that the effects of alcohol continue to accelerate after the person has gone to sleep. The occasional death that takes place during a drinking contest is attributed to this effect. The drinker drinks fast enough, before passing out, to receive a lethal dose. Table R1 shows the blood alcohol levels that correspond with progressively greater intoxication and 55 Table R2 shows the brain responses that occur at these blood levels.

Brain cells are particularly sensitive to excessive exposure to alcohol. The brain shrinks, even in people who drink only moderately. The extent of the shrinkage is proportional to the amount drunk. Abstinence, together with good nutrition, reverses some of the brain damage—possibly all of it if 60 heavy drinking has not continued for more than a few years—but prolonged

Table R1 Alcohol Doses and Blood Levels

Percent Blood Alcohol by Body Weight

Number of Drinks[a]	100 lb	120 lb	150 lb	180 lb	200 lb
2	0.08	0.06	0.05	0.04	0.04
4	0.15	0.13	0.10	0.08	0.08
6	0.23	0.19	0.15	0.13	0.11
8	0.30	0.25	0.20	0.17	0.15
12	0.45	0.36	0.30	0.25	0.23
14	0.52	0.42	0.35	0.34	0.27

[a]Taken within an hour or so.

Table R2 Alcohol Blood Levels and Brain Responses

Blood Level (%)	Brain Response
0.05	Judgment impaired
0.10	Emotional control impaired
0.15	Muscle coordination and reflexes impaired
0.20	Vision impaired
0.30	Drunk, totally out of control
0.35	Stupor
0.50–0.60	Total loss of consciousness, finally death

drinking beyond an individual's capacity to recover can cause severe and irreversible effects on vision, memory, learning ability, and other functions.

Anyone who has had an alcoholic drink knows that alcohol increases urine output. This is because alcohol depresses the brain's production of
65 **antidiuretic hormone.** Loss of body water leads to thirst. The only fluid that will relieve dehydration is water, but if alcohol is the only drink available, the thirsty person may choose another alcoholic beverage and worsen the problem. The smart drinker, then, alternates alcoholic beverages with nonalcoholic choices and when thirsty chooses the latter.
70   The water loss caused by hormone depression involves loss of more than just water. The water takes with it important minerals, such as magnesium, potassium, calcium, and zinc, depleting the body's reserves. These minerals are vital to the maintenance of fluid balance and to nerve and muscle action and coordination.

75 **Alcohol Arrives in the Liver**

The capillaries that surround the digestive tract merge into veins that carry the alcohol-laden blood to the liver. Here the veins branch and rebranch into capillaries that touch every liver cell. The liver cells make nearly all of the body's alcohol-processing machinery, and the routing of
80 blood through the liver allows the cells to go right to work on the alcohol. The liver's location at this point along the circulatory system guarantees that it gets the chance to remove toxic substances before they reach other body organs such as the heart and brain.

The liver makes and maintains two sets of equipment for metabolizing
85 alcohol. One is an enzyme that removes hydrogens from alcohol to break it down; the name almost says what it does—**alcohol dehydrogenase (ADH).***
This handles about 80 percent or more of body alcohol. The other alcohol-metabolizing equipment is a chain of enzymes (known as the **MEOS**) thought to handle about 10 to 20 percent of body alcohol. With high blood
90 alcohol concentrations, the MEOS activity is enhanced, as will be shown later. But let us look at the ADH system first.

The amount of alcohol a person's body can process in a given time is limited by the number of ADH enzymes that reside in the liver.† If more molecules of alcohol arrive at the liver cells than the enzymes can handle,
95 the extra alcohol must wait. It enters the general circulation and is carried

---

*There are actually two ADH enzymes, each for a specific task in alcohol breakdown. Enzyme 1, alcohol dehydrogenase, converts alcohol to acetaldehyde. Enzyme 2, acetaldehyde dehydrogenase, converts acetaldehyde to a common body compound, acetyl CoA, identical to that derived from carbohydrate and fat during their breakdown.

†Some ADH enzymes reside in the stomach, offering a protective barrier against alcohol entering the blood. Research shows that alcoholics make less stomach ADH, and so do women. Women may absorb about one-third more alcohol than men, even when they are the same size and drink the same amount of alcoholic beverage.

to all parts of the body, circulating again and again through the liver until enzymes are available to degrade it.

100

The number of ADH enzymes present is affected by whether or not a person eats. Fasting for as little as a day causes degradation of body proteins, including the ADH enzymes in the liver, and this can reduce the rate of alcohol metabolism by half. Prudent drinkers drink slowly, with food in their stomachs, to allow the alcohol molecules to move to the liver cells gradually enough for the enzymes to handle the load. It takes about an hour and a half to metabolize one drink, depending on a person's body

105

size, on previous drinking experience, on how recently the person has eaten, and on general health at the time. The liver is the only organ that can dispose of significant quantities of alcohol, and its maximum rate of alcohol clearance is fixed. This explains why only time will restore sobriety. Walking will not; muscles cannot metabolize alcohol. Nor will it help to

110

drink a cup of coffee. Caffeine is a stimulant, but it won't speed up the metabolism of alcohol. The police say ruefully that a cup of coffee will only make a sleepy drunk into a wide-awake drunk.

As the ADH enzymes break alcohol down, they produce hydrogen ions (acid), which must be picked up by a compound that contains the B vitamin

115

niacin as part of its structure. Normally this acid is disposed of through a metabolic pathway, but when alcohol is present in the system, this pathway shuts down. The niacin-containing compound remains loaded with hydrogens that it cannot get rid of and so becomes unavailable for a multitude of other vital body processes for which it is required.

120

The synthesis of fatty acids also accelerates as a result of the liver's exposure to alcohol. Fat accumulation can be seen in the liver after a single night of heavy drinking. **Fatty liver,** the first stage of liver deterioration seen in heavy drinkers, interferes with the distribution of nutrients and oxygen to the liver cells. If the condition lasts long enough, the liver cells die, and

125

fibrous scar tissue invades the area—the second stage of liver deterioration called **fibrosis.** Fibrosis is reversible with good nutrition and abstinence from alcohol, but the next (last) stage—**cirrhosis**—is not. All of this points to the importance of moderation in the use of alcohol.

The presence of alcohol alters amino acid metabolism in the liver cells.

130

Synthesis of some proteins important in the immune system slows down, weakening the body's defenses against infection. Synthesis of lipoproteins speeds up, increasing blood triglyceride levels. In addition, excessive alcohol increases the body's acid burden and interferes with normal uric acid metabolism, causing symptoms like those of **gout.**

135

Liver metabolism clears most of the alcohol from the blood. However, about 10 percent is excreted through the breath and in the urine. This fact is the basis for the breathalyzer test that law enforcement officers administer when they suspect someone of driving under the influence of alcohol.

Alcohol's Long-Term Effects

140   By far the longest term effects of alcohol are those felt by the child of a woman who drinks during pregnancy. Pregnant women should not drink at all. For nonpregnant adults, however, what are the effects of alcohol over the long term?

145   A couple of drinks set in motion many destructive processes in the body, but the next day's abstinence reverses them. As long as the doses taken are moderate, time between them is ample, and nutrition is adequate meanwhile, recovery is probably complete.

    If the doses of alcohol are heavy and the time between them is short, complete recovery cannot take place, and repeated onslaughts of alcohol
150 gradually take a toll on the body. For example, alcohol is directly toxic to skeletal and cardiac muscle, causing weakness and deterioration in a dose-related manner. Alcoholism makes heart disease more likely probably because alcohol in high doses raises the blood pressure. Cirrhosis can develop after 10 to 20 years from the additive effects of frequent heavy
155 drinking episodes. Alcohol abuse also increases a person's risk of cancer of the mouth, throat, esophagus, rectum, and lungs. Women who drink even moderately may run an increased risk of developing breast cancer. Although some dispute these findings, a reliable source tentatively ranks daily human exposure to ethanol as high in relation to other possible
160 carcinogenic hazards. Other long-terms effects of alcohol abuse include:

Ulcers of the stomach and intestines

Psychological depression

Kidney damage, bladder damage, prostate gland damage, pancreas damage

Skin rashes and sores

165   Impaired immune response

Deterioration in the testicles and adrenal glands, leading to feminization and sexual impotence in men

Central nervous system damage

Malnutrition

170   Increased risk of violent death

This list is by no means all inclusive. Alcohol has direct toxic effects, independent of the effect of malnutrition, on all body organs.

    The more alcohol a person drinks, the less likely that he or she will eat enough food to obtain adequate nutrients. Alcohol is empty calories, like
175 pure sugar and pure fat; it displaces nutrients. In a sense, each time you drink 150 calories of alcohol, you are spending those calories on a luxury item and getting no nutritional value in return. The more calories you spend this way, the fewer you have left to spend on nutritious foods. Table R3 shows the calorie amounts of typical alcoholic beverages.

Table R3 Calories in Alcoholic Beverages and Mixers

Beverage	Amount (oz)	Energy (cal)
Beer	12	150
Light beer	12	100
Gin, rum, vodka, whiskey (86 proof)	1 1/2	105
Dessert wine	3 1/2	140
Table wine	3 1/2	85
Tonic, ginger ale, other sweetened carbonated waters	8	80
Cola, root beer	8	100
Fruit-flavored soda, Tom Collins mix	8	115
Club soda, plain seltzer, diet drinks	8	1

180 Alcohol abuse not only displaces nutrients from the diet but also affects every tissue's metabolism of nutrients. Alcohol causes stomach cells to oversecrete both acid and an agent of the immune system, histamine, that produces inflammation. These changes make the stomach and esophagus linings vulnerable to ulcer formation. Intestinal cells fail to absorb thiamin,

185 folate, and vitamin B_{12}. Liver cells lose efficiency in activating vitamin D and alter their production and excretion of bile. Rod cells in the retina, which normally process vitamin A alcohol (retinol) to the form needed in vision, find themselves processing drinking alcohol instead. The kidneys excrete magnesium, calcium, potassium, and zinc.

190 Alcohol's intermediate products interfere with metabolism too. They dislodge vitamin B_6 from its protective binding protein so that it is destroyed, causing a vitamin B_6 deficiency and thereby lowered production of red blood cells.

Most dramatic is alcohol's effect on folate. When alcohol is present, it is

195 as though the body were actively trying to expel folate from all its sites of action and storage. The liver, which normally contains enough folate to meet all needs, leaks folate into the blood. As the blood folate concentration rises, the kidneys are deceived into excreting it, as though it were in excess. The intestine normally releases and retrieves folate

200 continuously, but it becomes damaged by folate deficiency and alcohol toxicity; so it fails to retrieve its own folate and misses out on any that may trickle in from food as well. Alcohol also interferes with the action of what little folate is left, and this inhibits the production of new cells, especially the rapidly dividing cells of the intestine and the blood. Alcohol abuse

205 causes a folate deficiency that devastates digestive system function.

Nutrient deficiencies are thus a virtually inevitable consequence of alcohol abuse, not only because alcohol displaces food but also because alcohol directly interferes with the body's use of nutrients, making them ineffective even if they are present. Over a lifetime, excessive drinking, whether or not accompanied by attention to nutrition, brings about deficits of all the nutrients mentioned in this discussion and many more besides.

210

Alcohol and Drugs

The liver's reaction to alcohol affects its handling of drugs as well as nutrients. In addition to the ADH enzymes, the liver possesses an enzyme system that metabolizes *both* alcohol and drugs—any compounds that have certain chemical features in common. As mentioned earlier, at low blood alcohol concentrations, the MEOS handles about 10 to 20 percent of the alcohol consumed. However, at high blood alcohol concentrations, or if repeatedly exposed to alcohol, the MEOS is enhanced.

215

As a person's blood alcohol concentration rises, the alcohol competes with—and wins out over—other drugs whose metabolism relies on the MEOS. If a person drinks and uses another drug at the same time, the drug will be metabolized more slowly and so will be much more potent. The MEOS is busy disposing of alcohol, so the drug cannot be handled until later; the dose may build up to where its effects are greatly amplified—sometimes to the point of killing the user.

220

225

In contrast, once a heavy drinker stops drinking and alcohol is not present to compete with other drugs, the enhanced MEOS metabolizes those drugs much faster than before. This can make it confusing and tricky to work out the correct dosages of medications. The doctor who prescribes sedatives every four hours, for example, unaware that the person has recently gone from being a heavy drinker to an abstainer, expects the MEOS to dispose of the drug at a certain predicted rate. The MEOS is adapted to metabolizing large quantities of alcohol, however. It therefore metabolizes the drug extra fast. The drug's effects wear off unexpectedly fast, leaving the client undersedated. Imagine the doctor's alarm should a patient wake up on the table during an operation! A skilled anesthesiologist always asks the patient about his drinking pattern before putting him to sleep.

230

235

This discussion has touched on some of the ways alcohol affects health and nutrition. Despite some possible benefits of moderate alcohol consumption, the potential for harm is great, especially with excessive alcohol consumption. Consider that over 50 percent of all fatal auto accidents are alcohol related. Translated to human lives, more than 25,000 people die each year in alcohol-related traffic accidents. The best way to avoid the harmful effects of alcohol is, of course, to avoid alcohol altogether. If you do drink, do so with care—for yourself and for others—and in moderation.

240

250

Step 3: Recall

Stop to self-test and relate. Your instructor may ask ten true-false questions to stimulate your recall.

SKILL DEVELOPMENT: READING GRAPHICS

Refer to the designated graphic and answer the following items with *T* (true) or *F* (false).

_F_ 1. According to Figure R1, alcohol first affects muscular control.

_F_ 2. According to Table R1, a person who has two drinks and weighs 120 pounds would have 13 percent blood alcohol level.

_T_ 3. According to Table R2, a blood alcohol level of 0.35 will cause a stupor.

_T_ 4. According to Tables R1 and R2, a person weighing 150 pounds who has eight drinks would have impaired vision.

_F_ 5. According to Table R3, vodka has more calories than rum.

COMPREHENSION QUESTIONS

After reading the selection, answer the following questions with *a, b, c,* or *d.*

_d_ 1. The best statement of the main idea of this selection is
   a. alcohol is involved in over half of the fatal auto accidents each year.
   b. alcohol is processed by the liver.
   c. alcohol is a drug rather than a food.
   d. alcohol is a drug that has a complex and interrelated impact on the body.

_c_ 2. When the stomach is full of food, alcohol
   a. goes directly to the liver.
   b. bypasses the liver for the bloodstream.
   c. affects the brain less immediately.
   d. rapidly diffuses through the walls of the stomach.

_d_ 3. The brain responds to elevated blood alcohol in all of the following ways except
   a. loss of consciousness.
   b. shrinking.
   c. sedating nerve cells.
   d. increasing production of antidiuretic hormones.

_A_ 4. Most of the body's processing of alcohol is done by the
a. liver.
b. brain.
c. stomach.
d. blood.

_D_ 5. Alcohol reaches the liver through
a. direct absorption.
b. vein and capillaries.
c. the intestines.
d. loss of body water.

_b_ 6. When enzymes are not available to degrade the total amount of alcohol consumed, this extra alcohol that cannot be immediately processed by the liver
a. waits in the liver for enzymes to become available.
b. circulates to all parts of the body.
c. is metabolized by the MEOS.
d. is sent to the stomach for storage.

_a_ 7. All of the following are true about ADH except
a. its production can be accelerated to meet increased demand.
b. it removes hydrogen from the alcohol.
c. the number of ADH enzymes is affected by the presence of food in the stomach.
d. ADH enzymes can reside in the stomach.

_B_ 8. The destruction of vitamin B_6 by alcohol results in
a. the excretion of bile.
b. a reduction in the number of red blood cells.
c. the oversecretion of acid and histamine.
d. loss of retinol by the rod cells in the eye.

_A_ 9. The negative influence of alcohol on the production of new cells is caused by
a. folate excretion.
b. ulcer formation.
c. esophagus inflammation.
d. carcinogenic hazards.

_C_ 10. If a doctor knows that a patient has recently progressed from a heavy drinker to an abstainer, the doctor should expect that prescribed drugs will be metabolized
a. at a normal rate.
b. slower than normal.
c. faster than normal.
d. only when the MEOS has returned to normal.

Answer the following with *T* (true) or *F* (false).

F 11. The sentence in the first paragraph, "All beverages ease conversation whether or not they contain alcohol" is a statement of fact.

T 12. Carbohydrate snacks slow alcohol absorption.

T 13. Alcohol can bypass the liver and flow directly to the brain.

T 14. High doses of alcohol can raise blood pressure.

F 15. Men absorb alcohol faster than women.

VOCABULARY

According to the way the italicized word was used in the selection, indicate *a, b, c,* or *d* for the word or phrase that gives the best definition.

a 1. "their nonalcoholic
counterparts" (7)
a. duplicates
b. sugars
c. energy sources
d. stimulants

d 2. "*diffuse* right through the walls" (22)
a. disappear
b. weaken
c. stick together
d. spread widely

A 3. "*sedating* inhibitory nerves"
(44)
a. soothing
b. connecting
c. closing
d. exciting

d 4. "receive a *lethal* dose"
(53)
a. complete
b. large
c. legal
d. deadly

C 5. "remove *toxic* substances"
(82)
a. inhibiting
b. foreign
c. poisonous
d. digestive

A 6. "MEOS activity is *enhanced*"
(90)
a. increased
b. condensed
c. redirected
d. consolidated

b 7. "*Prudent* drinkers" (101)
a. older
b. wise
c. experienced
d. addicted

C 8. "police say *ruefully*" (111)
a. happily
b. angrily
c. mournfully
d. humorously

d   9. "next day's *abstinence*" (145)
   a. headache
   b. sickness
   c. repentance
   d. giving up drinking

q   10. "*devastates* digestive system (205)
   a. destroys
   b. divides
   c. follows
   d. loosens

WRITTEN RESPONSE

Use information from the selection to write a letter to a friend who drinks and drives. **In a scientific manner explain to your friend why driving after having a few drinks is a danger.**

COLLABORATIVE CRITICAL THINKING

Drinking During Pregnancy

Read the following for information on the effects of alcohol on the unborn.

Drinking During Pregnancy

Drinking excess alcohol during pregnancy threatens the fetus with the irreversible brain damage and mental and physical retardation known as **fetal alcohol syndrome,** or **FAS.** The fetal brain is extremely vulnerable to a glucose or oxygen deficit, and alcohol causes both. In addition, alcohol itself crosses the placenta freely and is directly toxic to the fetal brain. FAS is not curable, only preventable.

Alcohol's Effects

Even before fertilization, alcohol may damage the ovum and so lead to abnormalities in offspring. In males the same is true—drinking before impregnation damages sperm and can also produce an infant of low birthweight.

Although the syndrome was named for damage evident at birth, it has been shown that children born with it remain damaged—they may live, but they never fully recover. About 1 to 3 in every 1000 children are victims of this preventable damage, making FAS the leading known cause of mental retardation in the world. Moreover, for every baby born with these symptoms, another may go undiagnosed until problems develop later in the preschool years. In addition, many others are born with **subclinical FAS.** The mothers of these children drank but not enough to cause visible, obvious effects. Even a child without external damage may have a lower IQ than peers.

Thus, apparently even moderate drinking can affect a fetus negatively. Oxygen is indispensable, on a minute-to-minute basis, to the development of the fetus's central nervous system, and a sudden dose of alcohol can halt the delivery of oxygen through the umbilical cord. During the first month of pregnancy, even a few minutes of such exposure can have a major effect on the fetal brain, which at that time is growing at the rate of 100,000 new brain cells a minute. Alcohol also interferes with placental transport of nutrients to the fetus.

Every container of beer, wine, or liquor for sale in the United States is now required to warn pregnant women of FAS. Before this, many women would have ceased drinking during pregnancy had they known the danger unwittingly damaged their infants.

Experts' Advice

The editors of the *Journal of the American Medical Association* have taken the position that women should stop drinking as soon as they *plan* to become pregnant. The editors of *Nutrition Today* magazine have stated the following:

> The pregnant woman who drinks is more likely to give birth to a baby with FAS defects.

> The woman who is pregnant should not drink.

> The woman who is addicted to alcohol should be advised to avoid pregnancy at all costs.

> From Eva May Nunnelley Hamilton, et al., *Nutrition*

Join in a collaborative group with two other classmates and **conduct a study on the extent to which alcohol's effects on the unborn are known.** Dividing work among group members, poll 15 women and 15 men, and ask each person the following questions:

1. Did you know that a pregnant woman can endanger the fetus by drinking alcohol?
2. Did you know that drinking before impregnation can damage sperm?
3. Did you know that drinking alcohol during pregnancy can affect the delivery of oxygen to the fetal brain?

Separately tally the responses for men and women on each of the three questions. Tally only "yes" answers to each question. Use the left side of the question numbers on the horizontal line to build a shaded bar upward for "yes" responses from women and use the right side of the mark to build an unshaded bar for men. Refer to the vertical line to indicate the number of affirmative responses. Write a title for the graph that reflects the information displayed, and identify each numbered question at the end with a short, meaningful phrase.

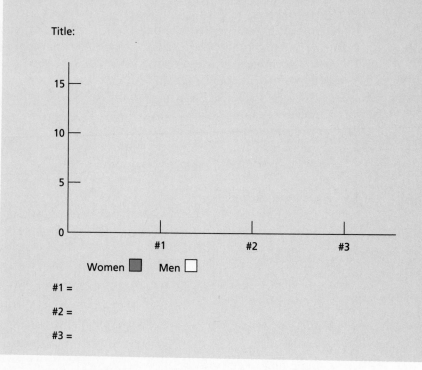

Title:

#1 =

#2 =

#3 =

LEARNING LOG
CHAPTER 8

Name _____

Answer the following to learn about your own learning and reflect on your progress. Your instructor may collect your responses.

Which of the graphic illustrations did you find easiest to understand?

_____

_____

When would you use a pie graph rather than a bar graph?

_____

_____

When would you use a flow-chart rather than a table?

_____

_____

When would you use a bar graph rather than a line graph?

_____

_____

Reflect on the Longer Selections

Total your short-answer responses for the selection.

Comprehension scores:
completed = ___   # correct = ___   # incorrect = ___   accuracy = ___%

How did the complex, technical nature of the material affect your comprehension?

_____

_____

How did your background in science help you with the selection?

_____

_____

Clip out and explain one question that you missed. Attach this question and your analysis to the Learning Log for your instructor.

Reflect on the Vocabulary

Total your vocabulary responses for the selection.

completed = ___   # correct = ___   # incorrect = ___   accuracy = ___%

List the words that you missed.

_____

Vocabulary Review

Review words that you missed in previous chapters. Your instructor may choose to give you a cumulative true-false exam.

Using the perforations, tear out the Learning Log for your instructor.

Rate Flexibility

What is your reading rate?

How fast should you read?

What are some techniques for faster reading?

How does concentration affect rate?

What is a regression?

How does knowledge of organizational patterns increase rate?

Why skim?

Why scan?

WHY IS RATE IMPORTANT?[1]

Professors of college reading are far more concerned with comprehension than with a student's rate of reading. They would say that you should not attempt to "speed read" textbooks, and they would be right.

Most students, however, when asked what they would like to change about their reading, say, "I read too slowly. I would like to improve my reading speed." Whether or not this perception is accurate, rate is definitely a concern of college students. Whether you are reading a magazine or a textbook, reading 150 words per minute takes twice as long as reading 300 words per minute. Understanding the factors that contribute to rate can both quell anxiety and help increase reading efficiency.

WHAT IS YOUR READING RATE?

Do you know how many words you read on the average each minute? To find out, read the following selection at your usual reading rate, just as you would have read it before you started thinking about speed. Time your reading of the selection so that you can calculate your rate. Read carefully enough to answer the ten comprehension questions that follow the selection.

Exercise 1   ASSESSING RATE

Directions: Time your reading of this selection so that you can compute your words-per-minute rate. To make the calculations easier, try to begin reading on the exact minute, with zero seconds. In other words, begin when the second hand points to twelve. Record your starting time in minutes and seconds and, when you have finished reading, record your finishing time in minutes and seconds. Then answer the questions that follow. Remember, read the selection at your normal rate.

Starting time: _12:55_ minutes ___5___ seconds

Sea Lions

"Hey, you guys, hurry up? They're gonna feed the seals!" No visit to the zoo or the circus would be complete without the playful antics of the trained "seal." However, the noisy animal that barks enthusiastically while balancing a ball on its nose is not really a seal at all. In reality, it is a small species of sea lion.

Like all mammals, sea lions are air breathers. Nevertheless, they spend most of their lives in the ocean and are skilled and graceful swimmers. Two

[1]Your instructor may choose to introduce this chapter much earlier in the course to assess rate and suggest strategies for continuous practice.

species live off the Pacific coast of North America. The California sea lion is the smaller and more southerly. This is the circus "seal." An adult male may measure over seven feet in length and weigh more than 500 pounds. Females are considerably smaller, with a length of six feet and a weight of 200 pounds.

The larger northern, or Steller, sea lion lives off the Alaskan shore in summer and off the California coast in winter. Bulls may weigh over a ton and reach a length of more than eleven feet. Cows weigh some 750 pounds and are about nine feet long. The northern sea lion is generally not as noisy as the California sea lion, but it can bellow loudly when it wants to make its presence known.

At one time, sea lions were hunted almost to extinction for their hides, meat, and oil. Eskimos even stored the valuable oil in pouches made from the sea lion's stomach. Today, sea lions are protected by law, but many fall prey to their natural enemies, the shark and the killer whale. Sea lions are often disliked and sometimes killed by fishermen who accuse them of eating valuable fish and damaging nets. For the most part, the accusations are untrue. The northern sea lion eats mostly "trash fish," which are of little commercial value. The California sea lion prefers squid. Although sea lions do eat salmon, they also eat lampreys, a snake-like parasitic fish that devours salmon in great numbers. By controlling the lamprey population, the sea lion probably saves more salmon than it eats.

Sea lions come ashore in early summer to give birth and to mate. First to arrive are the bulls, which immediately stake out individual territories along the beach. The cows follow and soon give birth to the single pup that each has been carrying since the previous summer. The newborn pup has about a dozen teeth. Its big blue eyes are open from birth and will turn brown after a few weeks.

The pup is born into a tumultuous world of huge, bellowing adults, and it must mature quickly to avoid being trampled by the teeming mob around it. It can move about within an hour, and can be seen scrambling nimbly among its elders within a few days. It doubles its weight in the first month or two. The quick weight gain is largely attributable to the extremely rich milk of the sea lion mother. Low in water and high in protein, the milk is almost 50 percent fat, whereas cow's milk is about 4 percent fat. Zookeepers have found it difficult to provide sea lion pups with adequate nourishment in the absence of the mother. At Marineland of the Pacific, an orphaned pup was successfully raised on a diet of whipping cream, liquified mackerel muscle, calcium caseinate, and a multivitamin syrup. Not a very delectable-sounding menu, perhaps, but the pup loved it.

Throw a human infant into the ocean and it would drown. So would a sea lion baby. The only mammals that are known to swim from birth are whales and manatees. Although it will spend most of its twenty-year life in the ocean, the sea lion pup is at first terrified of water. The mother must spend about two months teaching it to swim.

Mating is no quiet affair among the sea lions. Almost immediately after the birth of the pups the huge bulls begin to wage bloody battles, trying to keep control of their harems of about a dozen cows. Using their long canine teeth as weapons, they fight with great ferocity for possession of the females. Fighting and mating consume so much of the bulls' time and energy during this period that little time is left for sleeping or eating.

At the end of the summer, the sea lions return to the ocean. The bulls, thin and scarred after a busy breeding season, regain their lost weight with several months of active feeding. As the weather grows colder, the huge northern sea lions begin their southward migration; leaving deserted the northern beaches which in warm weather were covered with their massive dark bodies.

The sea lion has to adapt to a considerable range of climate conditions. Its thick blubber and rapid metabolism are assets in the cold northern waters. But the California sea lion ranges as far south as the Galápagos Islands off the coast of South America. How does it adapt to a hot and dry environment?

The most important thing that the sea lion does to stay cool is to sleep in the daytime and take care of business during the cooler night hours. Sea lions in warm climates spend a great deal of time sleeping on the wet sand. Their bodies are designed in such a way that a large surface of the torso comes in contact with the cool ground when the animal lies down. About 10 percent of body heat can be lost in this way. Furthermore, the animal produces nearly 25 percent less heat while it sleeps than it does when awake and active.

Unfortunately, none of the sea lion's cooling mechanisms are highly effective. Ultimately, the animal relies on immersion in the ocean to keep itself cool.

Victor A. Greulach and Vincent J. Chiappetta, *Biology*
958 Words

Finishing time: _1:09_ minutes _30_ seconds

Reading time in seconds _____

Words per minute _____ (see chart on page 393)

Mark each statement with *T* for true or *F* for false.

_F_   1. The author focuses mainly on the sea lion's insatiable appetite for high-protein food.

_F_   2. The larger northern sea lion is the circus "seal."

_T_   3. Sea lions eat lampreys, which eat salmon.

_F_   4. Sea lions both give birth and get pregnant in the summer.

Time (Min.)	Words Per Minute	Time (Min.)	Words Per Minute
3:00	319	5:10	185
3:10	303	5:20	180
3:20	287	5:30	174
3:30	274	5:40	169
3:40	261	5:50	164
3:50	250	6:00	160
4:00	240	6:10	155
4:10	230	6:20	151
4:20	221	6:30	147
4:30	213	6:40	144
4:40	205	6:50	140
4:50	198	7:00	137
5:00	190		

___T___ 5. Sea lion milk contains a higher percentage of fat than cow's milk.

___F___ 6. Baby sea lions, like whales and manatees, are natural swimmers.

___T___ 7. Male sea lions mate with more than one female.

___F___ 8. The cool ground provides the sea lion with a greater release of body heat than the ocean water.

___F___ 9. In warm climates sea lions sleep more at night than during the day.

___F___ 10. Sea lions are able to stay under water because they have gills.

Comprehension (% correct) _____ %

HOW FAST SHOULD YOU READ?

Reading specialists say that the average adult reading speed on relatively easy material is approximately 250 words per minute at 70 percent comprehension. The rate for college students tends to be a little higher, averaging about 300 words per minute on the same type of material with 70 percent comprehension. However, these figures are misleading for a number of reasons.

Anyone who says to you, "My reading rate is 500 words per minute" is not telling the whole story. The question that immediately comes to mind is, "Is that the rate for reading the newspaper or for the physics textbook?" For an efficient reader, no one reading rate serves for all purposes for all materials. Efficient readers demonstrate their flexibility by varying their rate according to their own purpose for reading or according to their prior knowledge of the material being read.

Rate Varies According to Prior Knowledge

One reason textbooks usually require slower reading than newspapers is that textbooks are more difficult; the vocabulary and ideas are new, and prior knowledge is limited. If you already have a lot of knowledge on a topic, you can usually read about it at a faster rate than if you are exploring a totally new subject. For example, a student who is already involved in advertising will probably be able to work through the advertising chapter in the business textbook at a faster rate than the chapter on a less familiar topic, like supply-side economics. The student may need to slow to a crawl at the beginning of the economics chapter in order to understand the new concepts, but as the new ideas become more familiar, the student can perhaps read at a faster rate toward the end of the chapter.

The "difficulty level" of a textbook is primarily measured by you according to your own prior knowledge of the subject. Another measure combines the length of the sentences and the number of syllables in the words. The longer sentences and words indicate a more difficult level of reading. Freshman textbooks vary greatly in difficulty from field to field and from book to book. Some are written at levels as high as 16th grade level (senior in college), whereas others may be on the 11th or 12th grade level. Even within a single textbook the levels vary from one section or paragraph to another. Unfamiliar technical vocabulary can bring a reader to a complete stop. Complex sentences are more difficult to read than simple, concise statements. Sometimes the difficulty is caused by the complexity of the ideas expressed and sometimes, perhaps unnecessarily, by the complexity of the author's writing style.

Before starting on the first word and moving automatically on to the second, third, and fourth at the same pace, take a minute to ask yourself, "Why am I reading this material?" and, based on your answer, vary your speed according to your purpose. Do you want 100 percent, 70 percent, or 50 percent comprehension? In other words, figure out what you want to know when you finish and read accordingly. If you are studying for an examination, you probably need to read slowly and carefully, taking time to monitor your comprehension as you progress. Because 100 percent comprehension is not always your goal, be willing to switch gears and move faster over low-priority material even though you may sacrifice a few details. If you are reading only to get an overview or to verify a particular detail, read as rapidly as possible to achieve your specific purpose.

TECHNIQUES FOR FASTER READING

Concentrate

Fast readers, like fast race car drivers, concentrate on what they are doing; they try to think fast while they take in the important aspects of the course before them. Although we use our eyes, we actually read with our minds. If our attention is veering off course, we lose some of that cutting-edge quickness necessary for success. Slow readers tend to become bored because ideas are coming too slowly to keep their minds alert. Fast readers are curious to learn, mentally alert, and motivated to achieve.

Distractions that interfere with concentration, as mentioned in Chapter 1, fall into two categories: external and internal. External distractions, the physical happenings around you, are fairly easy to control with a little assertiveness. You can turn the television off or get up and go to another room. You can ask people not to interrupt or choose a place to read where interruptions will be at a minimum. Through prior planning, set yourself up for success and create a physical environment over which you have control.

Internal distractions, the irrelevant ideas that pop into your head while reading, are more difficult to control. As mentioned in Chapter 1, a to-do list will help. Write down your nagging concerns as a reminder for action. Spend less time worrying and more time doing, and you will clear your head for success.

Visualize as you read so that you will become wrapped up in the material. Imagine the goslings following you around and see the bird in the nest that did not learn to fly. Use your five senses to increase your involvement with the material.

Stop Regressing

During your initial reading of material, have you ever realized halfway down the page that you have no idea what you have read? Your eyes were engaged, but your mind was not. Do you ever go back and reread sentences or paragraphs? Were you rereading because the material is difficult to understand, because you were tired and not concentrating, or because you were daydreaming? This type of rereading is called a **regression.**

Regression can be a crutch that allows you to make up for wasted time. If this is a problem for you, analyze when and why you are regressing. If you discern that your regression is due to thinking of something else, start denying yourself the privilege in order to break the habit. Say, "OK, I missed that paragraph because I was thinking of something else, but I'm going to keep on going and start paying close attention."

Rereading because you did not understand is a legitimate fix-up strategy used by good readers who monitor their own comprehension. Rereading because your mind was asleep is a waste of time and a habit of many slow readers.

Daydreaming is a habit caused by lack of involvement with the material. Be demanding on yourself and expect 100 percent attention to the task. Visualize the incoming ideas, and relate the new material to what you already know. Don't just read the words; think the ideas.

Expand Fixations

Your eyes must stop in order to read. These stops, called **fixations,** last a fraction of a second. On the average, 5 to 10 percent of the time is spent on fixations. Thus, reading more than one word per fixation will reduce your total reading time.

Research on vision shows that the eye is able to see about one-half inch on either side of a fixation point. This means that a reader can see two or possibly three words per fixation. To illustrate, read the following phrase.

in the car

Did you make three fixations, two, or one? Now read the following word.

entertainment

You can read this word automatically with one fixation. As a beginning reader, however, you probably stopped for each syllable for a total of four fixations. If you can read *entertainment,* which has thirteen letters, with one fixation, you can certainly read the eight-letter phrase *in the car* with only one fixation.

Use your peripheral vision on either side of the fixation point to help you read two or three words per fixation. In expanding your fixations, take in phrases or thought units that seem to go together automatically. To illustrate, the following sentence has been grouped into thought units with fixation points.

After lunch,   I studied   in the library   at a table.

By expanding your fixations, the sentence can easily be read with four fixations rather than ten and thus reduce your total reading time.

Monitor Subvocalization

Subvocalization is the little voice in your head that reads for you. Some experts say that subvocalization is necessary for difficult materials, and others say that fast readers are totally visual and do not need to hear the words. Good college readers will probably experience some of both. On easy reading you may find yourself speeding up to the point that you are not hearing every word, particularly the unimportant filler phrases. However, on more difficult textbook readings, your inner voice may speak every word. The voice seems to add another sensory dimension to help you comprehend. Because experts say that the inner voice can read up to about 400 words per minute, many college students can make a considerable improvement in speed while still experiencing the inner voice.

Vocalizers, on the other hand, move their lips while reading to pronounce each word. This is an immature habit and should be stopped. Putting a slip of paper or a pencil in your mouth while reading will alert you to lip movement and inspire you to stop.

Preview

Size up your reading assignment before you get started. If it is a chapter, glance through the pages and read the subheadings. Look at the pictures and notice the italicized words and boldface print. Make predictions about what you think the chapter will cover. Activate your schema or prior knowledge on the subject. Pull out your mental computer chip on acupuncture, for example, and prepare to bring something to the printed page.

Use Your Pen as a Pacer

The technique of using your pen or fingers as a pacer means pointing under the words in a smooth, flowing motion, moving back and forth from line to line. Although as a child you were probably told never to point to words, it is a very effective technique for improving reading speed. The technique seems to have several benefits. After you overcome the initial distraction, the physical act of pointing tends to improve concentration by drawing your attention directly to the words. The forward motion of your pen tends to keep you from regressing because rereading would interrupt your established rhythm. By pulling your eyes down the page, the pen movement helps set a rapid, steady pace for reading and tends to shift you out of word-by-word reading and move you automatically into phrase reading. Obviously, you cannot read a whole book using your pen as a pacer, but you can start out with this technique. Later, if you feel yourself slowing down, use your pen again to get back on track.

The technique is demonstrated in the following passage. Your pen moves in a *Z* pattern from one side of the column to the other. Because you are trying to read several words at each fixation, your pen does not have to go to the extreme end of either side of the column.

Rapid reading requires quick thinking
and intense concentration. The reader
must be alert and aggressive. Being
interested in the subject helps improve speed.

As you begin to read faster and become more proficient with the *Z* pattern, you will notice the corners starting to round into an *S*. The *Z* pattern is turning into a more relaxed *S* swirl. When you get to the point of using the *S* swirl, you will be reading for ideas and not be reading every word. You are reading actively and aggressively, with good concentration. Use the *Z* pattern until you find your pen or hand movement has automatically turned into an *S*. The following illustration compares the two.

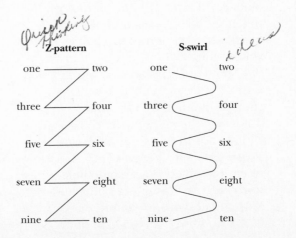

Push and Pace

Be alert and aggressive and try to read faster. Sit up straight and attack the text. Get uncomfortable and force yourself to hurry. Changing old habits is difficult. You will never read faster unless you try to read faster.

Set goals and pace yourself. Count the number of pages in your homework assignments and estimate according to your reading rate how many pages you can read in thirty minutes. Use a paper clip or an index card to mark the page you are trying to reach. Push yourself to achieve your goal.

Exercise 2   PACING

The following passages are written in columns with approximately six words on each line. Using your pen as a pacer, read each passage, and try to make only two fixations per line. A dashed line has been placed down the middle of the column to help you with the fixations. Record your time for reading each passage and then answer the comprehension questions.

Determine your rate from the rate chart at the end of the passage. Before reading, use the title and any clues in the passage to predict organization: Is it definition or description?

Skunks

Skunks are small, omnivorous
animals found throughout most of
the United States. Striped skunks
are at home in practically every
habitat in every state, living in dens
and often beneath abandoned
buildings. They can be seen
wandering around on cloudy days
and at sunset. They eat a variety of
fruits, berries, insects, earthworms,
other small invertebrates, and some
rodents. They sport many color
variations, from almost black to
almost white.

Spotted skunks are also found
throughout a good portion of the
country, but they are not common
in some of the more northerly states
and the northern part of the East
Coast. They eat a variety of
invertebrates, eggs, and sometimes
small birds. The hognose skunk and
the hooded skunk are found in the
Pacific Southwest and extend down

into Mexico and parts of Central America.

In a country where millions of dollars are spent every year on human deodorants, it is not to be wondered that the skunk is not favored. Then, too, the animal can carry rabies. Thus, removal procedures are the order of the day when skunks invade suburban areas or campgrounds in large numbers. They can be kept away from buildings by repellents—moth balls (paradichlorobenzene) are effective. Screens can prevent them from getting under buildings. Proper fencing will keep them from chicken coops or apiaries (skunks like honeybees). Removal of insects from golf-course grasses is useful.

Despite their bad reputation, skunks do help keep small rodent and insect populations in check.

Stanley Anderson, *Managing Our Wildlife Resources*

245 words

Time (Min.)	Words Per Minute	Time (Min.)	Words Per Minute
0:10	1470	0:40	368
0:20	735	0:50	294
0:30	490	1:00	245

Time _____ 5.0

Words per minute _____ 294

Mark each statement with *T* for true or *F* for false.

_T_ 1. Skunks eat rats and insects.

_T_ 2. Skunks are repelled by moth balls.

Exercise 3   PACING

Predict organization: Is it simple listing or comparison?

Special Solutions to the Water Problem

Some insects are able to survive for years enclosed in jars of dry pepper. They do this by utilizing metabolic water and excreting almost dry uric acid.

A camel can tolerate dry conditions by adopting a number of tactics. At night it drops its body temperature several degrees so that bodily processes slow down. In the heat of the day it doesn't begin to sweat until its body temperature reaches about 105° F. In addition, the camel can lose twice as much of its body water (40 percent) without ill effect than can most other mammals. Peculiarly, the thick coat of a camel acts as insulation to keep the heat out. Also when the camel does drink, it may hold prodigious amounts of water.

Some seabirds and turtles have sale removal glands. The huge tears that may appear in the eyes of sea turtles have nothing to do with the turtle's realization that we are poisoning the oceans. They are merely the result of specialized salt-removing glands. These glands, however, remove only sodium chloride from the blood.

The tiny kangaroo rat doesn't drink at all and it lives on dry plant material. It survives because it doesn't sweat and is active only in the cool of night. Its feces are dry and its urine is highly concentrated.

1:35

Most of its water loss is through the
lungs. Fats produce more metabolic
water than other foods, so it prefers
fatty foods. On the other hand,
soybeans are high in protein and
thus produce a lot of nitrogenous
waste for which a lot of water is
needed—so if a kangaroo rat is fed
only soybeans it will die of thirst.

        Robert Wallace, *Biology: The World of Life*

278 words

Time (Min.)	Words Per Minute	Time (Min.)	Words Per Minute
0:10	1668	0:40	417
0:20	834	0:50	334
0:30	556	1:00	278

Time _____ *50*

Words per minute _____ *334*

Mark each statement with *T* for true or *F* for false.

_____ 1. A camel will die if its body temperature rises above 105° F.

_____ 2. The kangaroo rat drinks no water.

Exercise 4   PACING

Predict organization: Is it sequence or description?

Can Humans Regenerate Missing Parts?

A few years ago a young boy was admitted to the
Children's Hospital in Sheffield, England. He had
accidentally cut off the end of his finger. Ordinarily
the part would have been reattached by a plastic
surgeon in the hope that it would grow back and that
the feeling would be restored. However, due to a
clerical error, the stub was simply bandaged and the
boy was ignored for several days. When the error was
discovered, anxious physicians unwrapped the finger
to see how extensive the damage had become. They
were stunned to see that the missing part was

regenerating. They carefully monitored the progress of the finger over the next few weeks until the damage had, for all practical purposes, repaired itself. The technique is now routinely used for young children. There are several instances of regrown fingers, complete with nails and fingerprints. But how? This was contrary to all medical expectations. Should it have been? After all, identical twins are formed when a developing human breaks apart at the two-cell stage, each part regenerating whatever was lost. But these enormous powers reside in embryos, and the regrown finger occurred on a young boy. It has not been found in adults, other than to a limited degree in wound healing. Subsequent research has shown that age does, in fact, have something to do with regeneration. It seems that children under the age of eleven have marked powers of regeneration, and these rapidly dissipate after this time. In the early 1970s it was demonstrated that electrical charges surrounding the tissues become reversed at about the time that regenerative powers dissipate. Research attention is now focusing on maintaining particular (young) electrical fields around those areas in which regeneration is being attempted. The time when humans can regenerate lost limbs is probably not near, but scientists have new reasons for optimism.

Robert Wallace, Biology: The World of Life

© 1997 Addison-Wesley Educational Publishers Inc.

309 words

Time (Min.)	Words Per Minute	Time (Min.)	Words Per Minute
0:20	927	1:00	309
0:30	618	1:10	265
0:40	464	1:20	232
0:50	371	1:30	206

Time _____ 2:00

Words per minute _____

Mark each statement with *T* for true or *F* for false.

_F_ 1. The young boy's finger was sewn back on by the surgeon.

_F_ 2. The regenerative powers seem to wane at age eleven.

Exercise 5   PACING

Predict organization: Is it simple listing or description?

Shy People

The shy person does not seem to take full advantage of social opportunities to meet new persons and cultivate friendships. In public, shy persons are usually silent. They avoid eye contact and speak quietly when they speak at all. They avoid others whenever possible and take refuge in a private project such as reading.

Privately, shy persons are supersensitive about what other people think about them. They worry about unpleasant aspects of social situations and about leaving others with a negative impression. Increased pulse rate, blushing, perspiration, and rapid heart rate are pronounced in people who are shy in public. But the major problem for shy persons, which distinguishes them from others who have only occasional bouts of shyness, is that they label themselves as being shy. If persons believe they are shy, then they are likely to be especially sensitive to social situations that might produce shyness.

Probably the key to overcoming shyness involves practicing new forms of behavior designed to provide the person with rewarding experiences when meeting others. The chronically shy person has developed a self-defeating pattern of behavior: "I am a shy person, so I am going to be silent and withdrawn when I meet other people. I meet other people and keep silent, and no one talks to me. Therefore, I must be odd and basically shy."

Valerian J. Derlega and Louis H. Janda, *Personal Adjustment*[2]

222 words

[2]From *Personal Adjustment*, Second Edition, by Valerian J. Derlega and Louis H. Janda, pp. 100–102. Copyright © 1981 by Scott, Foresman and Company, HarperCollins College Publishers.

Time (Min.)	Words Per Minute	Time (Min.)	Words Per Minute
0:20	666	0:50	266
0:30	444	1:00	222
0:40	333	1:10	190

Time _1:00_

Words per minute _222_

Mark each statement with *T* for true or *F* for false.

_T_ 1. Shy people tend to worry about what others think of them.

_T_ 2. Shy people do not usually think of themselves as shy.

SKIMMING

Skimming is a technique of selectively reading for the gist or the main idea. Because it involves processing material at rates of around 900 words per minute, it is not defined by some experts as reading. Skimming involves skipping words, sentences, paragraphs, and even pages. It is a method of quickly overviewing material to answer the question, "What is this about?"

Skimming and previewing are very similar in that both involve getting an overview. Previewing sets the stage for later careful reading, whereas skimming is a substitute for a complete reading. Skimming is useful for material that you want to know about but don't have the time to read. For example, you might want to skim some of the supplemental articles for a course that have been placed on reserve in the library because you know your professor is interested only in you understanding the main idea of each article and a complete reading would be unnecessary. Sometimes you may want to pick up a book and just "get the idea" but not read it completely. Skimming is a useful tool. The technique is as follows:

1. Read the title, subheadings, italics, and boldface print to get an idea of what the material is about.
2. Try to get an insight into the organization of the material to help you anticipate where the important points will be located. Some of the organizational patterns and their functions are:
   a. Listing: explains items of equal value.
   b. Definition and examples: defines a term and gives examples to help the reader understand the term.
   c. Time order or sequence: presents items in chronological order.
   d. Comparison-contrast: items are compared for their similarities and differences.

e. Description: characteristics of an item are explained.

f. Cause and effect: one item is shown to have produced another.

g. Problem-solution: explains the problem, causes, and effects as well as suggests a solution.

h. Opinion-proof: gives an opinion and then supports it with proof.

3. If the first paragraph is introductory, read it. If not skip to a paragraph that seems to introduce the topic.

4. Move rapidly, letting your eyes float over the words. Try to grasp the main ideas and the significant supporting details.

5. Notice first sentences in paragraphs and read them if they seem to be summary statements.

6. Skip words that seem to have little meaning, like *a, an,* and *the.*

7. Skip sentences or sections that seem to contain the following:

a. Familiar ideas.

b. Unnecessary details.

c. Superfluous examples.

d. Restatements or unneeded summaries.

e. Material irrelevant to your purpose.

8. If the last paragraph of a section is a summary, read it if you need to check your understanding.

SCANNING

Because scanning is a process of searching for a single bit of information, it is more of a locating skill than a reading skill. A common use of scanning is looking up a number in a telephone book. When scanning for information, you do not need to understand the meaning of the material, but instead you merely need to pinpoint a specific detail. For example, you might find that after reading a chapter on pricing in your marketing textbook that you cannot recall the definition of *price lining.* To locate the information, you would not reread, but scan the chapter to find the key phrase *price lining* and then review the definition.

A combination of skimming and scanning is used by researchers. If you are working on a research paper on paranoia, you might have a list of thirty books and articles to read. A complete reading of each reference is probably unnecessary. Instead, you can scan to locate the information relevant to your topic and skim to get the main idea.

The techniques of scanning are:

1. Figure out the organization of the material. Get an overview of which section will probably contain the information you are looking for.

2. Know specifically what you are looking for. Decide on a key expression that will signal your information, but be ready to switch to a related idea if that doesn't work.

3. Repeat the phrase and hold the image in your mind. Concentrate on the image so that you will recognize it when it comes into view.

4. Move quickly and aggressively. Remember, you are scanning, not reading.

5. Verify through careful reading. After locating your information, read carefully to make sure you have really found it.

SUMMARY POINTS

- Average adult reading speed on relatively easy material is approximately 250 words per minute at 70 percent comprehension.
- Rate should vary according to purpose and difficulty of the material.
- Faster readers concentrate, are curious to learn, stay mentally alert, and are motivated to achieve.
- Regressing because of inattention wastes time.
- Faster readers use peripheral vision and read two or three words per fixation.
- Subvocalizing is the little voice in your head that reads for you.
- Before reading, faster readers make predictions, anticipate organization, and activate schemata.
- Using the pen as a pacer is an important technique that can improve both concentration and rate.
- Skimming is a technique for getting an overview.
- Scanning is the process of searching for a single bit of information.

SELECTION 1

ESSAY

Skill Development: Skimming

Skim the selection and mark the following statements with *T* for true or *F* for false.

 1. The author is expressing her opinion.

_____ 2. The author is telling about her own experience in the school.

© 1997 Addison-Wesley Educational Publishers Inc.

Skill Development: Scanning

Scan to find each of the following details.

1. What was the number of her classroom?
2. What was her teacher's name?

Skill Development: Rate

Now read the selection in order to answer ten true-false items. Use your pen as a pacer and time your reading.

Starting time: —————— minutes —————— seconds

The Sanctuary of School[3]
Lynda Barry

I was 7 years old the first time I snuck out of the house in the dark. It was winter and my parents had been fighting all night. They were short on money and long on relatives who kept "temporarily" moving into our house because they had nowhere else to go.

5   My brother and I were used to giving up our bedroom. We slept on the couch, something we actually liked because it put us that much closer to the light of our lives, our television.

At night when everyone was asleep, we lay on our pillows watching it with the sound off. We watched Steve Allen's mouth moving. We watched
10   Johnny Carson's mouth moving. We watched movies filled with gangsters shooting machine guns into packed rooms, dying soldiers hurling a last grenade and beautiful women crying at windows. Then the sign-off finally came and we tried to sleep.

The morning I snuck out, I woke up filled with a panic about needing
15   to get to school. The sun wasn't quite up yet but my anxiety was so fierce that I just got dressed, walked quietly across the kitchen, and let myself out the back door.

It was quiet outside. Stars were still out. Nothing moved and no one was in the street. It was as if someone had turned the sound off on the world.
20   I walked the alley, breaking thin ice over the puddles with my shoes. I didn't know why I was walking to school in the dark. I didn't think about it. All I knew was the feeling of panic, like the panic that strikes kids when they realize they are lost.

That feeling eased the moment I turned the corner and saw the dark
25   outline of my school at the top of the hill. My school was made up of about 15 nondescript portable classrooms set down on a fenced concrete lot in a

[3]"The Sanctuary of School" appeared in *Education Life,* a special feature in *The New York Times,* on January 5, 1992.

rundown Seattle neighborhood, but it had the most beautiful view of the Cascade Mountains. You could see them from anywhere on the playfield and you could see them from the windows of my classroom—Room 2.

30   I walked over to the monkey bars and hooked my arms around the cold metal. I stood for a long time just looking across Rainier Valley. The sky was beginning to whiten and I could hear a few birds.

In a perfect world my absence at home would not have gone unnoticed. I would have had two parents in a panic to locate me, instead of two parents
35   in a panic to locate an answer to the hard question of survival during a deep financial and emotional crisis.

But in an overcrowded and unhappy home, it's incredibly easy for any child to slip away. The high levels of frustration, depression, and anger in my house made my brother and me invisible. We were children with the
40   sound turned off. And for us, as for the steadily increasing number of neglected children in this country, the only place where we could count on being noticed was at school.

"Hey there, young lady. Did you forget to go home last night?" It was Mr. Gunderson, our janitor, whom we all loved. He was nice and he was
45   funny and he was old with white hair, thick glasses, and an unbelievable number of keys. I could hear them jingling as he walked across the playfield. I felt incredibly happy to see him.

He let me push his wheeled garbage can between the different portables as he unlocked each room. He let me turn on the lights and raise
50   the window shades and I saw my school slowly come to life. I saw Mrs. Holman, our school secretary, walk into the office without her orange lipstick on yet. She waved.

I saw the fifth-grade teacher, Mr. Cunningham, walking under the breezeway eating a hard roll. He waved.

55   And I saw my teacher, Mrs. Clair LeSane, walking toward us in a red coat and calling my name in a very happy and surprised way, and suddenly my throat got tight and my eyes stung and I ran toward her crying. It was something that surprised both of us.

It's only thinking about it now, 28 years later, that I realize I was crying
60   from relief. I was with my teacher, and in a while I was going to sit at my desk, with my crayons and pencils and books and classmates all around me, and for the next six hours I was going to enjoy a thoroughly secure, warm, and stable world. It was a world I absolutely relied on. Without it, I don't know where I would have gone that morning.

65   Mrs. LeSane asked me what was wrong and when I said "Nothing," she seemingly left it at that. But she asked me if I would carry her purse for her, an honor above all honors, and she asked if I wanted to come into Room 2 early and paint.

She believed in the natural healing power of painting and drawing for
70   troubled children. In the back of her room there was always a drawing table and an easel with plenty of supplies, and sometimes during the day she

would come up to you for what seemed like no good reason and quietly ask if you wanted to go to the back table and "make some pictures for Mrs. LeSane." We all had a chance at it—to sit apart from the class for a while to
75   paint, draw, and silently work out impossible problems on 11 x 17 sheets of newsprint.

Drawing came to mean everything to me. At the back table in Room 2, I learned to build myself a life preserver that I could carry into my home.

We all know that a good education system saves lives, but the people of
80   this country are still told that cutting the budget for public schools is necessary, that poor salaries for teachers are all we can manage and that art, music, and all creative activities must be the first to go when times are lean.

Before- and after-school programs are cut and we are told that public schools were not made for baby-sitting children. If parents are neglectful
85   temporarily or permanently, for whatever reason, it's certainly sad, but their unlucky children must fend for themselves. Or slip through the cracks. Or wander in a dark night alone.

We are told in a thousand ways that not only are public schools not important, but that the children who attend them, the children who need
90   them most, are not important either. We leave them to learn from the blind eye of television, or to the mercy of "a thousand points of light" that can be as far away as the stars.

I was lucky. I had Mrs. LeSane. I had Mr. Gunderson. I had an abundance of art supplies. And I had a particular brand of neglect in my
95   home that allowed me to slip away and get to them. But what about the rest of the kids who weren't as lucky? What happened to them?

By the time the bell rang that morning I had finished my drawing and Mrs. LeSane pinned it up on the special bulletin board she reserved for drawings from the back table. It was the same picture I always drew—a sun
100 in the corner of a blue sky over a nice house with flowers all around it.

Mrs. LeSane asked us to please stand, face the flag, place our right hands over our hearts and say the Pledge of Allegiance. Children across the country do it faithfully. I wonder now when the country will face its children and say a pledge right back.

1300 words

Finishing time: _3:00_ minutes _434_ seconds

Min.	Words/Min.	Min.	Words/Min.	Min.	Words/Min.	Min.	Words/Min.
1:00	1300	4:00	325	5:20	244	6:40	195
2:00	650	4:10	312	5:30	236	6:50	190
3:00	434	4:20	300	5:40	230	7:00	186
3:10	410	4:30	289	5:50	223	7:10	181
3:20	390	4:40	279	6:00	217	7:20	177
3:30	371	4:50	269	6:10	211	7:30	173
3:40	355	5:00	260	6:20	205		
3:50	339	5:10	252	6:30	200		

COMPREHENSION QUESTIONS

Mark each statement with *T* for true or *F* for false.

_T_ 1. The author uses the word *sanctuary* to mean a place of protection.

_F_ 2. She and her brother slept on the couch because the house had only one bedroom.

_F_ 3. The story the author tells of leaving for school in the dark occurred in the winter.

_T_ 4. The school was made up of portable classrooms.

_F_ 5. The author's parents were in a panic to locate her when she left for school that morning alone.

_T_ 6. The author recognizes art as a kind of therapy.

_F_ 7. The author told Mrs. LeSane about her problems at home.

_T_ 8. The author uses an anecdote to support an argument.

_T_ 9. The author suggests that her picture reflected her dreams.

_T_ 10. The author feels that the government does not do enough to support the children who are falling through the cracks.

SELECTION 2

ESSAY

Skill Development: Skimming

Skim the selection and mark the following statements with *T* for true or *F* for false.

1. The author is probably at a college.

2. The article seems to list ten steps for successful interviews.

Skill Development: Scanning

Scan to find each of the following details.

1. The Softball Championship jacket was from what tavern?
2. The author mentions General Motors, Bendix, and what other company?

Skill Development: Rate

Now read the selection in order to answer ten true-false items. Use your pen as a pacer and time your reading.

Starting time: _____ minutes _____ seconds

How to Take a Job Interview[4]
Kirby W. Stanat

To succeed in campus job interviews, you have to know where that recruiter is coming from. The simple answer is that he is coming from corporate headquarters.

That may sound obvious, but it is a significant point that too many
5   students do not consider. The recruiter is not a free spirit as he flies from Berkeley to New Haven, from Chapel Hill to Boulder. He's on an invisible leash to the office, and if he is worth his salary, he is mentally in corporate headquarters all the time he's on the road.

If you can fix that in your mind—that when you walk into that bare-
10   walled cubicle in the placement center you are walking into a branch office of Sears, Bendix or General Motors—you can avoid a lot of little mistakes and maybe some big ones.

If, for example, you assume that because the interview is on campus the recruiter expects you to look and act like a student, you're in for a shock. A
15   student is somebody who drinks beer, wears blue jeans and throws a Frisbee. No recruiter has jobs for student Frisbee whizzes.

A cool spring day in late March, Sam Davis, a good recruiter who has been on the college circuit for years, is on my campus talking to candidates. He comes out to the waiting area to meet the student who signed up for an
20   11 o'clock interview. I'm standing in the doorway of my office taking in the scene.

Sam calls the candidate: "Sidney Student." There sits Sidney. He's at a 45 degree angle, his feet are in the aisle, and he's almost lying down. He's wearing well-polished brown shoes, a tasteful pair of brown pants, a light
25   brown shirt, and a good looking tie. Unfortunately, he tops off this well-

[4]"How to Take a Job Interview" by Kirby W. Stanat. From *Job Hunting Secrets and Tactics* by Kirby W. Stanat with Patrick Reardon. Copyright © 1977 by Kirby Stanat and Patrick Reardon. Reprinted with the permission of Westwind Press, a division of Raintree Publishers Limited.

coordinated outfit with his Joe's Tavern Class A Softball Championship jacket, which has a big woven emblem over the heart.

If that isn't bad enough, in his left hand is a cigarette and in his right hand is a half-eaten apple.

30   When Sam calls his name, the kid is caught off guard. He ditches the cigarette in an ashtray, struggles to his feet, and transfers the apple from the right to the left hand. Apple juice is everywhere, so Sid wipes his hand on the seat of his pants and shakes hands with Sam.

Sam, who by now is close to having a stroke, gives me that what-do-I-have-
35   here look and has the young man follow him into the interviewing room.

The situation deteriorates even further—into pure Laurel and Hardy. The kid is stuck with the half-eaten apple, doesn't know what to do with it, and obviously is suffering some discomfort. He carries the apple into the interviewing room with him and places it in the ashtray on the desk—right
40   on top of Sam's freshly lit cigarette.

The interview lasts five minutes. . . .

Let us move in for a closer look at how the campus recruiter operates.

Let's say you have a 10 o'clock appointment with the recruiter from the XYZ Corporation. The recruiter gets rid of the candidate in front of you at
45   about 5 minutes to 10, jots down a few notes about what he is going to do with him or her, then picks up your résumé or data sheet (which you have submitted in advance). . . .

Although the recruiter is still in the interview room and you are still in the lobby, your interview is under way. You're on. The recruiter will look
50   over your sheet pretty carefully before he goes out to call you. He develops a mental picture of you.

He thinks, "I'm going to enjoy talking with this kid," or "This one's going to be a turkey." The recruiter has already begun to make a screening decision about you.

55   His first impression of you, from reading the sheet, could come from your grade point. It could come from misspelled words. It could come from poor erasures or from the fact that necessary information is missing. By the time the recruiter has finished reading your sheet, you've already hit the plus or minus column.

60   Let's assume the recruiter got a fairly good impression from your sheet.

Now the recruiter goes out to the lobby to meet you. He almost shuffles along, and his mind is somewhere else. Then he calls your name, and at that instant he visibly clicks into gear. He just went to work.

As he calls your name he looks quickly around the room, waiting for
65   somebody to move. If you are sitting on the middle of your back, with a book open and a cigarette going, and if you have to rebuild yourself to stand up, the interest will run right out of the recruiter's face. You, not the recruiter, made the appointment for 10 o'clock, and the recruiter expects to see a young professional come popping out of that chair like today is a
70   good day and you're anxious to meet him.

At this point, the recruiter does something rude. He doesn't walk across the room to meet you halfway. He waits for you to come to him. Something very important is happening. He wants to see you move. He wants to get an impression about your posture, your stride, and your briskness.

75   If you slouch over to him, sidewinderlike, he is not going to be impressed. He'll figure you would probably slouch your way through your workdays. He wants you to come at him with lots of good things going for you. If you watch the recruiter's eyes, you can see the inspection. He glances quickly at shoes, pants, coat, shirt; dress, blouse, hose—the whole works.

80   After introducing himself, the recruiter will probably say, "Okay, please follow me," and he'll lead you into his interviewing room.

When you get to the room, you may find that the recruiter will open the door and gesture you in—with him blocking part of the doorway. There's enough room for you to get past him, but it's a near thing.

85   As you scrape past, he gives you a closeup inspection. He looks at your hair; if it's greasy, that will bother him. He looks at your collar; if it's dirty, that will bother him. He looks at your shoulders; if they're covered with dandruff, that will bother him. If you're a man, he looks at your chin. If you didn't get a close shave, that will irritate him. If you're a woman, he checks

90   your makeup. If it's too heavy, he won't like it.

Then he smells you. An amazing number of people smell bad. Occasionally a recruiter meets a student who smells like a canal horse. That student can expect an interview of about four or five minutes.

Next the recruiter inspects the back side of you. He checks your hair (is

95   it combed in front but not in back?), he checks your heels (are they run down?), your pants (are they baggy?), your slip (is it showing?), your stockings (do they have runs?).

Then he invites you to sit down.

At this point, I submit, the recruiter's decision on you is 75 to 80

100   percent made.

Think about it. The recruiter has read your résumé. He knows who you are and where you are from. He knows your marital status, your major and your grade point. And he knows what you have done with your summers. He has inspected you, exchanged greetings with you and smelled you.

105   There is very little additional hard information that he must gather on you. From now on it's mostly body chemistry.

Many recruiters have argued strenuously with me that they don't make such hasty decisions. So I tried an experiment. I told several recruiters that I would hang around in the hall outside the interview room when they took

110   candidates in.

I told them that as soon as they had definitely decided not to recommend (to department managers in their companies) the candidate they were interviewing, they should snap their fingers loud enough for me to hear. It went like this.

115   First candidate: 38 seconds after the candidate sat down: Snap!

Second candidate: 1 minute, 42 seconds: Snap!
Third candidate: 45 seconds: Snap!

120   One recruiter was particularly adamant, insisting that he didn't rush to judgment on candidates. I asked him to participate in the snapping experiment. He went out in the lobby, picked up his first candidate of the day, and headed for an interview room.

As he passed me in the hall, he glared at me. And his fingers went "Snap!"

1334 words

Finishing time: —————— minutes —————— seconds

Min.	Words/Min.	Min.	Words/Min.	Min.	Words/Min.	Min.	Words/Min.	Min.	Words/Min.
1:00	1334	3:40	364	4:40	286	5:40	235	6:40	200
2:00	667	3:50	348	4:50	276	5:50	229	6:50	195
3:00	445	4:00	334	5:00	267	6:00	222	7:00	191
3:10	421	4:10	320	5:10	258	6:10	216	7:10	186
3:20	400	4:20	307	5:20	258	6:20	211	7:20	182
3:30	381	4:30	296	5:30	243	6:30	205	7:30	179

COMPREHENSION QUESTIONS

Mark each statement with *T* for true and *F* for false.

_F_ 1. The author suggests that recruiters are less corporate in their thinking than the employees at their headquarters.

_T_ 2. According to the author, the recruiter has your data sheet in advance.

_F_ 3. In the example, Sidney Student put the apple in the trash can.

_T_ 4. The author suggests that the recruiter has formed an impression of you even before meeting you.

_T_ 5. The author suggests that you should look professional as you sit in the lobby and wait for your appointment.

_T_ 6. The author suggests that four or five minutes is the polite time allocated to an unacceptable applicant.

_T_ 7. The author suggests that the recruiter manipulates space in order to inspect applicants.

_F_ 8. The author believes that 75 percent of the recruiter's decision is made by the time you sit down in the office.

_F_ 9. The author suggests that most recruiters will readily admit that they make hasty decisions.

_T_ 10. The author found that a recruiter's decision could be made in as few as 45 seconds.

Name _____

Answer the following to learn about your own learning and reflect on your progress. Your instructor may collect your responses.

How would you describe your concentration on different reading materials? Give at least two examples.

_____

_____

When your mind wanders as you read, what are you usually thinking about?

_____

_____

If your rate of reading is a concern for you, how would you describe the problem?

_____

_____

Did the timed exercises help you read faster? Why or why not?

_____

_____

Will you continue to use your pen as a pacer to speed up your reading? Why or why not?

_____

_____

How much did your reading speed increase as you worked through this chapter?

_____

_____

Reflect on the Longer Selections

Total your short-answer responses for the longer selections.

Comprehension scores:

completed = ___   # correct = ___   # incorrect = ___   accuracy = ___%

How did your speed affect your comprehension?

_____

_____

Clip out and explain two questions that you missed. Attach these questions and your analysis to the Learning Log for your instructor.

Vocabulary Review

Review words that you missed in previous chapters. Your instructor may choose to give you a cumulative true-false exam.

Using the perforations, tear out the Learning Log for your instructor.

Test Taking

Can testwiseness help?

How should you prepare before the test?

What should you notice during a test?

What strategies should you use to read a comprehension passage?

How can you recognize the major question types?

What hints help with multiple-choice items?

How do you answer an essay question?

TESTS IN COLLEGE[1]

For college students, tests may seem at times to come from all directions and to fall into many areas, ranging from personality tests to blood tests. Although students and professors may joke about tests and bemoan the need for them, test taking is a serious part of the business of being a successful college student. In this chapter, two types of tests will be discussed: standardized reading tests and content area exams.

Standardized reading tests, like the reading portion of the SAT, have been developed and administered to large numbers of students in order to establish performance levels. When taking such a test, you are usually striving to perform at a certain level in order to demonstrate your ability to comprehend written material and your potential for college work. The SAT and the ACT are typically associated with college admission, but many colleges and states require additional standardized testing. Developmental studies students, for example, frequently find a statewide test to be part of their exit criteria. In addition, juniors in many states are required to pass a standardized test of reading proficiency in order to continue their work in college. Although the actual value of such testing programs can be questioned, the reality is that standardized reading tests exist and that students need to know how to perform well on them.

Content area exams, by contrast, are the midterms and final exams in courses like Psychology 101 and History 111. These tests are designed to measure how much psychology or history you know so that professors can assign your final course grades. Content exams may be multiple choice, essay, or a combination of the two. For the multiple-choice portion, questions are usually taken from an item pool provided by a textbook publishing company. For short-answer and essay tests, professors usually make up their own questions to reflect both the text material and the class lectures.

Standardized reading tests and content exams have both similarities and differences. Although intensive studying has always been considered a prerequisite for content testing, research has shown that preparation and practice can also improve standardized test scores. Both types of tests require you to be mentally and physically alert, aware of procedures, and aware of environmental factors that can affect your score. Both types of tests also use multiple-choice items. While standardized reading tests are almost exclusively multiple-choice, content exams may also make heavy use of multiple-choice items, especially in introductory courses. Therefore, many general observations and suggestions for answering multiple-choice items apply to both types of testing.

---

[1]Your instructor may choose to introduce this chapter much earlier in the course when specific test-taking challenges arise.

CAN TESTWISENESS HELP?

Receiving a passing grade on a test should not be the result of a trick; your grade should be a genuine assessment of the mastery of a skill or the understanding of a body of information. High scores, therefore, should depend on preparation, both mental and physical, and not on schemes involving length of responses or the likelihood of *b* or *c* being the right answer. Research has proven many such gimmicks don't work.[2] Tricks will not get you through college. For a well constructed examination, the only magic formula is mastery of the skill and an understanding of the material being tested.

Insight into test construction and the testing situation, however, will help you achieve at your highest potential. You will perhaps discover answers that you know but didn't think you knew.

The purpose of this material is to help you gain points by being aware. You can improve your score by understanding how tests are constructed and what is needed for maximum performance. Study the following and do everything you can both mentally and physically to gain an edge.

STRATEGIES FOR MENTAL AND PHYSICAL AWARENESS

Before Taking a Test

Get Plenty of Sleep the Night Before. How alert can you be with inadequate sleep? Would you want a physician operating on you who had only a few hours of sleep the night before? The mental alertness that comes from a good night's sleep could add two, four, or even six points to your score and mean the difference between passing or failing. Why take a chance by staying up late and gambling at such high stakes?

Arrive Five or Ten Minutes Early and Get Settled. If you run in flustered at the last second, you will spend the first five minutes of the test calming yourself rather than getting immediately to work. Do your nerves a favor and arrive early. Find a seat, get settled with pen or pencil and paper, and relax with some small talk about the weather to a neighbor.

Know What to Expect on the Test. Check beforehand to see if the test will be essay or multiple choice so that you can anticipate the format. Research has shown that studying for both types should stress main ideas, and that it is as difficult to get a good grade on one as it is on another.[3]

[2]W. G. Brozo, R. V. Schmelzer, and H. A. Spires, "A Study of Test-Wiseness Clues in College and University Teacher-Made Tests with Implications for Academic Assistance Centers," *College Reading and Learning Assistance,* Technical Report 84–01 (ERIC, 1984), ED 240928.

[3]P. M. Clark, "Examination Performance and Examination Set," in D. M. Wark, ed., *Fifth Yearbook of the North Central Reading Association* (Minneapolis: Central Reading Association, 1968), 114–122.

Have Confidence in Your Abilities. The best way to achieve self-confidence is to be well prepared. Be optimistic, and approach the test with a positive mental attitude. Lack of preparation breeds anxiety, but positive testing experiences tend to breed confidence. Research shows that students who have frequent quizzes during a course tend to do better on the final exam.[4]

Know How the Test Will Be Scored. If the test has several sections, be very clear on how many points can be earned from each section so that you can set priorities on your time and effort.

Find out if there is a penalty for guessing and, if so, what it is. Because most test scores are based on answering all of the questions, you are usually better off guessing than leaving items unanswered. Research shows that guessing can add points to your score.[5] Know the answers to the following questions and act accordingly:

Are some items worth more points than others?

Will the items omitted count against you?

Is there a penalty for guessing?

Plan Your Attack. At least a week before the test, take an inventory of what needs to be done and make plans to achieve your goals. Preparation can make a difference for both standardized tests and content area exams. Professors report that students gain awareness prior to content exams from truthfully writing answers to questions like the following:

1. How will the test look?
   How many parts to the test? What king of questions will be asked? How will points be counted?
2. What material will be covered?
   What textbook pages are covered? What lecture notes are included? Is outside reading significant?
3. How will you study?
   Have you made a checklist or study guide? Have you read all the material? Will you study notes or annotations from your textbook? Will you write down answers to potential essay questions? Will you include time to study with a classmate?
4. When will you study?
   What is your schedule the week before the test? How long will you need to study? How much of the material do you plan to cover each day? What are your projected study hours?
5. What grade are you honestly working to achieve?
   Are you willing to work for an *A,* or are you actually trying to earn a *B* or *C?*

[4]M. L. Fitch, A. J. Drucker, and J. A. Norton, "Frequent Testing as a Motivating Factor in Large Lecture Classes," *Journal of Educational Psychology* 42 (1951): 1–20.
[5]R. C. Preston, "Ability of Students to Identify Correct Responses Before Reading," *Journal of Educational Research* 58 (1964): 181–183.

During the Test

Concentrate. Tune out both internal and external distractions and focus your attention on the material on the test. Visualize and integrate old and new knowledge as you work. Read with curiosity and an eagerness to learn something new. If you become anxious or distracted, close your eyes and take a few deep breaths to relax and get yourself back on track.

On a teacher-made test, you may have a few thoughts that you want to jot down immediately on the back of the test so that you don't forget them. Do so, and proceed with confidence.

Read and Follow Directions. Find out what you are supposed to do by reading the directions. On a multiple-choice test, perhaps more than one answer is needed. Perhaps on an essay exam you are to respond to only three of five questions. Find out, and then do it.

Schedule Your Time. Wear a watch and plan to use it. When you receive your copy of the test, look it over, size up the task, and allocate your time. Determine the number of sections to be covered and organize your time accordingly. As you work through the test, periodically check to see if you are meeting your time goals.

On teacher-made tests, the number of points for each item may vary. Do the easy items first, but spend the most time on the items that will yield you the most points.

Work Rapidly. On a test every minute counts. Do not waste the time that you may need later by pondering at length over an especially difficult item. Mark the item with a check or a dot and move on to the rest of the test. If you have a few minutes at the end of the test, return to the marked items for further study.

Think. Use knowledge, logic, and common sense in responding to the items. Be aggressive and alert in moving through the test.

If you are unsure, use a process of elimination to narrow down the options. Double-check your paper to make sure you have answered every item.

Don't Be Intimidated by Students Who Finish Early. Early departures draw attention and can create anxiety for those still working, but calm yourself with knowing that students who finish early do not necessarily make the highest scores. Even though some students work more rapidly than others, fast students do not necessarily work more accurately. If you have time, review areas of the test where you felt a weakness. If your careful rethinking indicates another response, change your answer to agree with your new thoughts. Research shows that scores can be improved by making such changes.[6]

After the Test

Analyze Your Preparation. Question yourself after the test, and learn from the experience. Did you study the right material? Do you wish you had

[6]F. K. Berrien, "Are Scores Increased on Objective Tests by Changing the Initial Decision?," *Journal of Educational Psychology* 31 (1940): 64–67.

spent more time studying any particular topic? Were you mentally and physically alert enough to function at your full capacity?

Analyze the Test. Decide if the test was what you expected. If not, what was unexpected? Did the professor describe the test accurately or were there a few surprises? Why were you surprised? Use your memory of the test to predict the patterns of future tests.

Analyze Your Performance. Most standardized tests are not returned, but you do receive scores and subscores. What do these scores tell you about your strengths and weaknesses? What can you do to improve?

Content area exams are usually returned and reviewed in class. Ask questions and seek a clear understanding of your errors. Find out why any weak responses that were not wrong did not receive full credit. Do you see any patterns in your performance? What are your strengths and weaknesses? Plan to use what you learn to make an even higher grade on the perpetual "next test."

Meet with your professor if you are confused or disappointed. Ask the professor to analyze your performance and suggest means of improvement. Find out if tutorial sessions or study groups are available for you to join. Formulate a plan with your professor for improved performance on the next test.

STRATEGIES FOR STANDARDIZED READING TESTS

Read to Comprehend the Passage as a Whole

While discussing test-taking strategies a student will usually ask, "Should I read the questions first and then read the passage?" Although the answer to this is subject to some debate, most reading experts would advise reading the passage first and then answering the questions. The reasoning behind this position is convincingly logical. Examining the questions first arms the reader with a confusing collection of key words and phrases. Rather than reading to comprehend the author's message, the reader instead searches for many bits of information. Reading becomes fragmented and lacks focus. Few people are capable of reading with five or six purposes in mind. Not only is this method confusing, but it is also detail-oriented and does not prepare the reader for more general questions concerning the main idea and implied meanings.

Too many students muddle through test passages with only the high hopes that they will later be able to recognize answers. In other words, they passively watch the words go by with their fingers crossed for good luck. Get aggressive. Attach the passage to get the message. Predict the topic and activate your schema. Interact with the material as you read, and employ the thinking strategies of good readers. Monitor and self-correct. Function on a metacognitive level and expect success. Apply what you already know about the reading process to each test passage.

Read to understand the passage as a whole. Each passage has a central theme. Find it. If you understand the central theme or main idea, the rest of the ideas fall into place. The central theme may have several divisions that are developed in the different paragraphs. Attempt to understand what each paragraph contributes to the central theme. Don't worry about the details, other than understanding how they contribute to the central theme. If you find later that a minor detail is needed to answer a question, you can quickly use a key word to locate and reread for accuracy the sentence in which it appears.

Anticipate What Is Coming Next

Most test passages are untitled and thus offer no initial clue for content. Before reading, glance at the passage for a repeated word, name, or date. In other words, look for any quick clue to let you know whether the passage is about Queen Victoria, pit bulls, or chromosome reproduction.

Do not rush through the first sentence. The first sentence further activates your computer chip and sets the stage for what is to come. In some cases, the first sentence may give an overview or even state the central theme. Other times, it may simply pique your curiosity or stimulate your imagination. In any case, the first sentence starts you thinking, wondering, and anticipating. You begin to guess what will come next and how it will be stated.

Anticipating and guessing continue throughout the passage. Some guesses are proven correct and others are proven wrong. When necessary, glance back in the passage to double-check a date, fact, or event that emerges differently than expected. Looking back does not signal weak memory but instead indicates skill in monitoring one's own comprehension.

Read Rapidly, But Don't Allow Yourself to Feel Rushed

Use your pen as a pacer to direct your attention both mentally and physically to the printed page. Using your pen will help you focus your attention, particularly at the times of the test when you feel more rushed.

That uneasy, rushed feeling tends to be with you at the beginning of the test when you have not yet fixed your concentration and become mentally involved with the work. During the middle of the test, you may feel anxious again if you look at your watch and discover you are only half finished and half of your time is gone (which is where you should be). Toward the end of the test, when the first person finishes, you will again feel rushed if you have not yet finished. Check your time, keep your cool, and use your pen as a pacer. Continue working with control and confidence.

Read with Involvement to Learn and Enjoy

Reading a passage to answer five or six questions is reading with an artificial purpose. Usually you read to learn and enjoy, not for the sole purpose of quickly answering questions. Most test passages can be fairly interesting to a receptive reader. Try changing your attitude about reading the passages. Use the thinking strategies of a good reader to become involved in the material. Picture what you read and relate the ideas to what you already know. Think, learn, and enjoy—or at least, fake it.

Self-Test for the Main Idea

Pull it together before pulling it apart. At the end of a passage, self-test for the main idea. This is a final monitoring step that should be seen as part of the reading process. Work efficiently, with purpose and determination. Actively seek meaning rather than waiting for the questions to prod you. Take perhaps ten or fifteen seconds to pinpoint the focus of the passage and to tell yourself the point that the author is trying to make. Again, if you understand the main point, the rest of the passage will fall into place.

Pretend that the following passage is part of a reading comprehension test. Read it using the above suggestions. Note the handwritten reminders to make you aware of a few aspects of your thinking.

No title, so glance for key words. Dates? Names?

Practice Passage A

great image

In January 1744 a coach from Berlin bumped its way eastward over ditches and mud toward Russia. It carried Sophia, a young German princess, on a bridal journey. At the Russian border she was met with pomp, appropriate for one chosen to be married to Peter, heir to the Russian throne. The wedding was celebrated in August 1745 with gaiety and ceremony. *Why wait 1-1/2 years?*

Surprise!

Will he be tsar?

How?

For Sophia the marriage was anything but happy because the seventeen-year-old heir was "physically less than a man and mentally little more than a child." The "moronic booby" played with dolls and toy soldiers in his leisure time. He neglected his wife and was constantly in a drunken stupor. Moreover, Peter was strongly pro-German and made no secret of his contempt for the Russian people, intensifying the unhappiness of his ambitious young wife. This dreary period lasted for seventeen years, but Sophia used the time wisely. She set about "russifying" herself. She mastered the Russian language and avidly embraced the Russian faith; on joining the Orthodox church, she was renamed Catherine. She devoted herself to study, reading widely the works of Montesquieu, Voltaire, and other Western intellectuals. *what is that?* *what is she planning?*

Did she kill him?

When Peter became tsar in January 1762, Catherine immediately began plotting his downfall. Supported by the army, she seized power in July 1762 and tacitly consented to Peter's murder. It was announced that he died of "hemorrhoidal colic." Quickly taking over the conduct of governmental affairs, Catherine reveled in her new power. For the next thirty-four years the Russian people were dazzled by their ruler's political skill and cunning and her superb conduct of tortuous diplomacy. Perhaps even more, they were intrigued by gossip concerning her private life. *What gossip? Lovers?*

Ironic, since she's not Russian

Unusual term.

Long before she became empress, Catherine was involved with a number of male favorites referred to as her house pets. At first her affairs were clandestine, but soon she displayed her lovers as French kings paraded their mistresses. Once a young man was chosen, he was showered with lavish

© Addison-Wesley Educational Publishers Inc.

gifts; when the empress tired of him, he was given a lavish going-away present.

[handwritten: did she kill them?]

[handwritten margin note: Now moving from personal info to accomplishments]

Catherine is usually regarded as an enlightened despot. She formed the Imperial Academy of Art, began the first college of pharmacy, and imported foreign physicians. Her interest in architecture led to the construction of a number of fine palaces, villas, and public buildings and the first part of The Hermitage in Saint Petersburg. Attracted to Western culture, she carried on correspondence with the French *philosophes* and sought their flattery by seeming to champion liberal causes. The empress played especially on Voltaire's vanity, sending him copious praise about his literary endeavors. In turn this *philosophe* became her most ardent admirer. Yet while Catherine discussed liberty and equality before the law, her liberalism and dalliance with the Enlightenment was largely a pose—eloquent in theory, lacking in practice. The lot of serfs actually worsened, leading to a bloody uprising in 1773. This revolt brought an end to all talk of reform. And after the French Revolution, strict censorship was imposed.

[handwritten margin note: Double check years—not long]

[handwritten note: so, she did little towards human progress]

In her conduct of foreign policy, the empress was ruthless and successful. She annexed a large part of Poland and, realizing that Turkey was in decline, waged two wars against this ailing power. As a result of force and diplomacy, Russian frontiers reached the Black Sea, the Caspian, and the Baltic. Well could this shrewd practitioner of power politics tell her adopted people, "I came to Russia a poor girl. Russia has dowered me richly, but I have paid her back with Azov, the Crimea, and Poland." *[handwritten: What was the point?]*

[handwritten margin note: Changes to foreign policy accomplishments]

T. Walter Wallbank et al., *Civilization Past and Present*

Certainly your reading of the passage contained many more thoughts than those indicated on the page. The gossip at the beginning of the passage humanizes the empress and makes it easier for the reader to relate emotionally to the historic figure. Did you anticipate Peter's downfall and Catherine's subsequent relationships? Did you note the shift from gossip to accomplishments, both national and then international? The shift signals the alert reader to a change in style, purpose, and structure.

Take a few seconds to regroup and think about what you have read before proceeding to the questions that follow a passage. Self-test by pulling the material together before you tear it apart. Think about the focus of the passage and then proceed to the questions.

RECOGNIZE MAJOR QUESTION TYPES

Learn to recognize the types of questions asked on reading comprehension tests. Although the phraseology may vary slightly, most tests will include one or more of each of the following types of comprehension questions.

Main Idea

Main idea questions test your ability to find the central theme, central focus, gist, controlling idea, main point, or thesis. The terms are largely interchangeable in asking the reader to identify the main point of the passage. Main idea items are stated in any of the following forms:

The best statement of the main idea is. . . .

The best title for this passage is. . . .

The author is primarily concerned with. . . .

The central theme of the passage is. . . .

Incorrect responses to main idea items tend to fall into two categories. Some responses will be too general and express more ideas than are actually included in the passage. Other incorrect items will be details within the passage that support the main idea. The details may be attention-getting and interesting, but they do not describe the central focus of the passage. If you are having difficulty with the main idea, reread the first and last sentences of the passage. Sometimes, though not always, one of the two sentences will give you an overview or focus.

The following main idea items apply to the passage on Catherine the Great. Notice the handwritten remarks reflecting the thinking involved in judging a correct or incorrect response.

_D_   **The best statement of the main idea of this passage is**
   a. Peter lost his country through ignorance and drink. (Important detail, but focus is on her.)
   b. Gossip of Catherine's affairs intrigued the Russian people. (Very interesting, but a detail.)
   c. Progress for the Russian people was slow to come. (Too broad and general, or not really covered)
   d. Catherine came to Russia as a poor girl but emerged as a powerful empress and a shrewd politician. (Yes, sounds great)

_C_   **The best title for this passage is:**
   a. Catherine Changes Her Name. (Detail)
   b. Peter Against Catherine. (Only part of the story, so detail)
   c. Catherine the Great, Empress of Russia. (Sounds best)
   d. Success of Women in Russia. (Too broad—this is only about one woman)

Details

Detail questions check your ability to locate and understand explicitly stated material. Such items can frequently be answered correctly without a thorough understanding of the passage. To find the answer to such an item, note a key word in the question and then scan the passage for the word or a synonym.

When you locate the term, reread the sentence to double-check your answer. Stems for detail questions fall into the following patterns:

The author states that. . . .

According to the author. . . .

According to the passage. . . .

All of the following are true except. . . .

A person, term, or place is. . . .

Incorrect answers to detail questions tend to be false statements. Sometimes the test maker will trick the unsophisticated reader by using a pompous or catchy phrase from the passage as a distractor. The phrase may indeed appear in the passage and sound authoritative, but on close inspection it means nothing. Read the detail question on Catherine the Great and note the handwritten remarks. *Look for the only false item as the answer.*

*d*_____ **Catherine changed all of the following except**
   a. her religion. *(True, she joined the Orthodox church)*
   b. her name. *(True, from Sophia to Catherine)*
   c. Russia's borders. *(True, she gained seaports)*
   d. the poverty of the serfs. *(The serfs were worse off, but still in poverty, so this is the best answer.)*

Implied Meaning

Questions concerning implied meaning test your ability to look beyond what is directly stated and your understanding of the suggested meaning.

Items testing implied meaning deal with attitudes and feelings, sarcastic comments, snide remarks, the motivation of characters, favorable and unfavorable descriptions, and a host of other hints, clues, and ultimate assumptions. Stems for such items include the following:

The author believes (or feels or implies). . . .

It can be inferred from the passage. . . .

The passage or author suggests. . . .

It can be concluded from the passage that. . . .

To answer inference items correctly, look for clues to help you develop logical assumptions. Base your conclusions on what is known and what is suggested. Incorrect inference items tend to be false statements. Study the following question.

*a*_____ **The author implies that Catherine**
   a. did not practice the enlightenment she professed. *(Yes, "eloquent in theory but lacking practice")*
   b. preferred French over Russian architecture. *(not suggested)*
   c. took Voltaire as her lover. *(not suggested)*

d. came to Russia knowing her marriage would be unhappy. *(not suggested)*

Purpose

The purpose of a reading passage is not usually stated; it is implied. In a sense, the purpose is part of the main idea; you probably need to understand the main idea to understand the purpose. Generally, however, reading comprehension tests include three basic types of passages, and each type tends to dictate its own purpose. Study the following three types.

1. Factual
   Identification: gives the facts about science, history, or other subjects
   Strategy: If complex, do not try to understand each detail before going to the questions. Remember, you can look back.
   Example: textbook
   Purposes: to inform, to explain, to describe, or to enlighten
2. Opinion
   Identification: puts forth a particular point of view
   Strategy: The author states opinions and then refutes them. Sort out the opinions of the author and the opinions of the opposition.
   Example: newspaper editorial
   Purposes: to argue, to persuade, to condemn, or to ridicule
3. Fiction
   Identification: tells a story
   Strategy: Read slowly to understand the motivation and interrelationships of characters.
   Example: novel or short story
   Purposes: to entertain, to narrate, to describe, or to shock

b ___ ***The purpose of the passage on Catherine is***
   a. to argue. *(No side is taken)*
   b. to explain. *(Yes, because it is factual material)*
   c. to condemn. *(Not judgmental)*
   d. to persuade. *(No opinion is pushed)*

Vocabulary

Vocabulary items test your general word knowledge as well as your ability to use context to figure out word meaning. The stem of most vocabulary items on reading comprehension tests is as follows:

As used in the passage, the best definition of _____ is

Note that both word knowledge and context are necessary for a correct response. The item is qualified by "As used in the passage," and thus you must go back and reread the sentence (context) in which the word appears to be sure you are not misled by a multiple meaning. To illustrate, the word *sports* means *athletics* as well as *offshoots from trees*. As a test taker you would need to double-

© 1997 Addison-Wesley Educational Publishers Inc.

check the context to see which meaning appears in your test passage. In addition, if you knew only one definition of the word *sport*, rereading the sentence would perhaps suggest the alternate meaning to you and help you get the item correct. Note the following example.

> *C* *As used in the passage, the best definition of* **dreary** *is* (2nd paragraph)
>   a. sad. (Yes, <u>unhappiness</u> is used in the previous sentence)
>   b. commonplace. (Possible, but not right in the sentence)
>   c. stupid. (Not right in the sentence)
>   d. neglected. (True, but not the definition of the word)

STRATEGIES FOR MULTIPLE-CHOICE ITEMS

Consider All Alternatives Before Choosing an Answer

Read all the options. Do not rush to record an answer without considering all the alternatives. Be careful, not careless, in considering each option. Multiple-choice test items usually ask for the best choice for an answer, not any choice that is reasonable.

> *d* *Peter was most likely called a "moronic booby" because*
>   a. he neglected Catherine.
>   b. he drank too much.
>   c. he disliked German customs.
>   d. he played with dolls and toys.

Although the first three answers are true and reasonable, the last answer seems to be most directly related to that particular name.

Anticipate the Answer and Look for Something Close to It

As you read the beginning of a multiple-choice item, anticipate what you would write for a correct response. Develop an answer in your mind before you read the options, and then look for a response that corroborates your thinking.

> _____ *The author suggests that Catherine probably converted to the Russian Orthodox church because . . .* she wanted to rule the country and wanted the people to think of her as Russian, rather than German.
>   a. she was a very religious person.
>   b. Peter wanted her to convert.
>   c. she was no longer in Germany.
>   d. she wanted to appear thoroughly Russian to the Russian people.

The last answer most closely matches the kind of answer you were anticipating.

Avoid Answers with 100 Percent Words

All and *never* mean 100 percent, without exceptions. A response containing either word is seldom correct. Rarely can a statement be so definitely inclusive or exclusive. Other 100 percent words to avoid are:

no	none	only
every	always	must

 ___ ***Catherine the Great was beloved by all the Russian people.***
  Answer with *true* or *false*.

All means 100 percent and thus is too inclusive. Surely one or two Russians did not like Catherine, so the answer must be false.

Consider Answers with Qualifying Words

Words like *sometimes* and *seldom* suggest frequency but do not go so far as to say *all* or *none*. Such qualifying words can mean more than *none* and less than *all*. By being so indefinite, the words are difficult to dispute. Therefore, qualifiers are more likely to be included in a correct response. Other qualifiers are:

few	much	often	may
many	some	perhaps	generally

 ___ ***Catherine was beloved by many of the Russian people.***
  Answer with *true* or *false*.

The statement is difficult to dispute, given Catherine's popularity. An uprising against her occurred, but it was put down, and she maintained the support of many of the Russian people. Thus the answer would be *true*.

Choose the Intended Answer Without Overanalyzing

Try to follow logically the thinking of the test writer rather than overanalyzing minute points. Don't make the question harder than it is. Use your common sense and answer what you think was intended.

___ ***Catherine was responsible for Peter's murder.***
  Answer with *true* or *false*.

This is false in that Catherine did not personally murder Peter. On the other hand, she did "tacitly consent" to his murder, which suggests responsibility. After seizing power, it was certainly in her best interest to get rid of Peter permanently. Perhaps without Catherine, Peter would still be playing with his toys, so the intended answer is *true*.

True Statements Must Be True Without Exception

A statement is either totally true or it is incorrect. Adding an incorrect *and*, *but*, or *because* phrase to a true statement makes the statement false and thus an unacceptable answer. If a statement is half true and half false, mark it false.

F _____ *Catherine was an enlightened despot who did her best to improve the lot of all her people.*
Answer with *true* or *false*.

It is true that Catherine was considered an enlightened despot, but she did very little to improve the lot of the serfs. In fact, conditions for the serfs worsened. The statement is half true and half false, so it must be answered *false*.

If Two Options Are Synonymous, Eliminate Both

If *both* is not a possible answer and two items say basically the same thing, then neither can be correct. Eliminate the two and spend your time on the others.

b _____ *The purpose of this passage is*
a. to argue.
b. to persuade.
c. to inform.
d. to entertain.

Because *argue* and *persuade* are basically synonymous, you can eliminate both and move to the other options.

Study Similar Options to Figure Out the Differences

If two similar options appear, frequently one of them will be correct. Study the options to see the subtle difference intended by the test maker.

C _____ *Catherine was*
a. unpopular during her reign.
b. beloved by all of the Russian people.
c. beloved by many of the Russian people.
d. considered selfish and arrogant by the Russians.

The first and last answers are untrue. Close inspection shows that the 100 percent *all* is the difference between the second and third answer that makes the second answer untrue. Thus, the third answer with the qualifying word is the correct response.

Use Logical Reasoning If Two Answers Are Correct

Some tests include the options *all of the above* and *none of the above*. If you see that two of the options are correct and you are unsure about a third choice, then *all of the above* would be a logical response.

___d___ ***Catherine started***

a. the Imperial Academy of Art.
b. the first college of pharmacy.
c. the Hermitage.
d. all of the above.

If you remembered that Catherine started the first two but were not sure about the Hermitage, *all of the above* would be your logical option because you know that two of the above *are* correct.

Look Suspiciously at Directly Quoted Pompous Phrases

In searching for distractors, test makers sometimes quote a pompous phrase from the passage that doesn't make much sense. Students read the phrase and think, "Oh yes, I saw that in the passage. It sounds good, so it must be right." Beware of such repetitions and make sure they make sense before choosing them.

___a___ ***In her country Catherine enacted***

a. few of the progressive ideas she championed.
b. the liberalism of the Enlightenment.
c. laws for liberty and equality.
d. the liberal areas of the philosophers.

The first response is correct because Catherine talked about progress but did little about it. The other three answers sound impressive and are quoted from the text, but are totally incorrect.

Simplify Double Negatives by Canceling Out Both

Double negatives are confusing to unravel and, in addition, time consuming to think through. Simplify a double negative statement by first canceling out both negatives. Then reread the statement without the confusion of the two negatives, which at this point have canceled each other out, and decide on the accuracy of the statement.

___T___ ***Catherine's view of herself was not that of an unenlightened ruler.***
Answer with *true* or *false*.

Cancel out the two negatives, the *not* and the *un* in the word *unenlightened*. Reread the sentence without the negatives and decide on its accuracy: Catherine's view of herself was that of an enlightened ruler. The statement is correct so the answer is *true*.

Use Can't-Tell Responses If Clues Are Insufficient

Mark an item *can't tell* only if you are not given clues on which to base an assumption. In other words, there is no evidence to indicate the statement is either true or false.

   _F_   *Catherine the Great had no children.*

From the information in this passage, which is the information on which your reading test is based, you do not have any clues to indicate whether she did or did not have children. Thus, the answer must be *can't tell.*

Validate True Responses on "All of the Following Except"

In this type of question, you must recognize several responses as correct and find the one that is incorrect. Corroborate each response and, by the process of elimination, find the one that does not fit.

Note Oversights on Hastily Constructed Tests

Reading tests developed by professional test writers are usually well constructed and do not contain obvious clues to the correct answers. However, some teacher-made tests are hastily constructed and contain errors in test making that can help a student find the correct answer. Do not, however, rely on these flaws to make a big difference in your score because they should not occur in a well-constructed test.

Grammar. Eliminate responses that do not have subject-verb agreement. The tense of the verb as well as modifiers such as *a* or *an* can also give clues to the correct response.

   _b_   *Because of his described habits, it is possible that Peter was an*
    a. hemophiliac.
    b. alcoholic.
    c. Catholic.
    d. barbarian.

The *an* suggests an answer that starts with a vowel. Thus *alcoholic* is the only possibility.

Clues from Other Parts of the Test. Because the test was hastily constructed, information in one part of the test may help you with an uncertain answer.

   _b_   *Not only was Peter childlike and neglectful, but he was also frequently*
    a. abusive.
    b. drunk.
    c. dangerous.
    d. out of the country.

The previous question gives this answer away by stating that he was possibly an alcoholic.

Length. On poorly constructed tests, longer answers are more frequently correct.

___d___ *The word* **cunning** *used in describing Catherine suggests that she was*
a. evil
b. dishonest.
c. untrustworthy.
d. crafty and sly in managing affairs.

In an effort to be totally correct without question, the test maker has made the last answer so complete that its length gives it away.

Absurd Ideas and Emotional Words. Avoid distractors with absurd ideas or emotional words. The test maker probably got tired of thinking of distractors and in a moment of weakness included nonsense.

___c___ *As used in the passage, the term* **house pets** *refers to*
a. Peter's toys.
b. Catherine's favorite lovers.
c. the dogs and cats in the palace.
d. trained seals that performed for the empress.

Yes, the test maker has, indeed, become weary. The question itself has very little depth, and the last two answers are particularly flippant.

Pretend that the following selection is a passage on a reading comprehension test. Use what you have learned to read with understanding and answer the questions.

Practice Passage B

It seems odd that one of the most famous figures of antiquity—the founder of a philosophical movement—was a vagrant with a criminal record. Diogenes the Cynic began life as the son of a rich banker. This fact may not seem so strange when one remembers the rebellious young people of the late 1960s in America, many of whom also came from affluent families.

The turning point in Diogenes' life came when his father, Hikesios, treasurer of the flourishing Greek commercial city of Sinope in Asia Minor, was found guilty of "altering the currency." Since Hikesios was a sound money man concerned about maintaining the high quality of the Sinopean coinage, this was obviously a miscarriage of justice. The Persian governor of nearby Cappadocia had issued inferior imitations of the Sinopean currency, and Hikesios, who realized that this currency was undermining the credit of Sinope, ordered the false coins to be defaced in order to put them out of circulation. But a faction of Sinopean citizens—it is not clear whether for economic or political reasons—successfully prosecuted Hikesios. Hikesios was imprisoned, and Diogenes, who was his father's assistant, was exiled. He eventually settled in Athens.

The shock of this experience caused Diogenes to become a rebel against society—to continue "altering the currency," but in a different way. He decided to stop the circulation of all false values, customs, and conventions. To achieve this goal, he adopted the tactics that made him notorious—complete freedom in speaking out on any subject and a type of outrageous behavior that he called "shamelessness."

Diogenes called free speech "the most beautiful thing in the world" because it was so effective a weapon. He shocked his contemporaries with such statements as "Most men are so nearly mad that a finger's breadth would make the difference." He advocated free love, "recognizing no other union than that of the man who persuades with the woman who consents." He insisted that "the love of money is the mother of all evils"; when some temple officials caught someone stealing a bowl from a temple, he said, "The great thieves are leading away the little thief." He liked to point out that truly valuable things cost little, and vice versa. "A statue sells for three thousand drachmas, while a quart of flour is sold for two copper coins." And when he was asked what was the right time to marry, he replied, "For a young man not yet; for an old man never at all."

Diogenes' "shamelessness"—his eccentric behavior—was his second weapon against the artificiality of conventional behavior as well as his means of promoting what he called "life in accordance with nature," or self-sufficiency. He believed that gods are truly self-sufficient and that people should emulate them: "It is the privilege of the gods to want nothing, and of men who are most like gods to want but little." It was said that he "discovered the means of adapting himself to circumstances through watching a mouse running about, not looking for a place to lie down, not afraid of the dark, not seeking any of the things that are considered dainties." And he got the idea for living in a large pottery jar—his most famous exploit—from seeing a snail carrying its own shell. Above all, Diogenes admired and emulated the life-style of dogs because of their habit of "doing everything in public." For this reason he was called *Kynos,* "the Dog," and his disciples were called Cynics.

"We live in perfect peace," one Cynic wrote, "having been made free from every evil by the Sinopean Diogenes." Eventually the citizens of Sinope also came to honor their eccentric exile with an inscription in bronze:

> Even bronze grows old with time, but your fame, Diogenes, not all eternity shall take away. For you alone did point out to mortals the lesson of self-sufficiency, and the easiest path of life.

> T. Walter Wallbank et al., *Civilization Past and Present*

Identify each question type and answer with *a, b, c,* or *d.* Explain what is wrong with the incorrect distractors.

—— 1. The best statement of the main idea of this passage is

(Question type ——————)   (Explain errors)

a. the turning point in the life of Diogenes was the imprisonment of his father.   ——————

b. the eccentric Diogenes founded a philosophy and promoted self-sufficiency.   ——————

c. Diogenes became famous for living the life of a dog.   ——————

d. the Greek way of life and thought changed under the influence of Diogenes.   ——————

—— 2. The best title for this passage is

(Question type ——————)   (Explain errors)

a. Diogenes Shocks Athens.   ——————

b. Great Greek Philosophers.   ——————

c. The Eccentric Behavior of a Philosopher.   ——————

d. Diogenes, the Self-Sufficient Cynic.   ——————

—— 3. Diogenes's father

(Question type ——————)   (Explain errors)

a. was exiled from Athens.   ——————

b. destroyed counterfeit money.   ——————

c. stole from the treasury.   ——————

d. was treasurer of Sinope and Cappadocia.   ——————

—— 4. The author believes that Diogenes was all of the following except

(Question type ——————)   (Explain errors)

a. uninhibited by tradition.   ——————

b. insincere in not practicing what he preached.   ——————

c. angered by his father's persecution.   ——————

d. vocal in advocating free speech.   ——————

—— 5. The author's purpose is to

(Question type ——————)   (Explain errors)

a. argue.   ——————

b. inform.   ——————

c. ridicule.   ——————

d. persuade.   ——————

_____ 6. As used in the passage, the best definition of *affluent* is

(Question type _____)   (Explain errors)

    a. wealthy.   _____

    b. close-knit.   _____

    c. loving.   _____

    d. politically prominent.   _____

STRATEGIES FOR CONTENT AREA EXAMS

Almost all professors would say that the number one strategy for scoring high on content exams is to study the material. Although this advice is certainly on target, there are other suggestions that can help you gain an edge.

Multiple-Choice Items

Multiple-choice, true-false, or matching items on content area exams are written to evaluate the following three categories: factual knowledge, conceptual comprehension, and application skill. Factual questions tap your knowledge of names, definitions, dates, events, and theories. Conceptual comprehension questions evaluate your ability to see relationships, notice similarities and differences, and combine information from different parts of a chapter. Application questions provide the opportunity to generalize from a theory to a real-life illustration, and they are particularly popular in psychology and sociology. The following is an example of an application question from psychology.

An illustration of obsessive-compulsive behavior is

_____ a. Maria goes to the movies most Friday nights.

✓ b. Leon washes his hands over a hundred times a day.

_____ c. Pepe wants to buy a car.

_____ d. Sue eats more fish than red meat.

The second response is obviously correct, but such questions can be tricky if you have not prepared for them. To study for a multiple-choice test, make lists of key terms, facts, and concepts. Quiz yourself on recognition and general knowledge. Make connections and be sure you know similarities and differences. Lastly, invent scenarios that depict principles and concepts. Use your own knowledge, plus the previous suggestions for multiple-choice tests, to separate answers from distractors.

Short-Answer Items

Professors ask short-answer questions because they want you to use your own words to describe or identify. For such questions, be sure that you understand exactly what the professor is asking you to say. You do not want to waste time writing more than is needed, but on the other hand, you do not want to lose points for not writing enough. Study for short-answer items by making lists and self-testing, just as you do when studying for multiple-choice items.

Essay Questions

Essay answers demand more effort and energy from the test taker than multiple-choice items. Rather than simply recognizing correct answers, you must recall, create, and organize. On a multiple-choice test, all the correct answers are somewhere before you. On an essay exam, however, the only thing in front of you is a question and a blank sheet of paper. This blank sheet of paper can be intimidating to many students. Your job is to recall appropriate ideas for a response and pull them together under the central theme designated in the question. The following suggestions can help you respond effectively.

Translate the Question. Frequently the "question" is not a question at all. It may be a statement that you must first turn into a question. Read and reread this statement that is called a *question*. Be sure you understand it and then reword it into a question. Even if you begin with a question, translate it into your own words. Simplify the question into straight terms that you can understand. Break the question into its parts.

Convert the translated parts of the questions into the approach that you will need to use to answer the question. Will you define, describe, explain, or compare? State what you will do to answer. In a sense, this is a behavioral statement. The following example demonstrates the process.

Statement to Support: **It is both appropriate and ironic to refer to Catherine as one of the great rulers of Russia.**

Question: Why is it both appropriate and ironic to refer to Catherine as one of the great rulers of Russia?

Translation: The question has two parts:

1. What did Catherine do that was really great?
2. What did she do that was the opposite of what you would expect (irony) of a great Russian ruler?

Response Approach: List what Catherine did that was great and list what she did that was the opposite of what you would expect of a great Russian ruler. Relate her actions to the question.

Answer the Question. Your answer should be in response to the question that is asked and not a summary of everything you know about a particular subject. Write with purpose so that the reader can understand your views and relate your points to the subject. Padding your answer by repeating the same idea or including irrelevant information is obvious to graders and seldom appreciated.

Example: An inappropriate answer to the question "Why is it both appropriate and ironic to refer to Catherine as one of the great rulers of Russia?"

Catherine was born in Germany and came to Russia as a young girl to *marry Peter. It was an unhappy marriage that lasted for seventeen years. She . . .*

(This response does not answer the question: it is a summary.)

Organize Your Response. Do not write the first thing to pop into your head. Take a few minutes to brainstorm and jot down ideas. Number the ideas in the order that you wish to present them and use this plan as your outline for writing.

In your first sentence, establish the purpose and direction of your response. Then list specific details that support, explain, prove, and develop your point. Reemphasize the points in a concluding sentence and restate your purpose. Whenever possible, use numbers or subheadings to simplify your message for the reader. If time runs short, use an outline or a diagram to express your remaining ideas.

Example: To answer the previous question, think about the selection on Catherine and jot down the ideas that you would include in a response.

Use an Appropriate Style. Your audience for this response is not your best friend or buckaroo but your learned professor who is going to give you a grade. Be respectful. Do not use slang. Do not use phrases like "as you know" or "well." They may be appropriate in conversation, but they are not appropriate in formal writing.

I. *Appropriate*
1. Acquired land
2. Art, medicine, buildings
3. 34 years
4. Political skill & foreign diplomacy

II. *Ironic* (opposite)
1. Not Russian
2. Killed Peter
3. Serfs very poor
4. Revolt against her

Avoid empty words and thoughts. Words like *good, interesting,* and *nice* say very little. Be more direct and descriptive in your writing.

State your thesis, supply proof, and use transitional phrases to tie your ideas together. Words like *first, second,* and *finally* help to organize enumerations. Terms like *however* and *on the other hand* show a shift in thought. Remember, you are pulling ideas together, so use phrases and words to help the reader see relationships.

Study this response to the question for organization, transition, and style.

Catherine was a very good ruler of Russia. She tried to be Russian but she was from Germany. Catherine was a good politician and got Russia seaports on the Baltic, Caspian, and Black Sea. She had many boyfriends and there was gossip about her. She did very little for the Serfs because they remained very poor for a long time. She built nice buildings and got doctors to help people. She was not as awesome as she pretended to be.

(Note the total lack of organization, the weak language, inappropriate phrases, and the failure to use traditional words.)

Be Aware of Appearance. Research has shown that, on the average, essays written in a clear, legible hand receive a grade level higher score than essays written somewhat illegibly.[7] Be particular about appearance and considerate of the reader. Proofread for correct grammar, punctuation, and spelling.

Predict and Practice. Predict possible essay items by using the table of contents and subheadings of your text to form questions. Practice brainstorming to answer these questions. Review old exams for an insight both into the questions and the kinds of answers that received good marks. Outline answers to possible exam questions. Do as much thinking as possible to prepare yourself to take the test before you sit down to begin writing.

Notice Key Words in Essay Questions. This is a list of key words of instruction that appear in essay questions, with hints for responding to each:

Compare: list the similarities between things

Contrast: note the differences between things

Criticize: state your opinion and stress the weaknesses

Define: state the meaning so that the term is understood, and use examples

Describe: state the characteristics so that the image is vivid

Diagram: make a drawing that demonstrates relationships

Discuss: define the issue and elaborate on the advantages and disadvantages

Evaluate: state positive and negative views and make a judgment

Explain: show cause and effect and give reasons

Illustrate: provide examples

Interpret: explain your own understanding of a topic which includes your opinions

Justify: give proof or reasons to support an opinion

List: record a series of numbered items

Outline: sketch out the main points with their significant supporting details

Prove: use facts as evidence in support of an opinion

Relate: connect items and show how one influences another

Review: overview with a summary

Summarize: retell the main points

Trace: move sequentially from one event to another

View Your Response Objectively for Evaluation Points. Respond to get points. Some students feel that filling up the page deserves a passing grade. They do not understand how a whole page written on the subject of Catherine could receive no points.

[7]H. W. James, "The Effect of Handwriting upon Grading," *English Journal* 16 (1927): 180–185.

Although essay exams seem totally subjective, they cannot be. Students need to know that a professor who gives an essay exam grades answers according to an objective scoring system. The professor examines the paper for certain relevant points that should be made. The student's grade reflects the quantity, quality, and clarity of these relevant points.

Unfortunately, essay exams are shrouded in mystery. The hardest part of answering an item is to figure out what the professor wants. Ask yourself, "What do I need to say to get enough points to pass or to make an *A?*"

Do not add personal experiences or extraneous examples unless they are requested. You may be wasting your time by including information that will give you no points. Stick to the subject and the material. Demonstrate to the professor that you know the material by selectively using it in your response.

The professor scoring the response to the question about Catherine used the following checklist for evaluation.

Appropriate
1. Acquired land
2. Art, medicine, buildings
3. 34 years
4. Political skill and foreign diplomacy

Ironic
1. Not Russian
2. Killed Peter
3. Serfs very poor
4. Revolt against her

The professor determined that an *A* paper should contain all of the items. In order to pass, a student should give 5 of the 8 categories covered. Listing and explaining less than five would not produce enough points to pass. Naturally, the professor would expect clarity and elaboration in each category.

After the Test, Read an *A* Paper. Maybe the *A* paper will be yours. If so, share it with others. If not, ask to read an *A* paper so that you will have a model from which to learn. Ask your classmates or ask the professor. You can learn a lot from reading a good paper; you can see what you should and could have done.

When your professor returns a multiple-choice exam, you can reread items and analyze your mistakes to figure out what you did wrong. However, you cannot review essay exams so easily. You may get back a *C* paper with only a word or two of comment and never know what you should have done. Ideally, essay exams should be returned with an example of what would have been a perfect *A* response so that students can study and learn from a perfect model and not make the same mistakes on the next test, but this is seldom, if ever, done. Your best bet is to ask to see an *A* paper.

Study the following response to the previous question. The paper received an *A*.

To call Catherine one of the great rulers of Russia is both appropriate and ironic. It is appropriate because she expanded the borders of Russia. Through her cunning, Russia annexed part of Poland and expanded the frontier to the Black Sea, Caspian, and Baltic. Catherine professed to be enlightened and formed an art academy, a college of pharmacy, and imported foreign physicians. She built many architecturally significant buildings, including the Hermitage. For thirty-four years she amazed the Russian people with her political skill and diplomacy.

On the other hand, Catherine was not a great Russian, nor was she an enlightened leader of all the people. First, she was not Russian; she was German, but she had worked hard to "russify" herself during the early years of her unhappy marriage. Secondly and ironically, she murdered the legitimate ruler of Russia. When she seized power, she made sure the tsar quickly died of "hemorrhoidal colic." Third, she did nothing to improve the lot of the poor serfs and after a bloody uprising in 1773, she became even more despotic. Yet, Catherine was an engaging character who, through her cunning and intellect, has become known to the world in history books as "Catherine the Great."

(Note the organization, logical thinking, and use of transitions in this response.)

LOCUS OF CONTROL

Have you ever heard students say, "I do better when I don't study," or "No matter how much I study, I still get a *C*"? Rotter, a learning theory psychologist who believes that people develop attitudes about control of their lives, would interpret these comments as reflecting an external locus of control regarding test taking.[8] Such "externalizers" feel that fate, luck, or others control what happens to them. Since they feel they can do little to avoid what befalls them, they do not face matters directly and thus do not take responsibility for failure or credit for success.

People who have an internal locus of control, on the other hand, feel that they, rather than "fate," have control over what happens to them. Such students might evaluate test performance by saying, "I didn't study enough" or "I should have spent more time organizing my essay response." "Internalizers" feel their rewards are due to their own actions, and thus they take steps to be sure they receive those rewards. When it comes to test taking, be an "internalizer," take control, and accept the credit for your success.

SUMMARY

Test taking is a serious part of the business of being a college student. Preparation and practice can lead to improved scores on both standardized reading tests and content area exams. Both types of tests require you to be mentally and physically alert, aware of procedures, and aware of environmental factors that affect your score. Items on standardized reading tests tend to follow a predictable pattern and include five major question types. Observations and suggestions for multiple-choice items apply to both standardized and content exams. Essay exam questions demand effort, energy, and organization.

[8]J. Rotter, "External Control and Internal Control," *Psychology Today*, 5(1) (1971): 37–42.

Name _____

Answer the following questions to learn about your own learning and reflect on your progress. Your instructor may collect your responses.

How were you or were you not physically prepared for your last test?

_____

_____

How did you divide your time on the last test?

_____

_____

In what subjects do you have test anxiety? Why?

_____

_____

Do you have anxiety about public speaking? Why or why not?

_____

_____

Review your correct and incorrect responses to the comprehension questions in this text. What type of question seems to be most difficult for you?

_____

_____

What type of question do you usually get correct?

_____

_____

How would you diagnose your problems on multiple-choice tests?

_____

_____

How would you describe the difference in your preparation for a multiple-choice or an essay exam in history?

_____

_____

_____

Do you feel you score higher on multiple-choice or essay exams? Why?

_____

_____

How has this chapter changed your approach to test taking?

_____

_____

_____

Use the remaining space to write a paragraph "debriefing" the last big test that you took. Describe the test, evaluate your preparation and performance. What will you do differently next time?

Using the perforations, tear out the Learning Log for your instructor.

Textbook Application

Can you transfer your reading skills?

Can you plan your attack?

Can you succeed?

TRANSFER YOUR SKILLS

This book contains many exercises designed to teach reading skills. Each skill discussion is followed by short excerpts from college textbooks for practicing these skills. Your success with this textbook is certainly a measure of your reading ability. However, the true measure of success in college reading comes, not from your grade at the end of the reading course, but from your grades in the college courses in which you apply the skills.

At the end of your college reading course, your challenge is to transfer these skills to the real world. Can you read and understand textbook material? Can you present the information necessary to make a passing grade in a psychology, sociology, or history course?

MEET THE CHALLENGE

In order to encourage your transfer of skills, this last section of *Bridging the Gap* contains a chapter from a popular sociology text. The chapter titled "Racial and Ethnic Minorities" begins with an array of examples to sensitize the reader and heighten curiosity. Then words like *race, minority,* and *ethnicity* are defined from the perspective of a sociologist. Ways in which society accepts or rejects minorities are explained with accompanying examples, and the chapter concludes with a history of six different ethnic groups. In its approach the chapter is a combination of sociology and history.

Your challenge is to work systematically through the material using the skills you have learned, to study the material, and to present that knowledge on a test. Two tests have been prepared to cover this material. One is a multiple-choice test and the other is an essay exam asking for a written response to two out of three questions.

ORGANIZE YOUR STUDY

Another purpose of including this sociology chapter in *Bridging the Gap* is to give you the opportunity to work with a long piece of textbook material while you still have the advantage of college reading instruction. Use the skills you have learned over the past months and organize your study around the three stages of reading. Use the following suggestions as guides.

STUDY STRATEGIES

Before Reading
Stage 1: Preview
Read the table of contents.
Glance through the chapter for an overview.
Selectively read subheadings.

Predict content and organization.

Establish a purpose consistent with expectations.

Set goals.

Activate your computer chip.

While Reading

Stage 2: Integrate Knowledge

Use the five thinking strategies as you read.

1. Predict   2. Picture   3. Relate   4. Monitor   5. Fix up

Process the material; separate the major ideas from the minor ideas.

As you finish a section, annotate it for later study.

Take notes using a system that works for you.

After Reading

Stage 3: Recall to Self-Test

Recite what you have read.

Refer to the table of contents for an overview.

Identify the major trends.

Recognize similarities and differences that link issues.

Predict exam questions and practice written responses.

1. For multiple-choice tests, study the specifics.

2. For an essay exam, predict questions and outline possible responses.

Take the initiative with this chapter and coordinate your own reading and studying. Study strategy suggestions and questions are inserted, but they do not constitute all that is needed for you to master this material.

RACIAL AND ETHNIC MINORITIES[1]

Contents

[1]From Alex Thio, *Sociology: A Brief Introduction*, 1994.

Introduction

In this chapter, we will examine the criteria for identifying minorities and the nature of prejudice and discrimination against them. Then we will analyze the alternative ways in which a society may reject or accept a minority group. Finally, we will find out how various racial and ethnic groups have fared in the United States.

What are the major organizational sections of this chapter?

What is the purpose of each section?

How can you divide your reading and notetaking on this chapter?

In the summer of 1992 a deluge of horror stories about human cruelties shocked the world. They poured out of newly independent Bosnia and Herzegovina, the most ethnically diverse republic of what used to be Yugoslavia. The Serbs were reported to engage in an "ethnic cleansing" campaign by "driving Muslims and Croats from their homes, torturing and killing some of them, and abusing and terrorizing the rest." In a northern Bosnian town, armed Serbs, after rounding up 100 prisoners for a move from one detention camp to another, pulled out about 30 of them and shot them. At a camp, the family of one starving prisoner tried to bring him some food, but the guards took it away and then beat the prisoner in front of his relatives. In a town called Doboj, the Serbs sprayed insecticide on loaves of bread, which they fed to Muslim boys, making them violently ill. Near Tuzla in eastern Bosnia, three Muslim girls were stripped and chained to a fence "for all to use." After being raped for three days, they were doused with gasoline and set on fire. Other Muslim and Croatian girls had been used as sex slaves for months, and if they became pregnant they were set free to "have Serbian babies." While most reports focused on Serbian cruelties, some Muslims and Croats struck back with atrocities of their own in areas where they predominate (Watson, 1992).

Mistreatment of minorities does not, however, take place in Bosnia alone. In other parts of Eastern Europe, minorities—such as the Slovaks in Czechoslovakia, ethnic Albanians in Yugoslavia, ethnic Hungarians in Romania, and ethnic Turks in Bulgaria—also suffer. In Western Europe, too, Pakistanis, Turks, Algerians, and other non-European minorities are often subjected to random insults and hostile stares, which sometimes escalate into gang attacks or firebombs thrown from the streets. In Japan, the Koreans, Burakumin (sometimes called *Eta*, meaning "much filth"), and Konketsuji (American-Japanese mixed bloods) are also targets of considerable prejudice and discrimination. These are only a few of the countless cases of mistreatment suffered by minorities in various countries.

Identifying Minorities

Americans are accustomed to thinking of a minority as a category of people who are physically different and who make up a small percentage of the population. But the popular identification of minorities is often misleading. The Jews in China do not "look Jewish"—they look like other Chinese. Similarly, the Jews in the United States look like other white Americans. Jews cannot be differentiated from the dominant group on the basis of their physical characteristics, but they are considered a minority. In South Africa, blacks are a minority group, even though they make up a majority of the population. Neither physical traits nor numbers alone determine whether people constitute a minority group. To get a clearer idea of what a minority is, we need first to see what races and ethnic groups are.

Should you annotate and then take notes on this material?

Before reading what sociologists believe, how would you define *race, ethnicity,* and *minorities*?

Should you list an example to illustrate each definition?

Race

As a biological concept, race refers to a large category of people who share certain inherited physical characteristics. These characteristics may include particular skin color, head shape, hair type, nasal shape, lip form, or blood type. One common classification of human races recognizes three groups: Caucasoid, Mongoloid, and Negroid. Caucasoids have light skin, Mongoloids yellowish skin, and Negroids dark skin—and other physical differences exist among the three groups.

There are, however, at least two important problems with such a classification of races. First, some groups fit into none of these categories. Natives of India and Pakistan have Caucasoid facial features but dark skin. The Polynesians of Pacific Islands have a mixture of Caucasoid, Mongoloid, and Negroid characteristics.

Another problem with the biological classification of races is that there are no "pure" races. People in these groups have been interbreeding for centuries. In the United States, for example, about 70 percent of blacks have some white ancestry and approximately 20 percent of whites have at least one black ancestor (Sowell, 1983). Biologists have also determined that all current populations originate from one common genetic pool—one single group of humans that evolved about 30,000 years ago, most likely in Africa. As humans migrated all over the planet, different populations developed different physical characteristics in adapting to particular physical environments. Thus, the Eskimos' relatively thick layer of fat under the skin of their eyes, faces, and other parts of the body provides good insulation against the icy cold of Arctic regions. The Africans' dark skin offers protection from the burning sun of tropical regions. Yet there has not developed a significant genetic difference among the "races." As genetic research has indicated, about 95 percent of the DNA molecules (which make up the gene) are the same for all humans, and only the remaining 5 percent are responsible for all the differences in appearance (Vora, 1981). Even these outward differences are meaningless because the differences among members of the same "race" are greater than the average differences between two racial groups. Some American blacks, for example, have lighter skins than many whites, and some whites are darker than many blacks.

Since there are no clear-cut biological distinctions—in physical characteristics or genetic makeup—between racial groups, sociologists prefer to define race as a social rather than biological phenomenon. Defined sociologically, a **race** is a group of people who are *perceived* by a given society as biologically different from others. People are assigned to one race or another, not necessarily on the basis of logic or fact but by public opinion, which, in turn, is molded by society's dominant group. Consider an American boy whose father has 100 percent white ancestry and whose mother is the daughter of a white man and black woman. This youngster is considered "black" in our society, although he is actually more white than black because of his 75 percent white and 25 percent black ancestry. In many Latin American countries, however, this same child would be considered "white." In fact, according to Brazil's popular perception of a black as "a person of African descent who has no white ancestry at all," about three-fourths of all American blacks would *not* be considered blacks. They would be considered white because they have some white ancestry (Denton and Massey, 1989).

What is a race?

To what extent do we all share the same genetic pool?

Ethnicity

Jews have often been called a race. But they have the same racial origins as Arabs—both being Semites—and through the centuries Jews and non-Jews have interbred extensively. As a result, as we noted earlier, Jews are often physically indistinguishable from non-Jews. Besides, a person can become a Jew by choice—by conversion to Judaism. Jews do not constitute a race. Instead, they are a religious group or, more broadly, an ethnic group.

Whereas race is based on popularly perceived physical traits, ethnicity is based on cultural characteristics. An **ethnic group** is a collection of people who share a distinctive cultural heritage and a consciousness of their common bond. Members of an ethnic group may share a language, accent, religion, history, philosophy, national origin, or life-style. They always share a feeling that they are a distinct people. In the United States, members of an ethnic group typically have the same national origin. As a result, they are named after the countries from which they or their ancestors came. Thus, they are Polish-Americans, Italian-Americans, Irish-Americans, and so on.

For the most part, ethnicity is culturally learned. People learn the life-styles, cooking, language, values, and other characteristics of their ethnic group. Yet members of an ethnic group are usually born into it. The cultural traits of the group are passed from one generation to another, and ethnicity is not always a matter of choice. A person may be classified by others as a member of some ethnic group, for example, on the basis of appearance or accent. In fact, racial and ethnic groups sometimes overlap, as in the case of African- or Asian-Americans. Like race, ethnicity can be an ascribed status.

How does ethnicity differ from race?

Whom do you know who has dropped their ethnicity?

Who has maintained their ethnicity?

Minority

A **minority** is a racial or ethnic group that is subjected to prejudice and discrimination. The essence of a minority group is its experience of prejudice and discrimination. **Prejudice** is a negative attitude toward members of a minority. It includes ideas and beliefs, feelings, and predispositions to act in a certain way. For example, whites prejudiced against blacks might fear meeting a black man on the street at night. They might resent blacks who are successful. They might plan to sell their houses if a black family moves into the neighborhood.

Whereas prejudice is an attitude, **discrimination** is an act. More specifically, it is unequal treatment of people because they are members of some group. When a landlord will not rent an apartment to a family because they are African-American or Hispanic, that is discrimination.

What is a minority?

What is prejudice?

What is discrimination?

Are you a member of a minority?

QUESTIONS FOR DISCUSSION AND REVIEW

1. Why do sociologists define race as a social rather than a physical phenomenon?
2. What is ethnicity, and why do sociologists prefer to use this concept to explain the diverse behavior of minorities?
3. When does a racial or ethnic group become a minority group?

Racial and Ethnic Relations

Prejudice and discrimination are an integral part of the relations between the dominant group and minorities. But the amount of prejudice and discrimination obviously varies from one society to another. Hence the racial and ethnic relations may appear in different forms, ranging from peaceful coexistence to violent conflict. In the following sections we analyze the various ways in which a society's dominant group accepts or rejects its minorities, and we also look at minorities' various responses to the dominant group's negative action.

What is the focus of this section?

What is the pattern of organization under each subheading?

What will you need to know after reading this section?

How are the boldface words connected?

Forms of Acceptance

If a society treats its racial and ethnic groups in a positive way, it will grant them rights of citizenship. Still, its acceptance of these groups is not necessarily total and unconditional. The dominant group may expect other groups to give up their distinct identities and accept the dominant subculture. Acceptance of a racial or ethnic group may take three forms: assimilation, amalgamation, and cultural pluralism.

Assimilation Frequently, a minority group accepts the culture of the dominant group, fading into the larger society. This process, called **assimilation,** has at least two aspects. The first is **behavioral assimilation,** which means that the minority group adopts the dominant culture—its language, values, norms, and so on—giving up its own distinctive characteristics. Behavioral assimilation, however, does not guarantee **structural assimilation**—in which the minority group ceases to be a minority *and* is accepted on equal terms with the rest of society. German-Americans, for example, have achieved structural assimilation, but African-Americans have not. Taken as a whole, assimilation can be expressed as A + B + C = A, where minorities (B and C) lose their subcultural traits and become indistinguishable from the dominant group (A) (Newman, 1973).

When the dominant group is ethnocentric, believing that its subculture is superior to others', then minority groups face considerable pressure to achieve behavioral assimilation. How easily they make this transition depends on both their attitude toward their own subculture and the degree of similarity between themselves and the dominant group. Minority groups that take pride in their own subculture are likely to resist behavioral assimilation. This may explain why Jews and various Asian groups in the United States display a lot of ethnic solidarity. Groups that are very different from the dominant group may find that even behavioral assimilation does not lead to structural assimilation. Most members of the disadvantaged minorities look upon assimilation as a promise of their right to get ahead—economically and socially—in the United States (Hirschman, 1983).

What is behavioral assimilation? Name a personal example.

What is structural assimilation? Name a personal example.

What factors encourage and prevent behavioral and structural assimilation?

Amalgamation   A society that believes groups should go through the process of behavioral assimilation in order to be accepted as equals obviously has little respect for the distinctive traits of these groups. In contrast, a society that seeks amalgamation as an ideal has some appreciation for the equal worth of various subcultures. **Amalgamation** produces a "melting pot," in which many subcultures are blended together to produce a new culture, one that differs from any of its components. Like assimilation, amalgamation requires groups to give up their distinct racial and ethnic identities. But unlike assimilation, amalgamation demands respect for the original subcultures. Various groups are expected to contribute their own subcultures to the development of a new culture, without pushing any one subculture at the expense of another. Usually, this blending of diverse subcultures results from intermarriage. It can be described as A + B + C = D, where A, B, and C represent different groups jointly producing a new culture (D) unlike any of its original components (Newman, 1973).

More than 80 years ago, a British-Jewish dramatist portrayed the United States as an amalgamation of subcultures. "There she lies," he wrote, "the great melting pot—listen! . . . Ah, what a stirring and seething—Celt and Latin, Slav and Teuton, Greek and Syrian, Black and Yellow—Jew and Gentile" (Zangwill, 1909). Indeed, to some extent America is a melting pot. In popular music and slang you can find elements of many subcultures. And there has been considerable intermarriage among some groups—in particular, among Americans of English, German, Irish, Italian, and other European backgrounds. For the most part, however, the amalgamation is made up of these Western European peoples and their subcultures. Brazil, where interracial marriage is common, comes much closer than the United States to being a true melting pot of peoples.

What is amalgamation?

How does amalgamation differ from assimilation?

Cultural Pluralism   Switzerland provides an example of yet a third way in which ethnic groups may live together. In Switzerland, three major groups—Germans, French, and Italians—retain their own languages while living together in peace. They are neither assimilated nor amalgamated. Instead, these diverse groups retain their distinctive subcultures while coexisting peacefully. This situation is called **cultural pluralism.** It is the opposite of assimilation and requires yet greater mutual respect for other groups' traditions and customs than does amalgamation. And unlike either assimilation or amalgamation, cultural pluralism encourages each group to take pride in its distinctiveness, to be conscious of its heritage, and to retain its identify. Such pluralism can be shown as $A + B + C = A + B + C$, where various groups continue to keep their subcultures while living together in the same society (Newman, 1973).

To some extent, the United States has long been marked by cultural pluralism. This can be seen in the Chinatowns, Little Italies, and Polish neighborhoods of many American cities. But these ethnic enclaves owe their existence more to discrimination than to the respectful encouragement of diversity that characterizes true pluralism.

For many groups in America, cultural pluralism has become a goal. This became evident during the 1960s and 1970s, when blacks and white ethnics alike denounced assimilation and proclaimed pride in their own identities. Today the ethnic pride has fueled a social movement calling for a multicultural curriculum in American schools, which, however, has run into some opposition.

What is cultural pluralism?

What are the dangers of cultural pluralism?

Toward Multiculturalism?   **Multiculturalism** is the belief that all racial and ethnic cultures in the United States should be equally respected and cultivated. But according to its advocates, the United States has failed to practice multiculturalism, even though we are the most racially and ethnically diverse country in the world. Multiculturalists urge that American students study African, Asian, and Latin American civilizations as much as Western civilization.

Most Americans, including nonwhites, continue to accept Western civilization (such as the English language, Western legal system, and Western history and literature) as the dominant feature of American culture, though with less enthusiasm than before. Therefore, despite the inevitable increase in ethnic conflict, the United States still remains the most successful, stable large multiethnic nation in the world. This may be traced to the core of American culture, namely, the unique tolerance for diversity and conflict, which apparently is the product of a long history of being a plural nation.

What is multiculturalism?

Forms of Rejection

When a dominant group rejects racial and ethnic groups, those groups are restricted to the status of minorities. They are discriminated against to some degree. The three major forms of rejection, in order of severity, are segregation, expulsion, and extermination.

Segregation   **Segregation** means more than spatial and social separation of the dominant and minority groups. It means that minority groups, because they are believed inferior, are compelled to live separately, and in inferior conditions. The neighborhoods, schools, and other public facilities for the dominant group are both separate from and superior to those of the minorities.

The compulsion that underlies segregation is not necessarily official, or acknowledged. In the United States, for example, segregation is officially outlawed, yet it persists. In other words, *de jure* **segregation**—segregation sanctioned by law—is gone, but *de facto* **segregation**—segregation resulting from tradition and custom—remains. This is particularly the case with regard to housing for African-Americans. Like the United States, most nations no longer practice *de jure* segregation.

What is *de jure* segregation?

What is *de facto* segregation?

Expulsion   Societies have also used more drastic means of rejecting minorities, such as expulsion. In some cases, the dominant group has expelled a minority from certain areas. In other cases, it has pushed the minority out of the country entirely. During the nineteenth century, Czarist Russia drove out millions of Jews, and the American government forced the Cherokee to travel from their homes in Georgia and the Carolinas to reservations in Oklahoma. About 4000 Cherokee died on this "Trail of Tears." During the 1970s, Uganda expelled more than 40,000 Asians—many of them Ugandan citizens—and Vietnam forced 700,000 Chinese to leave the country (Schaefer, 1988).

What are examples of rejection by expulsion?

Can you add examples of others not mentioned?

Extermination   Finally, the most drastic action against minorities is to kill them. Wholesale killing of a racial or ethnic group, called **genocide,** has been attempted in various countries. During the nineteenth century, Dutch settlers in South Africa exterminated the Khoikhoin, or "Hottentots." Native Americans in the United States were slaughtered by white settlers. On the island of Tasmania, near Australia, British settlers killed the entire native population, whom they hunted like wild animals. Between 1933 and 1945, the Nazis systematically murdered 6 million Jews. In the early 1970s, thousands of Ibos and Hutus were massacred in the African states of Nigeria and Burundi. Also in the early 1970s, machine guns and gifts of poisoned food and germ-infected clothing were used against Indians in Brazil.

What is genocide?

What are examples of genocide?

QUESTIONS FOR DISCUSSION AND REVIEW

1. In what different ways can the majority group accept members of a minority group?
2. What can happen when a dominant group decides to reject a racial or ethnic minority?

Minority Groups in America

The United States is a nation of immigrants. The earliest immigrants were the American Indians, who arrived from Asia more than 20,000 years ago. Long after the Indians had settled down as Native Americans, other immigrants began to pour in from Europe and later from Africa, Asia, and Latin America. They came as explorers, adventurers, slaves, or refugees—most of them hoping to fulfill a dream of success and happiness. The British were the earliest of these immigrants and, on the whole, the most successful in fulfilling that dream. They became the dominant group. Eventually, they founded a government dedicated to the democratic ideal of equality.

What is the focus of this section?

What major groups are discussed?

What seems to be the pattern of organization for the discussion of each group?

How detailed should your notes be?

How much will you need to know for the test?

What do you already know about the Native Americans?

How have the Native Americans fared in their own country?

Native Americans

Native Americans have long been called Indians—one result of Columbus's mistaken belief that he had landed in India. The explorer's successors passed down many other distorted descriptions of the Native Americans. They were described as savages, although it was whites who slaughtered hundreds of thousands of them. They were portrayed as scalp hunters, although it was the white government that offered large sums to whites for the scalps of Indians. They were stereotyped as lazy, although it was whites who forced them to give up their traditional occupations. These false conceptions of Native Americans were reinforced by the contrasting pictures whites painted of themselves. The white settlers were known as pioneers rather than invaders and marauders; their taking of the Native Americans' land was called homesteading, not robbery.

When Columbus "discovered" America, there were more than 300 Native American tribes, with a total population exceeding a million. Of those he encountered around the Caribbean, Columbus wrote: "Of anything they have, if it be asked for, they never say no, but do rather invite the person to accept it, and show as much lovingness as though they would give their hearts" (Hraba, 1979). In North America, too, the earliest white settlers were often aided by friendly Native Americans.

Moving the Native Americans   As the white settlers increased in numbers and moved westward, however, Native Americans resisted them. But the native population was decimated by outright killing, by destruction of their food sources, and by diseases brought by whites, such as smallpox and influenza. With their greater numbers and superior military technology, the whites prevailed. Sometimes they took land by treaty rather than by outright force—and then they often violated the treaty.

During the last half of the nineteenth century, the U.S. government tried a new policy. It made the tribes its wards and drove them onto reservations. The land they were given was mostly useless for farming, and it made up only 2.9 percent of the United States. Even on the reservations, Native Americans were not free to live their own lives. The federal government was intent on assimilating them, replacing tribal culture with the white settlers' way of life. Native Americans were forced to become small farmers, though they had for centuries been hunting and herding. Some of the tribal rituals and languages were banned. Children were sent away to boarding schools and encouraged to leave the reservations to seek jobs in cities. In 1887 those Native Americans who lived away from the tribe and "adopted the habits of civilized life" were granted citizenship. The government also disrupted the tradition of tribal ownership by granting land to the heads of families (Franklin, 1981).

By 1890 the Native American population had been reduced to less than a quarter of a million. Changes in the government's policy toward them came slowly. In 1924 Congress conferred citizenship on all Native Americans. In 1934 the federal government reversed course and supported tribal culture by granting self-government rights to tribes, restoring communal ownership, and giving financial aid. In 1940 the Native American population, which had been reduced to 0.3 million, began to grow.

By 1990, there were nearly 2 million Native Americans. Slightly more than half lived on 278 reservations, mostly in the Southwest. The rest lived in urban areas. After more than two centuries of colonial subjugation, Native Americans today find themselves at the bottom of the ladder—the poorest minority in the United States. Their unemployment rates usually stay at a devastating 40 to 50 percent, compared with less than 10 percent among the general population. On some reservations, the unemployment rates are even higher.

"Red Power"   Since the early 1960s, Native Americans have begun to assert their "red power." In 1963 they started a vigorous campaign to have their fishing rights recognized in northwest Washington; these were eventually granted by the Supreme Court in 1968. In late 1960, they publicized their grievances by occupying Alcatraz, the abandoned island prison in San Francisco Bay, for 19 months. In 1972 they marched into Washington to dramatize the "trail of broken treaties" and presented the government with a series of demands for improving their lives. In 1973 they took over Wounded Knee, South Dakota, for 72 days, during which they were engaged in a shooting war with government troops. These dramatic actions were mostly symbolic, designed to foster Indian identity and unity. Since the early 1980s, however, Native Americans have been seeking more substantive goals. Thus, an increasing number of tribes have been filing lawsuits to win back lands taken from their ancestors. They have been fighting through federal courts to protect their water and mineral resources as well as hunting and fishing rights. They have also been demanding more government assistance with health, educational, and social programs.

To some extent, the U.S. government has heeded those demands. In 1988 a federal Indian policy was instituted "to promote tribal economic development, tribal self-sufficiency, and strong tribal government." Today, on some reservations Native Americans are exempted from paying taxes and further allowed to sell gasoline, cigarettes, and other items tax-free to non-Indians. About 59 percent of the reservations are also permitted to run highly profitable gambling operations that cater to non-Indians. New York's governor even treats Native Americans' lands within his state as if they were sovereign nations. In fact, the U.S. government has recently allowed seven tribes to govern themselves virtually as sovereign nations.

All this has sparked a national movement to recapture traditions, to make Native Americans feel proud of their cultural heritage. Virtually every tribe places a heavy emphasis on teaching the younger generation its native language, crafts, tribal history, and religious ceremonies. There used to be a lack of unity among the 300 tribes, but today intertribal visiting and marriage are common occurrences. Moreover, in the last 15 years, more than 500 Indian men and women have become lawyers—and more have successfully established themselves in the business and professional worlds. Of course, the majority of Native Americans still have a long way to go. Without a viable economic base to draw on, they still find themselves "powerless in the face of rising unemployment, deteriorating health care, and a falling standard of living."

How did government policies devastate Native Americans?

How has "red power" been asserted?

How have Native Americans been accepted and rejected by society?

African-Americans

There are more than 31 million African-Americans, constituting about 12.5 percent of the U.S. population. Blacks are the largest minority in the nation. In fact, there are more blacks in the United States than in any single African nation except Nigeria.

Their ancestors first came from Africa to North America as indentured servants in 1619. Soon after that they were brought here as slaves. During their two-month voyage across the ocean, they were chained and packed like sardines, often lying immobile for weeks in their own sweat and excrement. It was not unusual for half the slaves to die from disease, starvation, and suicide before reaching their destination.

From 1619 to 1820, about half a million slaves were taken to U.S. shores. Most lived in the southern states and worked on cotton, tobacco, or sugar-cane plantations. "Slave codes" that restricted their movement and conduct were enshrined in laws.

By the time the Civil War broke out in 1861, the number of enslaved African-Americans had reached 5 million. The end of the Civil War in 1865 brought not only the end of slavery but also other new opportunities for southern African-Americans. For the first time, they could go to public schools and state universities with whites. The greatest black advance came in politics, but little was done to improve the economic position of African-Americans.

Then, in 1877, federal troops were withdrawn from the South. White supremacy reigned, and whatever gains African-Americans had made during Reconstruction were wiped out. Many so-called **Jim Crow** laws were enacted, segregating blacks from whites in all kinds of public and private facilities—from restrooms to schools. These laws were supplemented by terror.

As southern farms were mechanized and as the demand for workers in northern industrial centers rose during World Wars I and II, many southern African-Americans migrated north. When the wars ended and the demand for workers decreased, however, they were often the first to be fired. Even in the North, where there were no Jim Crow laws, African-Americans faced discrimination and segregation.

The federal government itself sanctioned segregation. In 1896 the Supreme Court declared segregation legal. In 1913 President Wilson ordered the restaurants and cafeterias in federal buildings segregated. Even the armed forces were segregated until President Truman ordered them desegregated in 1948.

Desegregation   A turning point in American race relations came in 1954. In that year, the Supreme Court ordered that public schools be desegregated. The decision gave momentum to the long-standing movement against racial discrimination. In the late 1950s and 1960s, the civil rights movement launched marches, sit-ins, and boycotts. The price was high: many civil rights workers were beaten and jailed, and some were killed. But eventually Congress passed the landmark Civil Rights Act in 1964, prohibiting segregation and discrimination in virtually all areas of social life, such as restaurants, hotels, schools, housing, and employment (Schaefer, 1988).

In the last 30 years, the Civil Rights Act has ended many forms of segregation and paved the way for some improvements in the position of

African-Americans. Various studies have shown a significant decline in white opposition to such issues as school integration, integrated housing, interracial marriage, and voting for an African-American president. The proportion of African-American children attending white majority schools in the South rose from less than 2 percent in 1964 to 43 percent in 1980 and 75 percent in 1990. From 1961 to 1981, the number of African-Americans going to college soared by 500 percent, though their enrollment has declined steadily since the early 1980s. The number of African-Americans elected to various public offices more than quadrupled to over 7000 today. We can also see African-Americans holding positions of prominence in television and films and at major universities and colleges. Most impressive was Jesse Jackson's presidential candidacy in 1988, which would have been unthinkable a generation ago. The dramatic increase in social recognition for blacks can also be seen in the crowning of black women as Miss America, the sending of black astronauts into space, and the congressional proclamation of a national holiday to honor Dr. Martin Luther King, Jr. (Farley, 1985; Schuman et al., 1985; Marriott, 1990).

In sum, prejudice against African-Americans still exists. They still fall far behind whites in economics and housing, though they have shown significant gains in education and politics. It is true that, taking into account the long history of black oppression in America, the overall social status of African-Americans has improved dramatically, especially from 1939 to 1970, as a result of the civil rights movement and the nation's unprecedented economic growth. But since the early 1970s, though, black progress has slowed significantly (Jaynes and Williams, 1989; Hacker, 1992).

What were Jim Crow laws and what were the effects?

How have African-Americans been accepted and rejected by society?

Hispanic-Americans

In 1848 the United States either won in war or bought from Mexico what would become Texas, California, Nevada, Utah, Arizona, New Mexico, and Colorado. Thus, many Mexicans found themselves living in U.S. territories as American citizens. The vast majority of today's Mexican-Americans, however, are the result of immigration from Mexico since the turn of the century. The early immigrants came largely to work in the farmlands of California and to build the railroads of the Southwest. Then numerous Mexicans began to pour into the United States, driven by Mexico's population pressures and economic problems and attracted by American industry's need for low-paid, unskilled labor.

The United States also added Puerto Rico to its territory in 1898, by defeating the Spaniards in the Spanish-American War. In 1917 Congress conferred citizenship on all Puerto Ricans, but they may not vote in presidential elections and have no representation in Congress. Over the years, especially since the early 1950s, many Puerto Ricans have migrated to the U.S. mainland, lured by job opportunities and cheap plane service between New York City and San Juan. In the last two decades, though, more have returned to Puerto Rico than have come here.

Thus, a new minority group emerged in the United States—Hispanic-Americans, also called Latinos. The category actually includes several groups today. Besides the Mexican-Americans and Puerto Ricans, there are immigrants from Cuba, who began to flock to the Miami area since their country became communist in 1959. There are also the "other Hispanics"—immigrants from other Central and South American countries, who have come here as political refugees and job seekers. By 1990, the members of all these groups totaled about 22 million, constituting over 9 percent of the U.S. population. This made them our second largest minority. Because of their high birth rates and the continuing influx of immigrants, Hispanic-Americans could outnumber African-Americans in the next decade (Kenna, 1983; Davis, Haub, and Willette, 1983; Barringer, 1991a).

The Spanish language is the unifying factor among Hispanic-Americans. Another source of common identity is religion: at least 85 percent of them are Roman Catholic. There is an increasing friction, though, between Mexican-Americans and the newly arrived immigrants from Mexico. Many Mexican-Americans blame illegal aliens for lower salaries, loss of jobs, overcrowding of schools and health clinics, and deterioration of neighborhoods. According to one survey, for example, 66 percent of Mexican-Americans accused illegal immigrants of taking jobs from American citizens.

Differences in Hispanic Groups

There are, however, significant differences within the Hispanic community. Mexican-Americans are by far the largest group, accounting for 61 percent of the Hispanics. They are heavily concentrated in the Southwest and West. Puerto Ricans make up 15 percent and live mostly in the Northeast, especially in New York City. As a group, they are the poorest among the Hispanics, which may explain why many have gone back to Puerto Rico. Those born in the United States, however, are more successful economically than their parents from Puerto Rico. The Cubans, who constitute 7 percent of the Hispanic population, are the most affluent. They therefore show the greatest tendency toward integration with "Anglos"—white Americans. The remaining Hispanics are a diverse group, ranging from uneducated, unskilled laborers to highly trained professionals (Fitzpatrick and Parker, 1981; Nelson and Tienda, 1985; McHugh, 1989).

As a whole, Hispanics are younger than the general population. The median age is 23 for Hispanics, compared with 30 for other Americans. The youthfulness of the Hispanic population is due to relatively high fertility and heavy immigration of young adults. This is particularly the case with Mexican-Americans, who have the most children and are the youngest of all Hispanic groups. At the other extreme are Cubans, who have even fewer children and are older than non-Hispanic Americans, with a median age of 41.

Hispanics in general also lag behind both whites and blacks in educational attainment. Hispanic students are three times more likely to drop out of school than either their white or black peers. Among Hispanics aged 25 or older, only 10 percent have completed college, compared with 22 percent of other Americans (Kantrowitz, 1991). But some Hispanic groups are more educated than others. Cubans are the best educated, primarily because most of the early refugees fleeing communist Cuba were middle-class and professional people. Mexican-Americans and Puerto Ricans are less educated because they consist of many recent immigrants with much less schooling. The young, American-born Hispanics usually have more education. Lack of proficiency in English has retarded the recent Hispanic immigrants' educational progress. As many of 25 percent of Hispanics in public schools speak little or no English, which has resulted in their having higher dropout rates than non-Hispanic students (Bernstein, 1990). Nonetheless, most Hispanics believe that people who live in the United States should learn to speak English. This apparently reflects a desire for assimilation into mainstream American society.

In short, Hispanics as a group are still trailing behind the general population in social and economic well-being. However, the higher educational achievement of young Hispanics provides hope that more

© 1997 Addison-Wesley Educational Publishers Inc.

Hispanics—not just Cubans—will be joining the higher paid white-collar work force in the future. As shown by recent research, if Hispanics speak English fluently and have at least graduated from high school, their occupational achievement is close to that of non-Hispanics with similar English fluency and schooling (Stolzenberg, 1990). According to another study, the huge Latino population in Los Angeles is thriving, thanks to its traditionally stable families and community spirit. Nationwide, Hispanics are also already a growing force in American politics. They now have more members of Congress, more state governors, and more mayors of large cities than before. Most important, the states with the largest concentration of Hispanics—California, Texas, New York, and Florida—are highly significant for both state and national elections. It is no wonder that Hispanics were eagerly courted by both parties in the last two presidential elections. Interestingly, though, while most Hispanic leaders describe themselves as primarily liberal, the majority of ordinary Hispanics consider themselves moderate to conservative (Suro, 1992).

What commonalities unite Hispanics?

What are the different Hispanic groups?

How do the different Hispanic groups differ in their economic status in America?

Asian-Americans

Since 1980, Asian-Americans have been the fastest growing minority. Their population has increased by 108 percent, far higher than the next highest increase rate of 53 percent among Hispanics. (For even sharper contrast, the U.S. population as a whole has grown only 10 percent.) Nevertheless, Asian-Americans remain a much smaller minority—3 percent of the U.S. population—than Hispanics and African-Americans. There is tremendous diversity among Asian-Americans, whose ancestry can be traced to over 20 different countries. Filipinos are the most numerous, followed by Chinese, Vietnamese, Koreans, and Japanese (Butterfield, 1991). But it is the second and fifth largest groups—Chinese and Japanese—that are the best-known in the United States because before 1980 they had for a long time been the largest Asian-American groups.

The Chinese first came during the gold rush on the West Coast in 1849, pulled by better economic conditions in America and pushed by economic problems and local rebellions in China. Soon huge numbers of Chinese were imported to work for low wages, digging mines and building railroads. After these projects were completed, jobs became scarce, and white workers feared competition from the Chinese. As a result, special taxes were imposed on the Chinese, and they were prohibited from attending school, seeking employment, owning property, and bearing witness in court. In 1882 the Chinese Exclusion Act restricted Chinese immigration to the United States, and it stopped all Chinese immigration from 1904 to 1943. Many returned to their homeland (Kitano, 1981; Henry, 1990).

Immigrants from Japan met similar hostility. They began to come to the West Coast somewhat later than the Chinese, also in search of better economic opportunities. At first they were welcomed as a source of cheap labor. But soon they began to operate small shops, and anti-Japanese activity grew. In 1906 San Francisco forbade Asian children to attend white schools. In response, the Japanese government negotiated an agreement whereby the Japanese agreed to stop emigration to the United States, and President Theodore Roosevelt agreed to end harassment of the Japanese who were already here. But when the Japanese began to buy their own farms, they met new opposition. In 1913 California prohibited foreign-born Japanese from owning or leasing lands; other Western states followed suit. In 1922 the U.S. Supreme Court ruled that foreign-born Japanese could not become American citizens.

World War II   Worse events occurred during World War II. All the Japanese, aliens and citizens, were rounded up from the West Coast and confined in concentration camps set up in isolated areas. They were forced to sell their homes and properties; the average family lost $10,000. The action was condoned even by the Supreme Court as a legitimate way of ensuring that the Japanese-Americans would not help Japan defeat the United States. Racism, however, was the real source of such treatment. After all, there was no evidence of any espionage or sabotage by a Japanese-American. Besides, German-Americans were not sent to concentration camps, although Germany was at war with the United States and there *were* instances of subversion by German-Americans. In 1976, though, President Ford proclaimed that the wartime detention of Japanese-Americans had been a mistake, calling it "a sad day in American history." In 1983 a congressional commission recommended that each surviving evacuee be paid $20,000. In 1987, when the survivors sued the government for billions of dollars in compensation, the solicitor general acknowledged that the detention was "frankly racist" and "deplorable." And in 1988 the Senate voted overwhelmingly to give $20,000 and an apology to each of the surviving internees (Molotsky, 1988).

Reverence for Learning   Despite this history of discrimination, Chinese- and Japanese-Americans are educationally and professionally among the most successful minorities in the United States today. They have higher percentages of high school and college graduates than whites. Although Asians are only 3 percent of the U.S. population, they make up 8 percent of the student body at Harvard and 21 percent of the student body at the University of California at Berkeley. Among academics, scientists, and engineers, a higher proportion of Asians than whites have Ph.Ds. Asian professors also publish more than their white colleagues. Moreover, Asian-Americans as a whole have a higher percentage of white-collar jobs and a higher median family income than whites (Schwartz, 1987).

Officials at Berkeley, Stanford, Harvard, MIT, and other elite universities have also been charged with discriminating against Asian-Americans. At those universities, admission of Asian-Americans has stabilized or gone down, even though the number of qualified Asian applicants has risen substantially. Today, the proportion of admissions among Asian applicants is one-third lower than that among whites, despite comparable or higher academic qualifications. The university officials are apparently fearful of being "swamped" by Asian-American students, often pointing out that there are already numerous Asian-Americans on their campuses.

Now that they are being increasingly assimilated into the white culture, however, Asian-Americans have begun to assume a more confrontational stance on the issue of racism. They have complained to the U.S. Justice Department and to the press about discrimination at the universities. They have also sued companies for job discrimination. On the other hand, some corporations have begun to correct past wrongs. Aware that the Asian nations are becoming ever more powerful in the global economy, they realize that they can get the competitive edge by making use of Asian-

Americans' cultural backgrounds and language skills (Schwartz, 1987). Perhaps elite-university officials would follow suit by actively recruiting Asian-American students with excellent math and science skills, which the United States urgently needs today to retain its technological preeminence in the world. But those universities still prejudicially consider such students "too narrowly focused." They continue to use the "academic plus factor" (demonstration of interest in sports, music, and other extracurricular activities) to discriminate against Asian-Americans in admissions (U.S. Commission on Civil Rights, 1992).

What laws were passed against Asian-Americans?

How do Asian-Americans fare in the educational system?

Jewish-Americans

The first Jews came here from Brazil in 1654—their ancestors had been expelled from Spain and Portugal. Then other Jews arrived directly from Europe. Their numbers were very small, however, until the 1880s, when large numbers of Jewish immigrants began to arrive, first from Germany, then from Russia and other Eastern European countries. Here they were safe from the *pogroms* (massacres) they had faced in Europe, but they did confront prejudice and discrimination.

During the 1870s, many American colleges refused to admit Jews. At the turn of the century, Jews often encountered discrimination when they applied for white-collar jobs. During the 1920s and 1930s, they were accused of being part of an international conspiracy to take over U.S. business and government, and **anti-Semitism**—prejudice or discrimination against Jews—became more widespread and overt. The president of Harvard University called for quotas against Jews. Large real estate companies in New Jersey, New York, Georgia, and Florida refused to sell property to Jews.

The Jewish population in the United States rose as European Jews fled the Nazis' attempt to exterminate them. During and after World War II, anti-Jewish activities (such as bombings or bomb threats against Jewish property) subsided, but they increased again during the 1960s (Marden and Meyer, 1978). From 1964 to the present, however, anti-Semitism has declined sharply.

Jewish Success   Despite the past discrimination against them, Jewish-Americans as a group have become the most successful. They attain higher levels of education, occupation, and income than any other group. Fifty-eight percent of them have college degrees, compared with 29 percent of the total population. Fifty-three percent hold high-paying white-collar jobs, compared with 25 percent of all Americans. The median income of Jewish-Americans is 1.7 times higher than the median for the U.S. population as a whole (Waxman, 1981; Rose, 1983; Lipset, 1990a). Their success may stem from the emphasis Jewish culture gives to education, from a self-image as God's chosen people, and from parental pressure to succeed. Not all Jews are successful, though, They still have a significant amount of poverty in their midst—over 15 percent of New York City's Jewish population is poor. This poverty is largely due to the recency of their arrival in America, as can be seen in the experiences of three types of Jews. Most of the poor Jews are Orthodox, the most recent immigrants in the United States. Conservative Jews, who are more successful, have been in this country longer. Reform Jews, the wealthiest of the group, have been here the longest (Waxman, 1981; Schaefer, 1988).

Although Jews as a whole are prosperous, they are not conservative or inclined to vote Republican, as other prosperous Americans are. Instead, they tend more to be liberal—supporting welfare, civil rights, women's rights, civil liberties, and the like—and to vote Democratic. Perhaps this reflects their ability to identify with the dispossessed and oppressed, people like themselves when they came here to escape hunger and persecution in Europe. It also reflects the impact of Jewish norms underlying *tzedekah,* which requires the fortunate and the well-to-do to help individuals and communities in difficulty (Lipset, 1990a).

There is an irony about Jews being the most successful minority—and hence most successfully assimilated into American society. They are in danger of losing their traditional Jewish identity. There has been a substantial decline in affiliation with synagogues and in ritual observance. Today, about half of all Jews are not affiliated with a synagogue, and only 20 percent attend synagogue regularly. Marriage with non-Jews has increased greatly, with over half of all Jewish marriages involving a non-Jew and most children from such marriages being brought up as non-Jews. The Jewish birth rate has also declined. All this has caused consternation among some rabbis and Jewish communal workers. But Jewish sociologists point out that, despite all those changes in their lives, American Jews "have been able to maintain a stronger sense of group identity than most other ethnic groups" in the United States (Waxman, 1990). But the Jewish cohesion does not derive from traditional Jewish values. It comes from the situational forces of both occupational and residential concentration: Jews living together in urban areas and working in occupations with large numbers of Jews. By sharing similar residences, schools, occupations, organizations, and friends, Jews have been and continue to be able to maintain the highest level of cohesion (Zenner, 1985; Waxman, 1990).

What is anti-Semitism?

How have Jews been assimilated into society?

White Ethnics

Jews were not the only European immigrants to face discrimination. From about 1830 to 1860, European immigration surged, and conflict grew between the immigrants—especially Catholic immigrants—and native-born Americans, the majority of whom were Protestants. The Irish immigrants, who tended to be both poor and Catholic, faced especially strong hostility. The notice "No Irish Need Apply" was commonplace in newspaper want ads.

Toward the end of the nineteenth century, there was a new wave of immigrants. These people came not from northern and western Europe, as most of the earlier immigrants had, but from southern and eastern Europe. They were Poles, Greeks, Italians. Many native-born Americans proclaimed these new immigrants to be inferior people and treated them as such. This belief was reflected in the National Origins Act of 1924. It enacted quotas that greatly restricted immigration from southern and eastern Europe—a policy that was not altered until 1965.

Today, the Italians, Poles, Greeks, and others from eastern or southern Europe are called **white ethnics.** Even in the 1950s and 1960s, they faced jokes and stereotypes about "dumb Poles" or "criminal Italians".

Prejudice against white ethnics has been called "respectable bigotry." Liberal journalists often describe them as ultraconservative and prejudiced against African-Americans. The stereotype overlaps with the image of uneducated blue-collar workers. In fact, a rising number of white ethnics are middle class, and about half have attended college, the same proportion as many Anglo-Saxon Americans (Alba, 1981, 1985). Several surveys have further shown that white ethnics largely favor "liberal" policies such as welfare programs, antipollution laws, and guaranteed wages. They are also relatively free of racial prejudice, perhaps because they can easily identify with blacks since, like blacks, many have held low-paying manual jobs and been subjected to discrimination (Greeley and McCready, 1974). More significant, white ethnics by and large can no longer speak their immigrant parents' language, do not live in ethnic neighborhoods any more, and routinely marry into the dominant group. In short, they have become such an integral part of mainstream American society that it is difficult to tell them apart (Steinberg, 1981). Traces of prejudice toward some white ethnics still exist, though. Most Americans, for example, continue to associate Italian-Americans with organized crime, although people of Italian background make up less than 1 percent of the 500,000 individuals involved in such activities. In general, the young and highly educated white ethnics are particularly sensitive to ethnic stereotypes, because they identify themselves more strongly with their ethnicity than others do (Giordano, 1987; Alba, 1990).

What are the white ethnic groups?

What tends to be the economic status of white ethnics?

Conclusion

In conclusion, the status of all the minorities is generally better today than before. Getting closest to the American dream of success are Jews, Asians, and white ethnics, followed by blacks and Hispanics. Ironically, the original owners of this land—Native Americans—have experienced the least improvement in their lives. Of course, we still have a lot of prejudice and discrimination. But it is less than before, especially less than in South Africa, where racism has until recently been an official policy. It is also less serious than in Bosnia, India, and other countries; where a single incident of ethnic conflict often takes hundreds or thousands of lives. In fact, as black sociologist Orlando Patterson (1991) notes, "The sociological truths are that America, while still flawed in its race relations, is now the least racist white-majority society in the world; has a better record of legal protection of minorities than any other society, white or black; offers more opportunities to a greater number of black persons than any other society, including all those of Africa; and has gone through a dramatic change in its attitude toward miscegenation over the last 25 years."

However, Americans tend to focus on their own current racial problem, without comparing it with how things were in the past or with similar problems in other societies. Interestingly, although the lack of historical and cross-cultural concern may limit our understanding of race relations, it can intensify our impatience with our own racial inequality. This is good for American society because it compels us—especially the minorities among us—to keep pushing for racial equality. On the other hand, the historical and cross-societal analysis in this chapter, which shows some improvement in our race relations, is also useful. It counsels against despair, encouraging us to be hopeful that racial equality can be achieved.

QUESTIONS FOR DISCUSSION AND REVIEW

1. What different policies has the government adopted toward Native Americans, and why have they often been resisted?
2. Why are large numbers of black Americans still not fully equal?
3. Who are the different groups of Hispanic-Americans, and what factors unify all of them?
4. Why have Asian-Americans gained more educational and professional success than other minority groups?
5. How have the experiences of Jewish-Americans differed from those of other white ethnic groups?
6. Does the "American Dilemma" still exist, or have American intergroup relations improved?

STUDY STRATEGIES

1. Recall the focus of each section of this chapter.
2. Make a study sheet including words like "race," "assimilation," and "anti-Semitic." Define them and give examples.
3. Create scenarios with fictional characters to illustrate a list of words like "cultural pluralism" and "expulsion" in preparation for application questions.
4. Connect your new knowledge by discussing recent articles that deal with some of the same issues in this chapter.
5. Brainstorm possible essay questions that connect the different sections of the chapter. Practice by writing answers to your questions.
6. Plan your attack by answering the following questions:

   How will the test look?

   What material will be covered?

   How will you study?

   When will you study?

   What grade are you honestly working to achieve?

Study for Success!

Glossary

analogy: a comparison showing connections with and similarities to previous experiences

annotating: a method of using symbols and notations to highlight textbook material for future study

argument: assertions that support a conclusion with the intention of persuading

assertion: declarative statement

attention: uninterrupted mental focus

bar graph: an arrangement of horizontal or vertical bars in which the length of each represents an amount or number

believability: support that is not suspicious but is believable

bias: an opinion or position on a subject recognized through facts slanted towards an author's personal beliefs

cause and effect: a pattern of organization in which one item is shown as having produced another

chronological order: a pattern of organization in which items are listed in time order or sequence

cognitive psychology: a body of knowledge that describes how the mind works or is believed to work

comparison-contrast: a pattern of organization in which similarities and differences are presented

concentration: the focusing of full attention on a task

conclusion: interpretation based on evidence and suggested meaning

connotation: the feeling associated with the definition of a word

consistency: support that holds together and does not contradict itself

context clues: hints within the sentence which help unlock the meaning of an unknown word

Cornell method: a system of note taking that involves writing sentence summaries on the right side of the page with key words and topics indicated to the left

creative thinking: generating many possible solutions to a problem

critical thinking: deliberating in a purposeful, organized manner to assess the value of information or argument

deductive reasoning: thinking which starts with a previously learned conclusion and applies it to a new situation

definition: a pattern of organization devoted to defining an idea and further explaining it with examples

denotation: the dictionary definition of a word

description: a pattern of organization, listing characteristics of a person, place, or thing, as in a simple listing

details: information that supports, describes, and explains the main idea

diagram: drawing of an object showing labeled parts

external distractors: temptations of the physical world that divert the attention from a task

fact: a statement that can be proven true or false

fallacy: an inference that first appears reasonable, but closer inspection proves it to be unrelated, unreliable, or illogical

figurative language: words used to create images that take on a new meaning

fixation: a stop the eyes make while reading

flowchart: a diagram showing how ideas are related with boxes and arrows indicating levels of importance and movement

humorous: comical or amusing

idiom: figurative expression that does not make literal sense but communicates a generally accepted meaning

imagery: mental pictures created by figurative language

implied meaning: suggested rather than directly stated meaning

inductive reasoning: thinking based on the collection of data and the formulation of a conclusion based on it

inference: subtle suggestions expressed without direct statement

internal distractions: concerns that come repeatedly to mind and disturb concentration

irony: a twist or surprise ending that is the opposite of what is expected and elicits a bittersweet, cruel chuckle

knowledge network: a cluster of knowledge about a subject: a schema

lateral thinking: a way of creatively thinking around a problem or a redefining of the problem to seek new solutions

learning styles: preference for a particular manner of presenting material to be learned

line graph: a frequency distribution in which the horizontal scale measures time and the vertical scale measures amount

main idea: a statement of the particular focus of the topic in a passage

map: graphic designation or distribution

mapping: a method of graphically displaying material to show relationships and importance for later study

metacognition: knowledge of how to read as well as the ability to regulate and direct the process

metaphor: a direct comparison of two unlike things (without using the words *like* or *as*)

mnemonics: a technique using images, numbers, rhymes, or letters to improve memory

notetaking: a method of writing down short phrases and summaries to record textbook material for future study

opinion: a statement of personal views or judgment

outlining: a method of using indentations, Roman numerals, numbers, and letters to organize textbook material for future study

pattern of organization: the structure or framework for presenting the details in a passage

personification: attributing human characteristics to nonhuman things

pie graph: a circle divided into wedge-shaped slices to show portions totaling 100 percent

point of view: a position or opinion on a subject

premise: the thesis or main point of an argument

previewing: a method of predicting what the material is about in order to assess knowledge and need

prior knowledge: previous learning about a subject

propaganda: a systematic and deliberate attempt to persuade others to a particular doctrine or point of view

purpose: the author's underlying reason or intent for writing

rate: reading pace described in number of words per minute

recall: reviewing what was included and learned after reading material

regression: rereading material because of a lack of understanding

relevance: support that is related to the conclusion

sarcasm: a tone that is witty, usually saying the opposite of what is true, but with the purpose of cutting or ridicule

scanning: searching to locate single bits of information in reading material

schema: a skeleton or network of knowledge about a subject

simile: a comparison of two things using the words *like* or *as*

simple listing: a pattern of organization that lists items in a series

skimming: a technique for selectively reading for the gist or main idea

study system: a plan for working through stages to read and learn textbook material

subvocalization: use of a little voice in the head, your inner voice, that reads aloud for you, enabling you to hear the words

summary: concise statement of the main idea and significant supporting details

table: listing of facts and figures in columns for quick reference

tone: the author's attitude toward the subject

topics: a word or phrase that labels the subject of a paragraph

vertical thinking: a straightforward and logical way of thinking that searches for a solution to the stated problem

Credits

Suzanne Britt, "Neat People vs. Sloppy People," *Show and Tell*, 1992.

Patty Fisher, "The Injustice System," *San Jose Mercury News*, 3/25/92.

John Dacey and John Travers, *Human Development*, Second Edition, WCB Brown & Benchmark, 1994.

Edward S. Greenberg and Benjamin I. Page, *The Struggle for Democracy*, HarperCollins College Publishers, 1995.

"Working Backwards" from Henry Gleitman, *Psychology*, Fourth Edition, W. W. Norton & Company, 1995, page 299.

Excerpt from "Oranges" by John McPhee. Copyright © 1966, 1967 by John McPhee. Reprinted by permission of Farrar, Straus & Giroux, Inc.

"Why Handguns Must Be Outlawed" by Nan Desuka from *American Voices: Multicultural Literacy and Critical Thinking* by Dolores laGuardia and Hans P. Guth, copyright © 1993.

"Mother Savage," (approximately 2350 words, pages 265–273) from *Selected Short Stories* by Guy DeMaupassant, translated by Roger Colet (Penguin Classics, 1971). Copyright © Roger Colet, 1971. Reproduced by permission of Penguin Books Limited.

"Caged" by Lloyd Eric Reeve from *Practical English*, March 2, 1960.

"How to Take a Job Interview" by Kirby W. Stanat. From *Job Hunting Secrets and Tactics* by Kirby W. Stanat with Patrick Reardon. Copyright © 1977, Kirby W. Stanat and Patrick Reardon. Reprinted by permission of the author.

Louis E. Boone and David L. Kurtz, from *Contemporary Business*. Copyright © 1976 by The Dryden Press.

Rodolfo Acuna, "Legacy of Hate: The Myth of a Peaceful Belligerent" from *Myth and the American Experience,* Volume One, Third Edition, edited by Nicholas Cords and Patrick Gerater. New York, NY: HarperCollins Publishers, 1991, pages 285 and 301.

From *America and Its People* by James Kirby Martin et al., pages 15–16, 440, 785–6, 902–903, 951, 953–6, and 989. Copyright © 1989 James Kirby Martin, Randy Roberts, Steven Mintz, Linda O. McMurry, and James H. Jones. Published by HarperCollins Publishers, Inc.

From *American Government: Incomplete Conquest* by Theodore J. Lowi. © 1987 by Scott, Foresman and Company, HarperCollins College Publishers.

From *America Past and Present*, 2nd Edition, by Divine et al. © 1987 by Scott, Foresman and Company, HarperCollins College Publishers.

Maya Angelou, *I Know Why the Caged Bird Sings*. New York: Random House, Inc., 1969.

From Ambrose Bierce: *The Devil's Dictionary.*

From *Biology: The Science of Life* by Victor A. Greulach and Vincent J. Chiappetta. Copyright © 1977 Scott, Foresman and Company, HarperCollins College Publishers.

From *Biology: The Science of Life*, Fifth Edition by Robert A. Wallace et al., pages 189, 194–7, and 512. Copyright © 1990, 1987, 1981 Scott, Foresman and Company, HarperCollins College Publishers.

From *Business Today*, David Rackman and Michael Mescon.

Excerpt from *Civilizations of the World: The Human Adventure* by Richard L. Greaves. Copyright © 1990 by Harper & Row, Publishers, Inc. Reprinted by permission of HarperCollins Publishers.

Joseph R. Conlin, *The American Past: A Brief History*. Orlando, FL: Harcourt Brace Jovanovich, Publishers, 1991, pages 556–7, 71–75, 78–79, 98.

From *Civilization Past and Present* vol 2, by T. Walter Wallbank, et al. Copyright © 1987 Scott, Foresman and Company, HarperCollinsCollege Publishers.

From *Cultural Anthropology*, Fourth Edition by Serena Nanda, pages 300–301 and 323. Copyright © 1991 by Wadsworth, Inc. Reprinted by permission of Wadsworth Publishing Company, Inc.

John D. Cunningham, *Human Biology*, Second Edition. New York, NY, Harper & Row Publishers, Inc., 1989, pages 233, 237, and 247.

James West Davidson et al., *Nation of Nations: A Narrative History of the American Republic Volume II: Since 1965*. New York, NY: McGraw-Hill Publishing Company, 1990, page 752. Copyright © 1990 by McGraw-Hill, Inc. Reprinted by permission.

From *Essentials of Biology*, 2nd Edition by Willis H. Johnson, Louis E. DeLanney, Thomas A. Cole, and Austin E. Brooks. Copyright © 1969, 1972, and 1974 by Holt, Rinehart and Winston, Inc. Reprinted by permission of Holt, Rinehart and Winston.

From *A History of the Western World*, Second Edition by Shepard Clough, p. 596. Copyright © 1969 D. C. Heath.

Index